U0871858

|同|济|工|科|百|年|

Centennial Engineering Education of Tongji

同济大学百年卓越工程教育图史

An Illustrated History of Centennial Engineering Education of Tongji University

■ 顾问：周祖翼 裴钢
Consultants: Zhou Zuyi Pei Gang

■ 主编 : 周家伦
Editor-in-chief: Zhou Jialun

■ 副主编 : 陈小龙 马锦明 董琦
Deputy Editors-in-chief: Chen Xiaolong Ma Jinming Dong Qi

■ 执行编纂：朱大章 喻大翔 周黎萍
Executive Editors: Zhu Dazhang Yu Daxiang Zhou Liping

■ 英文翻译 : 李梅
English Translator: Li May

图书在版编目（CIP）数据

同济大学百年卓越工程教育图史 / 周家伦主编. --
上海 : 同济大学出版社， 2012.5
ISBN 978-7-5608-4071-0

Ⅰ. ①同… Ⅱ. ①周… Ⅲ. ①高等教育－工科（教育
）－教学研究－上海市 Ⅳ. ①G642.0

中国版本图书馆CIP数据核字(2012)第082610号

同济大学百年卓越工程教育图史

顾　　问　周祖翼 裴　钢
主　　编　周家伦
副 主 编　陈小龙 马锦明 董　琦
执行编纂　朱大章 喻大翔 周黎萍
英文翻译　李　梅
出　　品　支文军
责任编辑　赵泽毓
助理编辑　熊磊丽
责任校对　张德胜
装帧设计　欣诚艺阁

出版发行　同济大学出版社　www.tongjipress.com.cn
（地址：上海市四平路 1239 号　邮编：200092　电话：021-65985622）
经　　销　全国各地新华书店
印　　刷　上海雅昌彩色印刷有限公司
开　　本　889mm×1194mm　1/16
印　　张　19.5
字　　数　624 000
版　　次　2012 年 5 月第 1 版　2012 年 5 月第 1 次印刷
书　　号　ISBN 978-7-5608-4071-0

定　　价　298.00 元

前 言

“乘扁舟而济者，其身也安；粹大道而动者，其业也美。”（东汉·徐干），个人的修养如此，一校一城一国的发展也是如此。19 世纪末 20 世纪初，是中国近代高等教育发展的重要时期，和大多数中国近代大学取法日、英、美等国不同，同济大学的工程教育自开办之初就以其鲜明的德国特征闻名于世。

在中德两国政府的支持以及两国工商界人士的帮助下，1912 年 4 月，同济工科的创始人、特许工程师伯恩哈德·贝伦子先生带着德国各界捐赠的大量现代化机器、模型来到上海，开始工学堂的筹建工作。1912 年 6 月 12 日，“德文工学堂”正式开学，跟 1907 年创办的“同济德文医学堂”合称“同济德文医工学堂”，开始了同济工程教育的百年育人之路。

同济大学工程教育的一百年，是同舟共济，自强不息的一百年。一百年来，同济大学的工程教育从创建时的“机电”一科，发展到 1910 年代的“机电、土木、机师”三科鼎立；1920 年代以严谨的学风，全国首屈一指的硬件设备成为“德国科学技术的中心”和我国对德交流的窗口；1930 年代改工科为工学院，在全国高校中首先创办测量系，开创了我国民用测绘专业的先河；1930 年代末至 1940 年代中期，在抗日战争爆发后的八年中，同济辗转沪、浙、赣、湘、贵、粤、桂、滇、黔、川九省及越南，在六次迁校的艰辛中工程教育的规模不但没有缩小，反而得到进一步发展壮大，同济学子大多进入兵工厂，加入敌后的重大工程建设中去，成为科技抗日的主力军；1946 年回迁上海后发展成为拥有机械、电机、土木、测量、造船五个系，一个机械专门科，并附设实习工厂和高级工业职业学校，具有广泛社会影响力的工程教育名校。

同济大学工程教育的一百年，是继往开来、蓬勃壮大的一百年。新中国成立后，同济大学的工程教育得到了新的发展。经过 20 世纪 50 年代的院系调整，同济大学成为以土木建筑为主的单科性工程院校，为日后同济大学成为我国在土木建筑类的一面旗帜奠定了坚实的学科基础；尔后的二十七年，同济在工程教育方面积极探索、多方开拓，即使在正常的教学秩序受到影响的十年文革期间，学校仍然坚持在有限的专业实践中摸索前进；文革结束后，学校加强对德联系、重回综合性大学的发展轨道，以土木建筑等强势学科带动工程教育其他学科的建设，并抓住改革开放的良机全面发展，迎来了工程教育发展的新高潮。20 世纪末 21 世纪初，通过三次并校，学科结构得到了优化，工程教育的优势学科得到加强。新世纪以来，通过“211 工程”、“985 工程”的建设，同济大学的工程教育以优势学科为龙头，带动交叉学科的发展，呈现了学科设置集成化、人才培养复合化、合作办学国际化、科研创新产业化的大繁荣特征。

一百年来，同济大学的工程教育从第一届 6 名学生、1 位教师，发展到如今已有 10 多个学院，千余名教师，共培养工程人才近 20 万人。同济工科人秉持“厚国聚民先乎工”的抱负，为中国的现代化和工业化做出了巨大贡献，为我国高等工程教育的发展树立了典范，奠定了工程领域的“同济品牌”。总结百年同济大学工程教育的传统，有以下几个特点：

第一，注重基础教育。1949 年以前，同济大学的工预科学生须在学习 5 个学期物理、4 个学期化学、3 个学期力学、4 个学期图解代数、3 个学期微积分、2 个学期机件学的基础上，方可进入专业课程的学习。进入专业学习阶段后，还需要继续学习动力学、静力学、热动学、微分方程、机件学等基础课程。学生绘制机械图，必须由草图、零件图、装配图、实体图、总体图到施工明细图，画上几百张，技艺要求达到德国二等或三等技工的手艺水平，才能参加毕业考试。

第二，注重实践教育。在同济工程教育的创建历史上，实习工厂的建设要先于校舍的建设。工科创立之初，在机电科第一年的教学中，学生须先实习半年，再开展理论教学。1915 年学校增设机师科，初期学制为 4 年，其中第一年为半天课堂教学、半天工厂实习，后改为 2 年在工厂实习，2 年半学习理论。即使在抗战大迁徙中，学校也十分重视学生的实习，花了很大代价沿途搬迁各种实习设备。抗战胜利后，学校回迁上海，花巨资购买工厂设备，保证学生实习的质量。

第三，坚持国际标准。从创设初期的“德籍教师、德国学制、德文教材、德语教学”，到 1927 年 9 月同济工科毕业生学历获德国部分州认可，到 1936 年 4 月 1 日，柏林德国工程师学会来函，承认同济大学工学院毕业生与德国工业大学毕业生具有同等资格，同时成为该会上海分会的正式会员，同济的工程教育从一开始就奠定了国际化的道路。自 1998 年开始，学校先后成立了中德学院、中德工程学院、中法工程与管理学院、联合国环境规划署 - 同济大学环境与可持续发展学院、中意学院、中芬中心、中西中心等国际合作办学基地，坚持国际标准，走国际化办学的道路。

第四，与产业密切结合。同济大学的工程教育践行了一条以产助学、产学研结合的特色道路。同济的实习工厂除供给学生实习外，兼做校内各研究馆所需的设备及标本，并制造车床、刨床、抽水机、台钳等产品出售，还接受校外的各种订单，得到社会各界的广泛欢迎。1949 年后，尤其是改革开放以来，同济大学为适应国家经济快速发展需要，在过去校办工厂辅助教学、实习、科研并接受部分生产订单的基础上，创办了一批科技企业，促进科技成果产业化。新世纪以来，学校对校办企业进行改制、重组，形成了具有同济特色的科技产业集群。

第五，主动服务社会。南浦大桥的建设，是老校长李国豪的全力争取，才使它从设计到建设，成为拥有自主知识产权的“中国制造”；东方明珠电视塔天线和上海大剧院屋顶，是同济教授们运用自己研发的“超大构件计算机控制液压提升、顶升技术”，顺利地完成顶升安装；2010 年的上海世博会，同济工科人完成各类规划设计任务 90 多项，先后承担 170 多个相关科技项目。在城乡规划、建筑设计、历史建筑保护、桥梁工程、结构工程、土木工程、机械工程、环境工程、地下空间开发利用等中国城市建设的几乎所有相关领域，同济人术有专攻，做出了不可磨灭的贡献。

“同有耳目同有手足，同有心思才力，不作工，负了好教育”，正如早期同济校歌所言，我们总结同济工程教育百年来的经验，是为了继承和发扬同济工程教育的优良传统，为正在开展的工程教育改革提供思路和参考。作为一所有着悠久历史的工程教育名校，同济将更加注重基础，更加注重实践，认真开展工程教育改革，更加注重师生品德与人格塑造；同济将继续坚持国际标准，深化国际合作，紧密结合社会需求和未来发展，加强与中学、与企业、与国内外高校的合作，推进卓越人才计划，提高工程人才培养水平，为国家和社会培养出更多的有用之才，为实现民族复兴和人类的共同发展而努力。

Preface

As Master Xu Gan from Eastern Han Dynasty of ancient China put it, "one feels physically calm when he reaches the bank in a small boat; one enjoys his career when he makes progress to keep abreast of time." People follow this state of mind in pursuing their personal development, and the same holds true for the development of a university, a city and even a country. The time at the turn of the 19th and 20th century was of vital importance in the development of higher education in modern China. Different from most Chinese universities modeled a Japanese, British or American educational system, the engineering education of Tongji University has been well-known for its distinctive German features since it was initiated a hundred years ago.

In April 1912, Mr. Bernhard Berrens, a chartered engineer of Germany, arrived in Shanghai with plenty of donations of modern facilities and models from Germany. He started the preparatory work for the establishment of German Engineering School with support from both Chinese and German governments and help from the industry and business sectors of the two countries. The German Engineering School which started formally on June 12th of 1912 and the German Medical School which was established earlier in 1907 were referred to collectively as German Medical and Engineering School, which marked the beginning of a centennial engineering education at Tongji.

The one hundred years of engineering education at Tongji witnessed remarkable joint efforts and strong persistence of Tongji people. Over the hundred years, the engineering education of Tongji University developed initially from a program in Electrical and Mechanical Engineering to three programs in Electrical and Mechanical Engineering, Civil Engineering and in Mechanist Education in the 1910s. In the 1920s, Tongji boasted its strict educational style and most sophisticated facilities in China and became a Centre for German Science and Technology and served as a window for exchanges between China and Germany. In the 1930s, Engineering School was established on the basis of the engineering program. Soon came the establishment of the Department of Surveying, the first of its kind in China, marking the beginning of civil surveying in China. During the eight years of Anti-Japanese War from the end of 1930s to the mid-1940s, Tongji was forced to move from Shanghai to Zhengjiang Province, Jiangxi Province, Hunan Province, Guangzhou Province, Guangxi Province, through Vietnam to Yunnan Province, Guizhou Province, and eventually to Sichuan Province. Although Tongji experienced relocations as many as six times, its engineering education kept growing in size. Most of students started to work in weapons manufacturers behind the enemy lines or joined major construction projects, becoming the major force in fighting the Japanese with science and technology. After Tongji was eventually relocated back to Shanghai in 1946, it underwent rapid development and became an influential engineering university with five departments of Mechanical Engineering, Electromechanical Engineering, Civil Engineering, Surveying and Shipbuilding, and a professional program in Mechanics. In addition, an internship factory and an Affiliated Advanced Industrial Vocational School were also established at the university.

The one hundred years of engineering education at Tongji University experienced the endeavors made by Tongji people in keeping its traditions and exploring a future for vigorous development. The founding of new China brought more changes to the engineering education at Tongji University. After the nationwide restructuring of colleges and universities in the 50s of the 20th Century, Tongji University became a specified university with a focus on civil engineering, which laid a firm foundation for the leading position of the engineering education of Tongji University in China at a later stage. In the following 27 years, even during the Cultural Revolution when teaching was interrupted, Tongji University were active in exploring its way of further developing engineering education. After the Cultural Revolution, the university resumed its links with Germany and reshaped itself as a comprehensive university with civil engineering taking the lead in the development of engineering programs. Tongji sought an all-round development by taking advantage of the economic reform of the country and soon entered its first peak time in the development of engineering education. At the turn of the 20th and 21st century, the university made good use of its three mergers with other universities in optimizing its structure and strengthening its strong disciplines. Since the beginning of the new century, with the help of the 211 Project and the 985 Project, Tongji University managed to boost interdisciplinary development with the engineering education functioning as the dragonhead. The engineering education of Tongji University during this time was characterized by interdisciplinary integration, student cultivation complexity, international cooperation and technology transfer.

A hundred years ago, the engineering education of Tongji started with six students and one teacher. But today there are over a thousand teachers of engineering in more than ten engineering schools and about 200,000 students graduated from engineering programs. Tongji People had made tremendous contributions to the modernization and industrialization of China with a belief that technology would make the country and its people stronger. They set an example for the development of engineering education in China and paved the way for the creation of a Tongji brand name in the field of engineering. The tradition of engineering education at Tongji is summarized as follows.

I. Basic Education

Before 1949, students on a preparatory engineering course could proceed to their specialized engineering courses only after they had taken Physics for five terms, Chemistry for four terms, Mechanics for three terms, Graphic Algebra for four terms, Calculus for three terms and Mechanical Science for two terms. While they took the specialized engineering courses, they continued to learn such basic courses as Dynamics, Statics, Thermal Dynamics, Differential Equations and Mechanical Science. Students were required to produce sketches, drawings of parts, drawings of assembly, drawings of entities, overall drawings and drawings of construction details while they made mechanical drawings. Students could proceed to take their graduation examinations only after they had made hundreds of drawings and reached Level 2 or Level 3 in craftsmanship of the German standards.

II. Practice

In the history of engineering education of Tongji, the internship factory was built prior to its campus. At the initial stage of the engineering education, students had to practise in the internship factory for half a year before they started their theoretical study during their first year on the Electrical and Mechanical Engineering course. A four-year Mechanist program was established in 1915. At the initial stage of the program, students were asked to learn in the classroom for half a day and work in the internship factory for half a day during the first year of their study. Later the program extended to four and a half years with two years of practice and two and a half years of theoretical study. Even during the Anti-Japanese War when the university was on a constant move, the university managed to bring the facilities along at a very high cost to ensure the implementation of Practice in the curriculum. After the victory of the Anti-Japanese War when the university was relocated back to Shanghai, Tongji spent a fortune in purchasing facilities for the internship factory to guarantee the quality of student internship.

III. International Standards

The engineering education of Tongji was already on its way to international development when its first engineering program started with “German teachers, German curriculum, German textbooks and German language for teaching”. In September 1927, the graduation certificates of the engineering students of Tongji were acknowledged by some states in Germany and on 1st April 1936, a letter arrived from the German Society of Engineers in Berlin, stating that graduates from Engineering School of National Tongji University may become members of the Shanghai branch of the society, for the qualifications they obtained from National Tongji University were as good as the ones obtained by their counterparts from a Technical University of Germany. Since 1998, Tongji University has established joint international education bases like Sino-German College for Postgraduate Studies, Sino-German College of Applied Sciences, Sino-French Institute of Engineering and Management, UNEP-Tongji Institute of Environment for Sustainable Development, Sino-Italian Campus, Sino-Finnish Centre and Sino-Spanish Campus. Tongji was determined to abide by international standards for its international development.

IV. Close Links with Industry

The engineering education of Tongji University was marked with a distinctive feature of keeping close links with the industry by way of integrating industry with teaching and research. The internship factory served not only for student internship, for making apparatuses and samples needed for university research institutes, but also for manufacturing such products as lathes, planers, pumps and vises for sale. Orders of these products came for outside the university and were very popular among people from relevant walks of life. To keep abreast of the rapid economic development of the country, Tongji University established high-tech companies to promote technology transfer after 1949, especially since the implementation of the reform and opening-up policy. Since the beginning of the new century, a High-tech Industry Group was formed at the Tongji University on the basis of reform and restructure of the university-owned companies.

V. Service to Society

It was because of the great efforts made by the former President Li Guohao in securing the construction of Nanpu Bridge that made it possible for the design and construction of the bridge to be Made in China with our own Intellectual properties. The "computer-controlled hydraulic-pressure lifting technology for super-size components" developed by professors of Tongji was employed in the antenna jacking-up of Oriental Pearl Tower of Shanghai and the large-scale roof lifting of Shanghai Grand Theatre. Engineering teachers and students of Tongji University completed over 90 planning and design tasks of various nature and undertook over 170 technical projects for Shanghai Expo 2010. Tongji University has made indelible contributions to urban construction in China with its engineering strengths in urban planning, architectural design, preservation of historic buildings, bridge engineering, structural engineering, civil engineering, mechanical engineering, environmental engineering and underground space exploration.

As the old song of Tongji said, "we will live up to good education if we don't work hard since we are all physically and mentally strong". We are making a summary of our experience of engineering education over a hundred years to inherit and develop the legacy of the fine traditions of the engineering education of Tongji, and to provide food for thought for the engineering education reform in progress that is under way. As a leading university with a long history of engineering education, Tongji University will pay closer attention to basic education and practice and will fully implement the engineering education reform to enhance personal quality development of teachers and students. It will continue its international cooperation, abide by international standards, and strengthen its cooperation with middle schools, industry and its counterparts both at home and abroad. Meanwhile, it will promote the Excellent Talents Cultivation Program to improve the standards of engineering education so as to produce more engineering professionals and make more contributions to the national rejuvenation and the progress of human beings.

目　录

第三章

1937.7-1952.5 辗转颠簸，越挫越强

下篇 1952-2012：粹大道而动

第四章

1952.6-1976.9 土建单科，局部发展

第五章

1976.10-1991.12 两个转变，承前启后

第六章

1992.1-2012.5 百年辉煌，继往开来

后记

Contents

Chapter III

1937.7-1952.5 The Harder, the Stronger

Part II 1952-2012 : Making Progress to Keep Abreast of Time

Chapter IV

1952.6-1976.9 Further Development Against All Odds

Chapter V

1976.10-1991.12 Two Transformations Bridging Past and Future

Chapter VI

1992.1-2012.5 Exploration of a Brighter Future in Centennial Glory

上 篇
Part I
1912-1952

乘扁舟而济
Reaching the Bank in a Small Boat

本时期工程教育分三个阶段：第一阶段为 1912 年至 1927 年，确立了同济工程教育的德国模式；第二阶段为 1927 年至 1937 年，迎来了第一个蓬勃发展期，并形成了德国式工学教育传统；第三阶段为 1937 年至 1952 年，六次迁校，九年颠簸，但工学教育愈挫愈强，解放前后达到“五系一厂一职业学校”的辉煌。

The engineering education from 1912 to 1952 was divided into three stages. During the first stage from 1912 to 1927, it was decided that Tongji should follow a German model of engineering education; during the second stage from 1927 to 1937, the German tradition of engineering education was established, marking the first flourishing stage of engineering education at Tongji; and during the third stage from 1937 to 1952 when Tongji was relocated six times in nine years, the engineering education grew even larger and stronger against all odds; and there were already five departments, an internship factory and an affiliated vocational school by the time when China was liberated in 1949.

100

第一章 Chapter I（1912.6-1927.7）

中西同舟，德国模式
A German Model Integrating West with East

1912 年 3 月中旬，学校开始修建工厂，4 月初伯恩哈德·贝伦子到沪管理一切事务。6 月中旬工科举行第一届开学典礼。学校依靠德国工商界及教育界捐赠的大量先进设备与仪器，以德国委派的教师及德国驻上海的工程师为主要师资团队，先后设立了“机电科、土木科”，并附设职业教育的“机师科”，以德语为教学语言，采用德国原版教材、注重实践与实习，奠定了同济工程教育的德国模式。

Tongji started to build a factory in mid-March of 1912. Weeks later in early April, Mr. Bernhard Berrens arrived in Shanghai to assume the responsibilities of managing all affairs at Tongji. The first opening ceremony of German Engineering School was held in mid-June. Tongji started its programs successively in Mechanical and Electrical Engineering, and in Civil Engineering and a Mechanist program for vocational education with strong support from Germany. A large number of facilities at Tongji were donated by people from the business and education sectors in Germany, and the teachers at Tonjgi were all German who either were teachers sent to Shanghai from Germany or German engineers who worked in Shanghai. Gradually a German model of engineering education was shaped at Tongji with a focus on practice. German was the language of delivery in class and German textbooks were used for teaching.

一九一二，工科始创

German Engineering School Established in 1912

继1907年“德文医学堂”在上海建立后，1912年德国特许工程师伯恩哈德·贝伦子来沪，在“同济德文医学堂”总理奥斯卡·福沙伯的协助下，主持筹办“德文工学堂”，工学堂与医学堂共用语言学校，合称“同济德文医工学堂”。

Mr. Bernhard Berrens, a German chartered engineer, arrived in Shanghai, China in 1912 after the establishment of German Medical School in Shanghai in 1907. He was responsible for establishing German Engineering School with support from Mr. Oscar von Schab, President of German Medical School. German Medical School and German Engineering School shared the same language school; therefore, the two schools were referred to as Tongji German Medical and Engineering School.

1907年创办的“德文医学堂”，为工学堂的建立奠定了基础。

German Medical School, established in 1907, laid a foundation for the establishment of German Engineering School.

Der Ostasiatische Lloyd

報 新 文 德

Der Ostasiatische Lloyd
erscheint in Shanghai Sonnabends Morgens.
Herausgeber und verantwortlicher Redakteur: C. FINK.
Redaktion und Geschäftsstelle:
Nanking Road 25, Shanghai.
Telephon No. 347.
Telegrammadresse: Publicatio Shanghai.

Interessenten in Europa
wollen sich wegen Probenummern und Abonnements wenden an die
Generalvertretung für Deutschland:
Verlag des Berliner Aktionärs
G. Schweitzer. E. Busch.
Berlin SW., Lindenstrasse 47.
Alleinige Annahme von Inseraten in Deutschland.
Abonnement in Deutschland:
ℳ 7.50 vierteljährlich.

海 上 圖 中 設 館

Organ für die deutschen Interessen im fernen Osten.
Tägliche Telegrammausgabe in Shanghai, Tsingtau, Peking und Tientsin.

XXI. Jahrgang. Shanghai, 4. Oktober 1907. Nummer 40.

Inhaltsverzeichnis.

Das Erziehungswesen in China.

Das Erziehungswesen in China hat in den letzten Jahren mehrfache Wandlungen

1903年12月，《德文新报》出版商卡尔·芬克在致德国驻上海总领事威廉·克纳佩的一份备忘录中建议：在上海建一所附设语言学校的工科学校。

A memorandum presented to Mr. Wilhelm Knappe, Consul General of Germany in Shanghai in December 1903, in which Mr. Carl Fink, a publisher of *Der Ostasiatische Lloyd*, suggested establishing an engineering school with an affiliated language school in Shanghai.

威廉·克纳佩(1855-1910)，曾任德国驻上海总领事，在工学堂的创建中起到了轴心作用。

Mr. Wilhelm Knappe (1855-1910), Consul General of Germany in Shanghai, played a vital role in the establishment of German Engineering School.

伯恩哈德·贝伦子(1880-1927)，德国汉诺威大学机械系工程硕士，特许工程师，“德文工学堂”创办人。1915年被德国政府授予教授称号，1924年被但泽工业大学授予名誉博士称号。

Mr. Bernhard Berrens (1880-1927), a chartered engineer with an MSc degree in Mechanical Engineering from University of Hannover (Gottfried Wilhelm Leibniz Universität Hannover), Germany, was the founder of German Engineering School. He was awarded a professorship by the German Government in 1915 and an honorary doctorate by Gdańsk University of Technology in 1924.

奥斯卡·福沙伯(1862-1934)，医学博士，“同济德文医学堂”总监督，医工学堂合并后，任“同济德文医工学堂”总监督，被德国政府授予教授称号。

Mr. Oscar von Schab (1862-1934), MD, superintendent of German Medical School, became superintendent of Tongji German Medical and Engineering School following the merger of German Medical School and German Engineering School. He was awarded a professorship by the German Government in 1915.

德国师资，德国模式

A German Model with German Faculty

“德文工学堂”校舍位于金神父路（今陕西南路），由德国建筑设计师卡尔·贝德克尔设计，1914 年竣工。最初仅有贝伦子一名教师，自 1913 年开始，一批德籍工科教师陆续来校任教，1917 年达到 19 人，确立了以“德籍教师、德国学制、德文教材、德语授课”为特色的德国工程教育模式。

The campus of German Engineering School on Route Pere Robert (current South Shaanxi Road) was designed by Mr. Baedecker Carl, a German architect. Its construction was completed in 1914. Mr. Bernhard Berrens was the only teacher at the school when it first started. Since 1913, German teachers of engineering started to arrive at the school and the number of teachers increased to 19 by 1917. A German model of engineering education was gradually shaped with German faculty, German curricula, German textbooks and German delivery.

“德文工学堂”校舍的建筑设计师卡尔·贝德克尔
Mr. Carl Baedecker, architect of the campus of German Engineering School

1912 年“同济德文医工学堂”校门
Entrance of Tongji German Medical and Engineering School in 1912

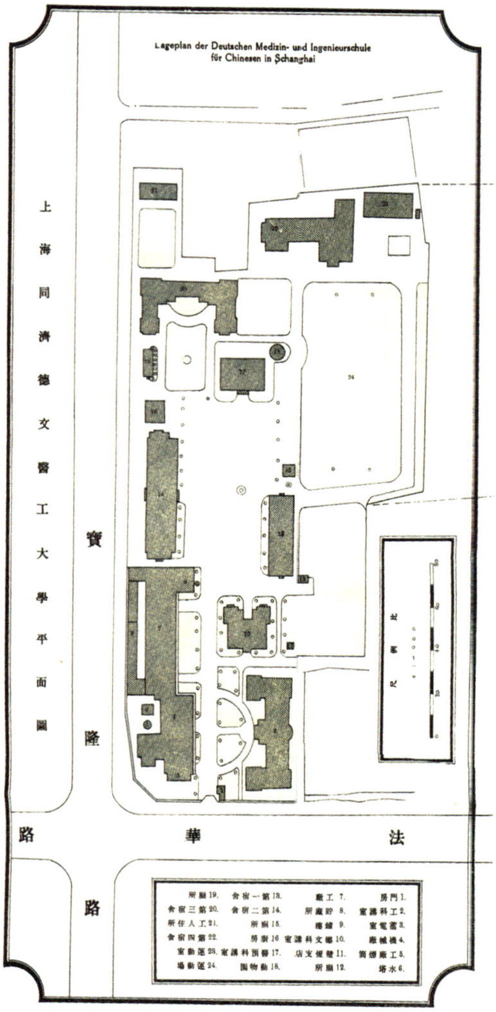

1916 年“上海同济德文医工大学”平面图
Plan of the Tongji German Medical and Engineering School in 1916

■ 1914 年“同济德文医工学堂”工科讲堂

A teaching building of Tongji Medical and Engineering School in 1914

■ “同济德文医工学堂”工科讲堂现址

（上海理工大学复兴路校区）

Current version of the old Teaching Building of Tongji German Medical and Engineering School (on the campus of University of Shanghai for Science and Technology on Fuxing Road)

■ 1916 年“同济德文医工学堂”工科教职员合影

Faculty of Tongji German Medical and Engineering School in 1916 (From left to right in turn is Architekt Schaffrath, Bauingenieur Jung, Dr.Drexler, Dipl.Ing. Beiderlinden, Prof.Baetz, Prof.Berrens, Dipl.Ing.De Grahl, Maschineningenieur Hohn, Tegierungsbaumeister Schoenwald, Michael)

学子六名，学制四年

Six Students on a Four-year Engineering Program

1912 年 6 月，“德文工学堂”第一次开学典礼举行，第一批工科学生一共六名，分别是从本校中学部转来的朱家骅、黄伯樵、舒震东、曹省之、刘荫椿和王道周。工学堂设机电一科，学制四年，同济大学的工程教育自此发端。

The first school opening ceremony of German Engineering School was held in June 1912. Six students were enrolled on the four-year program in mechanical and electrical engineering which marked the beginning of engineering education at Tongji University. They were Zhu Jiahua, Huang Boqiao, Shu Zhendong, Cao Xingzhi, Liu Yinkui and Wang Daozhou who were transferred to the school from the High School Affiliated to the German Engineering School.

■ 首届工科学生朱家骅（1893-1963），字骝先，浙江湖州人，民国时期教育界、学术界、外交界的耆宿。

Mr. Zhu Jiahua (1893-1963), alias Liuxian, a native of Huzhou, Zhejiang Province, was one of the first students of German Engineering School. He was a forerunner of the modernization of China and enjoyed a high reputation in the fields of education and foreign affairs in Republic of China.

■ 首届工科学生黄异（1890-1948），字伯樵，江苏太仓人，上海特别市首任公用局局长，我国铁路事业的先驱之一。

Mr. Huang Yi (1890-1948), alias Boqiao, a native of Taicang, Jiangsu Province, was one of the first students of German Engineering School. He acted as the first director of the Public Facilities Bureau of the Shanghai Special City and was a forerunner of the railway industry in China.

■ 首届工科学生舒震东（1893-1955），又名昌瑜，第一台有实用价值的中文打字机发明者。

Mr. Shu Zhendong (1893-1955), alias Changyu, was one of the first students of German Engineering School. He was an inventor of the first Chinese typewriter of practical value.

■ 首届工科学生曹省之，生卒年不详，中国机械工程学会上海分会主办学术刊物《机械世界》主编。

Mr. Cao Xingzhi, dates of birth and death unknown, was one of the first students of German Engineering School. He acted as editor-in-chief of *Mechanical World*, an academic journal published by the Shanghai Branch of the Society of Mechanical Engineering in China.

工学堂创办人伯恩哈德·贝伦子（后排右一）与工学堂首届学生在安装从德国运来的机器现场。

Mr. Bernhard Berrens (first from right in the back), founder of German Engineering School, ready to install machines from Germany with the first students of the school.

工学堂创办人伯恩哈德·贝伦子、工场指导诺斯与工学堂首届学生在机械馆工地。

Mr. Bernhard Berrens and Mr. Noss, a technical supervisor, on the site of the Machinery Laboratory with the first students of German Engineering School.

工学堂教室

A classroom of German Engineering School

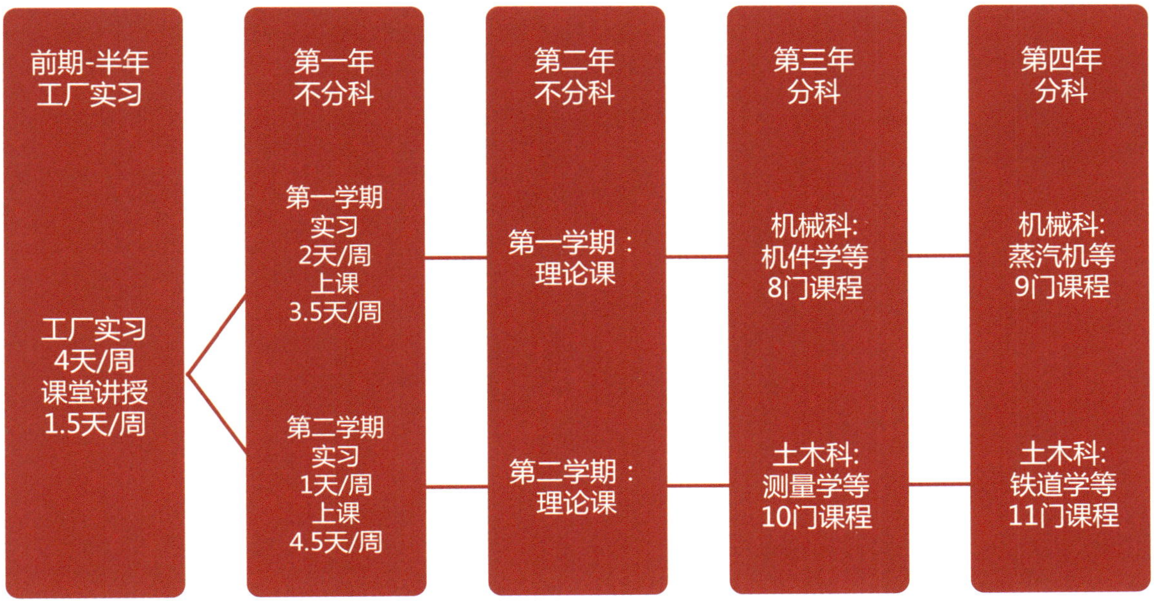

1917 年工科学制示意图

An illustration of the program in Engineering at German Engineering School in 1917

三科鼎立，各有所长

Three Programs with Distinctive Strengths

1914 年，日本攻占青岛，德中合办的“德华特别高等专门学堂”被迫停办，30 名土木科学生转至同济，学校为此特增设土木科。1915 年下半年，增设机师科，培养能讲德语、懂机械制造、又能为企业服务的人才，开创了我国工科职业教育的先河。

Sino-German Advanced Vocational School(Deutsch-Chinesische Hochschule), jointly run by Germany and China, was forced to close down in 1914 when Japan invaded Qingdao, China. Thirty students of Civil Engineering from the Hochschule were transferred to Tongji Medical and Engineering School which later expanded to include civil engineering as a separate program. In the later half of 1915, a program in Machinist Training was added to train professionals who had knowledge of machinery manufacturing and service skills for the industry with a good command of German, which was the first of its kind in vocational education of engineering in China.

图为 1909 年在青岛创办的“德华特别高等专门学堂”旧址，1914 年该校停办，工科学生大多转入同济

Sino-German Advanced Vocational School(Deutsch-Chinesische Hochschule), which was established jointly by Germany and China in Qingdao in 1909 and closed down in 1914 during the Japanese Invasion when most of the students had to transfer to Tongji Medical and Engineering School

由“德华特别高等专门学堂”转入同济的德国教师德士烈

Dr. Drexler, a German teacher who transferred to Tongji Medical and Engineering School from Sino-German Advanced Vocational School(Deutsch-Chinesische Hochschule)

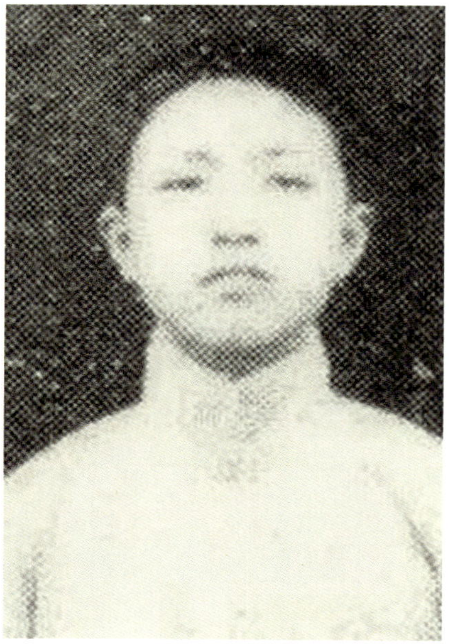

左：1914 年由“德华特别高等专门学堂”转入同济的工科学生杨继曾 (1898-1993)，曾任国民政府军工部兵工署署长，民国时期军工界的代表人物。

Left: Mr. Yang Jizeng (1898-1993), a student of civil engineering who transferred to Tongji Medical and Engineering School from Sino-German Advanced Vocational School (Deutsch-Chinesische Hochschule) in 1914, acted as director of the Ordnance Bureau of Military Industry Department of the Kuomintang Government. He was a leading figure in the military industry in Republic of China.

右：1914 年由“德华特别高等专门学堂”转入同济的工科学生沈怡 (1901-1980)，曾任上海市工务局局长、上海市特别市市长，著名水利学家。

Right: Shen Yi (1901-1980), a student of civil engineering who transferred to Tongji Medical and Engineering School from Sino-German Advanced Vocational School (Deutsch-Chinesische Hochschule) in 1914, acted as director of Works Bureau of Shanghai and mayor of Shanghai Special City. He was known as a famous expert in hydraulics.

机械科课堂

A mechanical class

土木科课堂

A civil engineering class

1916 年附设机师学校教员

Faculty with the Affiliated Machinist School in 1916

1916 年附设机师学校甲、乙班学生

Students from Classes 1 and 2 of the Affiliated Machinist School in 1916

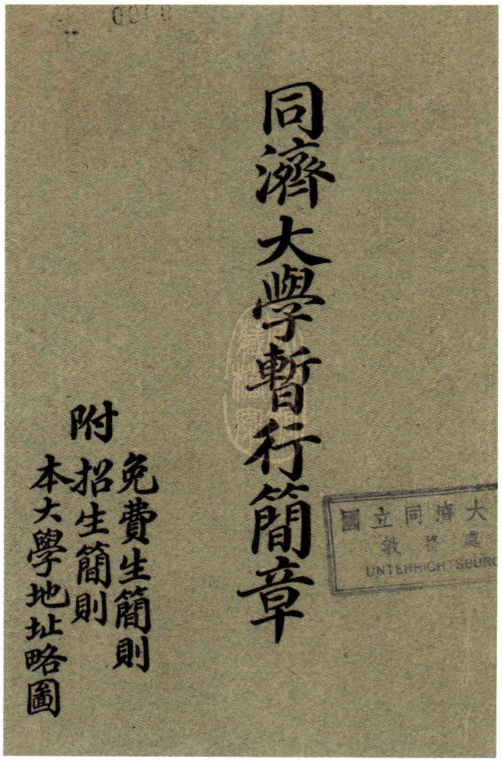
同濟大學暫行簡章

附
免費生簡則
招生簡則
本大學地址略圖

1922 年《同济大学暂行简章》，工科学制改为 5 年

The four-year engineering program changed to a five-year one in accordance with the *Provisional Regulations of Tongji University* in 1922

1923 年工科毕业生手绘树状结构图，树根为同济工科输送生源的各中学，主干为“同济大学工预科”，后按照专业分为土木科、机械科两分杈，树上所结果实为 1923 届毕业生。

A tree diagram drawn by graduates of engineering in 1916 with the roots standing for high schools that sent students to the Engineering School, the trunk for Engineering Preparation School of Tongji University, the two branches for civil engineering and mechanical engineering, and fruits as graduates of engineering in 1923.

一战影响，华人接办

School Taken Over by Chinese During World War I

1917 年，中德断交，同济濒危，“朝野人士莫不竭诚营救”。由于原法租界校舍被当局以种种借口不予归还，同济师生先后搬至吴淞中国公学、炮台湾海军学校上课。危机中，华人组成的校董会成为学校最高领导机构，经校董会公推，教育部同意，聘请阮尚介博士担任校长，但教务仍由德国教授负责。

Tongji was in crisis following China's diplomatic break with Germany in 1917. Enormous efforts were made to keep the school going. Teachers and students had to move first to the Chinese Public School in Wusong, then to the Paotaiwan Naval Academy, since the authorities refused to return to Tongji its campus at the French Concession. At this critical time, the Chinese members of the school board of trustees resumed the highest governance of the school. Approved by Ministry of Education, at the recommendation of the board of trustees, Dr. Ruan Shangjie was appointed as the president of the school and a German professor as the dean responsible for teaching administration.

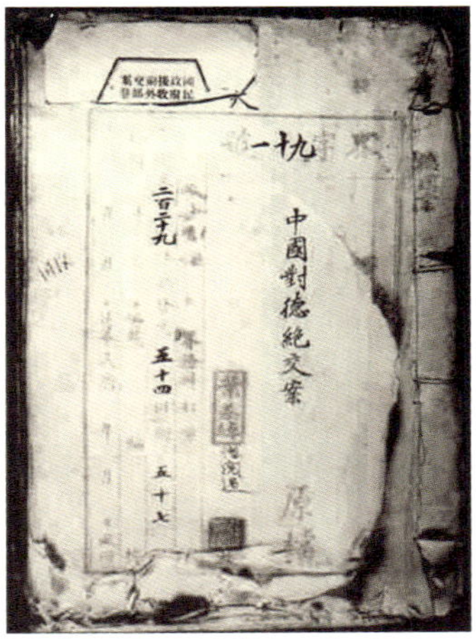

■ 左：北洋政府对德绝交档案

Left: Documents of China's diplomatic break with Germany

■ 右：1917 年 3 月 17 日下午，法捕房总巡率领安南兵大队，荷枪实弹，包围同济，强令学校解散，被称之为“三·一七”事件。

Right: On the afternoon of March 17th, 1917, the armed Annan Military Brigade led by a captain of the French Police Station surrounded the school and demanded that the school be dismissed, which was referred to as *March 17th Event*

危机中起重要作用的华人校董

Chinese members of the school board of trustees who played a critical role in a time of crisis

■ 首届华人校董朱葆三（1848-1926），曾在上海创办华安水火保险公司等企业，任中国通商银行总董等要职。

Mr. Zhu Baosan (1848-1926), a member on the first Chinese session of school board, founded Shanghai Hua'an Water and Fire Insurance Company and acted as Chairman of the Board of Directors of the Commercial Bank of China.

■ 首届华人校董虞洽卿（1867-1945），曾在上海成立四明银行、宁绍轮船公司等。

Mr. Yu Qiaqing (1867-1945), a member on the first Chinese session of the school board, founded Siming Bank and Ningshao Shipping Company in Shanghai.

■ 常务校董沈恩孚（1864-1944），历任江苏都督府民政司次长、江苏省教育会秘书长、上海市议会议长等职。

Mr. Shen Enfu (1864-1944), a standing member on the school board of trustees, acted as the undersecretary of Office of Home Affairs of Jiangsu Governor House, secretary general of Jiangsu Educational Association and chairman of Shanghai Council.

第二届华人校董贝仁元（1872-1947），昔日名闻上海滩的颜料大王。

Mr. Bei Renyuan (1872-1947), a member on the second Chinese session of the school board of trustees, was well-known as the Pigment King of Shanghai.

第二届华人校董唐元湛（1861-1921），著名的民族资本家、政治活动家。

Mr. Tang Yuanchen(1861-1921), a member on the second Chinese session of the school board of trustees, was a famous national capitalist and political activist.

校董李维格（1867-1929），我国钢铁冶金界的先驱，近代钢铁专家，汉阳铁厂的主要开拓者。

Mr. Li Weige (1867-1929), a member on the school board of trustees, was a forerunner in the metallurgy industry of China, a modern iron and steel expert and a pioneering founder of Hanyang Iron Works.

■ 常务校董袁希涛（1866-1930），曾任国民政府教育部次长，并两次代理部长职务。

Mr. Yuan Xitao (1866-1930), a standing member of the school board of trustees, was an undersecretary of the Ministry of Education, and was appointed twice as the acting minister.

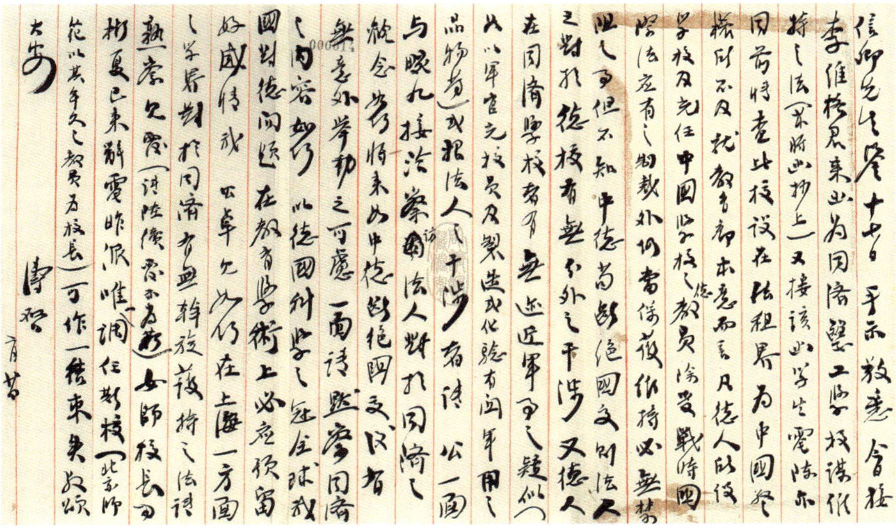

■ 袁希涛就法租借当局出兵强占同济校舍驱逐学生的“三·一七”事件复同济校董虞洽卿函。

A letter reply to Mr. Yu Qiaqing, a member on the school board of trustees, from Mr. Yuan Xitao about *March 17th Event* during which the authority from the French Concession sent troops to drive students away from Tongji campus.

赴南京请求维持学校的学生代表
Student representatives filing a petition to keep the school campus in Nanjing

■ 左：赵厚达（1886-1924），1914年至1918年就读于同济工科，中文打字机的发明者之一。

Left: Mr. Zhao Houda (1886-1924), one of the inventors of the Chinese typewriter, studied engineering at Tongji German Medical and Engineering School from 1914 to 1918.

■ 右：叶鼎，1915-1919年就读于同济工科，曾任“同济德文医工学堂”工科同志会会长。

Right: Mr. Ye Ding studied engineering at the Engineering School from 1915 to 1919. He acted as the chairman of Engineering Comrades Society of Tongji German Medical and Engineering School.

向同济伸出援手的各界代表
People from all walks of life who lent their support to Tongji in crisis

■ 援手同济的唐绍仪（1862-1938），字少川，广东珠海人，清末民初著名政治活动家、外交家，金星人寿保险有限公司创办人。

Mr. Tang Shaoyi (1862-1938), alias Shaochuan, a native of Zhuhai, Guangdong Province, and founder of Jinxing Life Insurance Company Ltd., lent a helping hand to Tongji. He was a famous political activist and diplomat in late Qing dynasty and early Republic of China.

■ 援手同济的简照南（1870-1923）、简玉阶（1875-1957）兄弟，南洋兄弟股份有限公司创办人。

Mr. Jian Zhaonan (1870-1923) and Mr. Jian Yujie (1875-1957), founders of Nanyang Brothers Co. Ltd., lent their support to Tongji.

■ 援手同济的中华书局，1912 年由中国近代著名教育家、出版家陆费逵（1886-1941）创立。

Zhonghua Book Company founded in 1912 by Mr. Lu Fei (1886-1941), a famous educator and publisher in Modern China, gave its support to Tongji.

国人接办后任命的首任校长阮尚介（1890-1960），字介藩，上海奉贤人，早年曾在日本留学，德国柏林工业大学造船系毕业。

Dr. Ruan Shangjie (1890-1960), alias Jiefan, a native of Fengxian, Shanghai, was the first president of the school after it was taken over by Chinese. He studied in Japan in his earlier years, and later graduatec from the Shipbuilding Department of Technical University of Berlin, Germany.

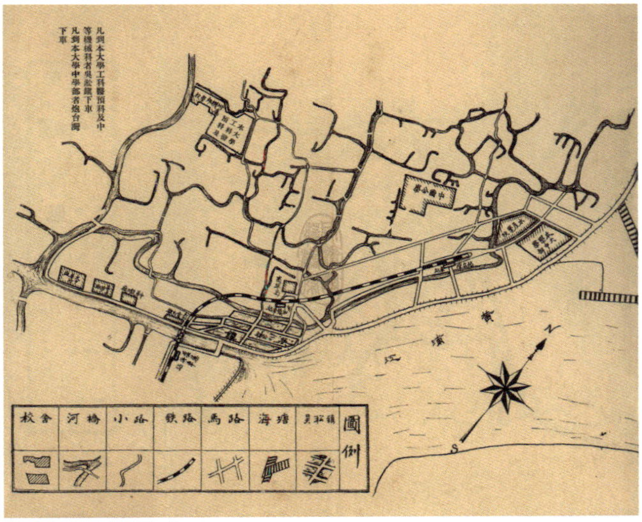

迁校吴淞中国公学后的学校各部分布图。工科大学部在炮台湾海军学校，实习工厂在中国公学。

Distribution of different parts of Tongji after its move to the Chinese Public School in Wusong: the internship factory at the Chinese Public School and the Engineering School at the Navy Academy in Paotaiwan.

迁校吴淞后，学校更名为“同济医工学校”，图为校门。

Entrance of the school which was renamed as Tongji Medical and Engineer ng School after its move to Wusong.

建新校舍，派新教师

A New Campus with New Teachers

1919 年，同济在吴淞购地 150 亩，1920 年开始新建校舍，由学校德籍建筑学教师埃里希·欧白兰设计。校董会和阮尚介校长通过与政府协商，使在同济任教的德籍教师不被遣送回国。同时受一战后德国对华文化政策的影响，德国派送到同济的教师质量进一步提高。

Tongji purchased 150 *mu* (1*mu*=666.7m²) of land in Wusong in 1919 and began to build a new campus in 1920, based upon a design by Mr. Erich Oberlein, a German teacher of architecture at the school. The school board of trustees and President Ruan Shangjie managed to keep the German teachers from being sent back to Germany through consultation with the government. Meanwhile, more and more better German teachers were sent to China owing to a German cultural policy favorable to China after World War I.

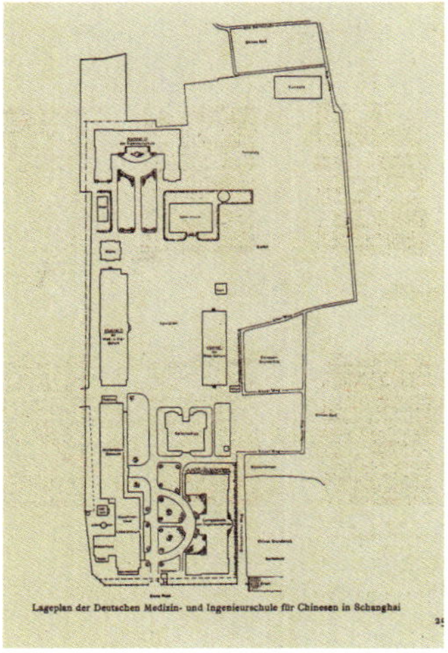

同济大学平面图 (1924)
Plan of Tongji University in 1924

吴淞校舍的设计师埃里希·欧白兰
Mr. Erich Oberlein, designer of the school campus in Wusong

大礼堂及工科讲堂（1924）
The school auditorium and the teaching building of engineering (1924)

工科宿舍（1924）
Dormitory for engineering students (1924)

实习工厂（1924）
The internship factory in 1924

■ 特许工程师裴宁，教授电工学、电工实习。

Mr. Böning, a chartered engineer who taught electrical engineering and supervised student practice in electrical engineering.

■ 特许工程师斐禄维，教授静力学、道路学、测量学和混凝土构造学。

Mr. Berlowitz, a chartered engineer who taught statics, road engineering, surveying and concrete structure.

■ 理学博士鲍尔德，教授化学

Dr. Bartelt, a chemistry teacher

■ 特许工程师阚尼格，教授水利学、力学。

Mr. Kienningers, a chartered engineer who taught hydraulics and mechanics.

■ 特许工程师吕霭，教授机件学、汽锅学和起重机。

Mr. Rühe, a chartered engineer who taught mechanical science, boilers and cranes.

■ 特许工程师施比禄，教授热动学、唧筒学和蒸汽涡轮学。

Mr. Spiro, a chartered engineer who taught thermal dynamics, rotary pumps and steam turbines.

■ 特许工程师丁克福，教授动力机、动力机实习。

Mr. Tenkhoff, a chartered engineer who taught engine-powered machines and supervised student practice in engine-powered machines.

■ 特许工程师史娄纳，教授铁道学、桥梁学、铁工建筑学和隧道建筑学。

Mr. Slonarin, a chartered engineer who taught railway engineering, bridge engineering, ironwork, and tunnel construction.

实习工厂，设备一流

An Internship Factory with Sophisticated Facilities

“德文工学堂”在开办之初就设立了实习工厂，1912 年，德国捐赠的大量现代化机器、模型运至上海，为实习工厂的建立奠定了基础。1913 年夏，校办实习工厂完工，首任工厂管理为德国人诺斯。1915 年新建模型练习所、物质试验所、电机试验室和土木工程模型陈列所等，实习工厂已臻完善。至 1925 年实习工厂已建成 10 个生产部门，成为展示纯正的德国技术及科学工作的一个样板，居当时国内大学一流水平。

An internship factory was built soon after the German Engineering School was established. A large number of modern machines and models donated by Germany were shipped to Shanghai in 1912 which laid a firm foundation for internship factory. In the summer of 1913, construction of the internship factory was completed and Mr. Noss from Germany acted as its first manager. In 1915, the factory was largely expanded by the addition of a model practice workshop, a material testing workshop, an electrical machinery laboratory and an exhibition room of civil engineering models. By 1925 with ten different workshops and rooms in place, the internship factory had become a model showcasing authentic German technology and science. The factory was widely acknowledged as a first class student internship factory among engineering schools in China.

“德文工学堂”创办之初，供教学和实习用的机械、模型由一艘北德劳埃德公司的货轮从德国运至上海。

Machinery and models for teaching and internship were shipped to Shanghai from Germany in a cargo ship of Germanischer Lloyd soon after the German Engineering School was founded.

胡厥文（1895-1989），近代著名爱国实业家，1919 年至 1921 年主持实习工厂，他在劳动纪律、财务制度和产品质量方面做了一系列改革，使校办工厂得到迅速发展。

Mr. Hu Juewen (1895-1989), a famous patriotic industrialist, was responsible for the management of the internship factory from 1919 to 1921. The factory developed rapidly after he made reforms in work regulations, financial system and product quality

实习工厂首任工厂管理德国人诺斯

Mr. Noss from Germany, the first manager of the internship factory

“德文工学堂”实习工厂（原法租界校舍），左图为建设中，右图为建成后。

The internship factory of German Engineering School (the old campus at the French Concession)
Lleft: during construction; Right: after completion of construction

1920 年工厂管理诺斯（前排中）指导学生实习结束后与学生合影
Mr. Noss (front middle) with students after supervising them on their internship in 1920

弱电试验室
Low voltage supply system laboratory

强电试验室
High voltage supply system laboratory

机械模型陈列室
An exhibition room of mechanical models

土木模型陈列室
An exhibition room of civil engineering models

锻冶所
A smelting and forging workshop

翻砂间
A foundry workshop

制电所
An electricity workshop

木工所
A carpentry workshop

冷凝机（Balke A.-G. 公司生产）
A condenser (produced by Balke A-G Company)

蒸汽发电机（Bosig-Lloyd-Dynamowerke 生产）
A steam generator (produced by Bosig-Lloyd-Dynamowerke)

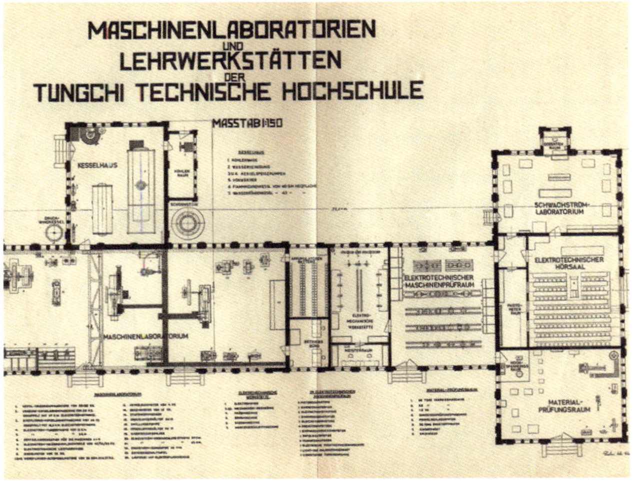

1924 年实习工厂部门及器械图示

A diagram of workshops and facilities at the internship factory in 1924

机器试验厂实习

Students on internship in a machinery laboratory

电工实习

Students on internship with electrical engineering

铁工实习

Students on internship with ironswork

测量实习

Students on internship with surveying

校长出访，升格大学

Presidential Visit to Germany and Promotion of University

一战结束后，同济继续加强对德联系。1920 年 7 月，阮尚介校长出访德国，得到了贝伦子和德国各界的大力支持，与德国远东协会签订了价值 400 万马克的仪器设备捐赠合同。1923 年 3 月，教育部下达训令，同意工科改为大学。1923 年 4 月 24 日，教育部下达指令，学校名称改为同济大学。

Tongji continued to strengthen its links with Germany after the First World War. President Ruan Shangjie visited Germany in July 1920. Strongly supported by Mr. Bernhard Berrens and people from all walks of life in Germany, he signed a contract for facility donations worth of 4 million DM with the Far East Association of Germany. In March, 1923, the Engineering School became a university with the authorization of the Ministry of Education. On April 24th, 1923, the university was officially renamed as Tongji University with the authorization of the Ministry of Education.

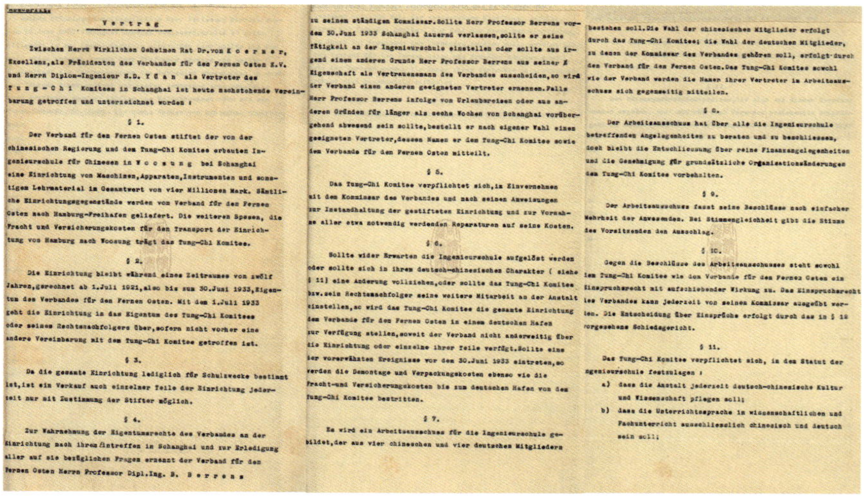

■ 1921 年 3 月 29 日阮尚介校长同德国远东协会签订的捐赠合同（德文）
A contract for facility donations (in German) signed by President Ruan Shangjie and the Far East Association of Germany on March 29th, 1921

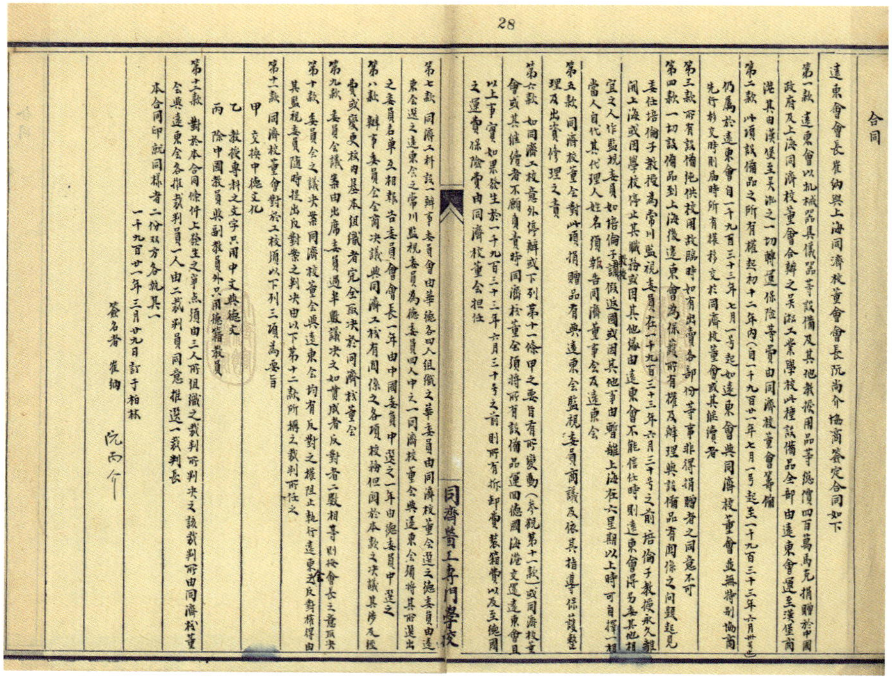

■ 1921 年 3 月 29 日阮尚介校长同德国远东协会签订的捐赠合同（中文）
A contract for facility donations (in Chinese) signed by President Ruan Shangjie and the Far East Association of Germany on March 29th, 1921.

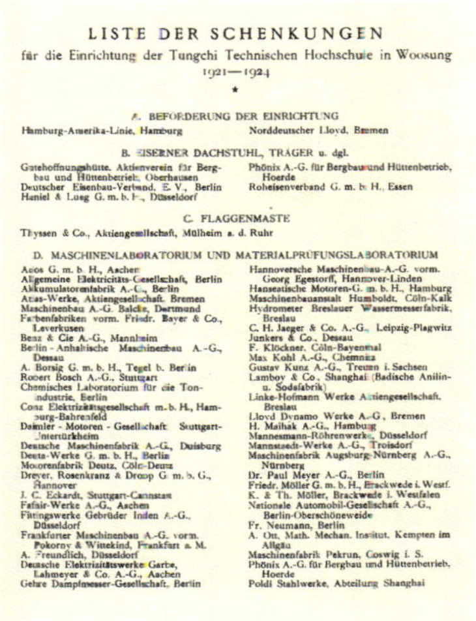

LISTE DER SCHENKUNGEN

für die Einrichtung der Tungchi Technischen Hochschule in Woosung

1921—1924

★

A. BEFÖRDERUNG DER EINRICHTUNG

Hamburg-Amerika-Linie, Hamburg
Norddeutscher Lloyd, Bremen

B. EISERNER DACHSTUHL, TRÄGER u. dgl.

Gutehoffnungshütte, Aktienverein für Bergbau und Hüttenbetrieb, Oberhausen
Deutscher Eisenbau-Verband, E. V., Berlin
Haniel & Lueg G. m. b. H., Düsseldorf
Phönix A.-G. für Bergbau und Hüttenbetrieb, Hoerde
Roheisenverband G. m. b. H., Essen

C. FLAGGENMASTE

Thyssen & Co., Aktiengesellschaft, Mülheim a. d. Ruhr

D. MASCHINENLABORATORIUM UND MATERIALPRÜFUNGSLABORATORIUM

Aeos G. m. b. H., Aachen
Allgemeine Elektricitäts-Gesellschaft, Berlin
Akkumulatorenfabrik A.-G., Berlin
Atlas-Werke, Aktiengesellschaft, Bremen
Maschinenbau A.-G. Balcke, Dortmund
Farbenfabriken vorm. Friedr. Bayer & Co., Leverkusen
Benz & Cie A.-G., Mannheim
Berlin-Anhaltische Maschinenbau A.-G., Dessau
A. Borsig G. m. b. H., Tegel b. Berlin
Robert Bosch A.-G., Stuttgart
Chemisches Laboratorium für die Tonindustrie, Berlin
Conz Elektrizitätsgesellschaft m. b. H., Hamburg-Bahrenfeld
Daimler-Motoren-Gesellschaft, Stuttgart-Untertürkheim
Deutsche Maschinenfabrik A.-G., Duisburg
Deuta-Werke G. m. b. H., Berlin
Motorenfabrik Deutz, Cöln-Deutz
Dreyer, Rosenkranz & Droop G. m. b. G., Hannover
J. C. Eckardt, Stuttgart-Cannstatt
Fafnir-Werke A.-G., Aachen
Fittingswerke Gebrüder Inden A.-G., Düsseldorf
Frankfurter Maschinenbau A.-G. vorm. Pokorny & Wittekind, Frankfurt a. M.
A. Freundlich, Düsseldorf
Deutsche Elektrizitätswerke Garbe, Lahmeyer & Co. A.-G., Aachen
Gehre Dampfmesser-Gesellschaft, Berlin
Hannoversche Maschinenbau-A.-G. vorm. Georg Egestorff, Hannover-Linden
Hanseatische Motoren-G. m. b. H., Hamburg
Maschinenbauanstalt Humboldt, Cöln-Kalk
Hydrometer Breslauer Wassermesserfabrik, Breslau
C. H. Jaeger & Co. A.-G., Leipzig-Plagwitz
Junkers & Co., Dessau
F. Klöckner, Cöln-Bayenthal
Max Kohl A.-G., Chemnitz
Gustav Kunz A.-G., Treuen i. Sachsen
Lamboy & Co., Shanghai (Badische Anilin- u. Sodafabrik)
Linke-Hofmann Werke Aktiengesellschaft, Breslau
Lloyd Dynamo Werke A.-G., Bremen
H. Maihak A.-G., Hamburg
Mannesmann-Röhrenwerke, Düsseldorf
Mannstaedt-Werke A.-G., Troisdorf
Maschinenfabrik Augsburg-Nürnberg A.-G., Nürnberg
Dr. Paul Meyer A.-G., Berlin
Friedr. Möller G. m. b. H., Brackwede i. Westf.
K. & Th. Möller, Brackwede i. Westfalen
Nationale Automobil-Gesellschaft A.-G., Berlin-Oberschöneweide
Fr. Neumann, Berlin
A. Ott, Math. Mechan. Institut, Kempten im Allgäu
Maschinenfabrik Pekrun, Coswig i. S.
Phönix A.-G. für Bergbau und Hüttenbetrieb, Hoerde
Poldi Stahlwerke, Abteilung Shanghai

■ 1921 年至 1924 年德国工商界对同济的捐赠清单（部分）

A page of the list of donations to Tongji by German businesses and commercial sector from 1921 to 1924

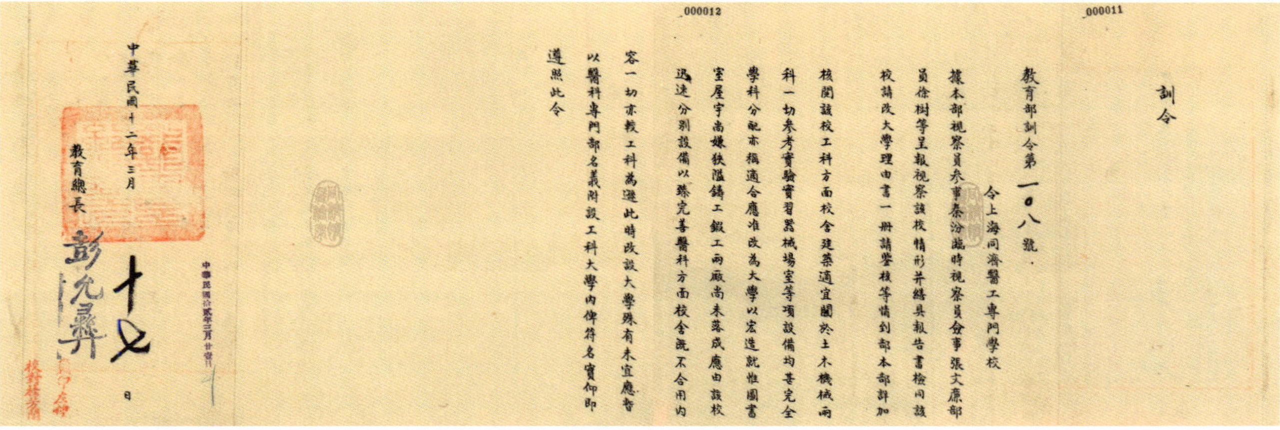

000011

000012

訓令

教育部訓令第一〇八號

令上海同濟醫工專門學校

據本部視察員參事秦汾臨時視察員僉事張文廉部員徐樹等呈報視察該校情形并繕具報告書檢同該校請改大學理由書一冊請鑒核等情到部本部詳加核閱該校工科方面校舍建築適宜關於土木機械兩科一切参考實驗實習器械場室等項設備均甚完全學科分配亦稱適合應准改為大學以宏造就惟圖書室屋宇尚嫌狹隘鑄工鍛工兩廠尚未落成應由該校迅速分別設備以臻完善醫科方面校舍既不合用內容一切亦較工科為遜此時改設大學殊有未宜應暫以醫科專門部名義附設工科大學內俾符名實仰即遵照此令

中華民國十二年三月十七日

教育總長 彭允彝

■ 1923 年 3 月，教育部同意同济工科改设大学，并附设医科专门部的训令。

Authorization of the Ministry of Education in March 1923 to change the engineering school to an engineering university with a medical training department affiliated to it

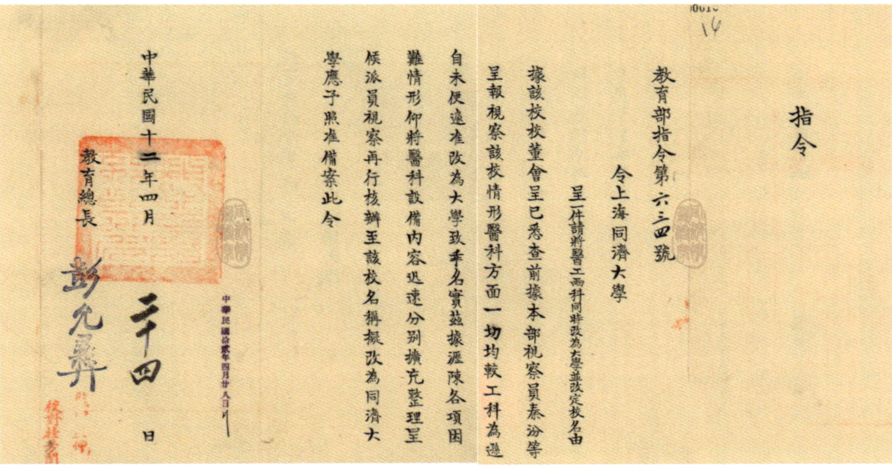

14

指令

教育部指令第六三四號

令上海同濟大學

呈一件請將醫工兩科同時改為大學並改定校名由

據該校校董會呈已悉查前據本部視察員秦汾等呈報視察該校情形醫科方面一切均較工科為遜自未便遽准改為大學致乖名實茲據瀝陳各項困難情形仰將醫科設備內容迅速分別擴充整理呈候派員視察再行核辦至該校名稱擬改為同濟大學應予照准備案此令

中華民國十二年四月二十四日

教育總長 彭允彝

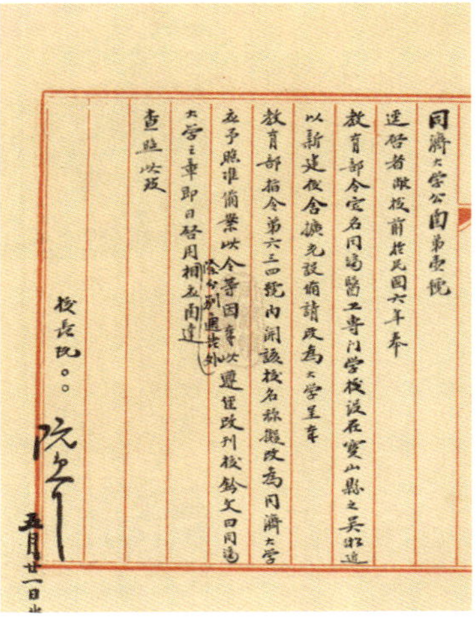

同濟大學公函第壹號

逕啓者敝校前於民國六年春

教育部令定名同濟醫工專門學校設在寶山縣之吳淞近以新建校舍擴充設備請改為大學呈奉

教育部指令第六三四號內開該校名稱擬改為同濟大學應予照准備案此令等因奉此除分別呈報外遵經改刊校鈐文曰同濟大學之章即日啓用相應函達

查照此致

校長阮○○

五月廿一日

■ 左：1923 年 4 月 24 日，教育部下达指令，学校名称改为同济大学。

Left: Authorization of the Ministry of Education on April 24th, 1923 to rename the University as Tongji University.

■ 右：1924 年 5 月 21 日，阮尚介校长签发的“同济大学公函第壹号”。

Right: *The First Official Document of Tongji University* endorsed by President Ruan Shangjie on May 21st, 1924.

奔赴各地，考察实业

Investigation of Industries in China

注重学生实践能力的培养，是同济工程教育的一大特色。除校办实习工厂是学生校内实习的重要基地外，校外参观和实习也是学生扩大视野、考察国情的重要途径。学校利用寒暑假，分组安排学生赴各地工厂参观，写出调查报告。

The engineering education of Tongji University was characterized by an emphasis on the training of student practical abilities. In addition to practice at the internship factory, students made investigations of companies and factories of investigation and did field research to broaden their horizons and to get first-hand information of the society. The university made the arrangements for the students to visit factories and const-uctions sites in groups during summer and winter holidays and asked them to write research reports on their investigations.

汉阳铁厂
Hanyang Iron Works

扬子机器公司
Yangtze Machinery Company

汉阳兵工厂
Hanyang Arsenal

武昌第一纺织有限公司
Wuchang First Textile Company Limited

汉冶萍公司
Hanyeping Company

湖北官矿局
Bureau of Geology and Mineral Resources of Hubei

财政部江南造币厂
Jiangnan Mint of Financial Ministry

海军鱼雷学校
Naval Torpedo School

■ 1921 年 6 月 28 日至 7 月 15 日，学生参观的工厂略表。
A list of factories that students visited from June 28th to July 15th, 1921

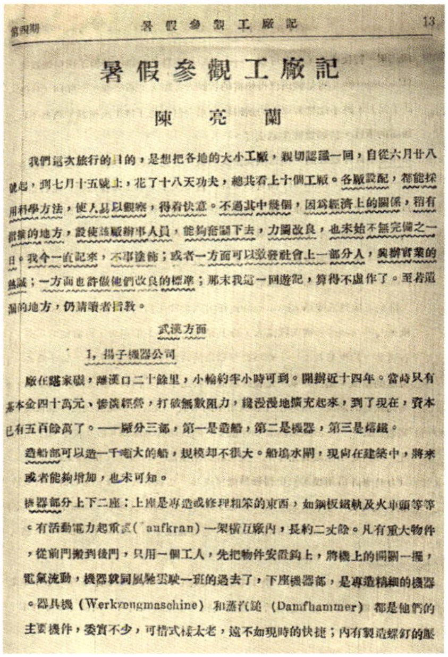

第四期　　暑假參觀工廠記　　13

暑假參觀工廠記

陳亮蘭

我們這次旅行的目的，是想把各地的大小工廠，親切認識一回，自從六月廿八號起，到七月十五號上，花了十八天功夫，總共看上十個工廠。各廠設配，都能採用科學方法，使人易以觀察，得着快意。不過其中幾個，因爲經濟上的關係，稍有拮据的地方，設使該廠辦事人員，能夠奮鬪下去，力圖改良，也未始不無完備之一日。我今一直記來，不事塗飾；或者一方面可以激發社會上一部分人，興辦實業的熱誠；一方面也許做他們改良的標準；那末我這一回遊記，算得不虛作了。至若遺漏的地方，仍請讀者指教。

武漢方面

1，揚子機器公司

廠在諶家磯，離漢口二十餘里，小輪約半小時可到。開辦近十四年。當時只有基本金四十萬元、慘淡經營，打破無數阻力，纔漫漫地擴充起來，到了現在，資本已有五百餘萬了。——廠分三部，第一是造船，第二是機器，第三是熔鐵。

造船部可以造一千噸大的船，規模却不很大。船塢水閘，現尚在建築中，將來或者能夠增加，也未可知。

機器部分上下二座：上座是專造或修理粗笨的東西，如鋼板鐵軌及火車頭等等。有活動電力起重機（aufkran）一架橫亘廠內，長約二丈餘。凡有重大物件，從前門搬到後門，只用一個工人，先把物件安置鈎上，將機上的開關一搖，電氣流動，機器就同風馳雲駛一班的過去了，下座機器部，是專造精細的機器。器具機（Werkzeugmaschine）和蒸汽鎚（Damfhammer）都是他們的主要機件，委實不少，可惜式樣太老，遠不如現時的快捷；內有製造螺釘的壓

■ 1921 年《同济杂志》刊载的《暑假参观工厂记》

An article about *Visits to Factories during Summer Vocation* published in *Tongji Journal* in 1921

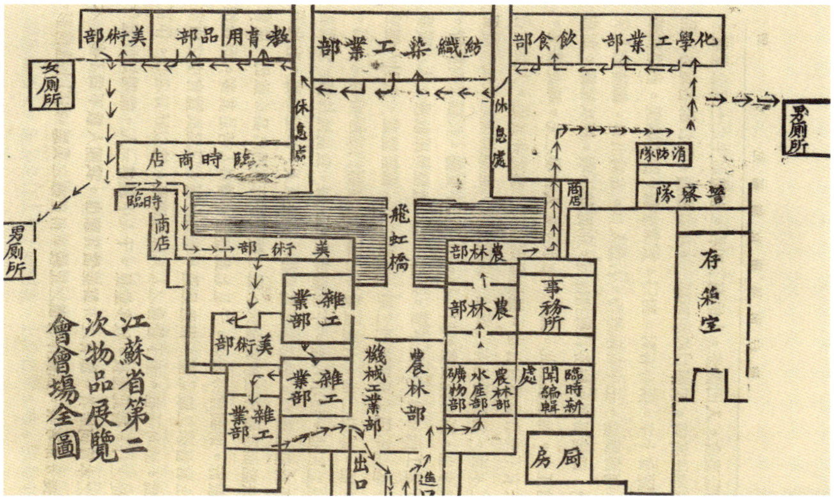

■ 1921 年工科机械专门科三年级学生所绘的江苏省第二次展览会会场图

A Guide Map of the Second Exhibition of Goods in Jiangsu Province, drawn by third-year students of Mechanical Engineering in 1921

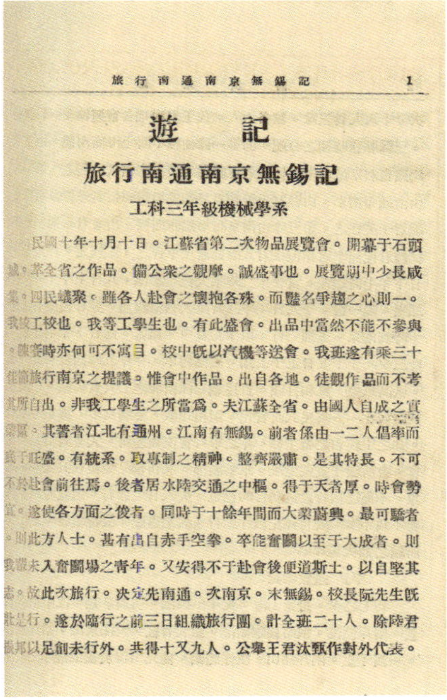

旅行南通南京無錫記　　1

遊　記

旅行南通南京無錫記

工科三年級機械學系

民國十年十月十日。江蘇省第二次物品展覽會。開幕于石頭城。萃全省之作品。備公衆之觀摩。誠盛事也。展覽期中少長咸集。四民蟻聚。雖各人赴會之懷抱各殊。而豔名爭趨之心則一。我校工校也。我等工學生也。有此盛會。出品中當然不能不參與。陳賽時亦何可不寓目。校中既以汽機等送會。我班遂有乘三十往簡旅行南京之提議。惟會中作品。出自各地。徒觀作品而不考其所自出。非我工學生之所當爲。夫江蘇全省。由國人自成之實業區。其著者江北有通州。江南有無錫。前者係由一二人倡率而臻于旺盛。有統系。取專制之精神。整齊嚴肅。是其特長。不可不於赴會前往焉。後者居水陸交通之中樞。得于天者厚。時會勢宜。遂使各方面之俊者。同時于十餘年間而大業蔚興。最可驚者。則此方人士。甚有出自赤手空拳。卒能奮鬪以至于大成者。則我儕未入奮鬪場之青年。又安得不于赴會後便道斯土。以自堅其志。故此次旅行。決定先南通。次南京。末無錫。校長阮先生旣許是行。遂於臨行之前三日組織旅行團。計全班二十人。除陸君振邦以足創未行外。共得十又九人。公舉王君汰甄作對外代表。

■ 《同济杂志》刊载的 1921 年工科机械专门科三年级学生《旅行南通南京无锡记》

An article on *Trips to Nantong, Nanjing and Wuxi* written by third-year students of Mechanical Engineering, published in *Tongji Journal* in 1921.

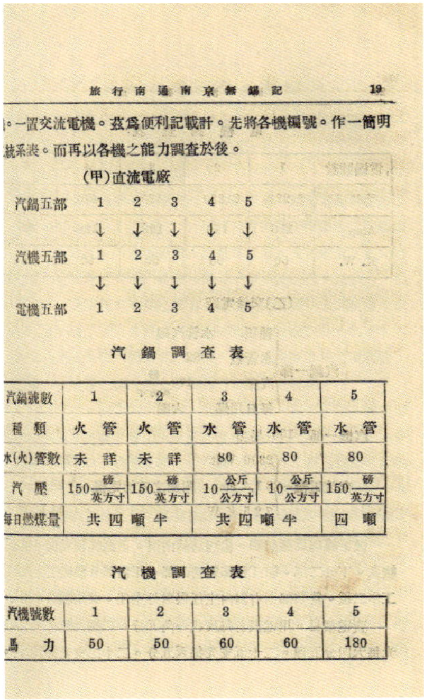

旅行南通南京無錫記　　19

一置交流電機。茲爲便利記載計。先將各機編號。作一簡明統系表。而再以各機之能力調查於後。

(甲)直流電廠

汽鍋五部　1　2　3　4　5
　　　　　↓　↓　↓　↓　↓
汽機五部　1　2　3　4　5
　　　　　↓　↓　↓　↓　↓
電機五部　1　2　3　4　5

汽鍋調查表

汽鍋號數	1	2	3	4	5
種類	火管	火管	水管	水管	水管
水(火)管數	未詳	未詳	80	80	80
汽壓	150 磅/英方寸	150 磅/英方寸	10 公斤/公方寸	10 公斤/公方寸	150 磅/英方寸
每日燃煤量	共四噸半		共四噸半		四噸

汽機調查表

汽機號數	1	2	3	4	5
馬力	50	50	60	60	180

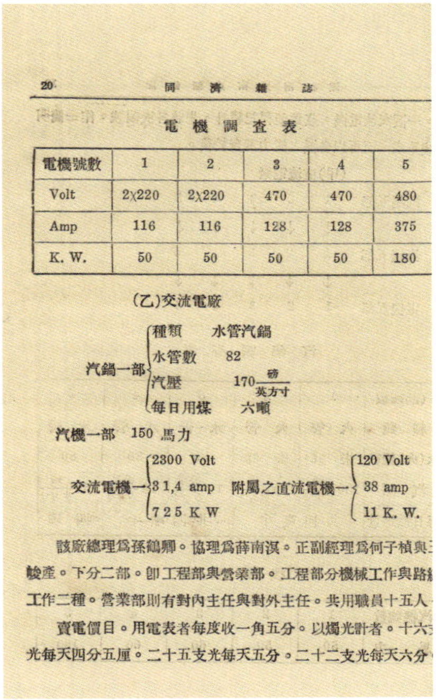

20　　同濟雜誌

電機調查表

電機號數	1	2	3	4	5
Volt	2χ220	2χ220	470	470	480
Amp	116	116	128	128	375
K. W.	50	50	50	50	180

(乙)交流電廠

汽鍋一部：種類　水管汽鍋；水管數　82；汽壓　170 磅/英方寸；每日用煤　六噸

汽機一部　150 馬力

交流電機一：2300 Volt；31,4 amp；725 K W　　附屬之直流電機一：120 Volt；38 amp；11 K. W.

該廠總理爲孫鶴卿。協理爲薛南溟。正副經理爲何子楨與

峻產。下分二部。卽工程部與營業部。工程部分機械工作與路

工作二種。營業部則有對內主任與對外主任。共用職員十五人

賣電價目。用電表者每度收一角五分。以燭光計者。十六

光每天四分五厘。二十五支光每天五分。二十二支光每天六分

■ 1921 年工科机械专门科三年级学生参观无锡耀明电灯厂所写的调查表

A completed questionnaire designed by third-year students of Mechanical Engineering on their visit to Wuxi Yaoming Lamp Factory in 1921

南通大生纺织公司
Nantong Dasheng Textile Company

南通广生榨油公司
Nantong Guangsheng Oil Extraction Company

南通资生冶铁厂
Nantong Zisheng Iron Factory

南京高等师范工艺实习场
Workshop of Nanjing Higher Normal School

南京皇城古物保存所
Nanjing Imperial Antique Preservation Institution

无锡振新纺织公司
Wuxi Zhenxin Textile Company

无锡茂新面粉厂
Wuxi Maoxin Flour Mill

无锡广勤机器纺织公司兼冶铁公司
Wuxi Guangqin Machine T

1921 年工科机械专门科三年级学生参观考察的工厂
Factories that third-year students of Mechanical Engineering visited in 1921

东游考工，西行问新

Knowledge of Engineering from East and West

为借鉴他国工程教育经验和工业发展成果，国外考察也是学校组织学生社会实践的途径。1923 年 7 月，阮尚介校长和施比禄教授带领机械科四年级 9 名学生，用 18 天时间到日本大坂、京都、东京、横滨，日光、足尾等城市参观了十几所工厂，写出了《东游考工记》的报告。此外，学校各类刊物上常发表留德同学在国外参观工厂、展览会的各种游记，向国内师友传达最新科学信息。

The university organized study trips abroad as part of social practice for students to learn about engineering education and the latest industrial development in other countries. In July 1923, nine fourth-year students of Mechanical Engineering headed by President Ruan Shangjie and Professor Spiro visited a over ten factories in Osaka, Kyoto, Tokyo, Yokohama, Nikko, Ashio, Japan in 18 days. They wrote a report on *Exploring Engineering in Japan* to share their experience with students at Tongji. Besides, students could update their knowledge of the development in science and technology in Germany by reading articles and reports published in Tongji newspapers and journals written by students who once studied in Germany.

■ 1923 年同济东游考察团出发时合影

Ready for an investigation trip to Japan in 1923

■ 足尾：铜矿制炼所

Ashio: Copper Mine Smelting Institution

■ 日光：日光电气精铜所

Nikko: Nikko Electrical Equipment and Refined Copper Instituion

■ 横滨：古河电气株式会社、电线制造所、护膜制造株式会社、户塚京滨电力株式会社变电所

Yokohama: Koga Electric Kabuskiki Kaisha, Wire Manufacturing Institution, Peristroma Manufacturing Kabuskiki Kaisha, Converting Station of Totsuka Keihin Electric Kabuskiki Kaisha

■ 东京：西门子电器株式会社东京总部

Tokyo: Tokyo Headquarter of Siemens Electric Kabuskiki Kaisha

■ 京都：帝国大学、宇治水电力发电所

Kyoto: Imperial University, Uji Hydroelectric Power Station

■ 大阪造币厂 - 大阪每日新闻社

Osaka: Mint, Mainichi Shimbun

■ 神户钟渊纺织株式会社

Kobe: Zhongyuan Textile Kabuskiki Kaisha

■ 1923 年同济东游考察团考察行程

Itinerary of Tongji Investigation Delegation to Japan in 1923

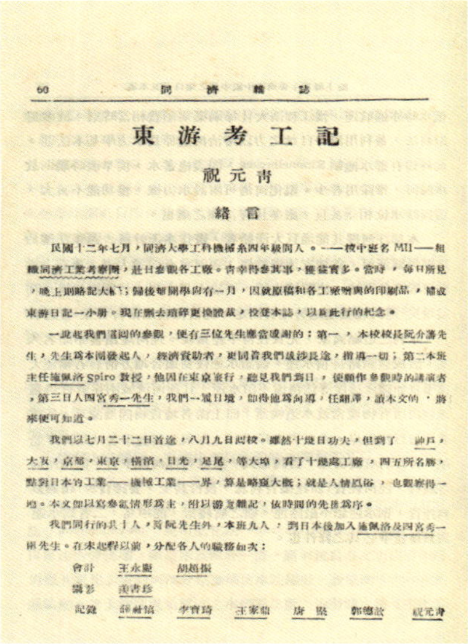

60 同 濟 雜 誌

東游考工記

祝元青

緒言

民國十二年七月，同濟大學工科機械系四年級同人。——校中班名 MII——組織同濟工業考察團，赴日參觀各工廠。青幸得參其事，獲益實多。當時，每日所見，晚上則略記大概；歸後離開學尚有一月，因就原稿和各工廠贈與的印刷品，補成東游日記一小册。現在删去瑣碎更換體裁，投登本誌，以贏此行的紀念。

一說起我們這回的參觀，便有三位先生應當感謝的：第一，本校校長阮介藩先生，先生爲本團發起人，經濟資助者，更同着我們跋涉長途，指導一切；第二本班主任施佩洛 Spiro 教授，他因在東京旅行，聽見我們到日，便願作參觀時的講演者，第三日人四宮秀一先生，我們一觸日境，即得他爲向導，任翻譯，讀本文的，將來便可知道。

我們以七月二十二日首途，八月九日回校。雖然十幾日功夫，但到了神戶，大阪，京都，東京，橫濱，日光，足尾，等大埠，看了十幾處工廠，四五所名勝，對到日本的工業——機械工業——界，算是略窺大概；就是人情風俗，也觀察得一些。本文即以寫參觀情形爲主，附以游覽雜記，依時間的先後爲序。

我們同行的共十人，爲阮先生外，本班九人；到日本後加入施佩洛及四宮秀一兩先生。在未起程以前，分配各人的職務如次：

會計　王永懇　胡超振

攝影　黃書珍

記錄　薛树镐　李寶琦　王家韞　唐　堅　郭總欲　祝元青

1923 年同济东游考察团成员祝元青所记载的考察报告《东游考工记》

A report on *Exploring Engineering in Japan* by Zhu Yuanqing, a student on the Tongji investigation trip to Japan in 1923

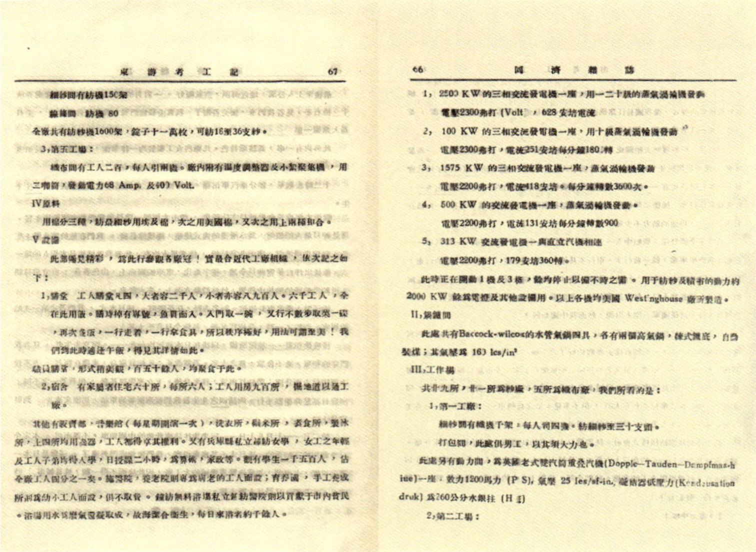

東 游 考 工 記 67

細紗間有紡機150架

線錘間　紡機 80

全廠共有紡紗機1600架，錠子十一萬枚，可紡16至36支紗。

3，第五工場：

織布間有工人二百，每人司兩機。廠內附有濕度調整器及小型聚塵機，用二喞筒，發動電力68 Amp. 及400 Volt.

IV原料

用棉分三種，紡最細紗用埃及棉，次之用美國棉，又次之用上兩種和合。

V設備

此部最見精彩，爲此行參觀各廠冠！實最合近代工廠組織，依次記之如下：

1，膳堂　工人膳堂凡四，大者容二千人，小者亦容八九百人。六千工人，全在此用飯。膳時掉有號牌，魚貫而入。入門取一碗，又行不數步取菜一碟，再次盛飯，一行走着，一行拿食具，所以秩序極好，用法可謂至美！我們到此時適逢午飯，得見其詳情如此。

職員膳堂，形式稍美觀，百五十餘人，均聚食于此。

2，宿舍　有家屬者住宅六十所，每所六人；工人用房九百所，攝地道以通工廠。

其他有販賣部，音樂館（每星期開演一次），洗衣所，縫紉所，養食所，製冰所，上四所均用機器，工人都得享其權利。又有兵庫縣私立鐘紡女學，女工之年輕及工人子弟均得入學，日授課二小時，爲算術，家政等。觀有學生一千五百人，佔全廠工人四分之一矣。施醫院，養老院則專爲病老的工人而設；育兒園，手工養成所則爲幼小工人而設，俱不取費。鐘紡無料浴場私立鐘紡醫院則以賈獻于市內貧民。浴場用水皆經氣壓濾取成，故極潔合衛生，每日來浴者約千餘人。

66 同 濟 雜 誌

1，2500 KW 的三相交流發電機一座，用一二十級的蒸氣渦輪機發動
電壓2300弗打（Volt），628 安培電流

2，100 KW 的三相交流發電機一座，用十級蒸氣渦輪機發動
電壓2300弗打，電流251安培每分鐘180轉

3，1575 KW 的三相交流發電機一座，蒸氣渦輪機發動
電壓2200弗打，電流418安培。每分鐘轉數3600次。

4，500 KW 的交流發電機一座，蒸氣渦輪機發動。
電壓2200弗打，電流131安培每分鐘轉數900

5，313 KW 交流發電機一與直立汽機相連
電壓2200弗打，179安培360轉。

此時正在開動 1 機及 3 機，餘均停止以備不時之需。用于紡紗及織布的動力約2000 KW 餘爲電燈及其他設備用。以上各機均美國 Westinghouse 廠所製造。

II，鍋爐間

此處共有Baccock-wilcox的水管氣鍋四具，各有兩個高氣鍋，鏈式爐底，自動裝煤；其氣壓爲 160 lcs/in²

III，工作場

共廿九所，廿一所爲紗廠，五所爲織布廠，我們所看的是：

1，第一工廠：

細紗間有機器千架，每人司四機。紡細紗至三十支頭。

打包間，此處俱男工，以其須大力也。

此處另有動力間，爲英國老式雙汽筒重叠汽機（Dopple-Tauden-Dempfmaschine）一座，馬力1200馬力（P S），氣壓 25 les/sf-in.，凝結器低壓力（Kondensationdruk）爲260公分水銀柱（H g）

2，第二工場：

1923 年同济东游考察团对钟渊纺织株式会社的考察记录

A report on Zhongyuan Textile Co. Ltd by a student on the Tongji Investigation trip to Japan in 1923

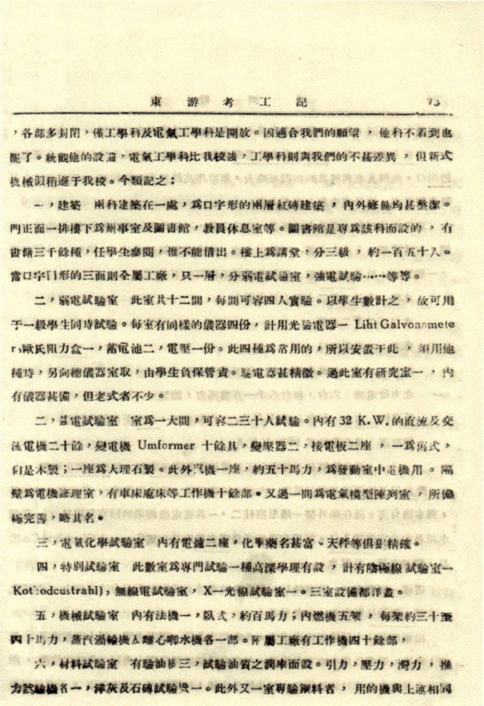

東 游 考 工 記 73

，各部多封閉，僅工學科及電氣工學科是開放。因適合我們的願望，他科不看到也罷了。統觀他的設備，電氣工學科比我校强，工學科則與我們的不甚差異，但新式機械似稍遜于我校。今類記之：

一，建築　兩科建築在一處，爲口字形的兩層紅磚建築，內外修飾均甚整潔。門正面一排樓下爲辦事室及圖書館，教員休息室等。圖書館是專爲該科而設的，有書籍三千餘種，任學生參閱，惟不能借出。樓上爲講堂，分三級，約一百五十人。當口字门形的三面則全屬工廠，只一層，分弱電試驗室，強電試驗……等等。

二，弱電試驗室　此室共十二間，每間可容四人實驗。以學生數計之，故可用于一級學生同時試驗。每室有同樣的儀器四份，計用光驗電器一 Liht Galvonometer，歐氏阻力盒一，蓄電池二，電壓一份。此四種爲常用的，所以安置于此，須用他種時，另向總儀器室取，由學生負保管責。驗電器甚精微。過此室有研究室一，內有儀器甚備，但老式者不少。

二，强電試驗室　室爲一大間，可容二三十人試驗。內有 32 K.W. 的直流及交流電機二十餘，變電機 Umformer 十餘具，變壓器二，接電板二座，一爲舊式，仍是木製；一座爲大理石製。此外汽機一座，約五十馬力，爲發動室中電機用。隔壁爲電機修理室，有車床磨床等工作機十餘部。又過一間爲電氣模型陳列室，所備極完善，略其名。

三，電氣化學試驗室　內有電爐二座，化學藥名甚富，天秤等俱甚精確。

四，特別試驗室　此數室爲專門試驗一種高深學理有設，計有陰極線試驗室一 Kotodcustrahl），無線電試驗室，X—光線試驗室一。三室設備都詳盡。

五，機械試驗室　內有汽機一，臥式，約百馬力；內燃機五架，每架約三十至四十馬力，蒸汽渦輪機及離心喞水機各一部。附屬工廠有工作機四十餘部，

六，材料試驗室　有驗油器三，試驗油質之潤滑而設。引力，壓力，滑力，推力試驗機各一，洋灰及石磚試驗器一。此外又一室專驗鋼料者，用的機與上述相同

1923 年同济东游考察团对京都帝国大学工科的考察记录

A report on the engineering program in Kyoto Imperial University by a student on the Tongji Investigation trip to Japan in 1923

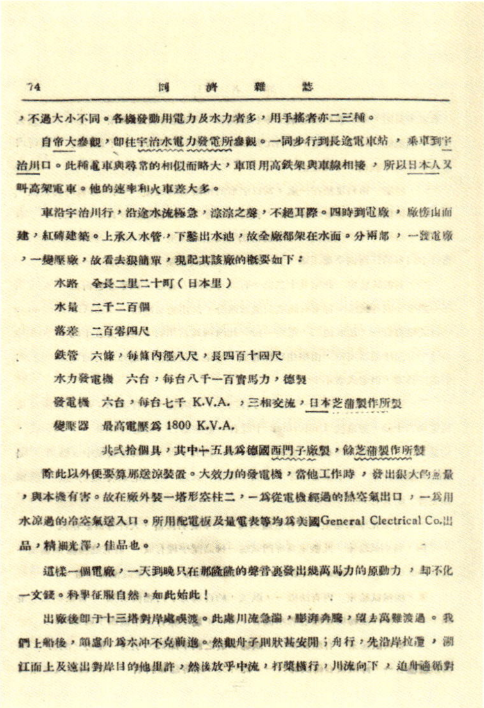

74 同 濟 雜 誌

，不過大小不同。各機發動用電力及水力者多，用手搖者亦二三種。

自帝大參觀，即往宇治水電力發電所參觀。一同步行到長途電車站，乘車到宇治川口。此種電車與尋常的相似而略大，車頂用高鐵架與車線相接，所以日本人又叫高架電車。他的速率和火車差大多。

車沿宇治川行，沿途水流極急，淙淙之聲，不絕耳際。四時到電廠，廠傍山而建，紅磚建築。上承入水管，下臨出水池，故全廠都架在水面。分兩部，一發電廠，一變壓廠，故看去狠簡單，現記其該廠的概要如下：

水路　全長二里二十町（日本里）

水量　二千二百個

落差　二百零四尺

鐵管　六條，每條內徑八尺，長四百十四尺

水力發電機　六台，每台八千一百實馬力，德製

發電機　六台，每台七千 K.V.A.，三相交流，日本芝浦製作所製

變壓器　最高電壓爲 1800 K.V.A.

共式拾個具，其中十五具爲德國西門子廠製，餘芝浦製作所製

除此以外便要算那送涼裝置。大效力的發電機，當他工作時，發出很大的熱量，與本機有害。故在廠外裝一塔形空柱二，一爲從電機經過的熱空氣出口，一爲用水涼過的冷空氣送入口。所用配電板及量電表等均爲美國General Clectrical Co.出品，精細光澤，佳品也。

這樣一個電廠，一天到晚只在那隆隆的聲音裏發出幾萬馬力的原動力，却不化一文錢。科學征服自然，如此如此！

出廠後即于十三塔對岸處渡渡。此處川流急湍，澎湃奔騰，望去萬難渡過。我們上船後，頗慮舟爲水冲不克前進。然觀舟子則狀甚安閒；舟行，先沿岸拉纜，溯江而上及遠出對岸目的地里許，然後放乎中流，打槳橫行，川流向下，追舟適循對

1923 年同济东游考察团对宇治水电力发电所的考察记录

A report on Uji Hydroelectric Power Station by a student on the Tongji Investigation trip to Japan in 1923

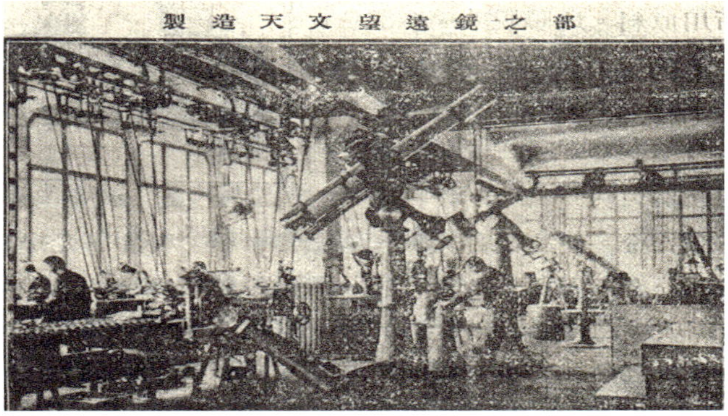

■ 留德学生张致果参观德国耶拿蔡司光学仪器厂后，向国内学子发回通讯，介绍参观详情，图为他记载的工厂全景。

A panoramic view of Jana Carl Zeiss Optical Instrument Factory, Germany as recorded in Zhang Zhiguo's report on his visit to the factory

■ 张致果在参观游记中记载的蔡司光学仪器厂场内工作场景

An astronomical telescope making workshop as recorded in Zhang Zhiguo's report on his visit to Jana Carl Zeiss Optical Instrument Factory, Germany

■ 张致果在参观游记中记载的蔡司光学仪器厂最新投影仪

A newly-released projector as recorded in Zhang Zhiguo's report on his visit to Jana Carl Zeiss Optical Instrument Factory, Germany

■ 张致果在参观游记中记载的蔡司光学仪器厂制造天文望远镜的厂房

A working scene as recorded in Zhang Zhiguo's report on his visit to Jana Carl Zeiss Optical Instrument Factory, Germany

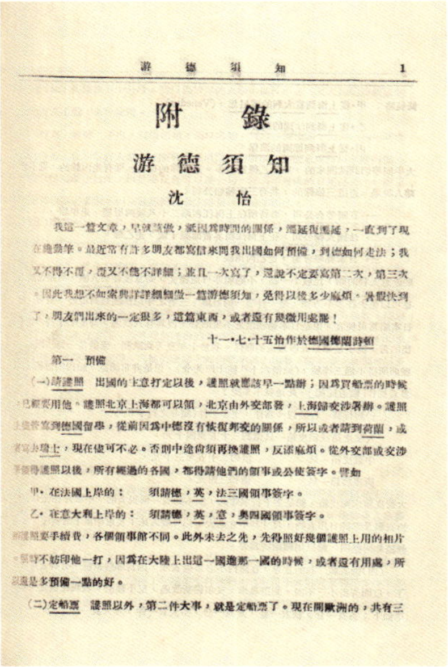

游德須知 1

附錄

游德須知

沈怡

我這一篇文章，早就該做，祇因爲時間的關係，遲延復遲延，一直到了現在纔動筆。最近常有許多朋友都寫信來問我出國如何預備，到德如何走法；我又不得不覆，覆又不能不詳細；並且一次寫了，還說不定要寫第二次，第三次。因此我想不如索興詳詳細細做一篇游德須知，免得以後多少麻煩。暑假快到了，朋友們出來的一定很多，這篇東西，或者還有幾微用處罷！

十一·七·十五怡作於德國德閑詩頓

第一 預備

(一)請護照 出國的主意打定以後，護照就應該早一點辦；因爲買船票的時候已經要用他。護照北京上海都可以領，北京由外交部發，上海歸交涉署辦。護照上也寫到德國留學，從前因爲中德沒有恢復邦交的關係，所以或者請到荷蘭，或者寫去瑞士，現在儘可不必。否則中途尚須再換護照，反添麻煩。從外交部或交涉署領得護照以後，所有經過的各國，都得請他們的領事或公使簽字。譬如

甲· 在法國上岸的： 須請德，英，法三國領事簽字。

乙· 在意大利上岸的： 須請德，英，意，奧四國領事簽字。

簽護照要手續費，各個領事館不同。此外未去之先，先得照好幾個護照上用的相片。照時不妨印他一打，因爲在大陸上出這一國進那一國的時候，或者還有用處，所以還是多預備一點的好。

(二)定船票 護照以外，第二件大事，就是定船票了。現在開歐洲的，共有三

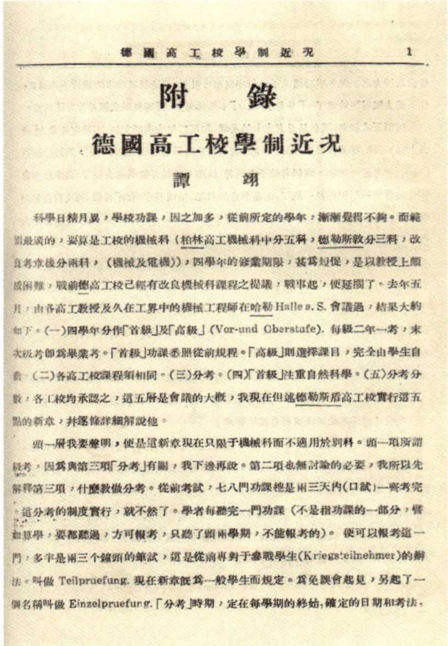

德國高工校學制近況 1

附錄

德國高工校學制近況

譚翊

科學日精月異，學校功課，因之加多，從前所定的學年，漸漸覺得不夠。而範圍最廣的，要算是工校的機械科（柏林高工機械科中分五科，德勒斯敦分三科，改良考章後分兩科，（機械及電機）），四學年的修業期限，甚爲短促，是以教授上頗感困難，戰前德高工校已經有改良機械科課程之提議，戰事起，便延擱了。去年五月，由各高工教授及久在工界中的機械工程師在哈勒 Halle a. S. 會議過，結果大約如下。(一)四學年分作「首級」及「高級」(Vor-und Oberstufe). 每級二年一考，末次級考即爲畢業考。「首級」功課悉照從前規程。「高級」則選擇課目，完全由學生自定。(二)各高工校課程須相同。(三)分考。(四)「首級」注重自然科學。(五)分考分數，各工校均承認之，這五層是會議的大概，我現在但述德勒斯盾高工校實行這五點的新章，并逐條詳細解說他。

頭一層我要聲明，便是這新章現在只限于機械科而不適用於別科。頭一項所謂級考，因爲與第三項「分考」有關，我下邊再說。第二項也無討論的必要，我所以先解釋第三項，什麼叫做分考。從前考試，七八門功課總是兩三天內(口試)一齊考完。這分考的制度實行，就不然了。學者每聽完一門功課（不是指功課的一部分，譬如算學，要都聽過，方可報考，只聽了頭兩學期，不能報考的）。便可以報考這一門，多半是兩三个鐘頭的筆試，這是從前專對于參戰學生(Kriegsteilnehmer)的辦法。叫做 Teilpruefung. 現在新章既爲一般學生而規定。爲免誤會起見，另起了一個名稱叫做 Einzelpruefung.「分考」時期，定在每學期的終始，確定的日期和考法，

左：同济工科留德学生沈怡在《同济杂志》上发表的《留德须知》

Left: *Guide to Study in Germany* published in *Tongji Journal* by Shen Yi, an engineering student of Tongji who studied in Germany.

右：同济工科留德学生谭翊在《同济杂志》上发表的《德国高工校学制近况》

Right: A report on *The Educational System in German Advanced Engineering Schools* published in *Tongji Journal* by Tan Yi, an engineering student of Tongji who studied in Germany.

1923 年 10 月，同济工科的魏时珍等中国留学生与朱德（前排右四）在哥廷根合影。

Mr. Zhu De (fourth front right) with Wei Shizhen, an engineering student of Tongji and other Chinese students who studied in Gottingen, Germany in October, 1923

创办刊物，交流学术

Academic Journals for Development in Research

1915 年，德籍教师德贵林、容固两人合建模型练习所、物质实验所，康拉德·白慈博士装置电机试验室。随着科研设备的完善，科研工作逐步开展。1917 年国人接管后，随着从医工专门学校向大学过渡，各项制度相继建立和健全，学术空气逐步形成。《同济》、《自觉月刊》、《同济杂志》等学术刊物相继创刊，学校和学生社团还组织编写了包含大量科研成果的其它出版物。

In 1915, German teachers Grahl G De and Jung A set up a model practice room and a material laboratory, and Dr. Baetz Konrad an electrical machinery laboratory. Research work gradually got under way when more research facilities were in place. An interest in academic research was aroused when new university regulations and rules were established following its change in status from a school to a university after the take-over of the school by Chinese in 1917. Such academic journals as *Tongji, Self-consciousness Monthly* and *Tongji Journal* came into being. In addition, other forms of publications were made by student societies as well as the university to promote research results.

■ 《同济》创刊于 1918 年 9 月 1 日，是学校编辑出版的第一本学报。

Tongji, the first issue of which was published on September 1st, 1918 was the first academic journal of Tongji University.

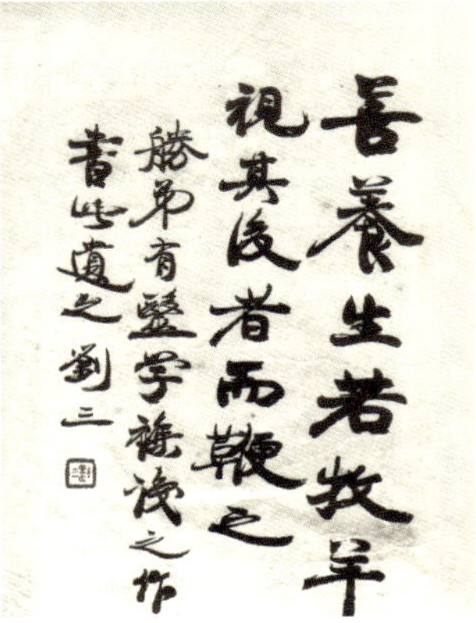

■ 清末著名书法家刘三为《同济》创刊号的题词：“善养生若牧羊，视其后者而鞭之”。

Inscription on the first issue of *Tongji* by Mr. Liu San, a famous calligrapher in late Qing Dynasty: Training students is like herding sheep, whip him only when he has fallen behind.

■ 中华民国首任教育总长蔡元培为《同济》杂志题词

Inscription for *Tongji* by Mr. Cai Yuanpei, the first Minister of Education of the Republic of China.

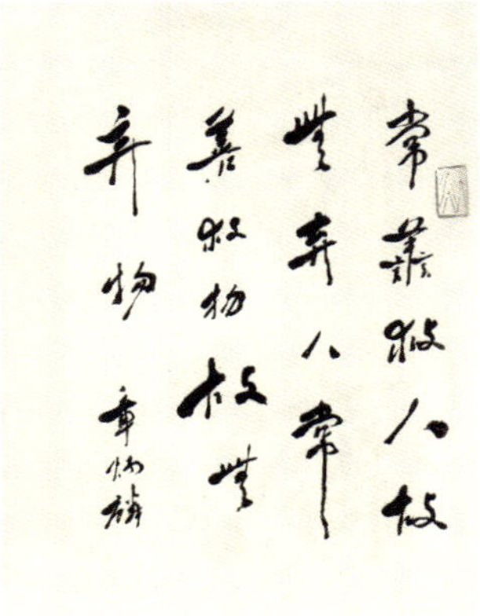

■ 清末民初民主革命家、思想家、著名学者章太炎为《同济》杂志题词。

Inscription for *Tongji* by Mr. Zhang Taiyan, a democratic revolutionary, a thinker and a famous scholar in late Qing Dynasty.

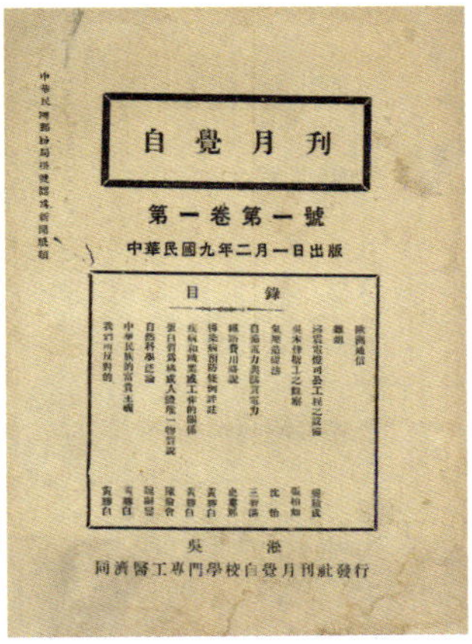

自覺月刊

第一卷第一號

中華民國九年二月一日出版

目錄

同濟醫工專門學校自覺月刊社發行

■ 1920 年创刊的《自觉月刊》

Self-consciousness Monthly published in 1920

自覺週報

■ 1919 年创刊的《自觉周报》，由同济自觉会主编。

Self-consciousness Weekly published in 1919 was edited by Tongji Self-consciousness Society.

1921 年 7 月 1 日创刊的《同济杂志》创刊号

The 1st issue of *Tongji Journal* on July 1st, 1921

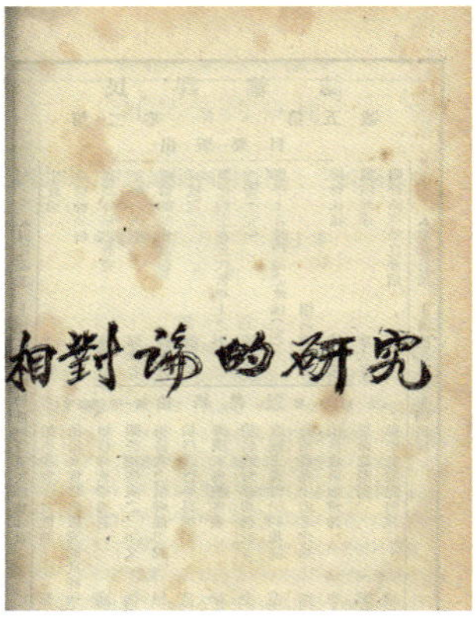

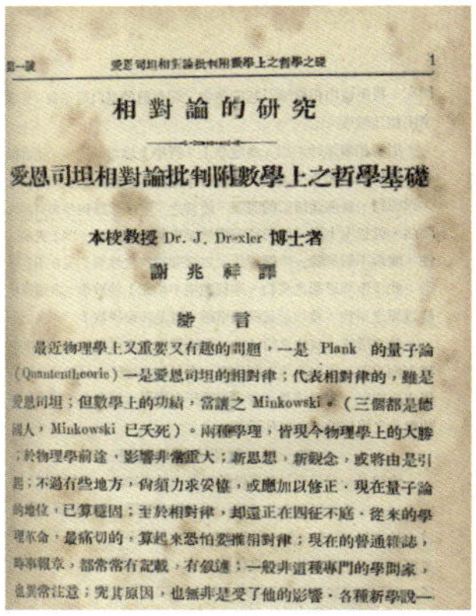

第一號 愛恩司坦相對論批判附數學上之哲學之礎 1

相對論的研究

愛恩司坦相對論批判附數學上之哲學基礎

本校教授 Dr. J. Drexler 博士著

謝兆祥譯

緒言

最近物理學上又重要又有趣的問題，一是 Plank 的量子論 (Quantentheorie) 一是愛恩司坦的相對律；代表相對律的，雖是愛恩司坦；但數學上的功績，當讓之 Minkowski。（三個都是德國人，Minkowski 已夭死）。兩種學理，皆現今物理學上的大勝；於物理學前途，影響非常重大；新思想，新觀念，或將由是引起；不過有些地方，尚須力求妥協，或應加以修正。現在量子論的地位，已算穩固；至於相對律，却還正在四征不庭。從來的學理革命，最痛切的，算起來恐怕要推相對律；現在的普通雜誌，時事報章，都常常有記載，有叙述；一般非這種專門的學問家，也異常注意；究其原因，也無非是受了他的影響。各種新學說—

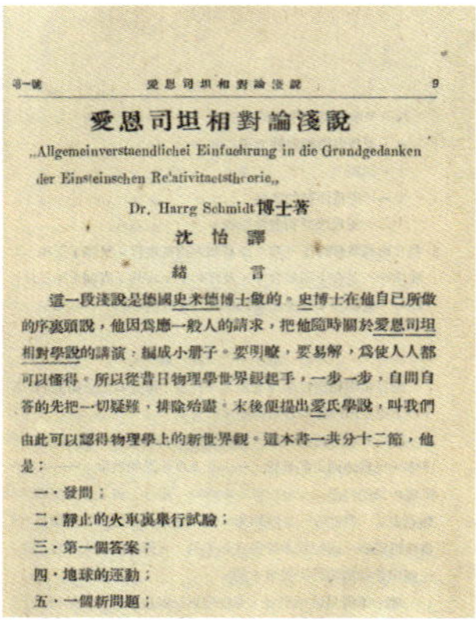

第一號 愛恩司坦相對論淺說 9

愛恩司坦相對論淺說

„Allgemeinverstaendlichei Einfuehrung in die Grundgedanken der Einsteinschen Relativitaetstheorie„

Dr. Harrg Schmidt 博士著

沈怡譯

緒言

這一段淺說是德國史米德博士做的。史博士在他自已所做的序裏頭說，他因爲應一般人的請求，把他隨時關於愛恩司坦相對學說的講演，編成小冊子。要明瞭，要易解，爲使人人都可以懂得。所以從昔日物理學世界觀起手，一步一步，自問自答的先把一切疑難，排除殆盡。末後便提出愛氏學說，叫我們由此可以認得物理學上的新世界觀。這本書一共分十二節，他是：

一．發問；
二．靜止的火車裏舉行試驗；
三．第一個答案；
四．地球的運動；
五．一個新問題；

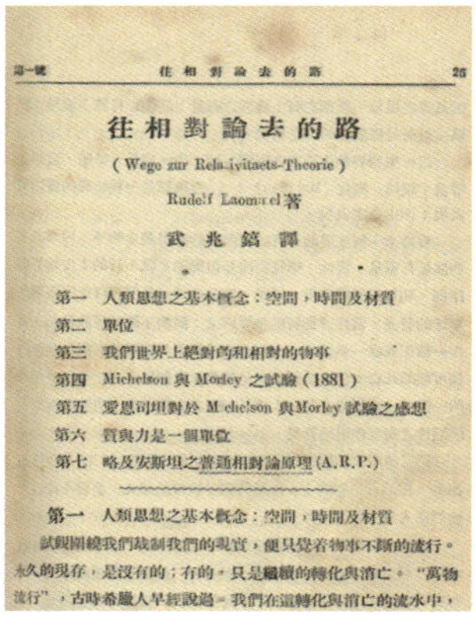

第一號 往相對論去的路 25

往相對論去的路

(Wege zur Relativitaets-Theorie)

Rudolf Laemmel 著

武兆鎬譯

第一 人類思想之基本概念：空間，時間及材質
第二 單位
第三 我們世界上絕對的和相對的物事
第四 Michelson 與 Morley 之試驗 (1881)
第五 愛恩司坦對於 Michelson 與 Morley 試驗之感想
第六 質與力是一個單位
第七 略及安斯坦之普通相對論原理 (A.R.P.)

第一 人類思想之基本概念：空間，時間及材質

試觀圍繞我們裁制我們的現實，便只覺着物事不斷的流行。永久的現存，是沒有的；有的，只是繼續的轉化與消亡。"萬物流行"，古時希臘人早經說過。我們在這轉化與消亡的流水中，

《同济杂志》创刊号刊载的“相对论的研究”专题

A special section on *Research on the Theory of Relativity* on the first issue *of Tongji Journal*

1928 年，德国柏林大学索默尔费尔德教授来同济演讲相对论。

A photo taken after a presentation on Theory of Relativity delivered at Tongji by Professor Sommerfeld from Berlin University, Germany, in 1928.

■ 《同济德文医工大学同学录》(1916)

Student Address Book of Tongji German Medical and Engineering School (1916)

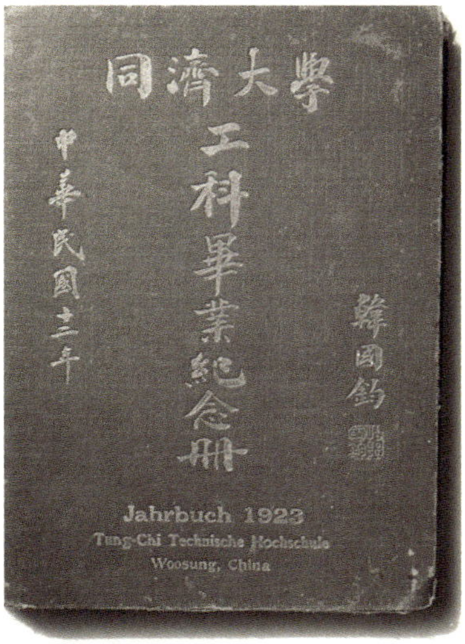

■ 《同济大学工科毕业纪念册》(1923)

Graduation Commemorative Album of Tongji Engineering Students (1923)

■ 《工科落成纪念册》(德文)

Commemorative Album of the Establishment of German Engineering School (in German)

■ 1916 年工科同志会合影。工科同志会最初由同济工科毕业生组成，后来范围进一步扩大，吸收工程领域相关人员入会，是行业内交流学问、联络感情的平台。

Students from Engineering Comrades Association in 1916. The association set up by a group of engineering graduates of Tongji attracted more and more people in the field of engineering and eventually became a platform of communications for professional in the engineering sector.

学有所长，造福社会

Knowledge and Skills for Social Service

随着学校声誉的提高和社会影响力的扩大，学生人数逐年增加。到 1927 年，机械和土木两科共有毕业生 187 人。中等机械科（机师科）共有毕业生 121 人。由于同济工科毕业生理论结合实际，动手能力较强，颇受社会各方面的欢迎。同济学子毕业后多数进入工务局、电话局等政府职能部门或在机械厂、电机厂、兵工厂当工程师或出国继续深造，致力于新旧交替的中国“改造与建设之使命”。

The number of students increased year by year when the university became more recognized and influential in the society. A total number of 187 students graduated from Mechanical and Civil Engineering programs by 1927 and 121 students from Secondary Mechanical Engineering (Machinist program). Graduates from Tongji were popular among employees since they had learnt both academic knowledge and technical skills at the university. Some graduates of Tongji University were employed in Works Bureau, Telephone Office and other government bodies while others as engineers in machinery factories, electric motor factories and arsenals. Still others chose to further their study in Germany to embark on a journey of constructing new China.

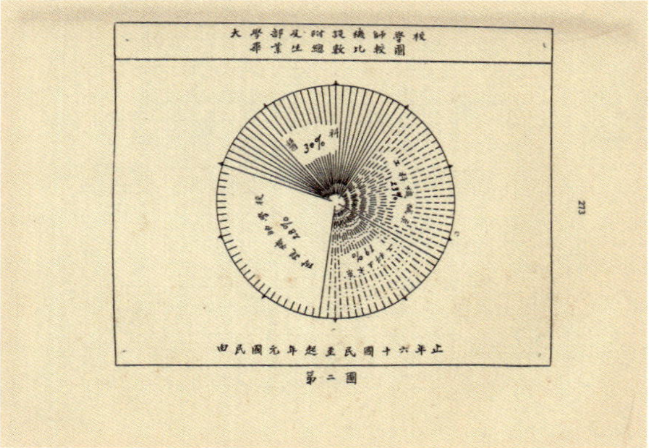

1912-1927 年大学部及附属机师学校毕业生总数比较图

A pie chart illustrating the total number of graduates from the university and the Affiliated Machinist School from 1912 to 1927

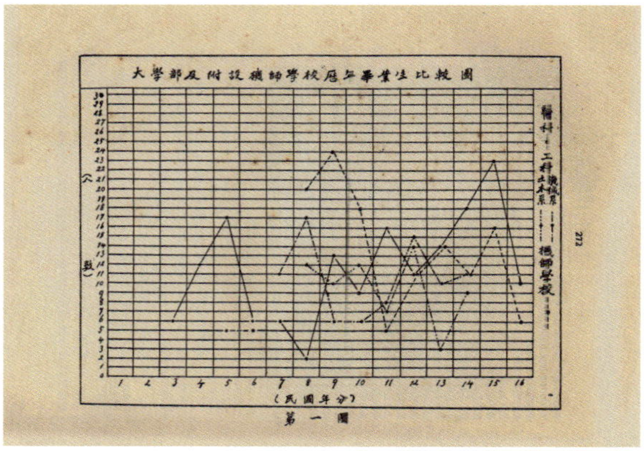

1912-1927 年大学部及附属机师学校历年毕业生比较图

A line diagram illustrating number of graduates from the university and the Affiliated Machinist School from 1912 to 1927

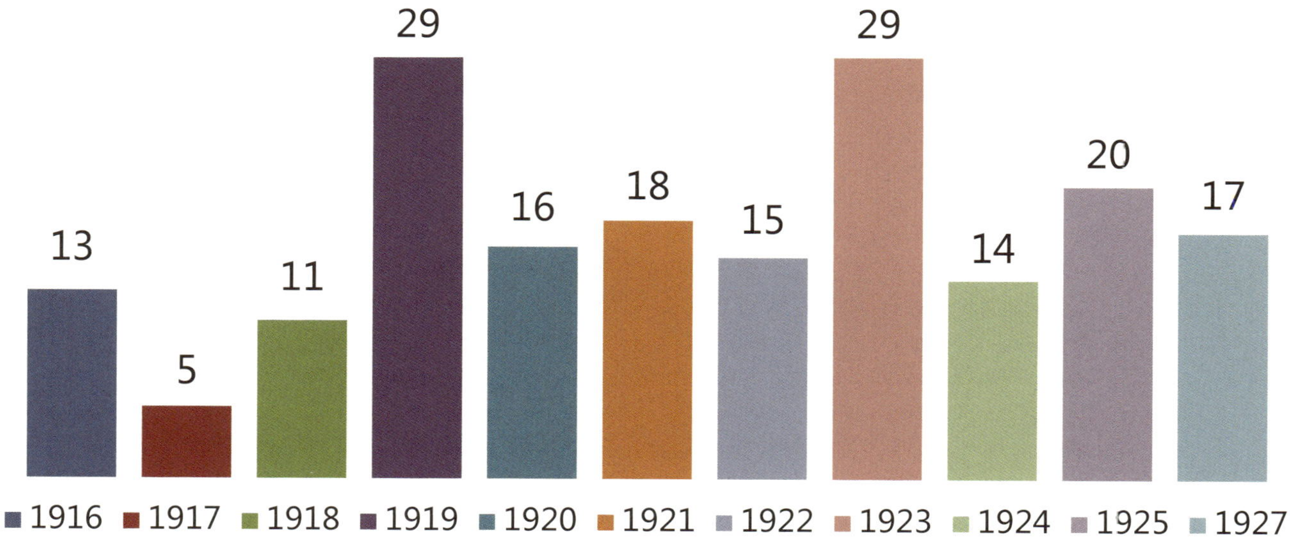

1916-1927 年工科（本科）毕业生人数

A bar chart illustrating engineering graduates from the university from 1916 to 1927

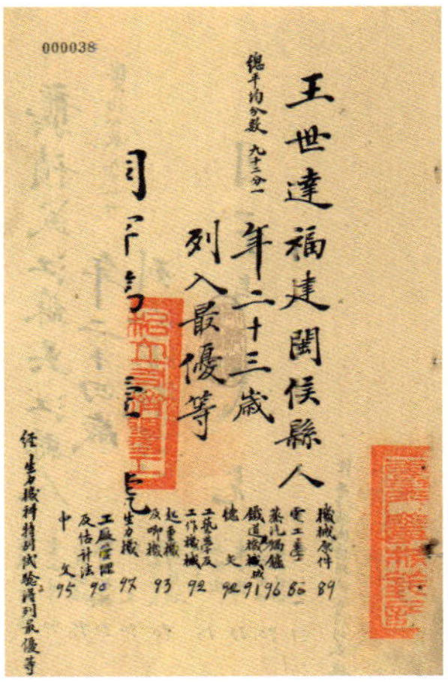
000038
王世達 福建閩侯縣人 年二十三歲 列入最優等

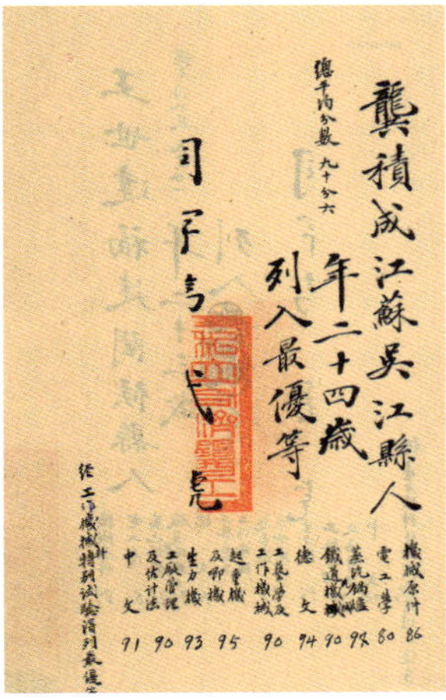
龔積成 江蘇吳江縣人 年二十四歲 列入最優等

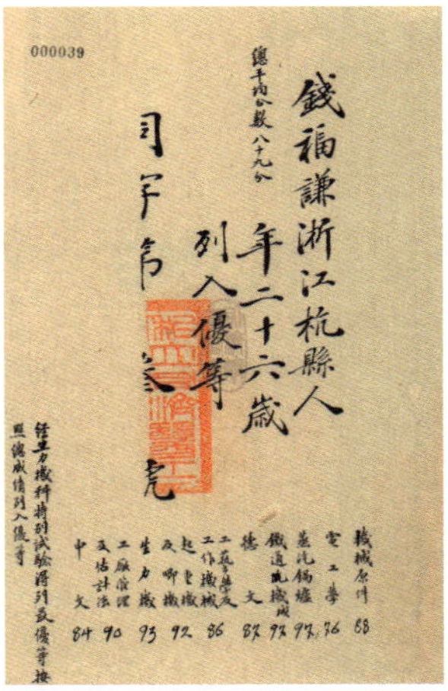
000039
錢福謙 浙江杭縣人 年二十六歲 列入優等

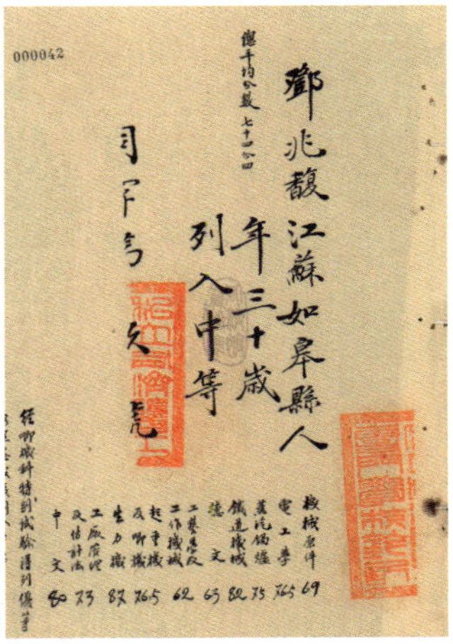
000042
鄧兆馥 江蘇如皋縣人 年三十歲 列入中等

1918 年夏季工科毕业生成绩单，分最优、优、中三等。

A transcript of an engineering graduate marked with Excellent, Good and Average in 1918

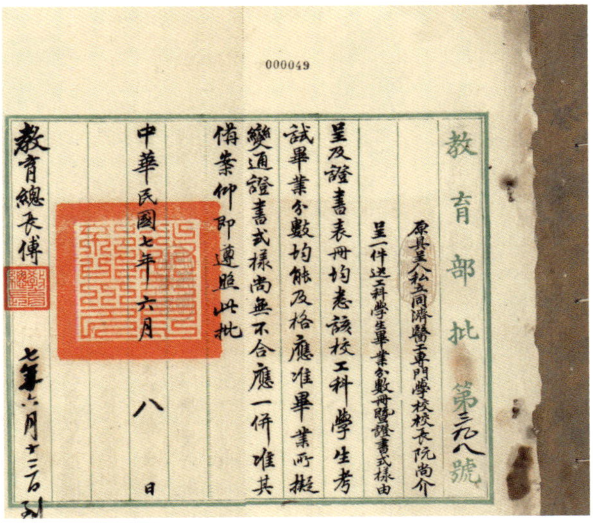
000049
教育部批 第三九八號
原具呈人私立同濟醫工專門學校校長阮尚介
呈一件送工科學生畢業分數冊暨證書式樣由
呈及證書表冊均悉該校工科學生考試畢業分數均能及格應准畢業所擬變通證書式樣尚無不合應一併准其備案仰即遵照此批
中華民國七年六月 八 日
教育總長傅

1918 年教育部下发的“私立同济医工专门学校”工科毕业生批函

Authorization of graduates from Tongji Medical and Engineering School issued by the Ministry of Education in 1918

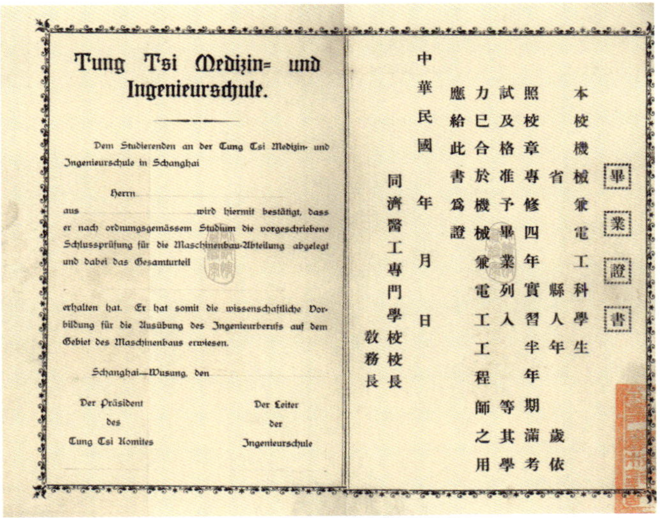
Tung Tsi Medizin- und Ingenieurschule.

Dem Studierenden an der Tung Tsi Medizin- und Ingenieurschule in Schanghai

Herrn

aus wird hiermit bestätigt, dass er nach ordnungsgemässem Studium die vorgeschriebene Schlussprüfung für die Maschinenbau-Abteilung abgelegt und dabei das Gesamturteil

erhalten hat. Er hat somit die wissenschaftliche Vorbildung für die Ausübung des Ingenieurberufs auf dem Gebiet des Maschinenbaus erwiesen.

Schanghai—Wusung, den

Der Präsident des Tung Tsi Komites

Der Leiter der Ingenieurschule

畢業證書

本校機械兼電工科學生
省 縣人年 歲依
照校章專修四年實習半年期滿考
試及格准予畢業列入 等其學
力已合於機械兼電工工程師之用
應給此書爲證
中華民國 年 月 日
同濟醫工專門學校校長
教務長

1918 年“同济医工专门学校”工科学生毕业证

A Graduation Certificate of an Engineering Student from Tongji Medical and Engineering School in 1918

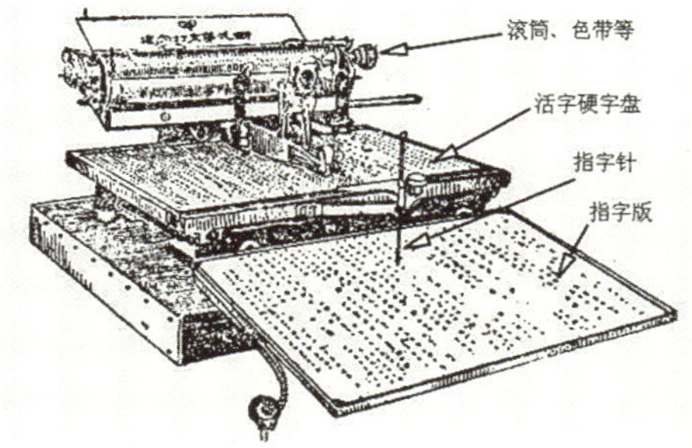

■ 1926年美国费城世博会上，同济首届工科毕业生舒昌瑜发明的第一台有实用价值的中文打字机夺得乙等荣誉奖章，图为舒式打字机构造图。

The first practical Chinese typewriter invented by Mr. Shu Changyu, one of first graduates from Tongji Engineering School, won a honorary medal of second class in World Expo 1926, Philadelphia, US. The structure of the Chinese typewriter is illustrated here.

■ 舒式打字机实景图

The Shu-style Chinese typewriter

■ 费城中国馆内景，左下角为舒式打字机的位置。

The Shu-style Chinese typewriter on the lower left shelf inside China Pavilion in Expo 1926, Philadelphia

■ 左：朱光彩（1899-1996），1922年毕业于同济工科，后留学德国柏林大学，获水利工程硕士、博士学位。1946年任黄河堵口复堤工程局局长时，出色完成堵口工程。曾荣获政府嘉奖和中国水利学会最高奖。

Left: Mr. Zhu Guangcai (1899-1996) graduated from the Engineering School of Tongji in 1922. He obtained his Master's and PhD degrees in hydraulics from Berlin University, Germany. He successfully completed the project of blocking the Yellow River while acting as director of the Bureau of Yellow River Blocking and Embankment Restoring. For his outstanding work, he won a special award issued by the Government and an award by the Chinese Hydraulic Society.

■ 右：李式白，1923年机械科毕业，任兵工署第50兵工厂厂长，曾主持研制60炮和57毫米无后座力炮，为解放西藏和抗美援朝立过功。

Right: Mr. Li Shibai, graduate of Mechanical Engineering in 1923, director of No. 50 Arsenal under Ordnance Department, was responsible for developing 60mm cannons and recoilless cannons of 57 mm. He was awarded for the great contributions he made to the Liberation of Tibet and the Korean War.

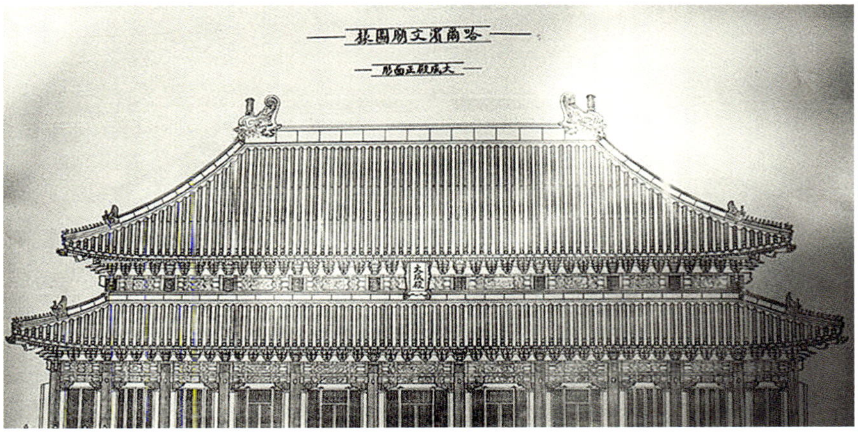

■ 同济工科毕业生陆士基、张象昺主持的哈尔滨文庙设计图。陆士基（1897-1989），江苏苏州人，1921 年毕业于同济医工专门学校土木系。曾任黑龙江松北市政局工程员，东北特别区行政长官公署技正。

A design of the Confucius Temple in Harbin headed by Lu Shiji and Zhang Xiangbing, engineering graduates of Tongji.
Mr. Lu Shiji(1897-1989), a native of Suzhou, Jiangsu Province, graduated from Civil Engineering Department of Tongji Medical and Engineering School in 1921. He acted as an engineer of Municipal Bureau of Songbei City, Heilongjiang Province, and the technician of the Chief Executive Office of the Northeast Special Administration.

■ 哈尔滨文庙现景，规模仅次于山东曲阜孔庙和北京孔庙，是全国现存最后一个建成的孔庙，是东北地区保存最完整的一座孔庙，被称为哈尔滨的“故宫”。

The Confucius Temple in Harbin today, biggest next to the Confucius Temples in Shangdong and in Beijing, is the last Confucius temple constructed in China and best preserved one in northeast China. It is therefore referred to as the Imperial Palace of Harbin.

■ 丁基实 (1903-1988)，1921 年考入同济医工专门学校预科土木专业，国共合作期间任国民党上海市第六区党部第三分部负责人。

Mr. Ding Jishi (1903-1988), admitted into the civil engineering program of Tongji Medical and Engineering School in 1921, acted as leader of the 3rd Division of the 6th District in Shanghai of Kuomingtang during its cooperation with Communist Party of China.

■ 尹景伊（1905-1925），1921 年秋考入同济医工专门学校机师科，1925 年加入中国共产主义青年团，“五卅运动”烈士。

Mr. Yin Jingyi (1905-1925), admitted into the Machinist program of Tongji Medical and Engineering School in 1921, joined the Communist Youth League of China in 1925 and died in the May 30th Movement.

■ 陈元达（1911-1931），1925 年秋考入同济大学机师科，在同济读书期间加入中国共产党，烈士。

Mr. Chen Yuanda (1911-1931), admitted into the Machinist program of Tongji University in 1925, joined the Communist Party of China and died during his time at Tongji University.

第二章 Chapter II（1927.8-1937.6）

蓬勃十年，渐成传统
Traditions Developed over Prosperous Ten Years

1927 年 7 月，同济成为南京国民政府确立的第一批国立大学，学校得到中德两国政府以及两国工商业界的大力支持，以德籍教授为主的中外师资阵容强大，由德国进口的硬件设备及实习条件堪称国内首屈一指，被称为“德国科学的一个中心”。1930 年工科改为工学院，增设了造船系与测量组，工程教育进入蓬勃发展阶段。

In July 1927, Tongji became one of the first national universities designated by the Nanjing National Government. Tongji obtained ardent support from both Chinese and German governments and from the business and commercial sector of the two countries. Its teaching staff was mainly composed of German professors. The facilities imported from Germany and the internship factory of Tongji were of top class in China, for which Tongji was referred to as a Center of German Sciences. In 1930, the engineering program was expanded to become an Engineering School of Tongji. When Department of Shipbuilding and Teaching Group of Surveying were added to the School, the engineering education entered a phase of rapid development.

国立同济，附设高职

National Tongji University with an Affiliated Advanced Vocational School

1927 年南京国民政府成立后，在时任大学院院长蔡元培的主持下，同济被列为国立大学。1931 年 8 月，国立劳动大学停办，同济接收了劳动大学工学院院舍及实习工厂厂房，恢复附设机师学校招生，改称高级职业学校，后更名为“同济大学附设高级工业职业学校”，办学规模进一步扩大。

After the founding of the Nanjing National Government in 1927, Tongji became one of the national universities in China under the leadership of Mr. Cai Yuanpei, Minister of Higher Education. National Labor University was closed down in August 1931 and its campus was allocated to National Tongji University. The Machinist School Affiliated to Tongji resumed its student recruitment under a new name: Advanced Vocational School. The school underwent steady development since then and was later renamed again as Advanced Vocational Industrial School Affiliated to Tongji University.

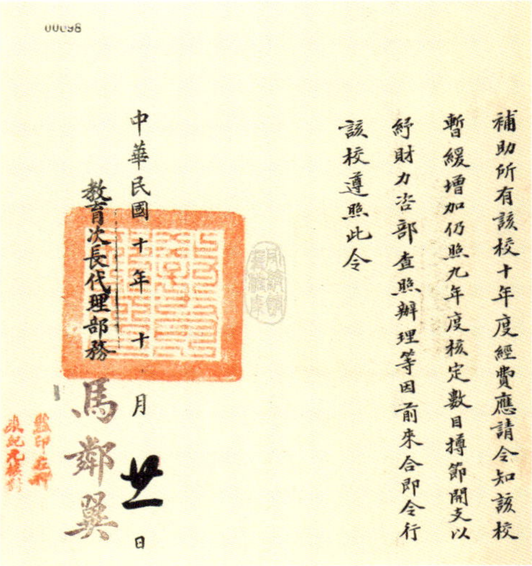

00098

補助所有該校十年度經費應請令知該校暫緩增加仍照九年度核定數目撙節開支以紓財力咨部查照辦理等因前來合即令行該校遵照此令

中華民國十年十月 日

教育次長代理部務 馬鄰翼

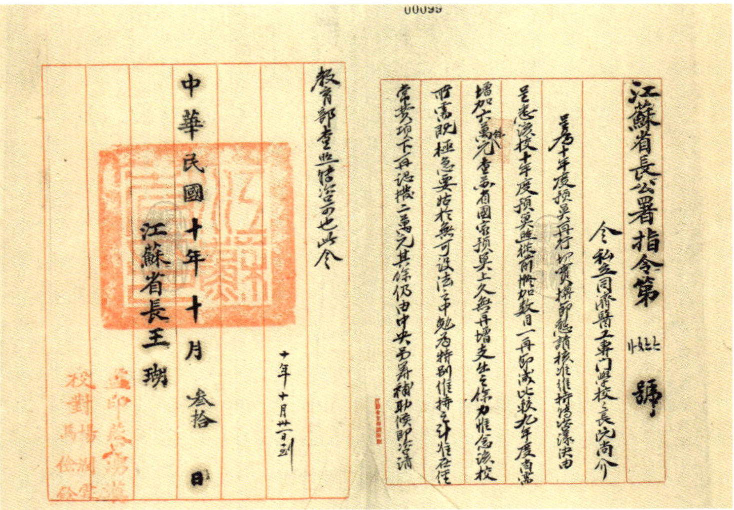

00099

江蘇省長公署指令第 號

令私立同濟醫工專門學校校長阮尚介

呈為十年度預算再行切實撙節懇請核准維持俾符原案由

呈悉。該校十年度預算照從前增加數目一再節減，比較九年度尚需增加六萬元。查省國家預算上久無再增支出之餘力，惟念該校所需既極急要，姑於無可設法之中勉為特別維持之計，准在經常費項下再認撥二萬元，其餘仍由中央另籌補助，候即咨請教育部查照辦理。此令。

中華民國十年十月 日

江蘇省長王瑚

■ 教育部、江苏省 1921 年 10 月关于“私立同济医工专门学校”次年预算的指令

An instruction on a next-year budget plan of Tongji Medical and Engineering School endorsed by Ministry of Education and Jiangsu Provincial government in October, 1921

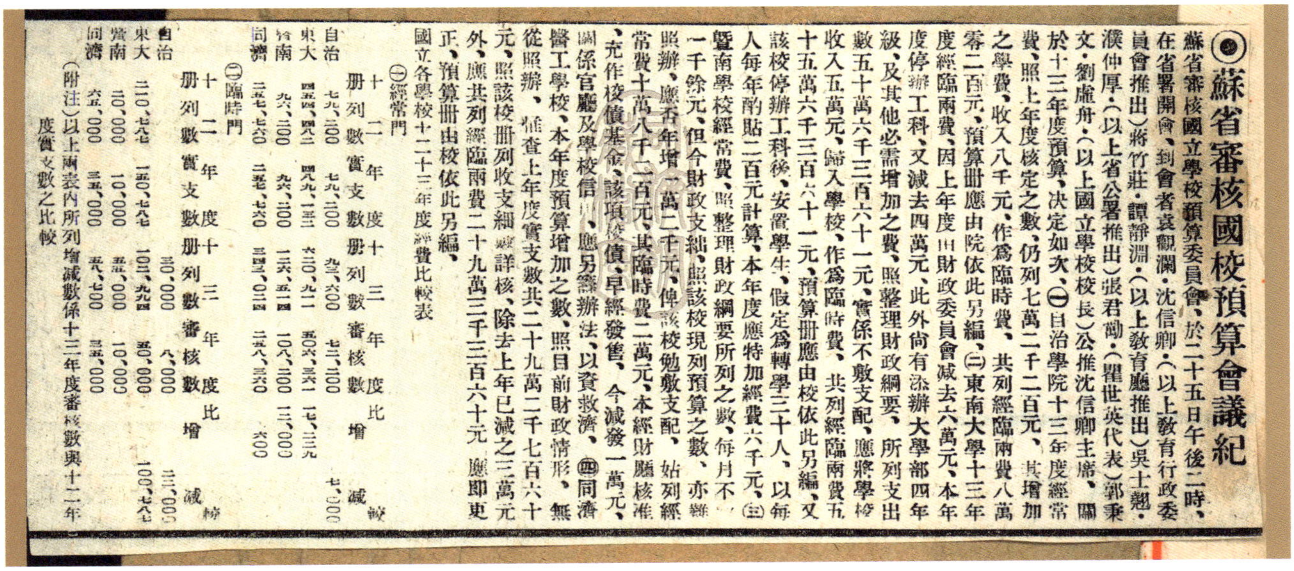

◉蘇省審核國校預算會議紀

蘇省審核國立學校預算委員會、於二十五日午後二時、在省署開會、到會者袁觀瀾・沈信卿・(以上敎育行政委員會推出)將竹莊・譚靜淵・(以上敎育廳推出)吳士翹・濮仲厚・(以上省公署推出)張君勱・(瞿世英代表)郭秉文・劉廬舟・(以上國立學校校長)公推沈信卿主席、關於十三年度預算、決定如次、㈠自治學院十三年度經常費、照上年度核定之數、仍列七萬二千二百元、其增加之學費、收入八千元、作爲臨時費、共列經臨兩費八萬零二百元、預算冊應由院依此另編、㈡東南大學十三年度經臨兩費、因上年度由財政委員會減去六萬元、本年度停辦工科、又減去四萬元、此外尚有添辦大學部四年級、及其他必需增加之費、照整理財政綱要、所列支出數五十萬六千三百六十一元、實係不敷支配、應將學校收入五萬元、歸入學校、作爲臨時費、共列經臨兩費五十五萬六千三百六十一元、預算冊應由校依此另編、又該校停辦工科後、安置學生、假定爲轉學三十八人、以每人每年酌貼二百元計算、本年度應特加經費六千元、㈢暨南學校經常費、照整理財政綱要所列之數、每月不敷一千餘元、但令財政支絀、照該校現列預算之數、亦難照辦、應在年增一萬二千元、俾該校勉敷支配、姑列經常費十萬八千二百元、其臨時費二萬元、本經財廳核准、充作校債基金、該項校債、早經發售、今減發一萬元、關係官廳及學校信用、應另籌辦法、以資救濟、㈣同濟醫工學校、本年度預算增加之數、照目前財政情形、無從照辦、准查上年度實支數共二十九萬二千七百六十元、照該校冊列收支細數詳核、除去上年已減之三萬元外、應共列經臨兩費二十九萬三千三百六十元 應即更正、預算冊由校依此另編、

國立各學校十二十三年度經費比較表

㈠經常門

	十二年度冊列數	十二年度實支數	十三年度冊列數	十三年度審核數	比較 增	比較 減
自治	七九、二00	七九、二00	九三、六00	七二、二00		七、000
東大	四五四、四六二	四八九、一三三	六二0、九二一	五0六、三六一	一七、二三九	
暨南	九六、二00	九六、二00	一三六、五二四	一0八、二00	一二、000	
同濟	二五七、七六0	二五七、七六0	三四三、0二四	二五八、三六0	六00	

㈡臨時門

	十二年度冊列數	十二年度實支數	十三年度冊列數	十三年度審核數	比較 增	比較 減
自治			三0、000	八、000		二二、000
東大	二一0、七八七	一五0、七八七	一0二、九九四	五0、000		一00、七八七
暨南	一0、000	一0、000	五五、000	一0、000		
同濟	六五、000	三五、000	五八、七00	三五、000		

(附注)以上兩表內所列增減數係十三年度審核數與十二年度實支數之比較

■ 1924 年《苏省审核国校预算会议纪》，“同济医工学校”已被列为国立学校。

Tongji Medical and Engineering School was referred to as a national university as indicated in the Minutes of Budget Plan Examination Meeting of National Universities in Jiangsu Province in 1924.

■ 蔡元培（1868-1940），留学德、法，民主主义革命家和教育家，中华民国首任教育总长，对推行“德国工程教育模式”的同济大学支持甚力。

Mr. Cai Yuanpei (1868-1940), a scholar who returned to China from his study in Germany and France, a democratic revolutionist and an educator, acted as the first Republic's Minister of Education. He lent ardent support to National Tongji University for its promotion of a German Model of Engineering Education.

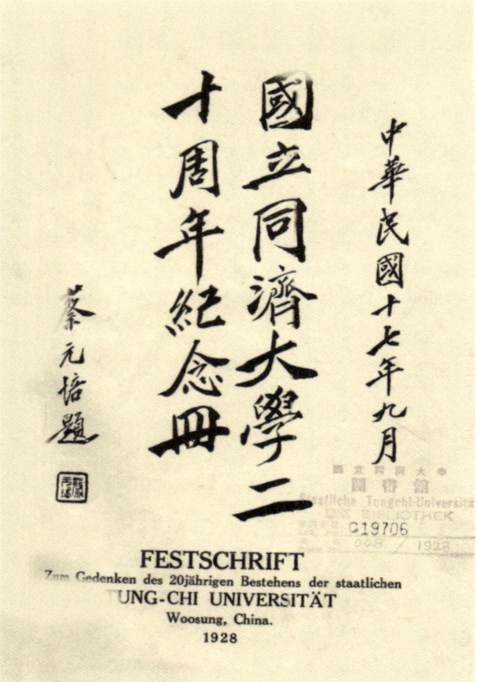

■ 蔡元培为《国立同济大学二十周年纪念册》题词

An inscription by Mr. Cai Yuanpei on *The 20th Anniversary Commemorative Album of National Tongji University*

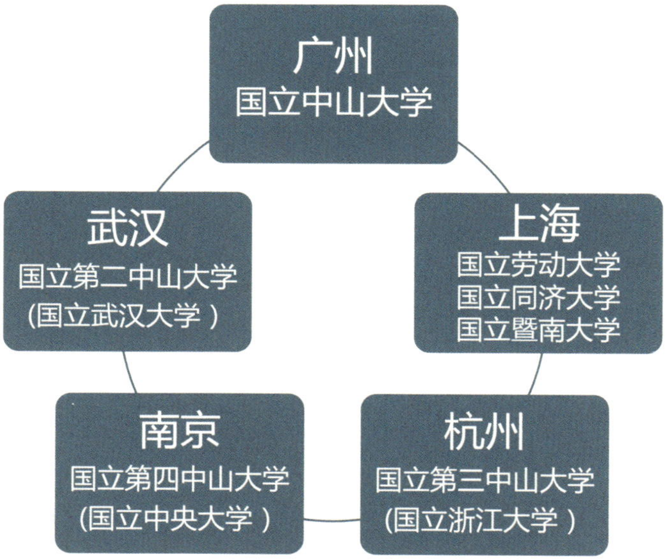

■ 1927 年南京国民政府成立后，所立国立大学名录。其中同属上海地区的“国立劳动大学”于 1931 年解散，校舍划归“国立同济大学”。

National universities in different cities in 1927 after the Nanjing National Government was established, among which National Labor University under Shanghai was closed and its campus was allocated to National Tongji University.

■ 1931 年，在“国立劳动大学”原址成立的“国立同济大学附设高级职业学校”，图为国立同济大学附设高级职业学校校门。
Entrance of Advanced Vocational School Affiliated to National Tongji University which was established on the campus former National Labor University

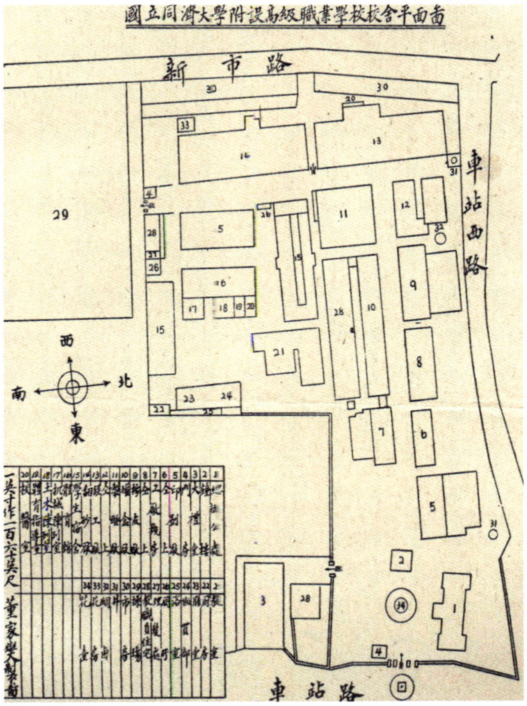

■ 1933 年 11 月，国立同济大学附设高级职业学校平面图。
Plan of Advanced Vocational School Affiliated to National Tongji University in November, 1933

■ 国立同济大学附设高级职业学校钟楼及工厂
The Bell Tower before the internship factory of Advanced Vocational School Affiliated to National Tongji University

■ 国立同济大学附设高级职业学校办公室及图书馆
An office building with a library of Advanced Vocational School Affiliated to National Tongji University

■ 国立同济大学附设高级职业学校教室
A teaching building of Advanced Vocational School Affiliated to National Tongji University

校长掌校，规范管理

Government Appointed President Supported by Standardized Management

国立之后，校董会的作用从决策机构变为咨询机构，由国民政府直接任命校长，规范了以校长为核心的组织管理制度，全面领导学校的校务和教务，为此阶段工程教育的发展壮大创造了条件。

When Tongji University became a national university with its president being appointed by the National Government, the function of the university board of trustees changed from decision-making to counseling. A standardized management system led by the president who played a central role in teaching administration and university operation paved the way for further development of engineering education at the university.

■ 张仲苏，国立同济大学校长（1927. 9-1929. 3），1879年生，河北清苑人，留学德国，回国后，历任教育部佥事、京师学务局局长、河北省教育厅长。

Mr. Zhang Zhongsu born in Qingyuan of Heibei Province in 1879, was the president of National Tongji University from September 1927 to March 1929. He returned to China following his study in Germany and served as section chief of the Ministry of Education, Chair of the Capital Department of Education Affairs, and director of the Education Department of Heibei Province.

■ 张群，国立同济大学校长（1929.3-1929.6），1889年生，执掌同济校长数月后，任上海特别市市长。

Mr. Zhang Qun, born in 1889, acted as president of National Tongji University from March 1929 to June 1929. Soon afterwards, he was appointed the mayor of Shanghai Special City.

■ 胡庶华，国立同济大学校长（1929.6-1932.9），1886年生，1913年考取公费留学德国，1920年获柏林工业大学铁冶金博士学位，著名教育家，冶金学家。

Dr. Hu Shuhua, born in 1886, a famous educator and an expert in metallurgy, was president of National Tongji University from June 1929 to September 1932. He studied, with financial support from the government, in Technical University of Berlin, Germany and obtained his PhD degree in iron metallurgy in 1920.

■ 翁之龙，国立同济大学校长（1932. 9-1939. 4），1896年生，1920年毕业于同济医科，1922年获德国法兰克福大学医学博士学位。

Dr. Weng Zhilong, born in 1896, was president of National Tongji University from September 1932 to April 1939. He graduated from the Medical School of Tongji in 1920 and obtained his PhD degree in Medicine from Frankfurt University, Germany in 1922.

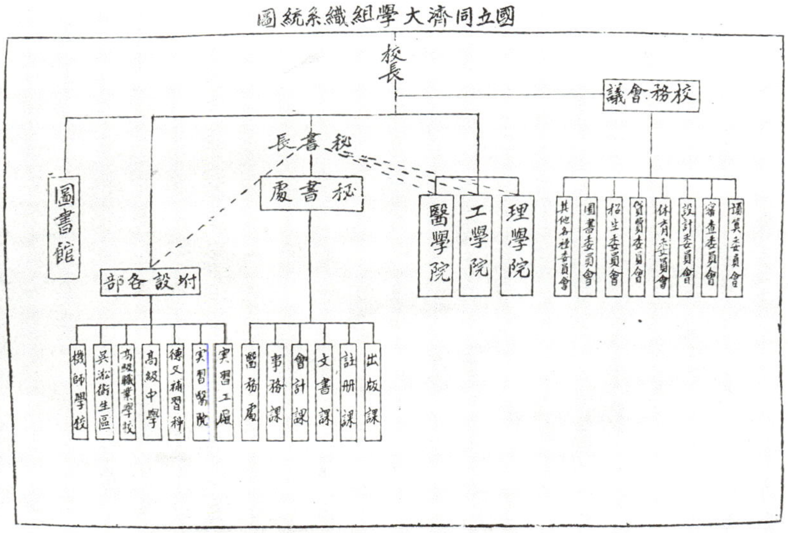

■ 1934 年国立同济大学组织系统图

Organizational structure of National Tongji University in 1934

■ 左一：计宗型，国立同济大学首任办公室主任（1927-1929），1883 年生，历任国民政府外交部帮办、上海市政府科长。

1st from left: Mr. Ji Zongxing, born in 1883, was the first director of the Administration Office, National Tongji University (1927-1929) . He served as an assistant in the Ministry of Foreign Affairs in the National Government and later a section chief in the Shanghai Government.

■ 左二：谭伯羽，国立同济大学首任秘书长（1929-1930），1900 年生，同济大学肄业，后赴德国留学，在同济经济困难时期，曾得其父亲谭延闿的资助。

2nd from left: Mr. Tan Boyu, born in 1900, was the first secretary-general of National Tongji University (1929-1930). He studied first in Tongji University, then continued his study in Germany. Tongji University received fundings from his father Tan Yanchang when experiencing a financially difficult time.

■ 左三：陈雨苍，国立同济大学秘书长（1931-1932），1889 年生，德国柏林医科大学博士，中国共产党党员，“一 · 二八”事变后，对学校的恢复起了重要作用。

3rd from left: Dr. Chen Yucang, born in 1889, obtained his PhD degree in Medicine from Medical University of Berlin, Germany. He was a member of Communist Party of China (CPC) and the secretary-general of National Tongji University (1931-1932) who played an important role in restoration of the university after the *January 28th Incident*.

■ 左四：周尚，国立同济大学秘书长（1932-1934；1936-1937），1898 生，德国汉诺威大学工程硕士，曾与周恩来同时赴法国勤工俭学，著名水利学家。

4th from left: Mr. Zhou Shang, born in 1898, obtained his Master's degree in Engineering from University of Hannover, Germany and became a renowned scholar in hydraulics. He was the secretary-general of National Tongji University (1932-1934; 1936-1937) and was with Mr. Zhou Enlai during his study in France.

■ 左五：杜殿英，国立同济大学秘书长（1934-1936），1893 年生，同济首届工科毕业生，德国慕尼黑工业大学机械专业博士，中国铁合金先驱之一。

5th from left: Dr. Du Dianying, born in 1893, obtained his PhD in Mechanical Engineering from Technical University of Munich , Germany and became one of the pioneers in ferroalloy industry in China. He acted as the secretary-general of National Tongji University (1934-1936) and was one of the first graduates of Tongji Engineering School.

图书馆
University library

图书馆中文书库
Books in Chinese in the library

图书馆西文书库
Books in other languages in the library

阅览室
A reading room

报纸阅览室
A newspaper reading room

期刊阅览室
A journal reading room

中外师资，阵容强大

Strong Faculty from Home and Abroad

此阶段仍以德籍教师为主，受聘者必须具有德国大学教授资格。此期间在同济大学任教后来成为德国大学校长的教授有欧根 · 弗雷格勒、卡尔·哈恩以及埃里希·罗鲁。与此同时，学校逐步大量聘请有留德背景的中国教授，一大批同济毕业后留学德国的学子如叶雪安、唐英、薛祉镐、吴之翰、郭德歆、王寿宝等回到母校就职，为同济的工程教育做出了贡献。

During this time, teachers of Tongji were mostly German professors from German universities. Professors Flegler Eugen, Hahn Karl, and Reuleaux Erich who taught at Tongji became presidents of German universities later. Meanwhile, the university started to employ Chinese professors who had educational background in Germany. A number of graduates from Tongji who continued their further study in Germany returned to the university to teach and made great contributions to the engineering education at Tongji. They were Ye Xue'an, Tang Ying, Xue Zhigao, Wu Zhihan, Guo Dexin and Wang Shoubao.

二之影合員職教校本

■ 1934 年全体教职员合影

All teachers at Tongji in 1934

■ 工科教务长史娄纳

Mr. Slotnarin, dean of Engineering School

■ 工科代理教务长施比禄

Mr. Spiro, Acting Dean of Engineering School

■ 工科代理教务长裴宁

Mr. Böning, Acting Dean of Engineering School

此期间在同济大学工学院任教回国后成为德国大学校长的教授
Professors who taught at Tongji and later became presidents of German universities

欧根·弗雷格勒（1897-1981），1936 年 9 月至 1938 年 10 月在同济大学工学院任教授，1954 年 7 月 1 日至 1956 年 9 月 30 日任德国亚琛工业大学校长。1977 年 5 月 23 日被授予德国联邦大十字勋章。

Mr. Eugen Flegler (1897-1981), a professor with Engineering School of Tongji University from September 1936 to October 1938, acted as president of RWTH Aachen University, Germany from July 1st, 1954 to September 30th, 1956. He was awarded Grand Cross of the Order of Merit of the Federal Republic of Germany on May 23rd, 1977.

卡尔·哈恩（1899-1960），1934 年 3 月至 1938 年在同济大学工学院任教授。二次大战结束前任德累斯顿工业大学校长。

Mr. Karl Hahn (1899-1960), a professor with Engineering School of Tongji University from 1934 to 1938, acted as president of Dresden University of Technology before the end of World War II.

此期间在工学院任职的部分德籍教授
German professors with Engineering School of Tongji University

Dr. Bartelt
理學博士鮑爾德先生
教授　化學
兼授醫科化學

Oberingenieur Hohn
工程師洪恩先生
本校工廠主任，教授估價術
工廠組織法兼附設機師
學校教員

Dr. Ing. Haasler
工學博士郝士蘭先生
教授
水利學　市政工程
建築學　測量學

Dr. Ing. Berrer
工學博士貝勒先生
教授
靜力學　鐵筋三和土建築學

Dr. Ing. Kraus
工學博士
葛樂士先生
教授
起重機　汽鍋學
抽水機　機械原件

Dr. Ing. List
工學博士李士特先生
教授
原動機　原動機實習

Dipl.-Ing. Kapper
特許工程師卡勃先生
教授　高等數學

工学院副教授唐英，毕业于德国柏林工业大学，建筑师，原国立劳动大学工学院院长。

Mr. Tang Ying, an architect who graduated from Technical University of Berlin, Germany. He was an associate professor with Engineering School of Tongji University and had been dean of the Engineering School of National Labor University.

工学院副教授薛祉镐，1924 年毕业于同济，曾任同济大学教务长。

Mr. Xue Zhigao, an associate professor with Engineering School who graduated from Tongji University in 1924. He became dean of Tongji University later.

高职教师王世达，1919 年毕业于同济。

Mr. Wang Shida, a teacher with Advanced Vocational School who graduated from Tongji University in 1919.

高职教师杨崇雅，1921 年毕业于同济。

Mr. Yang Chongya, a teacher with Advanced Vocational School who graduated from Tongji University in 1921.

高职教师祝元青，1924 年毕业于同济。

Mr. Zhu Yuanqing, a teacher with Advanced Vocational School who graduated from Tongji University in 1924.

高职教师周修齐，1927 年毕业于同济。

Mr. Zhou Xiuqi, a teacher with Advanced Vocational School who graduated from Tongji University in 1927.

高职教师王寿宝，1927 年毕业于同济。

Mr. Wang Shoubao, a teacher with Advanced Vocational School who graduated from Tongji University in 1927.

高职教师吴之敬

Mr. Wu Zhijing, a teacher with Advanced Vocational School.

广泛合作，保障生源

Cooperation with High Schools

为使更多青年学生进同济读书，学校向教育部递交报告，从 1927 年秋季开始学费减半。从 1932 年起，学校陆续与全国多所著名中学签订合作协定。因此，工学院学生人数不断增加，1930 年为 66 人，1933 年为 110 人，1937 年增加到 291 人。

In 1927 National Tongji University submitted a report to the Ministry of Education asking for permission of cutting the tuition fees by half so that more young people could afford to study at the university. The university had signed agreements with a number of leading high schools in China since 1932, which resulted in a gradual increase in the number of engineering students at National Tongji University. The intake of engineering students was 66 in 1930, 110 in 1933, and 291 in 1937.

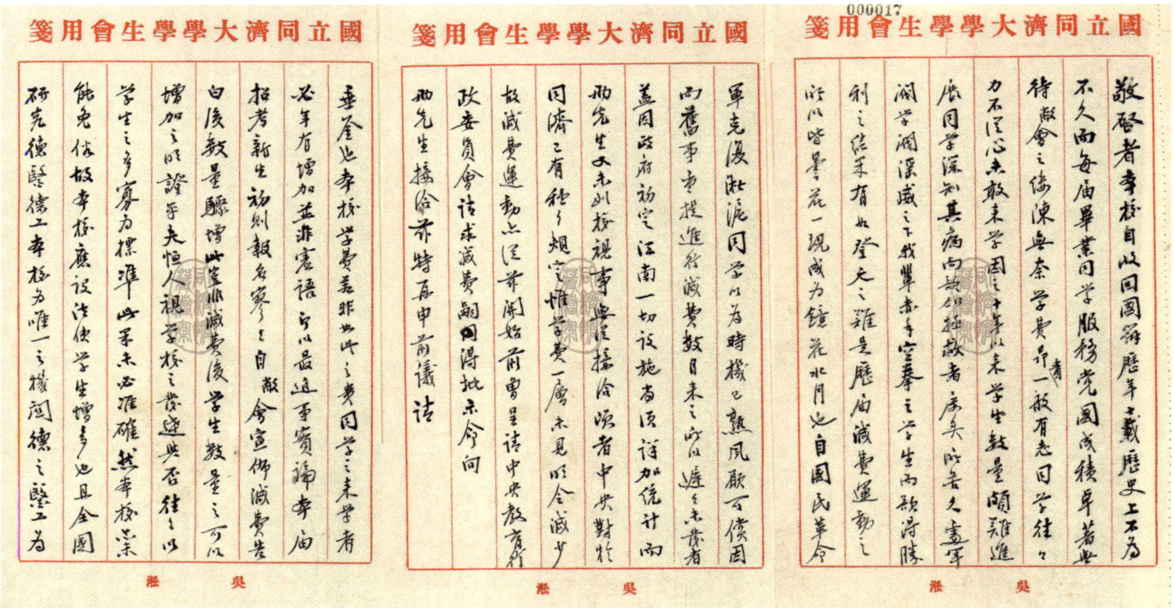

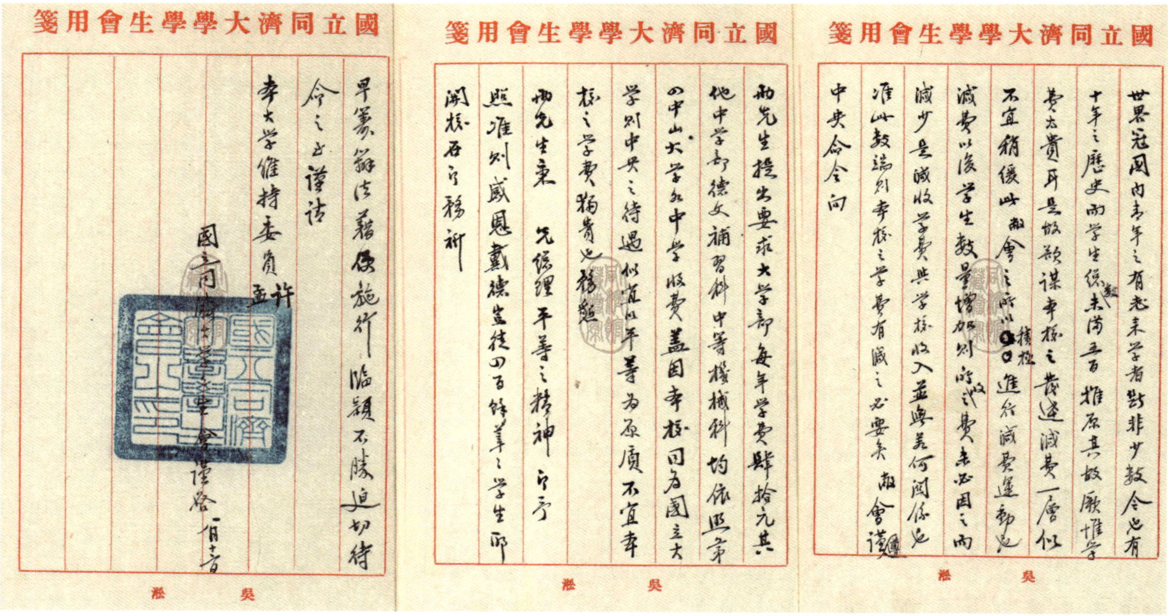

1927 年国立同济大学学生会向校务维持委员会递交的学费减半请求函

Letter submitted to the University Council by the Students Union of National Tongji University requesting a reduction in tuition fees by half in 1927

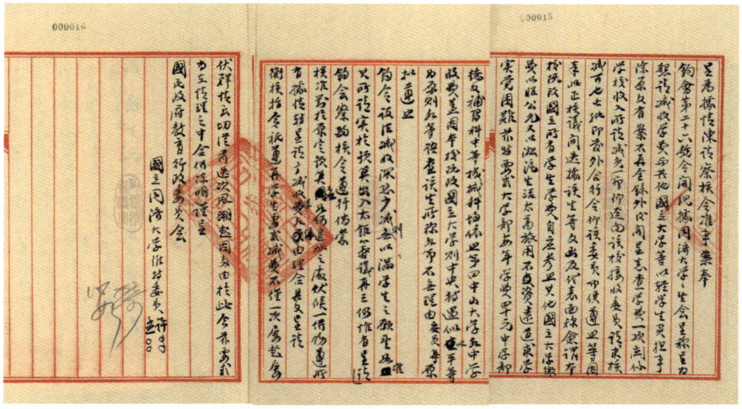

■ 1927 年国立同济大学向南京国民政府教育部呈请减免学费的函

Letter submitted to Ministry of Education of the Nanjing National Government by National Tongji University requesting a reduction in tuition fees by half in 1927

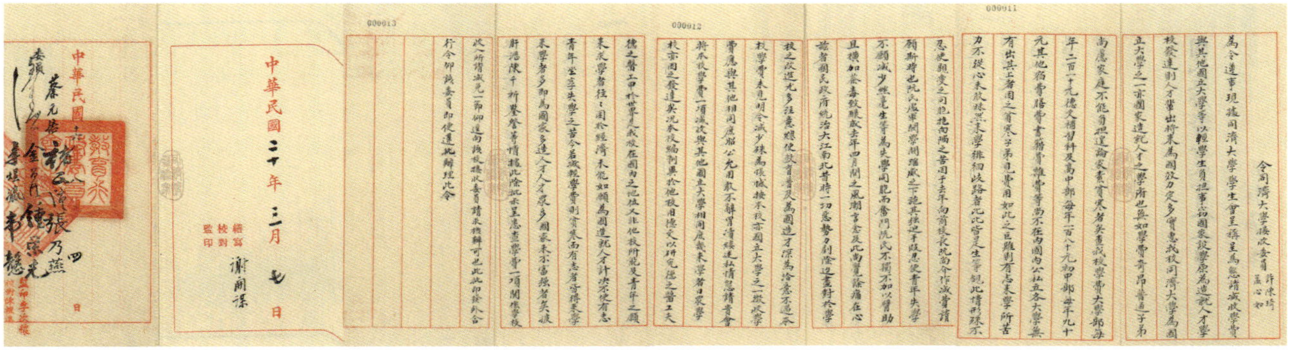

■ 1927 年南京国民政府就国立同济大学请求减免学费的批复函

Reply to National Tongji University from the Nanjing National Government on its request for reduction in tuition fees in 1927

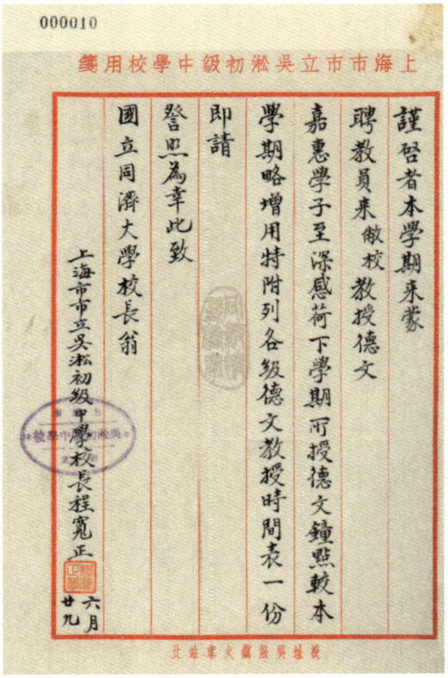

000010

上海市立吳淞初級中學校用箋

謹啓者本學期來蒙
聘教員來敝校教授德文
嘉惠學子至深感荷下學期所授德文鐘點較本
學期略增用特附列各級德文教授時間表一份
即請
詧照為幸此致
國立同濟大學校長翁
上海市市立吳淞初級中學校長程寬正
六月廿九

■ 上海市立吴淞初级中学与国立同济大学关于增加德文课程的函

Letter to National Tongji University from Shanghai Wusong High School requesting more German teachers for more German classes

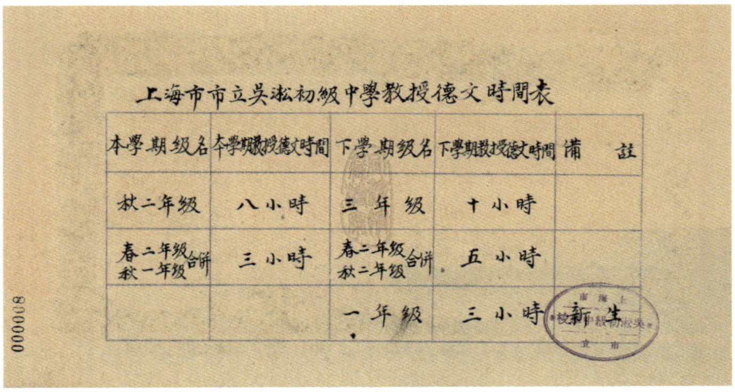

上海市市立吳淞初級中學教授德文時間表

本學期級名	本學期教授德文時間	下學期級名	下學期教授德文時間	備註
秋二年級	八小時	三年級	十小時	
春二年級 秋一年級 合併	三小時	春二年級 秋二年級 合併	五小時	
		一年級	三小時	新生

000008

■1933 年上海市立吴淞初级中学德文授课时间表

Timetable of German classes at Shanghai Wusong High School in 1933

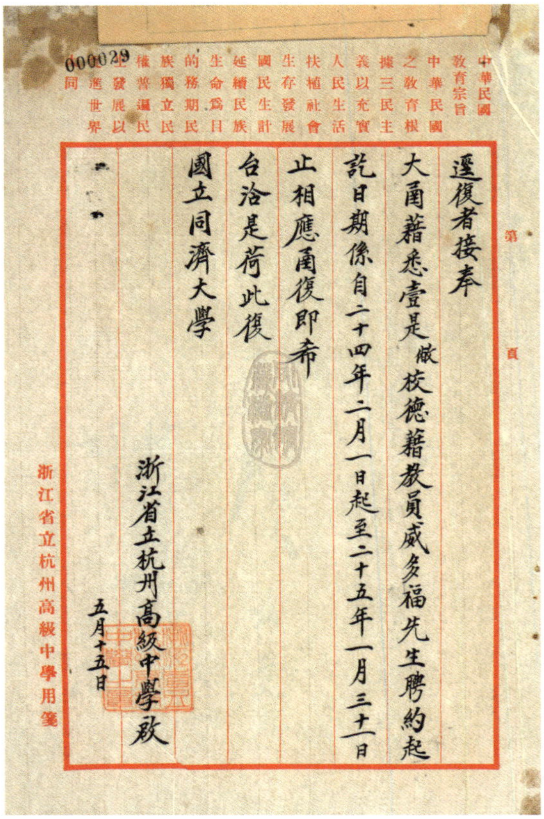

000029

中華民國教育宗旨
中華民國之教育根據三民主義以充實人民生活扶植社會生存發展國民生計延續民族生命為目的務期民族獨立民權普遍民生發展以促進世界大同

第　頁

逕復者接奉
大函藉悉壹是敝校德籍教員威多福先生聘約起
訖日期係自二十四年二月一日起至二十五年一月三十一日
止相應函復即希
台洽是荷此復
國立同濟大學
浙江省立杭州高級中學啟
五月十五日

浙江省立杭州高級中學用箋

■ 杭州高级中学聘请同济德籍教师威多福的函

Letter of employment from Hangzhou Senior High School for Mr. Wiethoff, a German teacher of National Tongji University

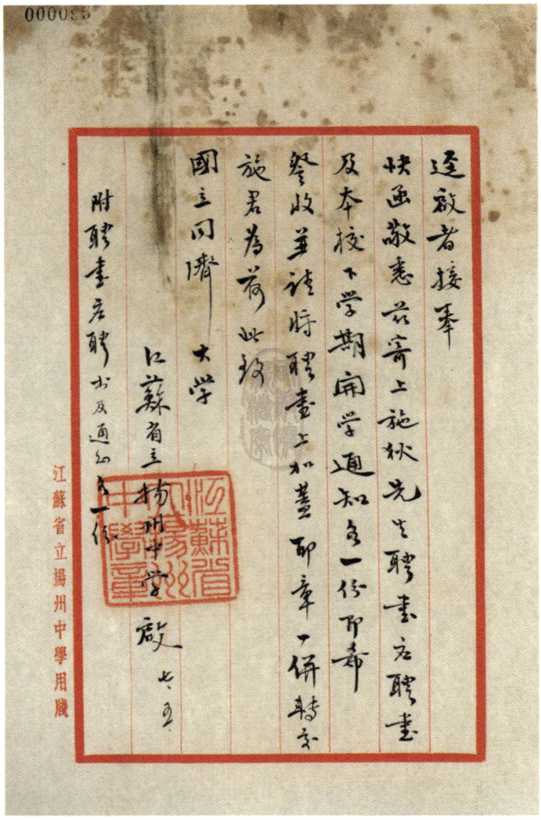

逕啟者接奉
快函敬悉前寄上施秋先生聘書存聘書
及本校下學期開學通知各一份即希
察收並請將聘書上加蓋印章一併轉交
施君為荷此致
國立同濟大學
江蘇省立揚州中學啟　七、五
附聘書存聘書及通知各一份

江蘇省立揚州中學用牋

■ 江苏省立扬州高级中学与国立同济大学教育合作往来函（聘请德籍教师）

A letter to National Tongji University from Yangzhou Senior High School of Jiangsu Province for employment of German teachers

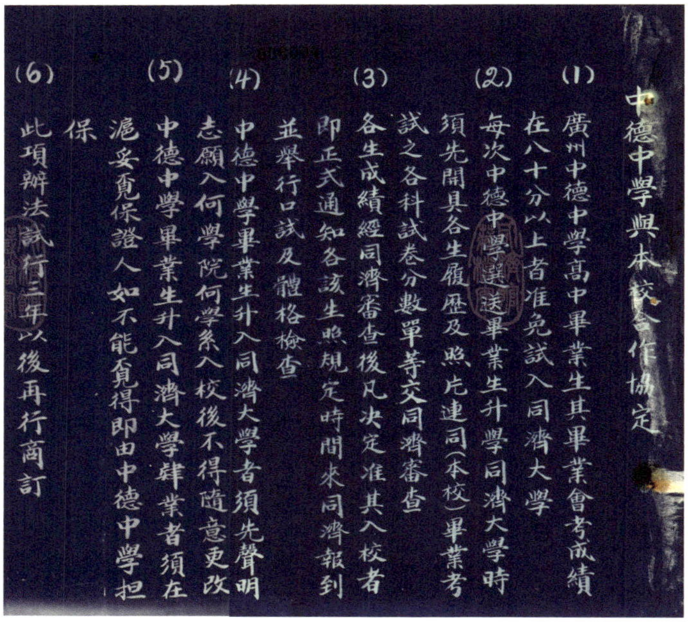

中德中學與本校合作協定

(1) 廣州中德中學高中畢業生其畢業會考成績在八十分以上者准免試入同濟大學

(2) 每次中德中學選送畢業生升學同濟大學時須先開具各生履歷及照片連同(本校)畢業考試之各科試卷分數單等交同濟審查

(3) 各生成績經同濟審查後凡決定准其入校者即正式通知各該生照規定時間來同濟報到並舉行口試及體格檢查

(4) 中德中學畢業生升入同濟大學者須先聲明志願入何學院何學系入校後不得隨意更改

(5) 中德中學畢業生升入同濟大學肄業者須在滬妥覓保證人如不能覓得即由中德中學担保

(6) 此項辦法試行三年以後再行商訂

■ 中德中学与国立同济大学合作协定

An Agreement of Cooperation between Sino-German High School and National Tongji University

(一)最近五年招生人數比較圖表

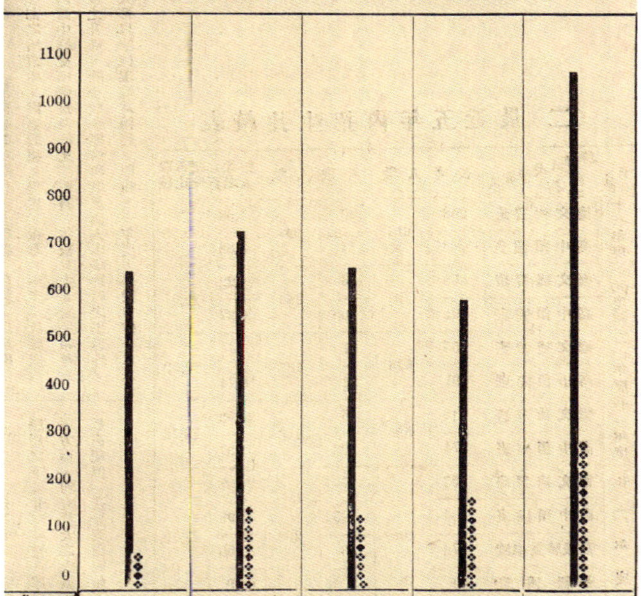

比較 年度	十八年度	十九年度	二十年度	廿一年度	廿二年度
投考人數	641	727	646	585	1068
考取人數	64	143	133	168	290
百分比	9,98	19,67	20,59	28,72	27,15

投考人 考取人

■ 国立同济大学 1929-1933 年招生人数比较图

A diagram illustrating student intakes of National Tongji University from 1929 to 1933

(一)七年內各級學生人數比較表

科別 / 級別 / 年度	工學院					醫學院					附設德文補習科		附設高中				附設初中			附設機師學校					附設高級職業學校		全校合計
	一	二	三	四	五	一	二	三	四	五	一	二	預	一	二	三	一	二	三	一	二	三	四	五	土木科	機械科	
十六年度	9	14	23	14		48	17	19	13	7	160	45		12	12	16	20	41	31	44	22	23	13				603
十七年度	9	9	14	23	13	41	47	17	19	13	29	150		28	12	12	42	20	36	31	40	22	22				649
十八年度	25	9	10	9	21	72	42	33	12	20	23	44	29	24	28	13		27	16		24	25	29	13			548
十九年度	13	24	9	11	9	43	73	33	31	23	36	26	78	42	19	29			32		20	24	21	12			608
二十年度	24	14	21	9	9	34	58	49	33	30	43	38	85	93	39	20						22	16				637
廿一年度	19	27	13	19	9	35	37	42	48	33	94	34	123	61	80	30							20	1			735
廿二年度上學期	24	16	15	13	19	36	35	28	45	48	87	86	105	112	61	77								20	39	57	933

附註 廿二年度上學期各級人數因在造表時補考尚未完竣未能十分固定

■ 1927-1933 年工学院各级人数比较图

A diagram illustrating numbers of students from different years at National Tongji University from 1927 to 1933

改工学院，设测量系

Department of Surveying Established with Engineering School

1930 年同济工科改为工学院，1935 年工学院教务长改称院长，首任院长由担任工科教务长的德国达姆斯塔特工业大学前任校长、国际著名铁道工程专家埃里希·罗鲁博士担任。1933 年秋高等测量系成立 (1935 年 1 月改名为测量系)，同济成为全国第一所设立测量系的高校，成为我国民用测绘的发祥地。同济大学测量系的校友有 9 位前后当选为中国科学院或工程院院士。

In 1930, all engineering programs were incorporated into the Engineering School and the dean responsible for the teaching administration of the the engineering program changed its official title to Dean of the School. Dr. Erich Rouleaux, an internationally well-known scholar in railway engineering who had been the dean responsible for the teaching administration of the engineering program and the former president of Technical University Darmstadt, Germany, was appointed the first Dean of the Engineering School in 1935. Advanced Department of Surveying was established in the autumn of 1933 and was renamed as Department of Surveying in January 1935. This department was the first of its kind in universities in China and therefore rendered National Tongji University the cradle for civil surveying and mapping. Among students who graduated from this department over the years, nine outstanding scholars became members of Chinese Academy of Sciences or of Chinese Academy of Engineering.

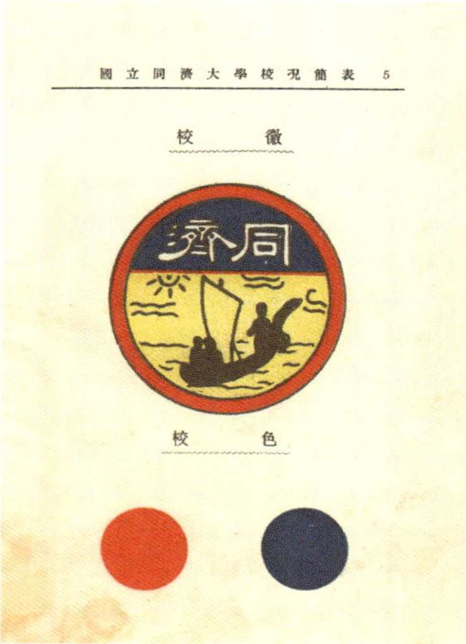

■ 左：1930 年国立同济大学校徽及校色，红色代表医学院，蓝色代表工学院。

Left: Emblem and colors of National Tongji University in 1930, with red for Medical School, and blue for Engineering School.

■ 右：1930 年国立同济大学校歌，第一段内容为工学，第二段内容为医学。

Right: Anthem of National Tongji University in 1930, with the first part on engineering, and the second on medicine.

■ 埃里希·罗鲁（1883-1967），工科改为工学院后首任院长。柏林工业大学工学硕士，卡斯鲁厄工业大学名誉博士。1934 年至 1936 年在同济大学工科任教授兼工学院院长，主讲土木工程学，兼任中国政府铁道部顾问。1937 年至 1952 年任达姆施塔特工业大学教授。1953 年被授予联邦十字勋章。

Dr. Erich Reuleaux (1883-1967) who obtained his Master's degree in Engineering from Technical University of Berlin, and his honorary PhD degree from Technical University of Karlsruhe, Germany, taught civil engineering and concurrently acted as the first Dean of Engineering School with National Tongji University from 1934 to 1936. He also served as a consultant to the Ministry of Railway of the National Government. After he returned to Germany, he was employed as a professor with Technical University of Darmstadt, Germany from 1937 to 1952, and was awarded the Grand Cross of the Order of Merit of the Federal Republic of Germany in 1953.

■ 工学院第二任院长贝勒

Mr. Berrer, second Dean of Engineering School of Tongji University

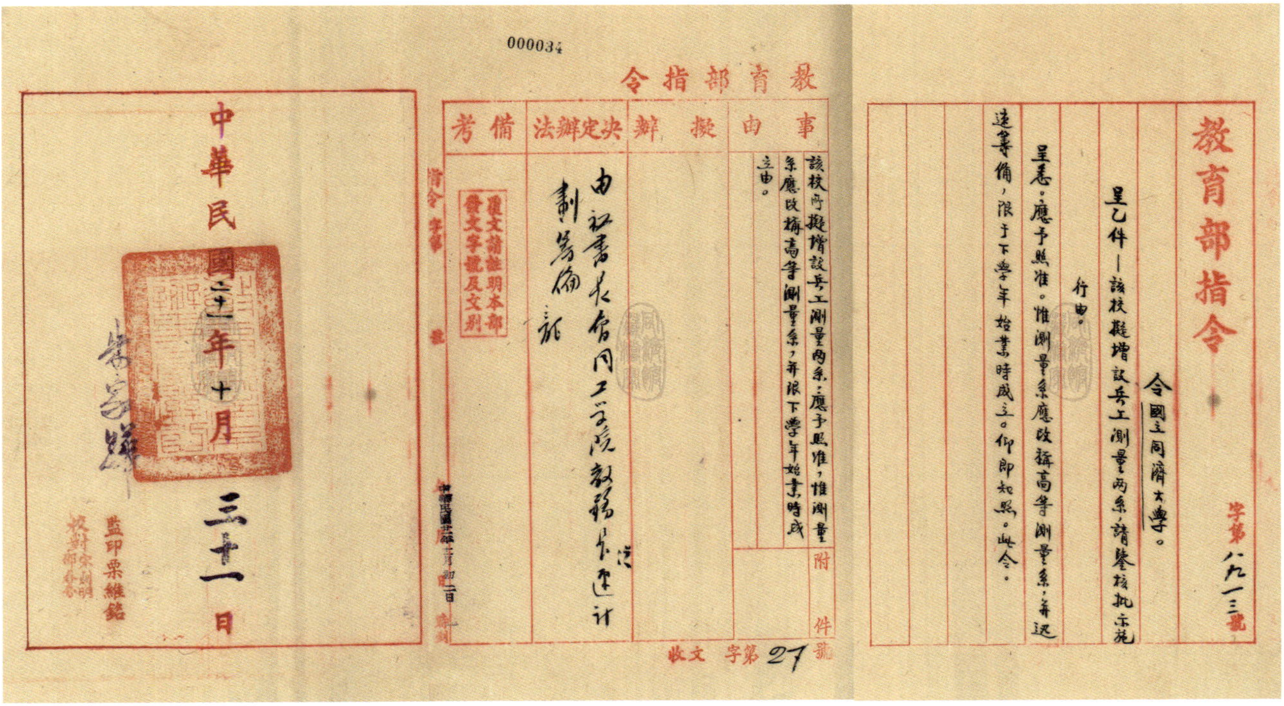

■ 1932 年教育部批准国立同济大学成立测量系的指令

Authorization from the Ministry of Education to establish the Department of Surveying at National Tongji University in 1932

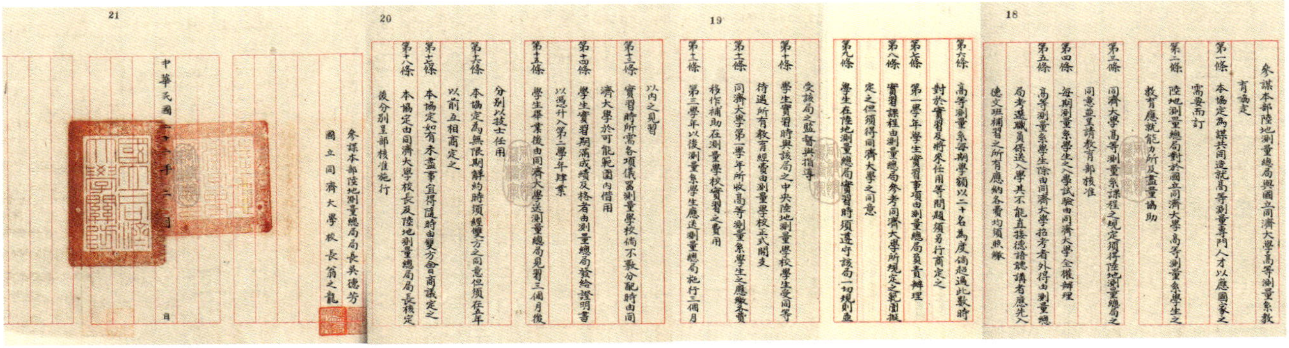

■ 学校同测量总局的协议

An agreement between the university and the Bureau of Survey

姓名 Name	在测量系工作时间 Time of Employment	职称 Academic Titles	简况 A brief introduction
诺伊迈尔 Neumaier	1934年秋 - 1936年春 Autumn of 1934 - spring of 1936	教授 Professor	奥地利测量专家 An expert in surveying from Austria
曾广梁 Zeng Guangliang	1936年春 - 1937年春 Spring of 1936 - spring of 1937	兼任教授 Adjunct professor	1925年同济大学土木工程系毕业，中央测量学校主任教官 A core teacher with Central School of Surveying who graduated from Civil Engineering Department of National Tongji University in 1925
	1939年2月 - 1940年夏 Feb 1939 to summer of 1940 February 1939 to summer of 1940	教授 Professor	
范远 Feyer	1936年春 - 1938年夏 Spring of 1936 to summer of 1938	教授 Professor	德籍航空测量学家，1936年 - 1938年主持测量系工作 A German expert in aviation survey who was responsible for the work at the department from 1936 to 1938
费理勒 Fliegner	1936年9月 - 1938年夏 September 1936 to summer of 1938	教授 Professor	德籍测量专家 An expert in surveying from Germany
叶雪安 Ye Xue'an	1937年2月 - 1956年 February 1937 to 1956	教授 Professor	1938年 - 1956年系主任 Head of Department of Surveying from 1938 to 1956

■ 测量系设立初期的师资

Faculty at the Department of Surveying in its Initial Stages

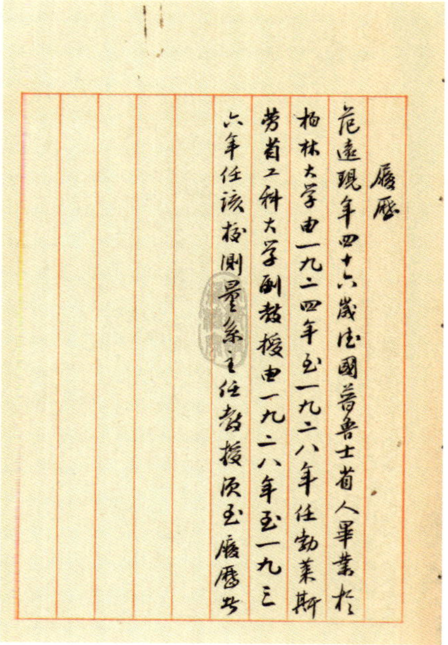
履歷
范遠現年四十六歲德國普魯士省人畢業於
柏林大學由一九二四年至一九二八年任勃萊斯
勞省工科大學副教授由一九二八年至一九三
六年任該校測量系主任教授及至履歷如

■ 埃迪文·范远教授简历

Resume of Professor Edwin Feyer

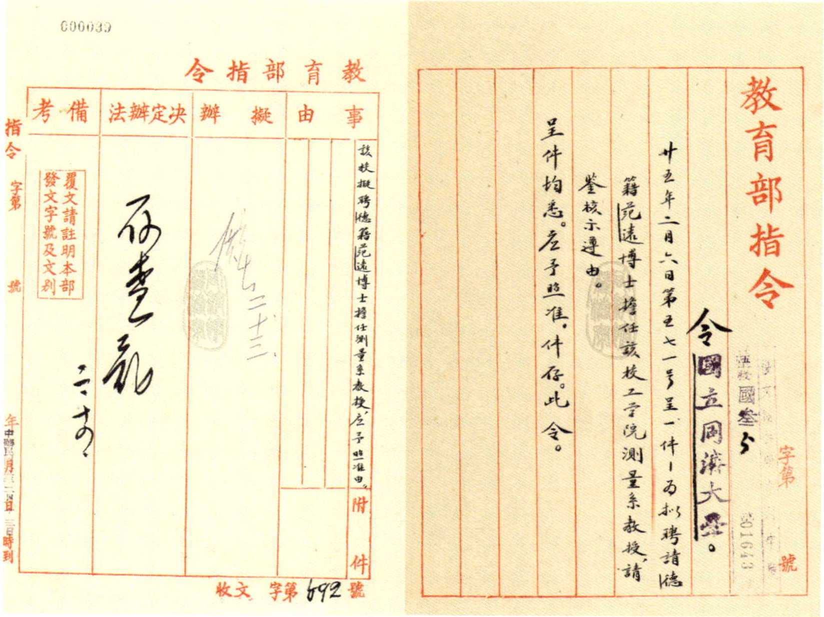
教育部指令
事由　擬辦　決定辦法　備考
該校擬聘德籍范遠博士擔任測量系教授，應予照准由。
附件
發文請註明本部文字號及文別
收文 字第692號

教育部指令
令國立同濟大學
廿五年二月六日第三七一號呈一件，為擬聘請德籍范遠博士擔任該校工學院測量系教授，請鑒核示遵由。
呈件均悉。應予照准。件存。此令。

■ 教育部同意聘用范远教授的指令

Authorization from the Ministry of Education to employ Professor Feyer

筹兵工系，增造船组

Teaching and Research Group in Shipbuilding

筹建测量系的同时，工学院还一度准备筹建兵工系，并且得到了教育部的批准，后因故未果。鉴于电工机械系设备完善，1934 年 5 月，增设造船和飞机课程，积极筹建造船飞机机械系。1936 年 8 月，电工机械系内增设造船组，聘请德国汉堡造船专门学校教授吴罗伯博士开设造船专业课程。

During the process of establishing Department of Surveying, efforts were made in preparation for the establishment of Department of Ordnance with the authorization of the Ministry of Education, but in vain for some reason. In May 1934, while courses in shipbuilding and aircraft engineering were offered at the Department of Electromechanics which boasted comprehensive facilities, preparations were made for the establishment of Department of Mechanical Engineering in Shipbuilding and Aircraft. In August 1936, a Teaching and Research Group in Shipbuilding was added to Department of Electromechanics and Dr. Wrobbel from the Shipbuilding School of Hamburg, Germany was employed to teach the courses in shipbuilding.

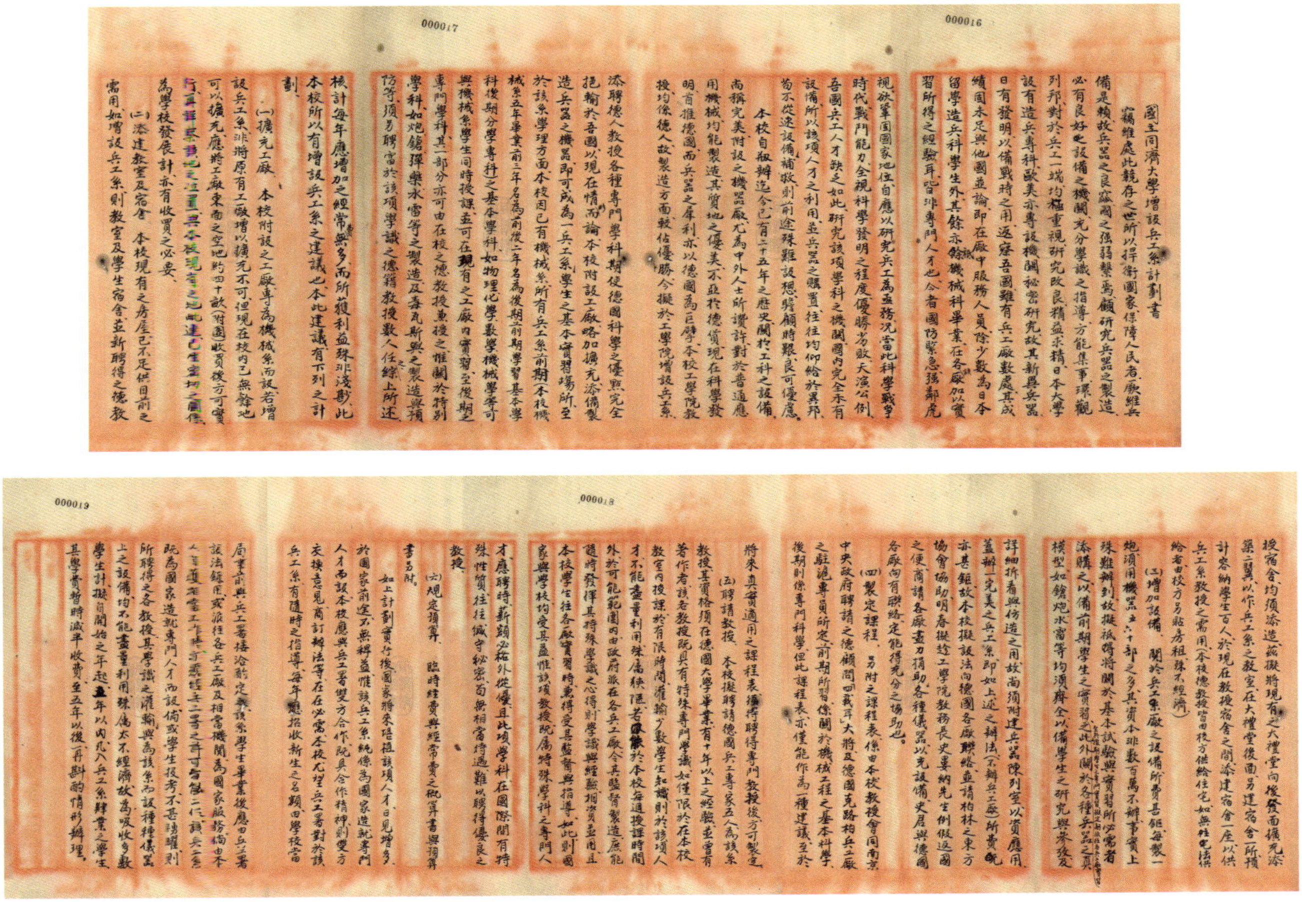

国立同济大学增设兵工系计划书

Plan for the establishment of Department of Ordnance at National Tongji University

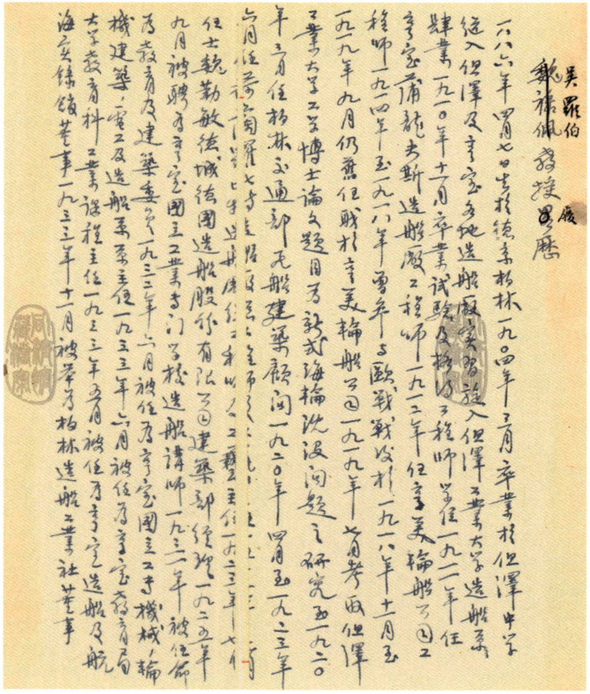

为新设立的造船组开设造船专业课程的德国汉堡造船学校教授吴罗伯博士简历

Introduction of Dr. Wrobbel from the Shipbuilding School of Hamburg, Germany, who was employed to offer courses in shipbuilding for the Teaching and Research Group in Shipbuilding.

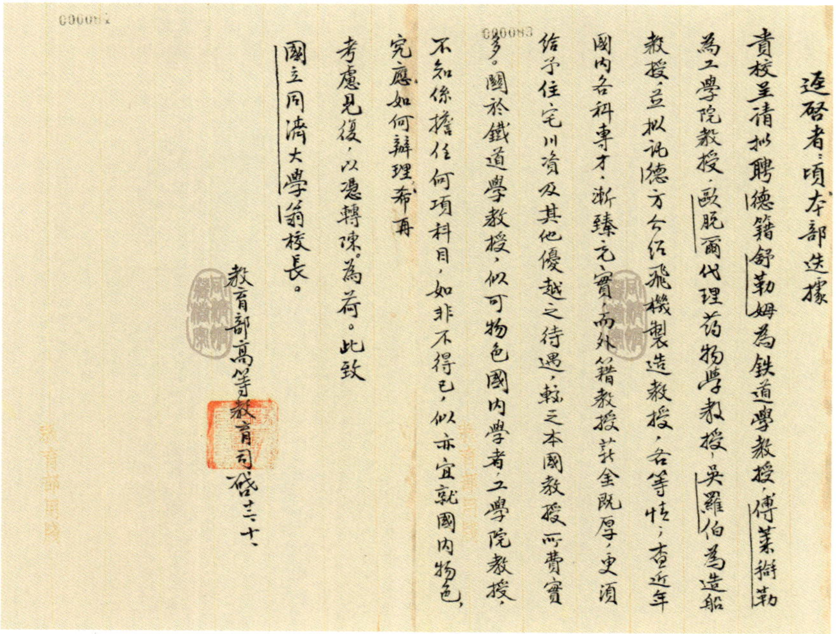

逕啓者：頃本部迭據
貴校呈請拟聘德籍舒勒姆為铁道學教授，傅萊衎勒為工學院教授，歐脫爾代理药物學教授，吳羅伯為造船教授，並拟託德方介绍飛機製造教授，各等情；查近年國内各科專才，漸臻充實，而外籍教授薪金既厚，更須給予住宅川資及其他優越之待遇，較之本國教授所費實多。關於鐵道學教授，似可物色國内學者，工學院教授，不知係擔任何項科目，如非不得已，似亦宜就國内物色，究應如何辦理，希再考慮見復，以憑轉陳。為荷。此致
國立同濟大學翁校長。

教育部高等教育司啓 三十、

中华民国教育部高等教育司同意聘请吴罗伯博士等的函

Authorization from the Ministry of Education of the National Government to employ German teachers at National Tongji University

日军轰炸，重伤吴淞

Wusong Campus Devastated by Japanese Bombardment

1932 年“一·二八”淞沪战争爆发，吴淞地区许多工厂、学校在日军的狂轰滥炸中毁于一旦。同济大学的主要建筑如大礼堂、实习工厂等被毁，图书、机器、标本、模型等设备损失严重，全校师生暂迁市区巨濑达路（今巨鹿路）民生坊，租赁民房上课。经过半年的抢修，被毁校舍才恢复旧貌。1932 年 8 月 25 日，学校迁回吴淞。

On January 28th, 1932, many factories and schools in Wusong area were destroyed by Japanese bombardments, which was later known as *January 28th Incident*. Main buildings at National Tongji University such as the auditorium and the internship factory were destroyed and books and facilities including machines, specimens and models were fatally damaged. As a result, teachers and students were forced to move to Minsheng Quarters on Julaida Road (the current Julu Road) in the city centre, and classes were taught in rented residential quarters. The university did not resume its operation at its campus in Wusong until half a year later after urgent repair work on its buildings and facilities was completed. On August 25th, 1932, the university was relocated back to the campus in Wusong.

1932 年淞沪战争爆发前

Before the *January 28th Incident*

■ 国立同济大学的前门与后门

Front and back entrances of National Tongji University

■ 国立同济大学大礼堂、总办公室及工学院教室

The main building which accommodated the auditorium, administration office and classrooms of Engineering School at National Tongji University

国立同济大学教授宿舍
Hall of Residence for professors of National Tongji University

国立同济大学女生宿舍
Hall of Residence for girl students of National Tongji University

1932 年淞沪战争爆发后
After the *January 28th Incident*

吴淞校区遭到日军炮轰
Wusong campus bombarded by Japanese

工厂外部被炸情形
Ruins outside the factory after Japanese bombardments

工厂内部被炸情形
Ruins inside the factory after Japanese bombardments

教师宿舍被炸情形
Teachers' Hall of Residence after the bombardment

生理馆被炸情形
Ruins of Physiological Laboratory after the Japanese bombardments

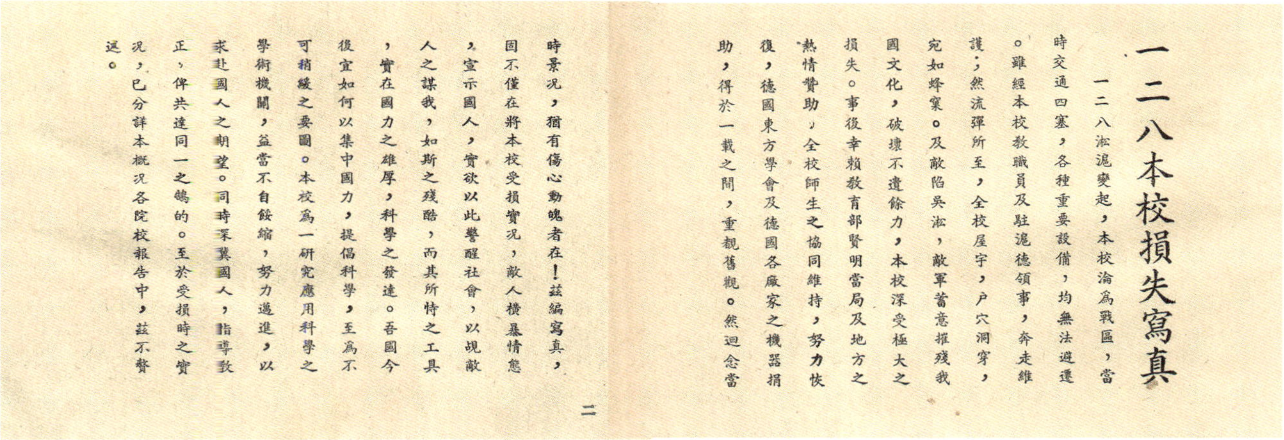

一二八本校損失寫真

一二八淞滬變起，本校淪爲戰區，當時交通四塞，各種重要設備，均無法避遷。雖經本校教職員及駐滬德領事，奔走維護；然流彈所至，全校屋宇，户穴洞穿，究如蜂窠。及敵陷吳淞，敵軍蓄意摧殘我國文化，破壞不遺餘力，本校深受極大之損失。事後幸賴教育部賢明當局及地方之熱情贊助，全校師生之協同維持，努力恢復，德國東方學會及德國各廠家之機器捐助，得於一載之間，重覩舊觀。然迴念當時景況，猶有傷心動魄者在！茲編寫真，固不僅在將本校受損實況，敵人橫暴情態，宣示國人，實欲以此警醒社會，以覘敵人之謀我，如斯之殘酷，而其所恃之工具，實在國力之雄厚，科學之發達。吾國今後宜如何以集中國力，提倡科學，至爲不可稍緩之要圖。本校爲一研究應用科學之學術機關，益當不自餒縮，努力邁進，以求赴國人之朝望。同時深冀國人，指導教正，俾共達同一之鵠的。至於受損時之實況，已分詳本概況各院校報告中，茲不贅述。

二

同济大学“一·二八”事件损失写真

Record of damage at National Tongji University during January 28th Incident

修缮后的被毁建筑

Buildings restored after the bombardments

1933年6月“国立同济大学大学部校舍全景摄影”

A panoramic view of the campus of National Tongji University in June 1933

学术创新，以助实业

Academic Innovation for Development of Industry

此阶段的学术创新，主要“以科研助实业”为指导思想。1930 年 3 月 1 日《工学会季刊》创刊，“鼓吹建设之思潮，阐明科学之原理，苟能焕发精神，锲而不舍，将有裨于工业”。1931 年 7 月，工学院创办《国立同济大学工学院报告》，内容分为机械工程、电工工程及理化三部分，每期 2000 份，分送国内外有关研究院（室）和图书馆。至 1937 年 5 月 18 日共出了 8 期，发表师生学术论文 61 篇。

The academic innovation during this time was guided by the principle of Developing Industry through Research. On March 1st, 1930, the first issue of the academic journal of *Engineering Society Quarterly* was published, which “advocated the idea that strong will and persistence inspired by spirit of construction and principles of science would benefit the development of industry”. In July 1931, the Engineering School published the first issue *of Reports from Engineering School of National Tongji University* which was composed of three parts: mechanical engineering, electrical engineering and basic sciences in physics and chemistry. By May 18th, 1937, a total of 61 academic papers by teachers and students were published in eight issues of the Reports. For each issue, 2000 copies were printed and sent to relevant research institutes/groups and libraries both at home and abroad.

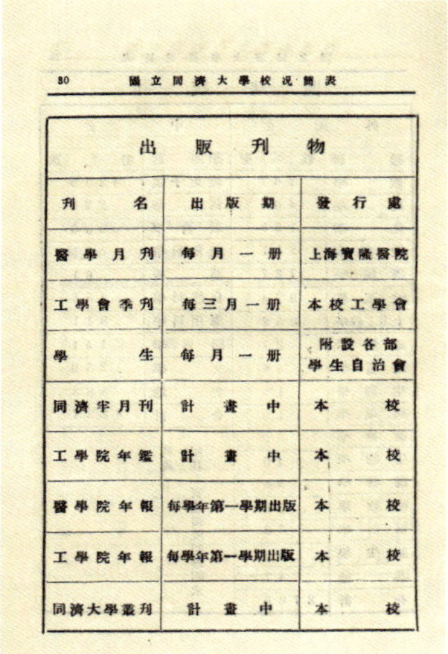

80　國立同濟大學校況簡表

出版刊物

刊名	出版期	發行處
醫學月刊	每月一册	上海寶隆醫院
工學會季刊	每三月一册	本校工學會
學生	每月一册	附設各部學生自治會
同濟半月刊	計畫中	本校
工學院年鑑	計畫中	本校
醫學院年報	每學年第一學期出版	本校
工學院年報	每學年第一學期出版	本校
同濟大學叢刊	計畫中	本校

1934 年国立同济大学出版刊物

A list of journals published by National Tongji University in 1934

1928 年工学会在校全体会员合影

Members of the Engineering Society of National Tongji University in 1928

同济大学工学会执监委员合影

Members of Executive Committee of Engineering Society of National Tongji University

■ 1928 年同济大学机师学会全体职员

All members of Machinist Society of National Tongji University in 1928

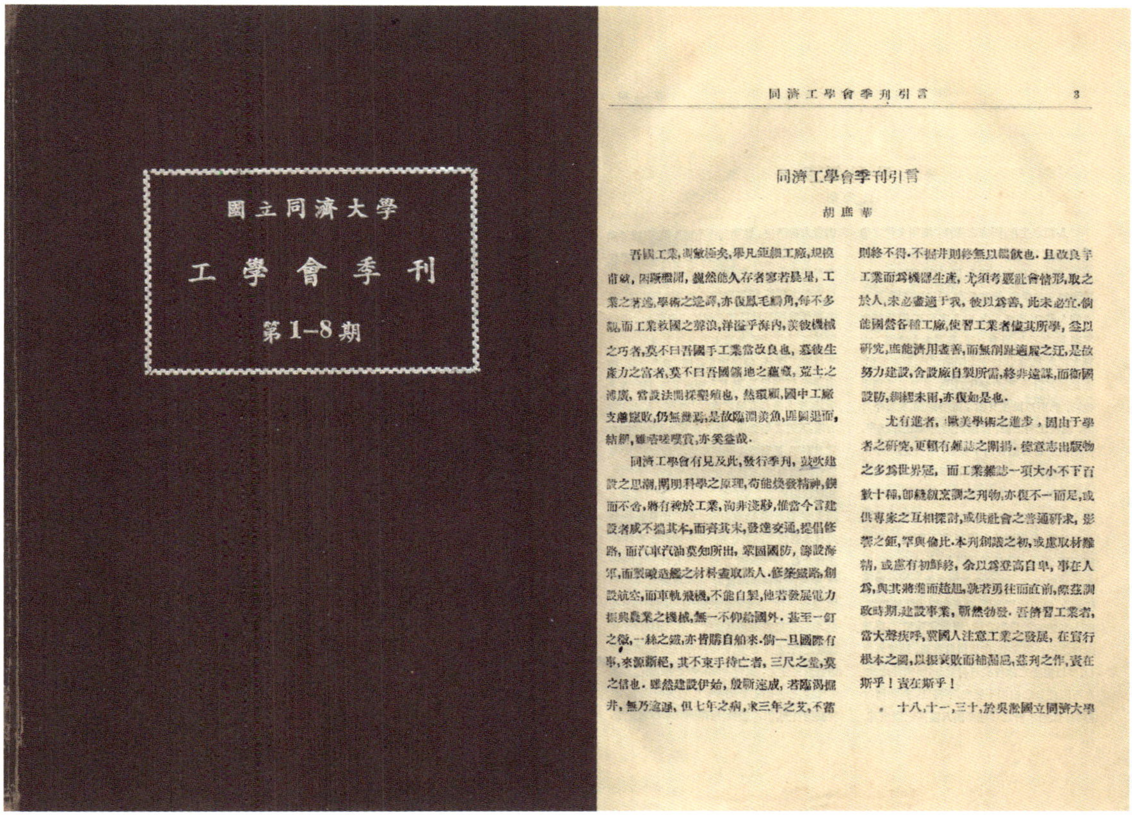

同濟工學會季刊引言 3

同濟工學會季刊引言

胡庶華

吾國工業，凋敝極矣，舉凡鉅細工廠，規模甫啟，困蹶繼開，鮮能久存者寥若晨星，工業之著述，學術之迻譯，亦復鳳毛麟角，每不多覯，而工業救國之聲浪，洋溢乎海內，羨彼機械之巧者，莫不曰吾國手工業當改良也，慕彼生產力之富者，莫不曰吾國礦地之蘊藏，荒土之溥廣，當設法開採墾殖也，然環顧國中工廠支離窳敗，仍無發端；是故臨淵羨魚，匪圖退而結網，雖咨嗟嘆賞，亦奚益哉．

同濟工學會有見及此，發行季刊，鼓吹建設之思潮，闡明科學之原理，苟能煥發精神，鍥而不舍，將有裨於工業，尚非淺尠，惟當今言建設者咸不揣其本，而齊其末，發達交通，提倡修路，而汽車汽油莫知所出，鞏固國防，籌設海軍，而製礮造艦之材料盡取諸人．修築鐵路，創設航空，而車軌飛機，不能自製，他若發展電力振興農業之機械，無一不仰給國外．甚至一釘之微，一絲之纖，亦皆購自舶來．倘一旦國際有事，來源斷絕，其不束手待亡者，三尺之童，莫之信也．雖然建設伊始，殷斯速成，若臨渴掘井，無乃遼遠，但七年之病，求三年之艾，不蓄則終不得．不掘井則終無以需飲也．且改良手工業而為機器生產，尤須考覈社會情形，取之於人，未必盡適于我，彼以為善，此未必宜．倘能國營各種工廠，使習工業者儘其所學，益以研究，庶能濟用盡善，而無削趾適履之迂，是故努力建設，合設廠自製所需，終非遠謀，而衛國設防，綢繆未雨，亦復如是也．

尤有進者，歐美學術之進步，固由于學者之研究，更賴有雜誌之闡揚．德意志出版物之多為世界冠，而工業雜誌一項大小不下百數十種，即纖細冗調之刊物，亦復不一而足，或供專家之互相探討，或供社會之普通研求，影響之鉅，罕與倫比．本刊創議之初，或慮取材難精，或慮有初鮮終，余以為登高自卑，事在人為，與其將進而趦趄，孰若勇往而直前，際茲訓政時期，建設事業，蔚然勃發．吾儕習工業者，當大聲疾呼，喚國人注意工業之發展，在實行根本之圖，以振衰敗而補罅漏，茲刊之作，責在斯乎！責在斯乎！

十八，十一，三十，於吳淞國立同濟大學

■ 《工学会季刊》合订本封面与胡庶华校长的引言

Foreword to the bound volume of *Engineering Society Quarterly* by President Hu Shuhua

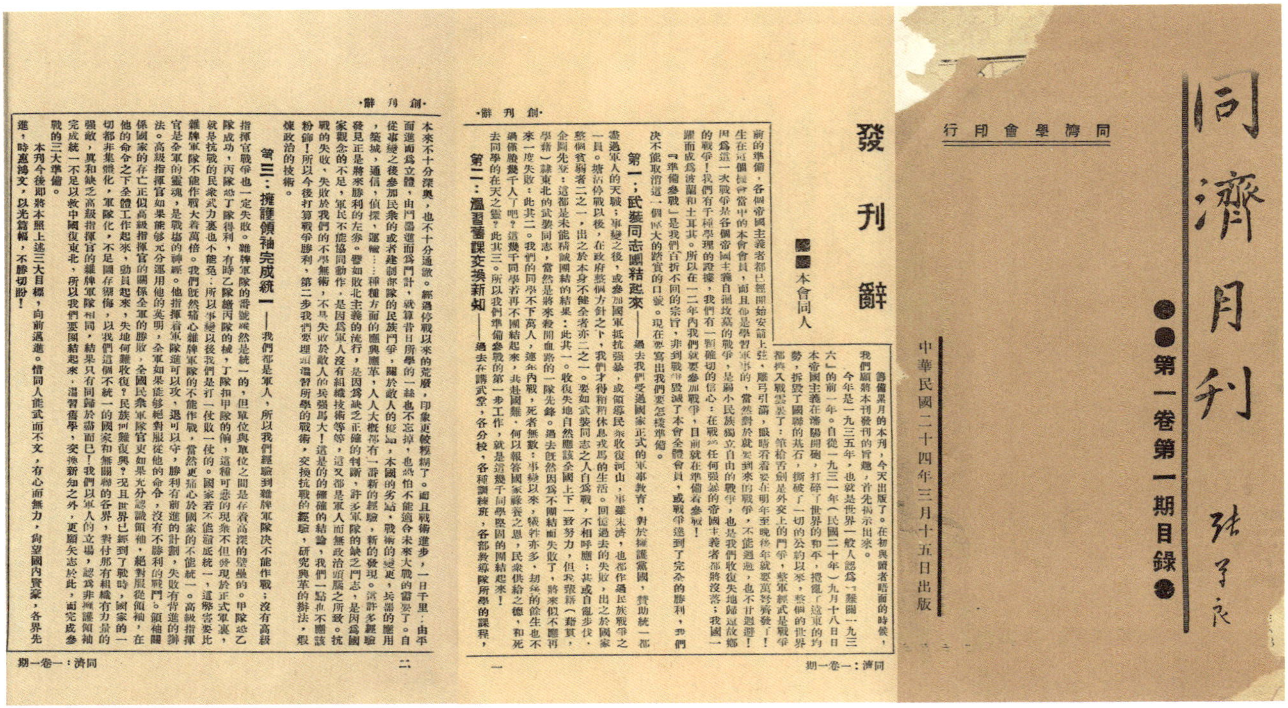

同濟月刊　張子良

●第一卷第一期目錄●

同濟學會印行

中華民國二十四年三月十五日出版

·創刊辭·

發刊辭

本會同人

籌備累月的本刊，今天出版了。在初與讀者晤面的時候，我們願將本刊發刊的旨趣，首先揭示出來。

今年是一九三五年，也就是世界一般人認為「難關一九三六」的前一年。自從一九三一年（民國二十年）九月十八日日本帝國主義在瀋陽開砲，打碎了世界的和平，推倒了遠東的均勢，拆毀了國聯的基石，撕破了一切的公約以來，整個的世界都捲入戰雲裏了：筆槍舌劍是外交上的鬥爭，整軍經武是戰爭前的準備，各個帝國主義者都已經開始安箭上弦，彎弓引滿，眼睛看着要在明年至晚後年就要萬弩齊發了！生在這個機會當中的本會會員，而且都是學習軍事的，當然對於就要到來的戰爭，不能迴避，也不甘迴避！因為這一次戰爭是各個帝國主義自掘坟墓的戰爭，也是弱小民族獨立自由的戰爭，是我們收復失地歸返故鄉的戰爭！我們有千種學理的證據，我們有一顆確切的信心：在戰爭中任何強暴的帝國主義者都將沒落；我國一躍而成為波蘭和土耳其。所以在一二年內我們就要參加戰爭，目前就在準備着參戰！

『準備參戰』是我們百折不回的宗旨，非到戰爭毀滅了本會全體會員，或戰爭達到了完全的勝利，我們決不能取消這一個偉大的踏實的口號。現在要寫出我們要怎樣準備。

第一：武裝同志團結起來——過去我們受過國家正式的軍事教育，對於擁護黨國，贊助統一都盡過軍人的天職；事變之後，或參加國軍抵抗強暴，或領導民眾收復河山，事雖未濟，也都作過民族戰爭之一員。塘沽停戰以後，在政府整個方針之下，我們才得稍稍休息戎馬的生活。回憶過去的失敗，出之於國家整個貧弱者二之一，出之於本身不健全者亦二之一。要如武裝同志之人自為戰，不相呼應；甚或自亂步伐，企圖先登：這都是未能精誠團結的結果：此其一。收復失地自然應該全國上下一致努力，但我們籍（一籍貫，學籍）隸東北的武裝同志，當然是將來殺開血路的一隊先鋒。過去既然因為不團結而失敗了，將來似不應再來一度失敗：此其二。我們的同學不下萬人，連年內戰，死者無數；事變以來，犧牲亦多，劫後的餘生也不過僅僅幾千人了吧？這幾千同學若再不團結起來，共赴國難，何以報答國家豢養之恩，民眾供給之德，和死去同學的在天之靈？此其三。所以我們準備參戰的第一步工作，就是這幾千同學堅固的團結起來！

第二：溫習舊課交換新知——過去在講武堂，各分校，各種訓練班，各部教導隊所學的課程，

同濟：一卷一期　一

·創刊辭·

本來不十分深奧，也不十分通徹。經過停戰以來的荒廢，印象更較模糊了。而且戰術進步，一日千里：由平面進而為立體，由鬥器進而為鬥計，就算昔日所學的一絲也不忘掉，也恐怕不能適合未來大戰的需要了。自從事變之後參加民眾的或者建制部隊的民族鬥爭，關於敵人的優點，本國的劣點，戰術的變更，兵器的應用，築城，通信，偵探，運輸……種種方面的應興應革，人人大概都有一番新的經驗，新的發現。這許多經驗發見正是將來勝利的左券。譬如敗北主義的流行，是因為缺乏正確的判斷，許多軍隊的缺乏鬥志，是因為國家觀念的不足，軍民不能協同動作，是因為軍人沒有組織技術等等，這又都是軍人而無政治頭腦之所致。抗戰的失敗，失敗於我們的不學無術，不是失敗於敵人的兵強馬大！這是的的確確的結論，我們一點也不應該粉飾！所以今後打算戰爭勝利，第二步我們要埋頭溫習所學的戰術，交換抗戰的經驗，研究興革的辦法，鍛煉政治的技術。

第三：擁護領袖完成統一——我們都是軍人，所以我們經驗到雜牌軍隊決不能作戰；沒有高級指揮官戰爭也一定失敗。雜牌軍隊的番號縱然是統一的，但單位與單位之間是存着高深的壁壘的。甲隊恐乙隊成功，丙隊恐丁隊得利，有時乙隊繳丙隊的械，丁隊扣甲隊的餉，這種可悲的現象不但發現於正式軍裏，就是抗戰的民眾武力裏也不能免：所以事變以後我們是打一仗敗一仗的。國家若不能澈底統一，這弊害要比雜牌軍隊不能作戰大着萬倍。我們既然痛心雜牌軍隊的不能作戰，當然更痛心於國家的不能統一。高級指揮官是全軍的靈魂，是戰場的神經。他指揮着軍隊進可以攻，退可以守，勝利有前進的計劃，失敗有背進的辦法。高級指揮官如果能夠充分運用他的英明，全軍如果能夠絕對服從他的命令，沒有不勝利的戰鬥。領袖關係國家的存亡正似高級指揮官的關係全軍的勝敗，全國民眾軍隊官吏如果充分認識領袖，絕對服從領袖，在他的命令之下全體工作起來，動員起來，失地何難收復？民族何難復興？況且世界已經到了戰時，國家的一切都非集體化，軍隊化，不足圖存禦侮，以我們這個不統一的國家和無關聯的各界，對付那有組織有力量的強敵，真和缺乏高級指揮官的雜牌軍隊相同，結果只有同歸於盡而已！我們以軍人的立場，認為非擁護領袖完成統一不足以救中國復東北，所以我們要團結起來，溫習舊學，交換新知之外，更願矢志於此，而完成參戰的三大準備。

本刊今後即將本照上述三大目標，向前邁進。惜同人能武而不文，有心而無力，尚望國內賢豪，各界先進，時惠鴻文，以光篇幅，不勝切盼！

同濟：一卷一期　二

《同济月刊》创刊号及发刊词

Foreword to the first issue of *Tongji Monthly*

《同济月刊》创刊号所载“同济学会成立纪念会摄影”

A group photo marking the establishment of Tongji Society on the first issue of *Tongji Monthly*

五馆一厂，领先全国

Leading Universities in China with Five Laboratories and a Factory

至 1937 年，实习工厂占地 4500 平方米，内有木工场、焊工场、铸工场、钳工场、锻工场、淬火工场、机器工场及圬工场各 1 所，除供给学生实习外，兼做校内各研究馆所需的设备及标本，并制造车床、刨床、抽水机、台钳等产品出售。除实习工厂外，还设有电工试验馆、机器试验馆、水利试验馆，材料试验馆、测量馆等专业实验室。

By 1937, the internship factory had an area of 4,500m² with workshops for carpentry, welding, foundry, benchwork, forging, quenching, machinery, and plastering. These workshops not only served for student internship, but also produced instruments and samples for laboratories at the university. Besides, lathes, planers, water pumps and bench vices were manufactured at the factory for sale. In addition to the internship factory, there were five professional laboratories for electrical testing, machine testing, hydraulic testing, material testing and surveying at the university.

机器试验馆

Machine Testing Laboratory

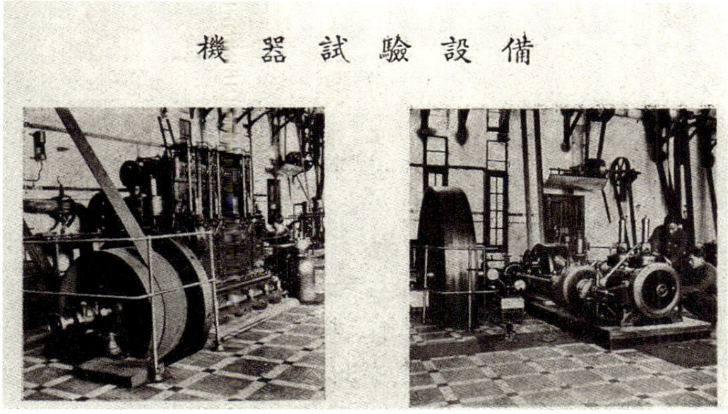

原動室之二

■ 机器试验馆占地 800m²，备有町发动之原动机多辆，除教学使用外，同时也供给全校水电及原动力。馆内空地有飞机引擎试验场所，有两座飞机机头，一为 90 马力“V”形的 Curtiss 机，一为 550 马力的星座式 BMWHornet 机。

The Machine Testing Laboratory, which covered an area of 800m², was equipped with several field mobilized prime movers for teaching and for supply of water and power at the university. Inside the laboratory, there were two aircraft prows, one of which being a V-shaped 90 horsepower Curtiss plane, and the other a 550 horsepower Constellation BMW Hornet plane as well as a space for testing aircraft engines.

鐵道儀型之二

鐵道儀型之一

电工试验馆
Electrical Laboratory

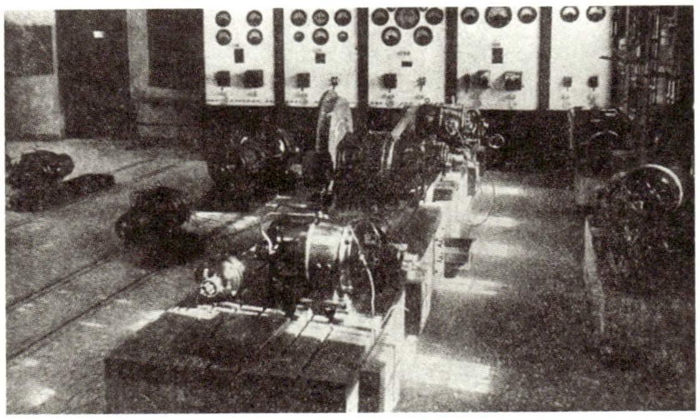

电工试验馆设有电机室、高压电室等。电机室有各种马达及发动机，有直流、交流之全部电动发动机组。高压电室包括高压试验室及高压开关器二部，内有各种高压及高频率弧光试验等设备。

There was an electric engine room and a high-voltage room in the Electrical Testing Laboratory. The electrical machinery room was equipped with various kinds of motors and engines, AC and DC electric engines whereas the high-voltage suite had a high-voltage testing room and two high-voltage switchgears with high-voltage and high-frequency equipments for arc experiments.

水利试验馆
Hydraulic Laboratory

水利试验馆利用回水槽建一升水设备，经过三种不同的活动堰，将水面升至三种不同的高度，这种活动水堰在国内属首创。

At the Hydraulic Laboratory, a water-lifting device was built by means of a return flume. The device lifted the water to three different levels through three different movable weirs, which were the first of its kind in China.

材料试验馆
Material Testing Laboratory

■ 材料试验馆占地 500m^2，内分钢铁强性试验部、金属显微室、钢骨水泥试验部和钢铁化验部等四个部分。

Material Testing Laboratory, which covered an area of 500m², was divided into four parts for steel strength testing, metal microscopy, reinforced concrete testing and steel testing.

测量馆
Surveying Laboratory

■ 测量馆于 1937 年建成，仪器设备包括大地测量、摄影测量和复照制版三部分。

The Surveying Laboratory built in 1937 was equipped with three kinds of facilities for geodedic surveying, photogrammetric surveying and duplicated plate making.

实习工厂

The internship factory

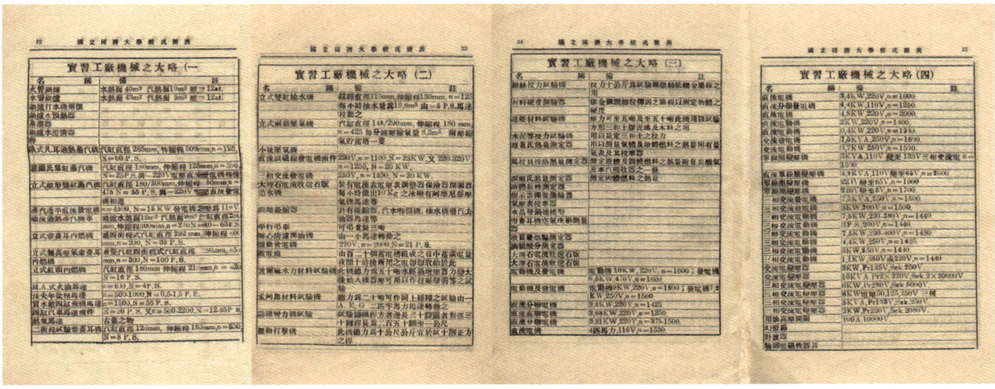

實習工廠機械之大略(一)

實習工廠機械之大略(二)

實習工廠機械之大略(三)

實習工廠機械之大略(四)

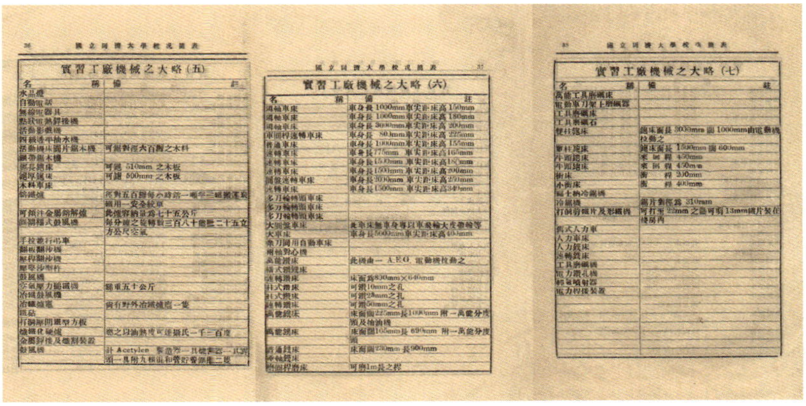

實習工廠機械之大略(五)

實習工廠機械之大略(六)

實習工廠機械之大略(七)

■ 实习工厂器械概况（1934 年）

A list of facilities at the internship factory (1934)

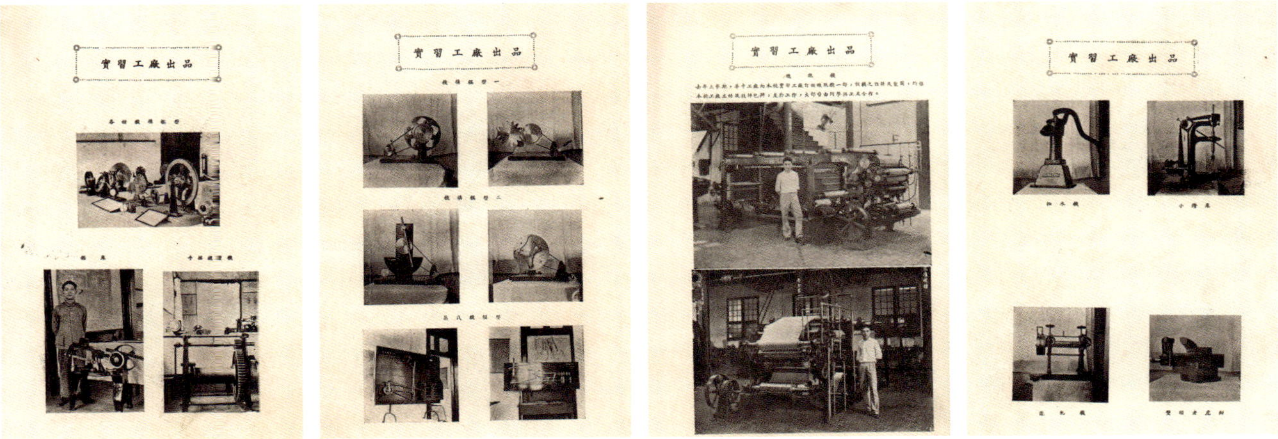

■ 由学校实习工厂生产出售的部分机器

Machines manufactured for sale at the internship factory

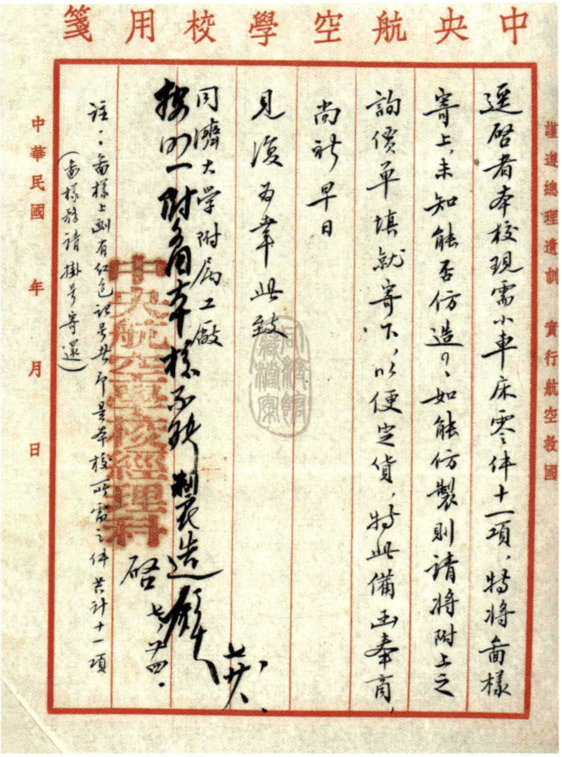

中央航空學校用箋

謹遵總理遺訓 實行航空救國

逕啓者本校現需小車床零件十一項，特將备樣寄上，未知能否仿造？如能仿製則請將附上之詢價單填就寄下，以便定貨，特此備函奉商，尚祈早日見復為幸，此致

同濟大學附属工廠

中央航空學校經理科 啓 七月廿四

註：备樣上剛有红色記号者即是本校所需之件，共計十一項（备樣務請掛号寄還）

中華民國 年 月 日

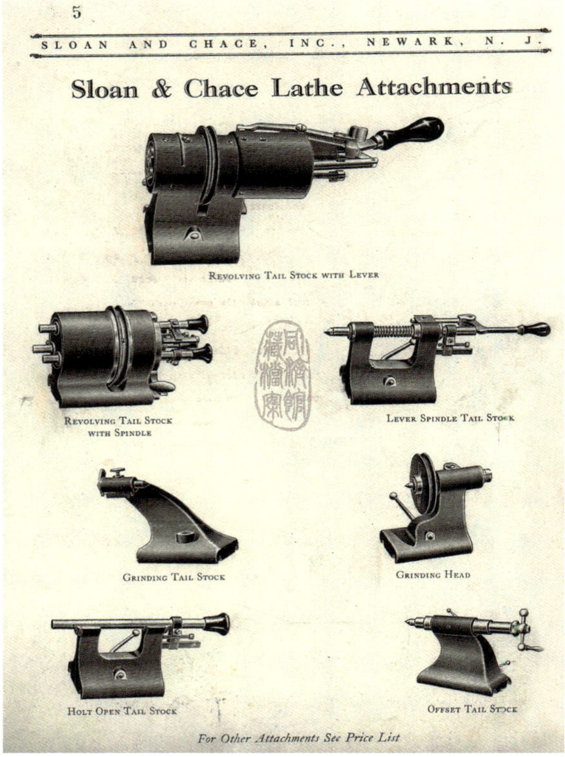

5

SLOAN AND CHACE, INC., NEWARK, N. J.

Sloan & Chace Lathe Attachments

For Other Attachments See Price List

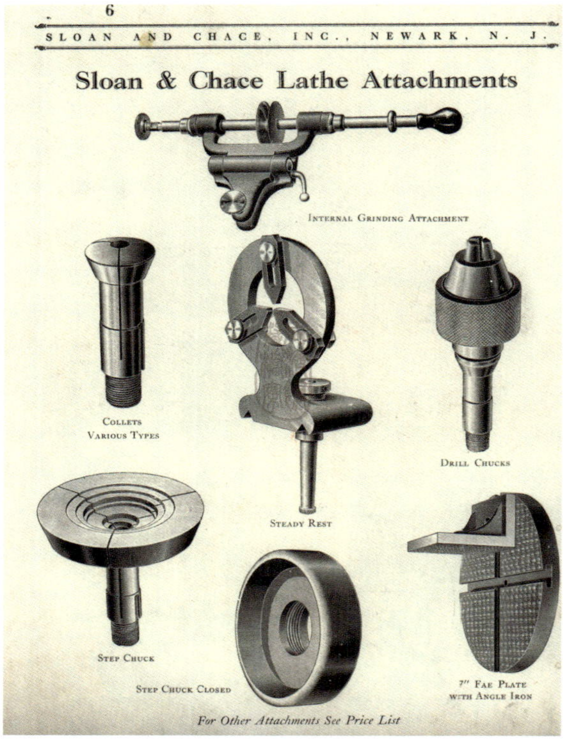

6

SLOAN AND CHACE, INC., NEWARK, N. J.

Sloan & Chace Lathe Attachments

For Other Attachments See Price List

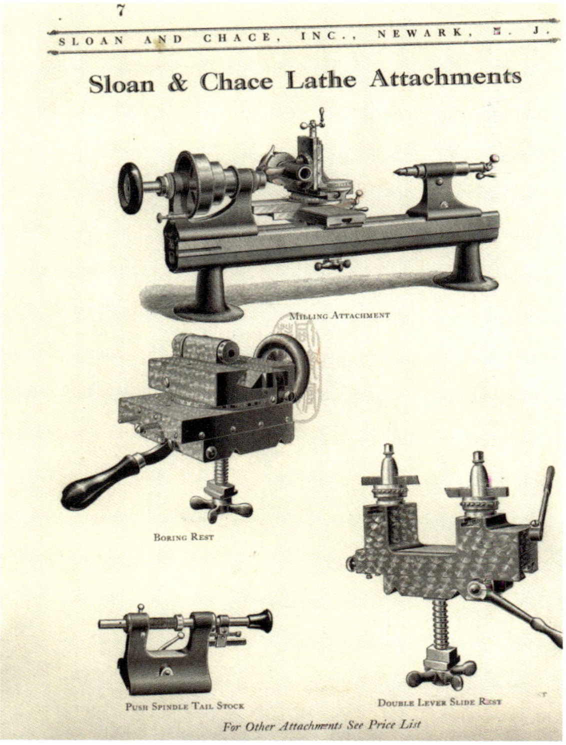

7

SLOAN AND CHACE, INC., NEWARK, N. J.

Sloan & Chace Lathe Attachments

For Other Attachments See Price List

■ 中央航空学校订单
An order from Central Aeronautical School

学以致用，求严求实

Practice-oriented Learning Under Strict Discipline

工学院一年级新生先进工厂，依照教学大纲规定程序，轮流至各工场实习。实习内容包括模型木工、铸工、钳工、锻工、淬火、机器工、焊工及土木工等。为增加学生工作兴趣，实习工作除练习一般方法外，尽量结合实用，增加创造性内容。因此，同济工科毕业生以动手能力强、适应岗位快受到社会各界欢迎。

According to the teaching curriculum, first-year students of Engineering School started to practise in different workshops to learn skills in model carpentry, foundry, benchwork, forging, quenching, latche work, welding and masonry at the internship factory. To stimulate students' interest, the learning of practical skills was coupled with real projects to keep students' mind open for creativity. Therefore, the engineering graduates of Tongji who were good at using their hands were very popular among employers from different walks of life.

■ 建筑实习

Students at work on a construction site

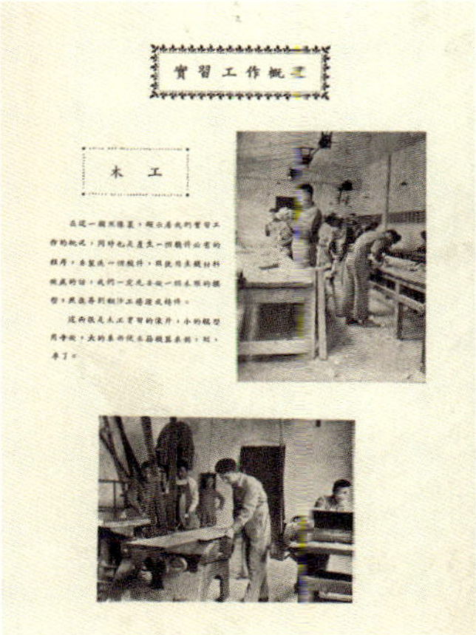

■ 木工实习

Students at work in a carpentry room

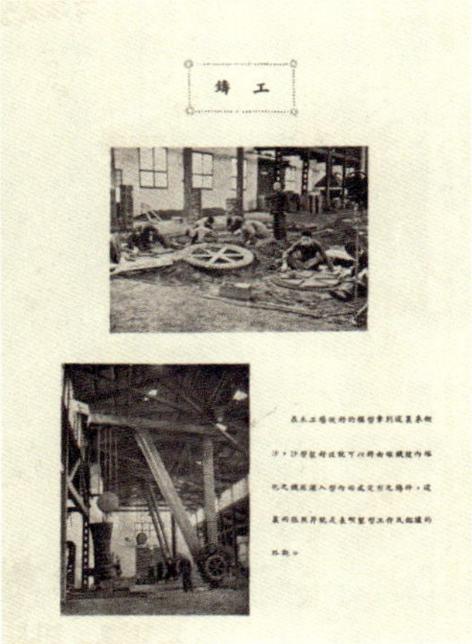

■ 铸工实习

Training in foundry

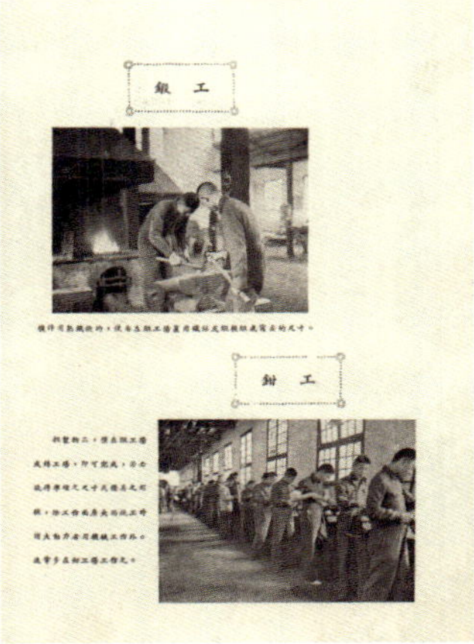

■ 钳工、锻工实习

Training in benchwork and forging

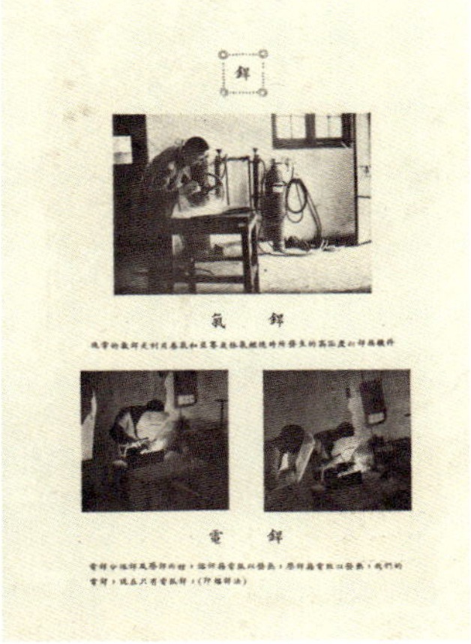

■ 焊工实习

Training in welding

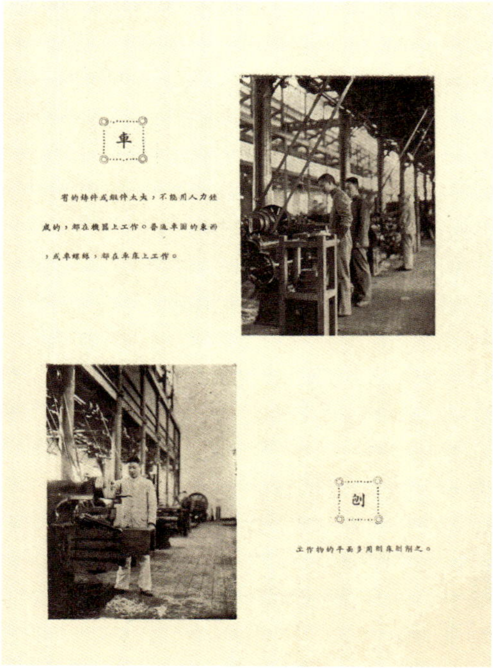

車

有的鑄件或鍛件太大，不能用人力鏟成的，都在機器上工作。普通車圓的東西，或車螺絲，都在車床上工作。

刨

工作物的平面多用刨床刨削之。

车、刨实习

Training in latche work

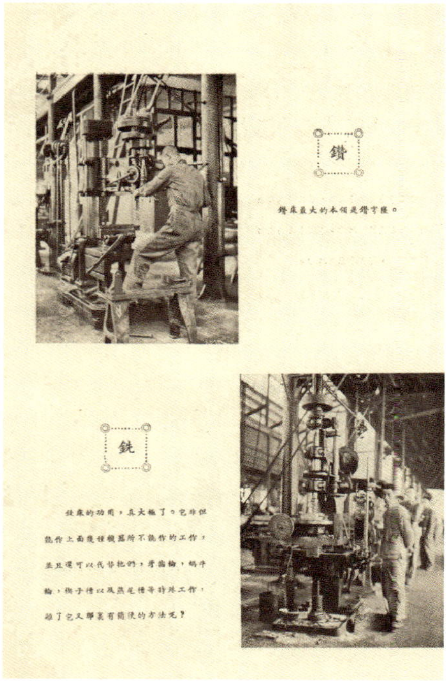

鑽

鑽床最大的本領是鑽穿眼。

銑

銑床的功用，真大極了。它非但能作上面幾種機器所不能作的工作，並且還可以代替牠們，牙齒輪，蝸牛輪，銷子槽以及燕尾槽等特殊工作，離了它又哪裏有簡便的方法呢？

铣、钻实习

Training in milling and drilling

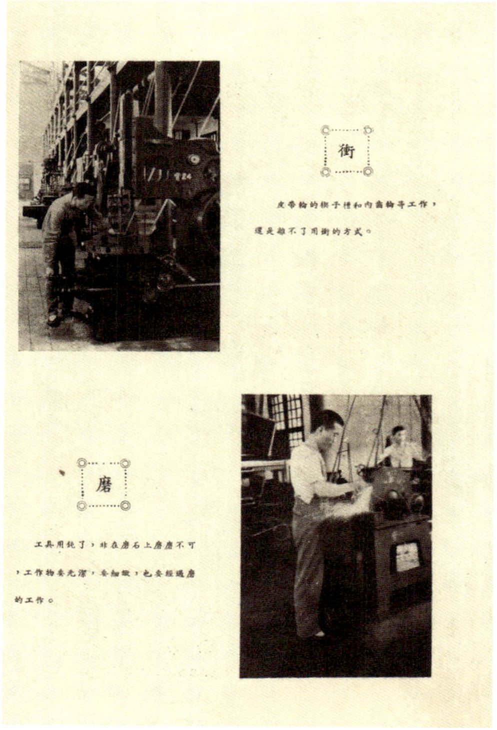

衝

皮帶輪的銷子槽和內齒輪等工作，還是離不了用衝的方式。

磨

工具用鈍了，非在磨石上磨磨不可，工作物要光潔，要細緻，也要經過磨的工作。

冲、磨实习

Training in punching and polishing

汽车驾驶实习

Training in driving

原动力实习

Training in generating motive power

三十而立，国家盛事

Grand Celebration on 30th Anniversary of Tongji University

1937年5月20日，同济大学三十周年纪念会隆重举行。参加典礼者有中外来宾及全校师生员工计三千余人。校长翁之龙介绍校务，向各界代表报告同济建校三十年来的成绩。蒋介石、林森、朱家骅、王世杰、俞鸿钧等分别题词，以示祝贺。德国柏林各报也发表纪念文章，赞扬同济为增进中德文化事业所作的努力。

On May 20th, 1937, a grand ceremony was held to celebrate the 30th anniversary of Tongji University. Over 3,000 participants from home and abroad including teachers and students at Tongji attended the ceremony. President Weng Zhilong gave an introduction of the development of the university and achievements that Tongji had made over the last thirty years. VIPs of the Nanjing National Government including Chiang Kai-shek, Lin Sen, Zhu Jiahua, Wang Shijie, and Yu Hongjun made inscriptions respectively to mark the occasion. Newspapers in Berlin, Germany published commemorative articles, highly commending National Tongji University for its efforts to promote Sino-German culture.

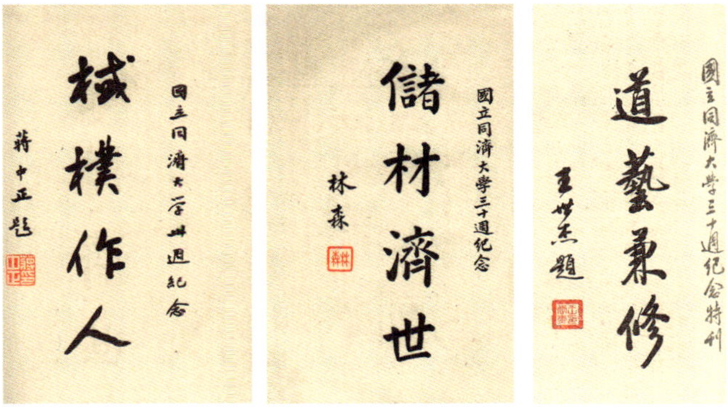

中华民国政府政要题字

Inscriptions by VIPs of the Nanjing National Government

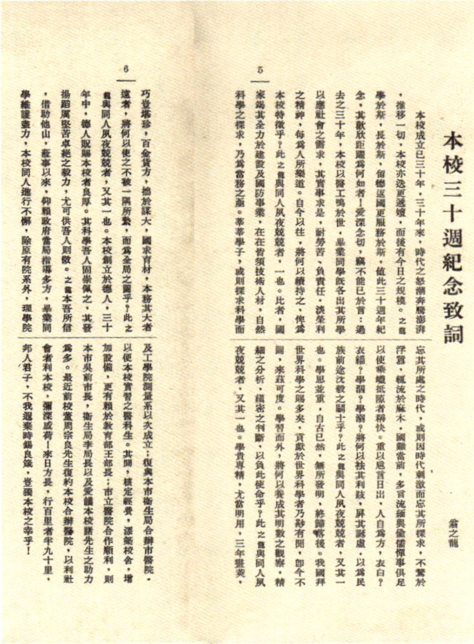

本校三十週紀念致詞

翁之龍

同济大学三十周年纪念会翁之龙校长致辞

Speech of President Weng Zhilong delivered on the 30th Anniversary of National Tongji University

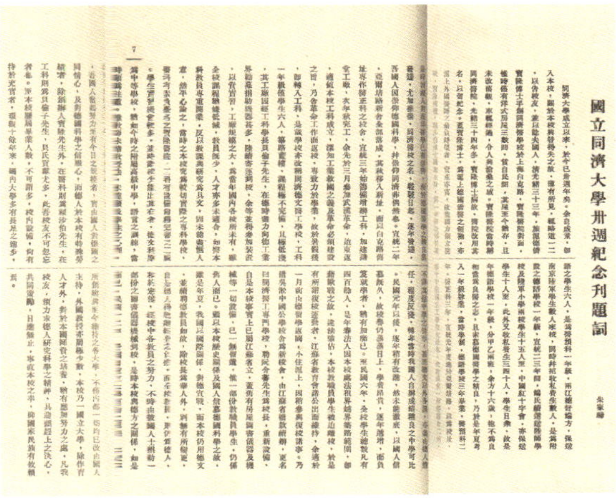

國立同濟大學卅週紀念刊題詞

朱家驊

朱家骅校友致《国立同济大学卅周纪念题词》

Inscription by alumna Zhu Jiahua for the 30th Anniversary of National Tongji University

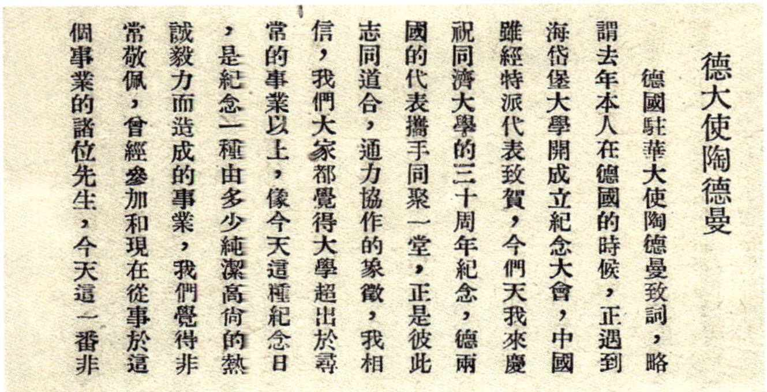

德大使陶德曼

德國駐華大使陶德曼致詞，略謂去年本人在德國的時候，正遇到海俗堡大學開成立紀念大會，中國雖經特派代表致賀，今們天我來慶祝同濟大學的三十周年紀念，德兩國的代表攜手同聚一堂，正是彼此志同道合，通力協作的象徵，我相信，我們大家都覺得大學超出於尋常的事業以上，像今天這種紀念日，是紀念一種由多少純潔高尚的熱誠毅力而造成的事業，我們覺得非常敬佩，曾經參加和現在從事於這個事業的諸位先生，今天這一番非

德国大使陶德曼发言概要

Speech by German Ambassador Dr. Oskar Paul Trautmann

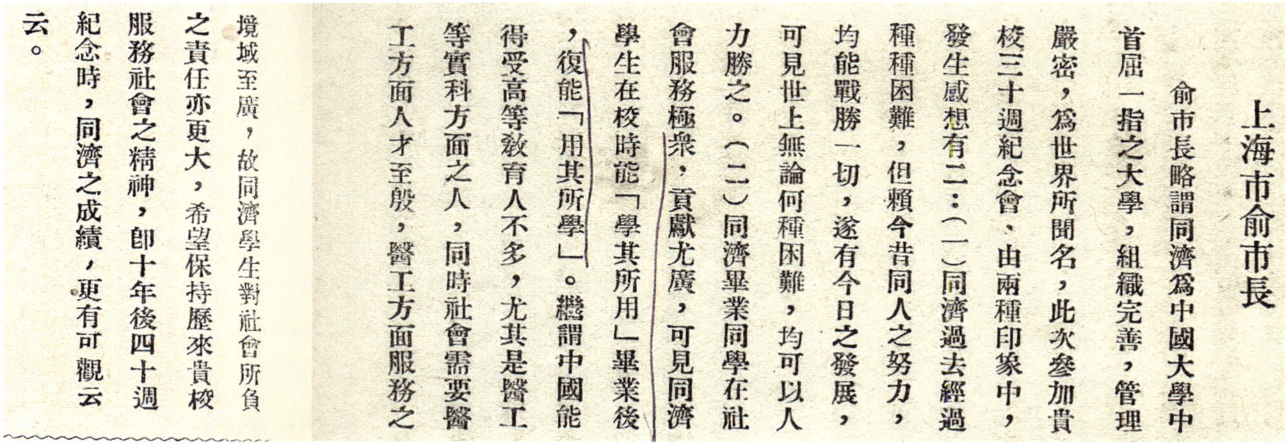

上海市俞市長

俞市長略謂同濟爲中國大學中首屈一指之大學，組織完善，管理嚴密，爲世界所聞名，此次參加貴校三十週紀念會，由兩種印象中，發生感想有二：(一)同濟過去經過種種困難，但賴今昔同人之努力，均能戰勝一切，遂有今日之發展，可見世上無論何種困難，均可以人力勝之。(二)同濟畢業同學在社會服務極衆，貢獻尤廣，可見同濟學生在校時能「學其所用」畢業後，復能「用其所學」。繼謂中國能得受高等教育人不多，尤其是醫工等實科方面之人，同時社會需要醫工方面人才至殷，醫工方面服務之境域至廣，故同濟學生對社會所負之責任亦更大，希望保持歷來貴校服務社會之精神，即十年後四十週紀念時，同濟之成績，更有可觀云云。

■ 上海市市长俞鸿钧发言概要

Speech summary by Mr. Yu Hongjun, Mayor of Shanghai

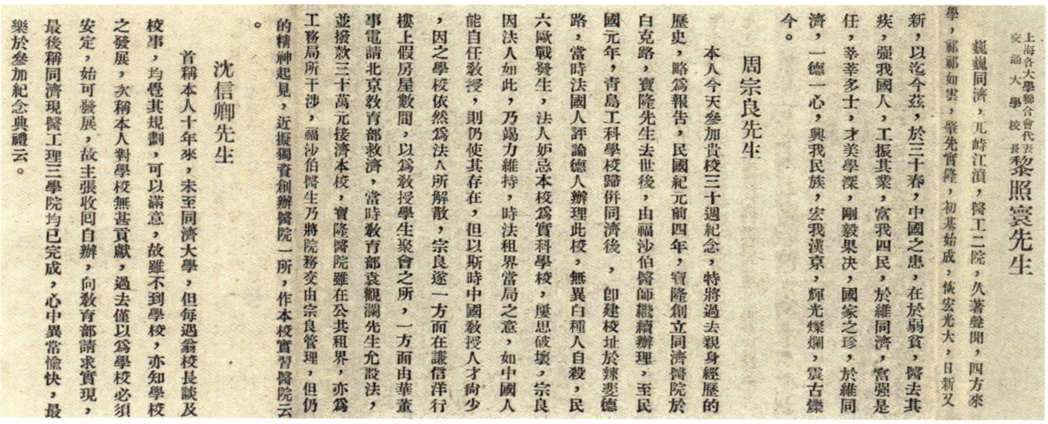

上海各大學聯合會代表 交通大學校長 黎照寰先生

巍巍同濟，几峙江濆，醫工二院，久著聲聞，四方來學，鄗鄗如雲，肇先寶隆，初基始成，恢宏光大，日新又新，以迄今茲，於三十春，中國之患，在於弱貧，醫去其疾，强我國人，工振其業，富我四民，於維同濟，實强是任，莘莘多士，才美學深，剛毅果决，國家之珍，於維同濟，一德一心，興我民族，宏我漢京，輝光燦爛，震古爍今。

周宗良先生

本人今天參加貴校三十週紀念，特將過去親身經歷的歷史，略爲報告，民國紀元前四年，寶隆創立同濟醫院於白克路，寶隆先生去世後，由福沙伯醫師繼續辦理，至民國元年，青島工科學校歸併同濟後，即建校址於辣斐德路，當時法國人評論德人辦理此校，無異白種人自殺，民六歐戰發生，法人妒忌本校爲實科學校，屢思破壞，宗良因法人如此，乃竭力維持，時法租界當局之意，如中國人能自任教授，則仍使其存在，但以斯時中國教授人才尚少，因之學校依然爲法人所解散，宗良遂一方面在謙信洋行樓上假房屋數間，以爲教授學生聚會之所，一方面由華董事電請北京教育部救濟，當時教育部袁觀瀾先生允設法，並撥款三十萬元接濟本校，寶隆醫院雖在公共租界，亦爲工務局所干涉，福沙伯醫生乃將院務交由宗良管理，但仍的精神起見，近擬獨資創辦醫院一所，作本校實習醫院云。

沈信卿先生

首稱本人十年來，未至同濟大學，但每遇翁校長談及校事，均覺其規劃，可以滿意，故雖不到學校，亦知學校之發展，次稱本人對學校無甚貢獻，過去僅以爲學校必須安定，始可發展，故主張收回自辦，向教育部請求實現，最後稱同濟現醫工理三學院均已完成，心中異常愉快，最樂於參加紀念典禮云。

■ 校董周宗良、沈信卿和上海交通大学校长黎照寰致辞

Speeches by university board members Mr. Zhou Zongliang and Mr. Shen Xinqing, and by Mr. Li Zhaohuan, President of Shanghai Jiaotong University

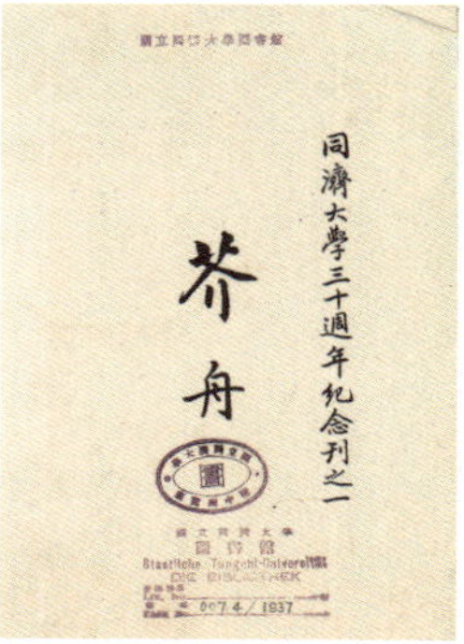

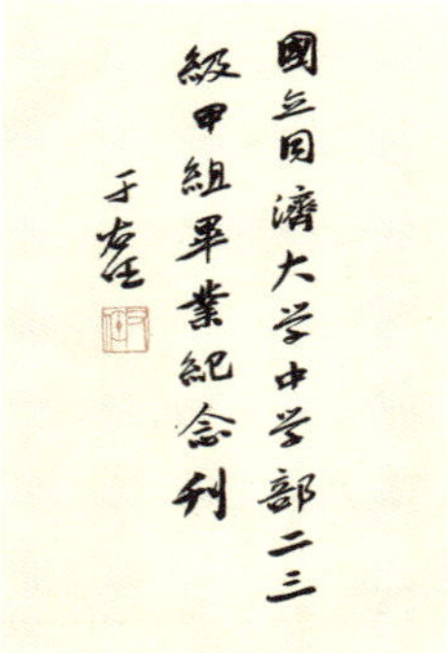

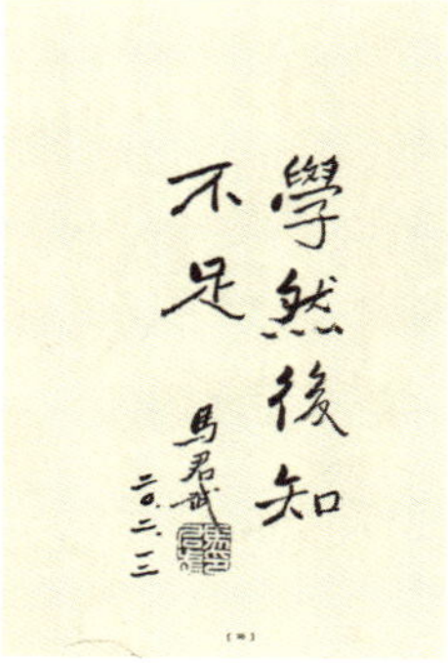

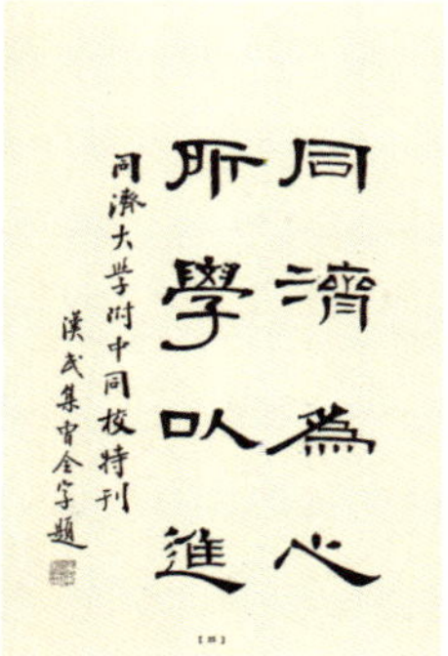

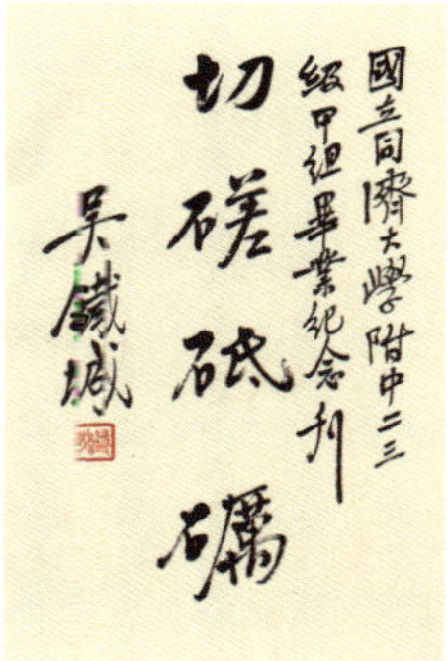

■ 校庆三十周年纪念刊《芥舟》中的部分题词

Inscriptions on the commemorative issue of the journal *Jiezhou* for the 30th anniversary of National Tongji University

本校三十週紀念蒙各軍政長官，機關團體，校友同學，或賜隆禮，或頒函電，隆情盛意，至堪感戴，茲依各件收到先後爲序，登載如下：

禮物

上海市教育會	銀盾一座	阮希堯先生	鏡框一方
上海市第八區黨部	鏡框一方	鞏縣兵工廠及分廠校友十八人	銀屏一具
魯主席韓復渠先生	銀盾一座	李驥騏先生	立軸一幅
同濟校友會	鏡扁一只	浙江省立杭州高級中學	銀盾一座
社會局局長潘公展先生	對聯一副	工學院民二五級同學	大鏡一面
兩路局局長黃伯樵先生	立軸一幅	蔡耀年先生	鏡架一件
國立暨南大學	同右	中國醫學院	立軸一幅
中國公學正校長吳鐵城副校長陳濟成	對聯一副	王承曾先生	鏡框一只
新聞報館	鏡架一只	留汴醫工兩科畢業同學贈中華書局出品	日歷掛鐘一具
中華醫學會	立軸一幅	吳淞市政委員辦事處	立軸一幅
上海美專校校長劉海粟先生	同右	留鎮江畢業同學方杲等三十五人贈銅質	校牌一塊
劉銓法先生	同右	唐承宗先生	花籃一只
鄒肇經先生	同右	附中學生自治會	扁額一塊

謹布頌忱！

弟張羣皓印

德國外交部長賀電：

Der Tung Chi Universitaet spreche ich zur Feier ihres 30 jaehrigen Bestehens meine besten Glueckwuensche aus und hoffe, dass sie ihre erfolgreiche Wecksamkeit zum Nutzen fuer China und im Sinne einer kulturellen Verbindung zwischin China und Deutschland auch weiterhin fortsezen moege.

Der Reichsminister des Auswaertigen

Freiherr Von Neurath

Berlin

吳淞鎮北，同濟大學

翁校長勛鑒，頃接喜柬，欣悉貴校卅週年紀念，謹電伸賀！

廈門弟林文慶叩

上海吳淞同濟大學鑒，接奉華箋，敬諗貴校創立適屆卅週，彰往策來，宏敷菁莪之化，日新月異，彌殷葵藿之傾，遙企申江，謹電奉賀！

國立山東大學校長林濟青叩敬

上海吳淞同濟大學，創校卅年，馳名中外，舉行紀念，無任欽仰，將來進展未可限量，謹布賀忱，伏維察督！

金陵大學校長陳裕光皓

上海同濟大學鑒

貴校成立屆卅周，棫樸作人，爲中華之模範，菁莪造士，毓黨國之棟樑，遙企宏規，謹電馳賀

杭州德奧瑞同學會叩

吳淞國立同濟大學

母校三十週紀念，同心濟世。

旅平同濟同學會恭祝

上海吳淞鎮北，同濟大學公鑒，

貴校卅週紀念，謹賀嘉績萬千，

濟南齊大劉世傳叩灰

德國遠東協會賀電：

Anlaesslich heutigen dreissigsten Jahrestages senden wir der Tung Chi Universitaet und Ihnen persönlich unsere aufrichtigsten Glueckwuensche. Moege die Universitaet sich weiterhin auf der beste entwickeln und Ihrem Vaterland viele tuechtige Maenner ausbilden, die beitragen zu Chinas Ruhm und Croesse

Fernostverband

Dr. Diehn (Praesident)

Dr. Linde (Vizepraesident)

德國外國研究院賀電：

Fuer Zukunft herzliche Wuensche Wissenschaftsarbeit

Deutshhes Auslandsinstitut

德國國家銀行賀電：

Zur 30 Wiederkehr des Gruendungstages neber sende ich beste Glueckwuensche Moege die Universitaet lebendigen Ausdruck fuer erfolgreiche deutsch Chinesische Gemeinschaftsarbeit, auch weiterhin eine glueckliche Entwicklung.

Reichsbank-praesident

■ 三十周年校庆各界人士贺电及礼物单

A list of presents and congratulatory letters and messages from all walks of life for the 30th Anniversary of National Tongji University

锻炼体质，全面发展

Physical Education for All-round Development

“康健之精神必寓健康之身体，惟有健康之身体，方能阐发深邃之学理”，同济的工科教育，注重学生全面发展。学校将体育课列为必修课，每年举行一次全校性各种球类比赛。校内体育设施有大运动场、田径场、网球场、篮球场、排球场、手球场、国术场、游泳池、乒乓室、游艇等，以便青年学生在课余之暇，强身健体，陶冶性情。

“A healthy mind resides in a healthy body; and a healthy body inspires profound thoughts”. The engineering education was balanced by a focus on allround development of students at National Tongji University. PE (Physical Education) was among the compulsory courses and a sports meeting of ball games was held every year. Available to students for their physical exercises on campus were a large playground, a track and field ground, tennis courts, basketball courts, volleyball courts, a handball pitch, a martial arts field, a swimming pool, table tennis rooms and yachts.

篮球队

University Basketball Team

排球队

University Volleyball Team

足球队

University Football Team

■ 网球队

University Tennis Team

■ 台球队

University Billiard Team

■ 田径队

University Track and Field Team

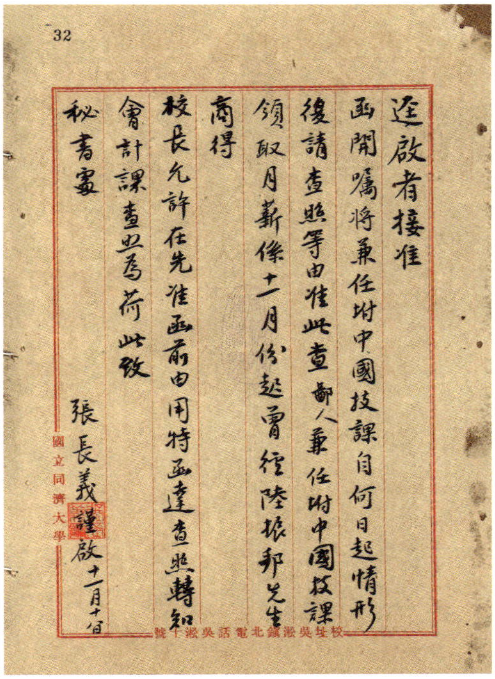

32

逕啟者接准

函開囑將兼任附中國技課自何日起情形

後請查照等由准此查鄙人兼任附中國技課

領取月薪係十一月份起曾經陸振邦先生

商得

校長允許在先准函前由用特函達查照轉知

會計課查照為荷此致

秘書處

張長義謹啟 十一月十日

國立同濟大學

校址吳淞鎮北電話吳淞十號

■ 1929 年学校聘第一届国术国考最优获得者张长义为专职国术教练，图为张长义任职时的公文。

In 1929, Mr. Zhang Changyi, the first prize winner of the First National Examination of Martial Arts, was employed as a full-time coach of martial arts by the university. The official document for employment of Mr. Zhang Changyi is on show here.

学校各项体育运动

Different kinds of sports activities on campus

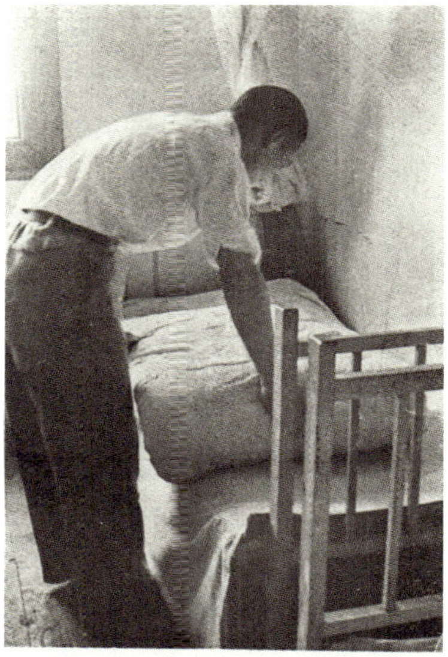

趕 快 起 床

將………

達 帝 達

蓮 蓮 蓮………

唱 得 夠 味 兒

獨　奏

工科学历，德国认可

Programs in Engineering Recognized by Germany

受这一时期学校机械设备精良、治学态度严谨、学术风气自由的影响，有些同学在二、三年级时就有发明创造成果，受到各界嘉奖。1936年4月1日，柏林德国工程师学会来函，承认同济大学工科毕业生与德国工业大学毕业生具有同等资格，可为该会上海分会正式会员，反映了当时国外教育界对同济工程教育的认可。

Due to the sophisticated facilities, strict disciplines and academic freedom at the university, students made innovative achievements during their second and third years of study and were awarded with prizes from various sources. On April 1st, 1936, a letter from the German Society of Engineers in Berlin arrived in recognition of the engineering education at Tongji. According to the letter, graduates of engineering programs from Tongji were entitled to the membership of the Shanghai branch of the society in the same way as their German counterparts from a Technical University, which revealed the acknowledgement of the engineering education of Tongji in the field of education abroad.

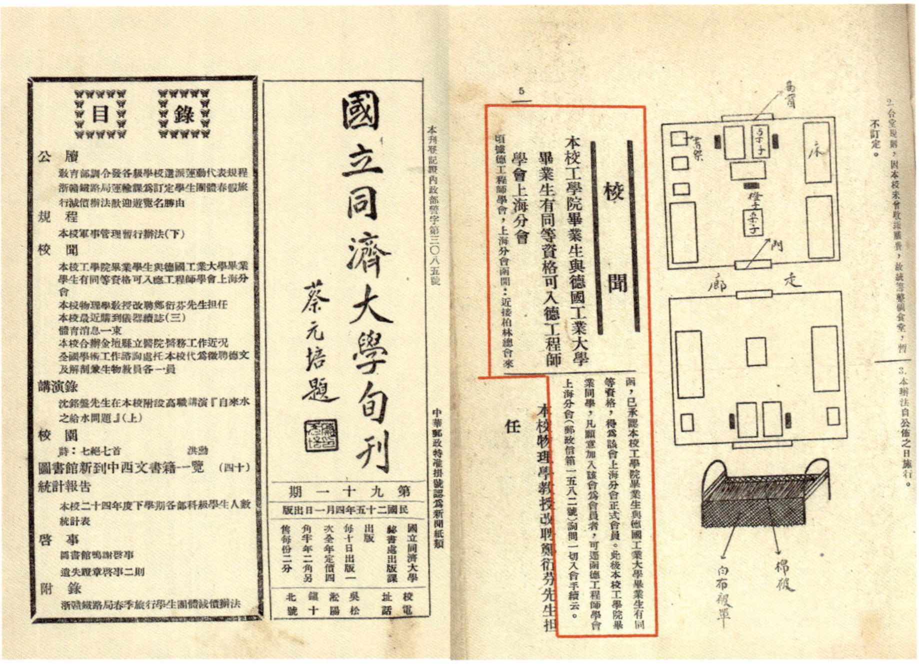
目錄

公牘
敎育部訓令發各級學校選派運動代表規程
浙贛鐵路局運輸課爲訂定學生團體春假旅行減價辦法歡迎遊覽名勝由

規程
本校軍事管理暫行辦法(下)

校聞
本校工學院畢業學生與德國工業大學畢業學生有同等資格可入德工程師學會上海分會
本校物理學教授改聘鄭衍芬先生担任
本校最近購到儀器續誌(三)
體育消息一束
本校合辦金塘縣立醫院醫務工作近況
全國學術工作諮詢處托本校代爲徵聘德文及解剖兼生物教員各一員

講演錄
沈銘盤先生在本校附設高職講演『自來水之給水問題』(上)

校園
詩：七絕七首　洪勁

圖書館新到中西文書籍一覽　(四十)

統計報告
本校二十四年度下學期各部科級學生人數統計表

啓事
圖書館鳴謝啓事
遺失證章啓事二則

附錄
浙贛鐵路局春季旅行學生團體減價辦法

國立同濟大學旬刊

蔡元培題

5

校聞

本校工學院畢業生與德國工業大學畢業生有同等資格可入德工程師學會上海分會

頃據德工程師學會，上海分會函開：近接柏林總會來函，已承認本校工學院畢業生與德國工業大學畢業生有同等資格，得爲該會上海分會正式會員。此後本校工學院畢業同學，凡願意加入該會爲會員者，可逕函德工程師學會上海分會（郵政信箱一五八二號）詢問一切入會手續云。

本校物理學教授改聘鄭衍芬先生担任

■《国立同济大学旬刊》1936年4月1日刊载的“本校工学院毕业生与德国工业大学毕业生有同等资格”的报道

A report on the letter from the German Society of Engineering in recognition of the engineering education at Tongji published in *University Xunkan* (journal published every ten days) on April 1st, 1936.

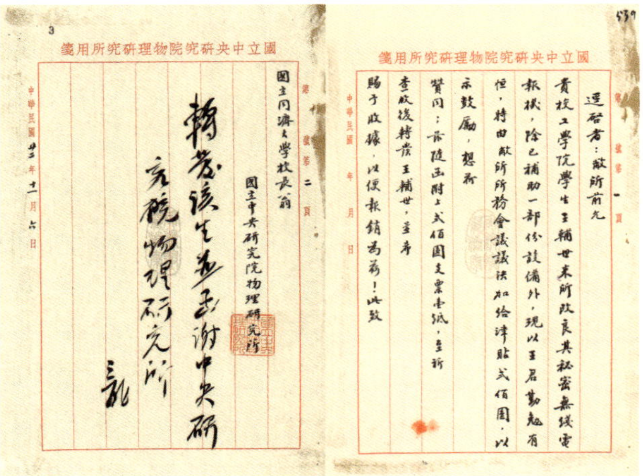
國立中央研究院物理研究所用箋

逕啓者：敝所前允
貴校工學院學生王輔世來所改良其秘密無線電報機，除已補助一部份設備外，現以王君勤勉有恒，特由敝所所務會議議決加給津貼貳佰圓，以示鼓勵，想荷
贊同；茲隨函附上貳佰圓支票壹紙，至祈
查收後轉發王輔世，並希
賜予收據，以便報銷爲荷！此致

國立中央研究院物理研究所用箋

國立同濟大學校長翁
國立中央研究院物理研究所

■ 国立中央研究院物理研究所关于同济学生王辅世发明秘密无线电的函

Letter from Physics Research Institute of Academia Sinica about the invention of a secret wireless radio by Mr. Wang Fushi, a student from National Tongji University

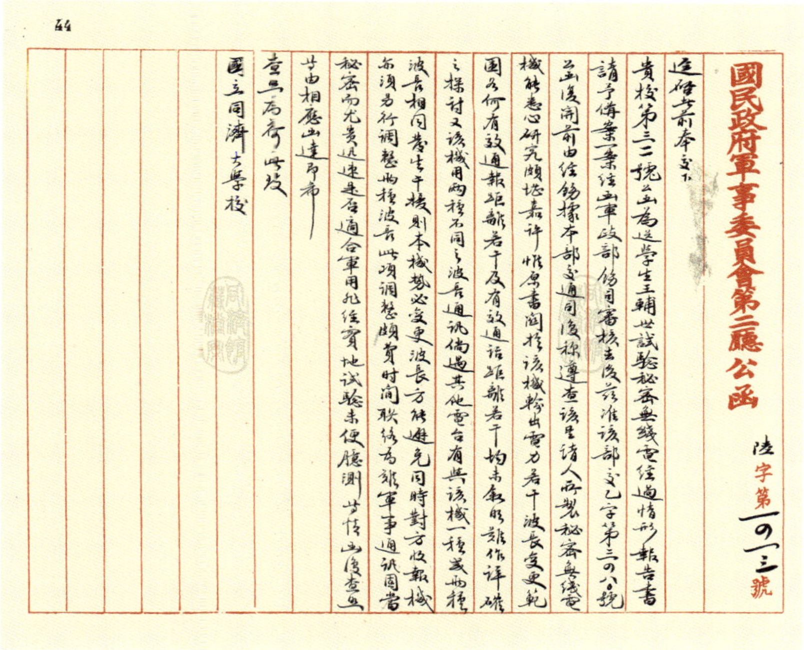
國民政府軍事委員會第二廳公函

■ 南京国民政府军事委员第二厅关于王辅世发明秘密无线电的公函

Letter from the Military Committee of the Nanjing National Government about the invention of a secret wireless radio by Mr. Wang Fushi

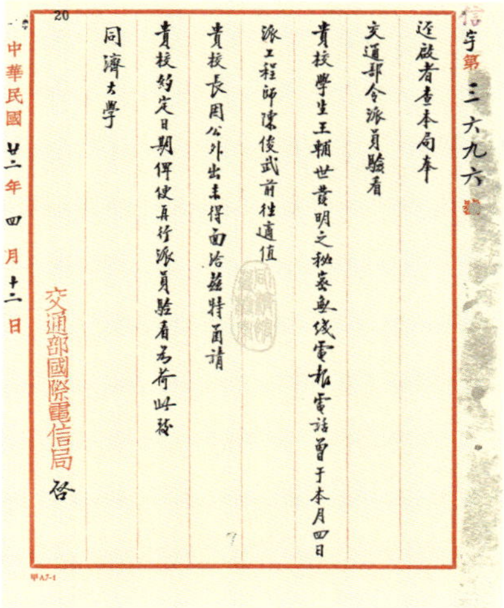
交通部國際電信局

■ 南京国民政府交通部关于同济学生王辅世发明秘密无线电的函

Letter from the Ministry of Communications about the invention of a secret wireless radio by Mr. Wang Fushi, a student from National Tongji University

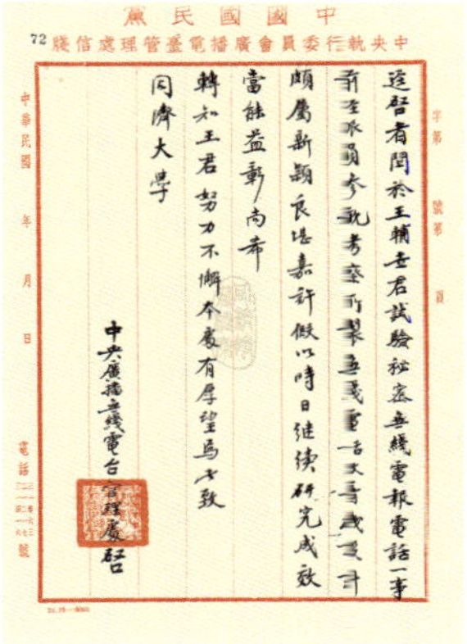
中國國民黨中央執行委員會廣播電臺管理處信牋

■ 中央广播无线电台管理处关于王辅世发明秘密无线电函

Letter from the Administration Office of Central Broadcasting Radio Station about the invention of a secret wireless radio by Mr. Wang Fushi

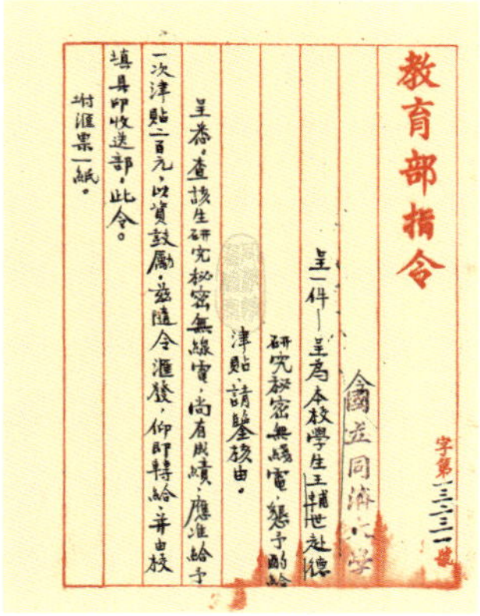
教育部指令

■ 南京国民政府教育部关于王辅世发明秘密无线电的嘉奖令

Order of Merit from the Ministry of Education of The Nanjing National Government about the invention of a secret wireless radio by Mr. Wang Fushi

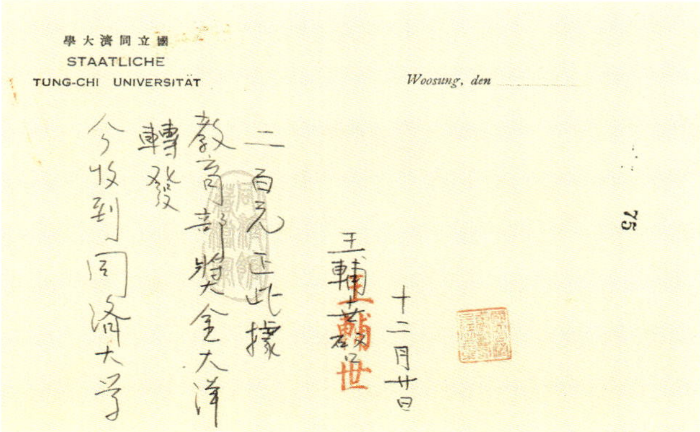
國立同濟大學
STAATLICHE
TUNG-CHI UNIVERSITÄT
Woosung, den

今收到同濟大學轉發教育部奬金大洋二百元正此據

王輔世

十二月廿日

■ 王辅世收领 200 元奖金的签收单

Receipt by Mr. Wang Fushi for an award of 200 yuan

幼树成材，支撑两岸

Contributions of Outstanding Alumni to Both Sides of China

1928至1937年十年间，同济工科共有215名毕业生，其中李国豪后来成为中国科学院和中国工程院院士。除此之外，还有“中国汽车工业之父”饶斌、台湾成功大学校长倪超等多位杰出校友，他们或从事工程建设、或从事教学科研、或自己创业，为我国经济与社会的发展做出了杰出贡献。

A total of 215 students graduated from the engineering programs of National Tongji University from 1928 to 1937, among whom Dr Li Guohao became a member of Chinese Academy of Sciences and of Chinese Academy of Engineering. Other outstanding alumni including Mr. Rao Bin known as "father of the automobile industry in China" and Mr. Ni Chao, president of Cheng Kung University in Taiwan, made great contributions to economic and social development in both side of China by engaging themselves in engineering construction, teaching and research or by starting their own businesses.

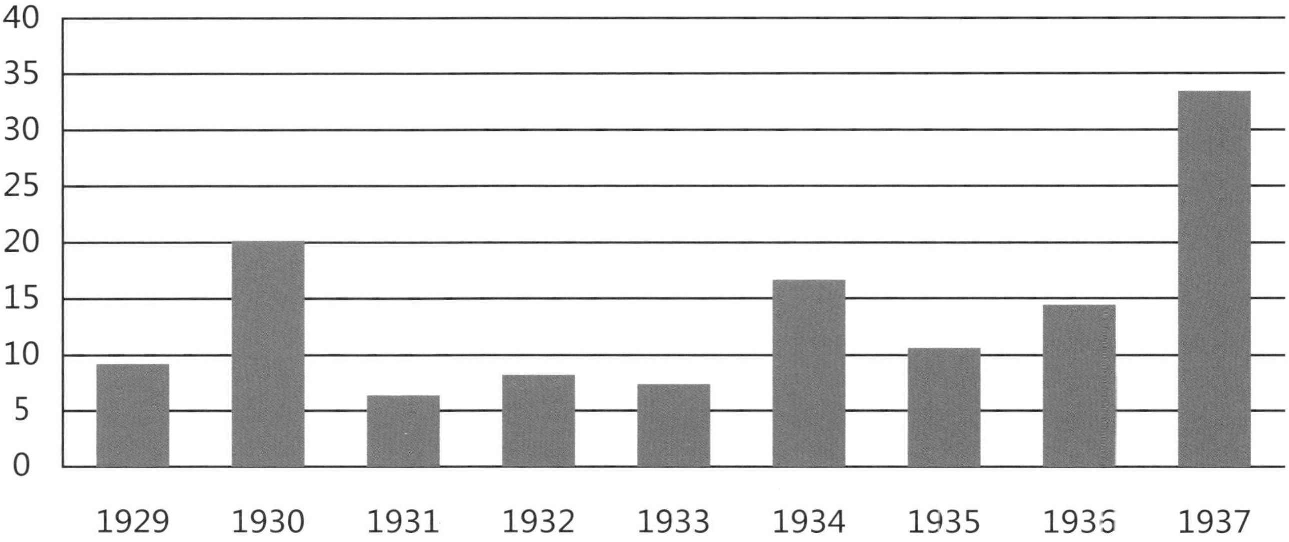

1929-1937年同济工科历年毕业人数
Numbers of graduates from engineering programs of National Tongji University from 1929 to 1937

李国豪（1913-2005），1936年毕业于同济大学工学院土木工程系，1940年获德国达姆施塔特工业大学工学博士学位，1977年至1984年任同济大学校长，中国科学院院士，中国工程院院士。

Dr. Li Guohao (1913-2005), a member of Chinese Academy of Sciences and of Chinese Academy of Engineering, graduated from National Tongji University in 1936. He obtained his PhD degree in engineering from Technical University of Darmstadt, Germany in 1940. He was the president of Tongji University from 1977 to 1984.

倪超（1905-1996），1933年毕业于同济大学工学院土木工程系，德国汉诺威工业大学工学博士，1971年至1978年任台湾成功大学校长。

Dr. Ni Chao (1905-1996), graduated from Civil Engineering Department of Engineering School, National Tongji University in 1933. He obtained his PhD degree in engineering from Technical University of Hannover, Germany. He acted as president of Cheng Kung University in Taiwan from 1971 to 1978.

■ 饶斌 (1913-1987)，1931 年进入同济大学学习，曾任一汽、二汽厂长，中国汽车工业的奠基人，被誉为“中国汽车工业之父”。

Mr. Rao Bin (1913-1987),known as "father of automobile industry in China", was admitted to study at National Tongji University in 1931. He acted as director of No. 1 Automobile Factory of China and No. 2 Automobile Factory of China and was the founder of the automobile industry in China.

■ 张继正 (1918-)，1937 年毕业于同济大学土木工程系，后赴德国和美国留学，1942 年获博士学位。曾任台湾大学教授、台湾“交通部、财政部部长“和”行政院秘书长“、“中央银行总裁”等职。

Dr. Zhang Jizheng (1918-), one of the pioneering members of KMT, graduated from Civil Engineering Department of Tongji University and went to Germany and USA for further study. He got his PhD degree in 1942. He was employed as a professor of Taiwan University, and acted as "minister" of Ministry of Communications and the Ministry of Finance, "secretary general" of the Executive Department and president of Central Bank in Taiwan.

■ 马雄冠（1905-1985），1929 年毕业于同济大学机械系，上海解放后任华东工业部上海通用机器厂（现上海汽轮机厂）第一任厂长、国家一级工程师。

Mr. Ma Xiongguan (1905-1985) graduated from Mechanical Department of National Tongji University in 1929. After the liberation of Shanghai, he served as the first director of Shanghai General Machinery Factory (the current Shanghai Turbine Factory) of East China Ministry of Industry. He was a Class A engineer at the national level.

■ 严庆龄（1909-1981），1931 年毕业于同济大学机械系。后留学德国柏林工业大学，裕隆汽车制造公司创办人，台湾机械工程学会、工程师学会理事长，带动台湾地区工业发展的先躯型企业家。

Mr. Yan Qingling (1909-1981) graduated from Mechanical Department of National Tongji University in 1931, and went to Technical University of Berlin, Germany for further study. He was the founder of Yulong Automobile Manufacturing Company, director-general of Taiwan Society of Mechanical Engineering and Society of Engineers, and a pioneering entrepreneur leading the industrial development in Taiwan.

■ 张象贤 (1901-2008)，1929 年毕业于同济大学机械系，留学意大利国立都灵大学航空工程研究院，获博士学位，1941 年回母校任教，曾任机械工程系主任。1948 年去台湾后，任成功大学教授。

Dr. Zhang Xiangxian (1901-2008) graduated from Mechanical Department of Tongji University in 1929, and obtained his PhD degree from the Research Institute of Aeronautical Engineering of National University of Turin, Italy. In 1941, he returned to Tongji University for teaching and later acted as head of Mechanical Engineering Department. He went to Taiwan in 1948 and became a professor in Cheng Kung University.

■ 叶雪安（1905-1966），1929 年毕业于同济大学土木工程系。1933 年公费留学德国，学习测量，1937 年回国任教于同济大学测量系，我国大地测量学理论的开拓者。

Mr. Ye Xuean(1905-1966) graduated from Civil Engineering Department of National Tongji University in 1929, and went to Germany for further study in surveying with financial support from the government. In 1937, he returned to Surveying Department of Tongji University for teaching and became known as a pioneer of Geodesy in China.

亦文亦武，保家卫国

Protection of Motherland with both Pens and Weapons

内忧外患的年代，同济工科学子积极参与爱国学生运动，为祖国的命运和前途奔走呼吁。1929 年 10 月中共同济地下支部建立，第一任支部书记是附设机师学校学生朱觉。1931 年“九·一八”事变后，同济学子赴南京请愿，要求政府出兵抗日，并参加学生救国宣传团，组织抗日青年团、同济大学救国会、无线电研究会等进步爱国组织。

During the hard time when China suffered both from the civil war and from foreign aggressions, engineering students of National Tongji University took an active part in patriotic student movements to fight for the fate and future of the nation. In October 1929, an underground branch of CPC was established in National Tongji University and Mr. Zhu Jue, a student from the affiliated Machinist School was appointed as the party secretary. After the *September 18th Incident* in 1931, Tongji students went to Nanjing to petition the National Government for deployment of troops in the fight against Japan. In addition, the students joined national student salvation campaigns and set up patriotic organizations including Anti-Japanese Youth League, the National Salvation Association of National Tongji University and Radio Society.

中国共产党同济支部第一任支部书记朱觉（1911-1932），1928 年 7 月考入同济大学附属机师学校，1929 至 1930 年担任中共同济大学支部书记，带领党员和进步同学从事革命斗争。

Mr. Zhu Jue, first party secretary of the underground branch of CPC of National Tongji University (1911-1932), was admitted to study at Machinist School Affiliated to Tongji University in July 1928. He was the party secretary of the underground branch of CPC of Tongji from 1929 to 1930, leading the party members and progressive students in the revolutionary struggles.

汪 珊，字 海 粟（1912-1993），1933 至 1937 年在同济大学德文补习科和电工机械系学习，1936 年参加共产党，上海学生救国会领导人之一，同济学生救国会负责人，南京工学院首任院长。

Mr. Wang Shan, alias Haisu (1912-1993), a student on a German supplementary course and in Department of Electromechanics of National Tongji University from 1933 to 1937. He joined the Communist Party in 1936 and was one of the leaders of the National Student Salvation Association of Shanghai and director of the National Student Salvation Association of Tongji. Later he became the first president of Nanjing Institute of Technology.

高职机械科第一届学生景智德、郑香山、郑文道发起读书会，学习革命文学和革命理论书籍。左图为郑香山，右图为郑文道。

Mr. Jing Zhide, Mr. Zheng Xiangshan and Mr. Zheng Wendao, first students on mechanical program of Advanced Vocational School who organized a reading club to study revolutionary literature and theories.

Left: Mr. Zheng Xiangshan; Right: Mr. Zheng Wendao

■ 1931 年“九 · 一八事变”后，上海学生赴南京请愿，要求政府出兵抗日，同济大学工学院曹玉祥参加该代表团。

After the *September 18th Incident* in 1931, a Shanghai student delegation went to Nanjing to petition the National Government for deployment of troops in the fight against Japan. Mr. Cao Yuxiang, a student from Engineering School of National Tongji University joined the delegation in their petition.

■ 上海学生在昆山宣传抗日

Students from Shanghai promoting anti-Japanese activities in Kunshan

■ 上海学生举行示威游行，并向上海当局请愿要求抗日救国。

Students from Shanghai on a demonstration petitioning to save China by fighting against Japan

1931 年 11 月 20 日，各校学生七八千人在上海市政府门前请愿，要求政府出兵抗日。
Over 7,000 students in a petition for deployment of troops in the fight against Japan in front of the Shanghai Government on November 20th 1931.

左：张凡，原名顾德熙，1936 年加入中国共产党，任同济大学学生救国会负责人，领导学生进行抗日爱国活动。
Left: Mr. Zhangfan, formerly known as Gu Dexi, joined the Communist Party in 1936 and acted as chairman of the National Student Salvation Association of Tongji University, leading students in their patriotic anti-Japanese activities.

右：朱惟善 (1917-)，1936 年加入中国共产党。曾任同济大学工学院党支部书记，1939 年 2 月至 3 月任中共义乌县委代书记。
Right: Mr. Zhu Weishan (1917-) joined the Communist Party in 1936 and acted as party secretary of the CPC branch in Engineering School of Tongji University. He was the acting party secretary of the CPC Yiwu County Committee from February to March 1929.

■ 同济无线电研究会，以修理无线电为掩护，开展抗日救亡活动。

Tongji Radio Society active in anti-Japanese activities under the disguise of radio repairs

■ 1935 年上海市各大中学学生救国宣传团。同济工科学生李欣、王国宾、钟思等人参加第三团。

Mr. Li Xin, Mr. Wang Guobin and Mr. Zhong Si, engineering students of Tongji on the third group of National Student Salvation Promotion Groups of Shanghai in 1935

■ 1935 年 12 月 24 日，上海学生支援北京“一二·九”运动，组织游行请愿。在火车站被阻两天后，同济高职机械科学生郑香山、景智德用低速把列车开到昆山，由同济学生代表在昆山车站向上海各报记者发表谈话，说明请愿的目的和意义。

On December 24th 1935, students from Shanghai organized a demonstration and a petition in support of the *December 9th Student Movement* in Beijing. After being blocked at the railway station for two days, Mr. Zheng Xiangshan and Mr. Jing Zhide, students on mechanical program of the Advanced Vocational School managed to drive a train at low speed to Kunshan where Tongji students spoke to the media of Shanghai about the purpose and significances of the petition at Kunshan Railway Station.

第三章 Chapter III（1937.7-1952.5）

辗转颠簸，越挫越强
The Harder, the Stronger

1937 年 7 月 7 日日寇侵华，同济大学辗转一万多公里，一路西迁办学。困境重重中，沿途招生，沿途就业，工学院扩充为机械、电机、土木、测量、造船 5 个系、1 个机械专修科，并附设高级工业职业学校。培育大批工程机械人才支援前线，为抗敌救国做出巨大贡献。1946 年回迁上海并迎接解放，全体师生投入到新中国大规模建设事业中。

The Japanese invaded China on July 7th, 1937. As a result of devastating bombardments by Japanese air force, Tongji University was forced to move about ten thousand kilometers westwards. In spite of the extreme difficulties along the way, Tongji never stopped its efforts in both student recruitment and employment upon their graduation. Moreover, the Engineering School was expanded to include five more departments of mechanical engineering, electrical engineering, civil engineering, surveying and shipbuilding, and a professional program in mechanics. An affiliated Advanced Industrial Vocational School was also set up. A large number of professionals who graduated from the engineering school of Tongji University went to the frontline of the anti-Japanese war and made great contributions to the fight against the Japanese for the country. All the teachers and students devoted themselves to the construction of a new China after Tongji was relocated back to Shanghai in 1946.

日军侵华，吴淞被毁

Campus in Wusong Devastated by Japanese Bombardment

1937 年 8 月 28、29 日，日本飞机接连轰炸吴淞地区，同济大学大礼堂、工学院、电机馆、材料试验室、实习工厂、教授住宅及学生宿舍等建筑均遭破坏，损失惨重。

In 1937, the Japanese air force bombarded Wusong District, Shanghai for two days from August 28th to 29th. The auditorium, Engineering School, Electromechanical Laboratory, Material Laboratory, Internship Factory, Hall of Residence of Teachers and student dormitory of Tongji University were severely damaged, resulting in an enormous loss.

大礼堂主楼被炸成空壳

The main building of the auditorium was blasted into an empty shell.

实习工厂成为一片焦土

The internship factory was razed to the ground.

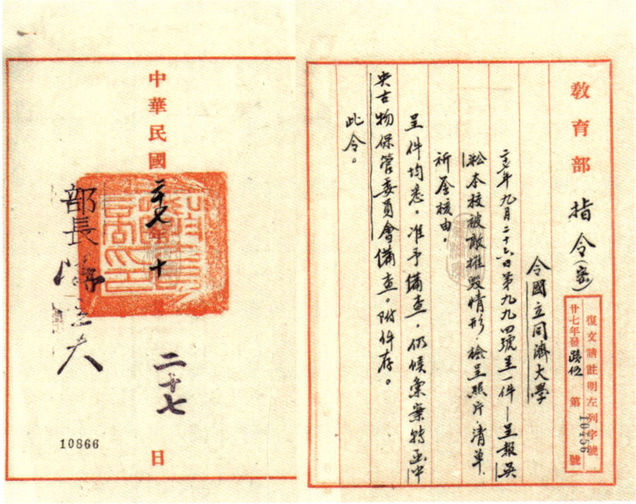

教育部指令(密)

廿七年發 復文請註明左列字號 第 10456 號

令國立同濟大學

廿六年九月二十八日第九九四號呈一件—呈報吳淞本校被敵摧毀情形，檢呈照片、清單，祈鑒核由。

呈件均悉。准予備查。仍候彙案轉函中央古物保管委員會備查。附件存。

此令。

部長 陳立夫

中華民國廿七年十月二十七日

10866

南京国民政府教育部令国立同济大学上报被日军轰炸被毁情形的指令

Instruction from the Ministry of Education of the Nanjing National Government to National Tongji University for a report of damage after the Japanese bombardment

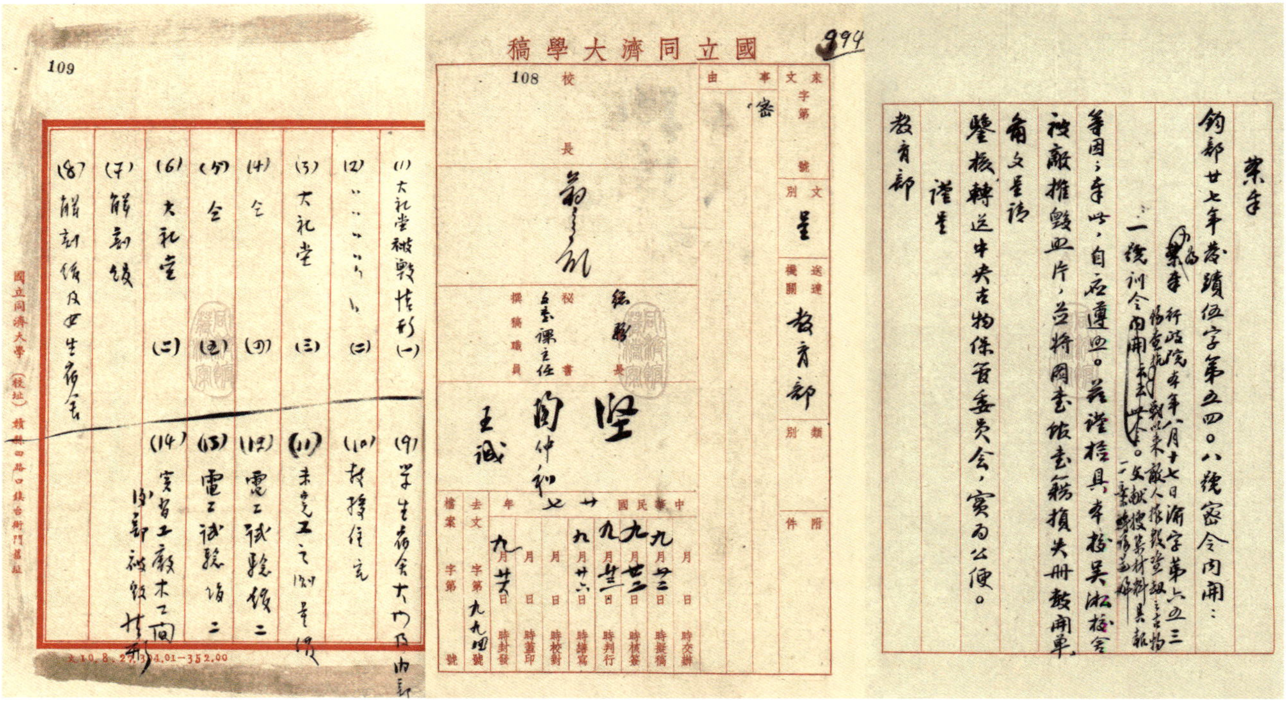
國立同濟大學稿

国立同济大学上报南京国民政府教育部被日军炸毁校舍情形

Report of National Tongji University submitted to the Ministry of Education of the Nanjing National Government on the devastated campus after the bombardment by the Japanese air force.

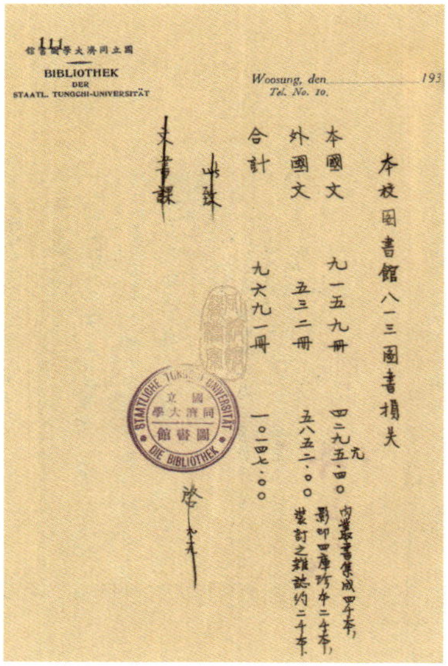
BIBLIOTHEK
DER
STAATL. TONGCHI-UNIVERSITÄT
本校圖書館八一三圖書損失

1937 年“八·一三”事件中学校图书损失情况

A record of loss of books at Tongji University in *August 13th Incident* in 1937

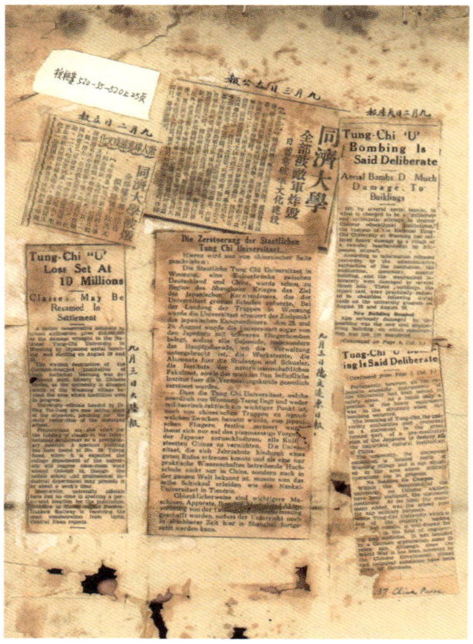
刊载同济大学被炸毁消息的中外剪报

Newspaper reports at home and abroad on the destruction of Tongji University by the Japanese bombardment.

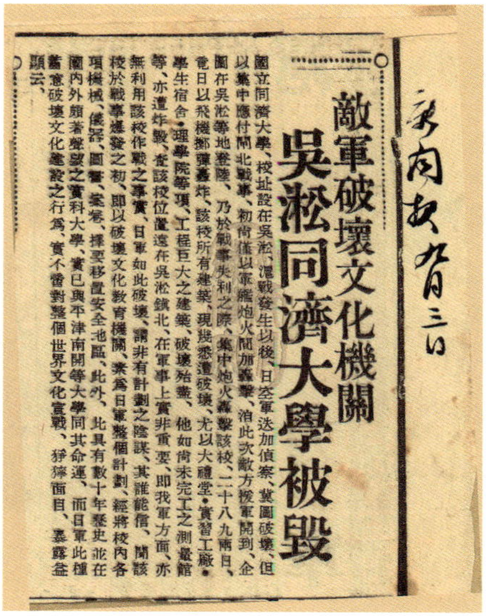
敵軍破壞文化機關
吳淞同濟大學被毀

《新闻报》刊载的消息《敌军破坏文化机关——吴淞同济大学被毁》

News from *News Daily*: “Tongji University in Wusong devastated by bombardment - The Japanese army destroyed an institution of higher learning”

六次迁校，教育长征

Long March of Education with Six Relocations

8 年抗战期间，同济师生历经 6 次迁校，辗转沪、浙、赣、湘、粤、桂、滇、黔、川 9 省以及越南，越过千山万水，忍受颠沛流离和饥寒交迫，总行程 11000 多公里。在此艰难时刻，同济师生秉持同舟共济的精神，竭尽所能保障教学工作的开展，沿途招生就业，为祖国输送了大批军工机械人才。

During the eight years of Anti-Japanese War, Tongji teachers and students were forced to move for six times across nine provinces and even to Vietnam, from Shanghai to Zhejiang, to Jiangxi, to Hunan, to Guangdong, to Guangxi, to Yunan, to Guizhou, and eventually to Sichuan. They walked and waded over mountains and rivers, covering 11,000 km and suffering miserably from hunger and cold on the way. At a time of extreme difficulty, Tongji teachers and students encouraged themselves with Tongji spirit of fighting towards the same goal on the same boat and tried everything possible to keep teaching and learning going. They recruited students along the way and managed to produce a large number military and mechanical personnel for the motherland.

六次迁校示意图

Map illustrating the six relocations of the university

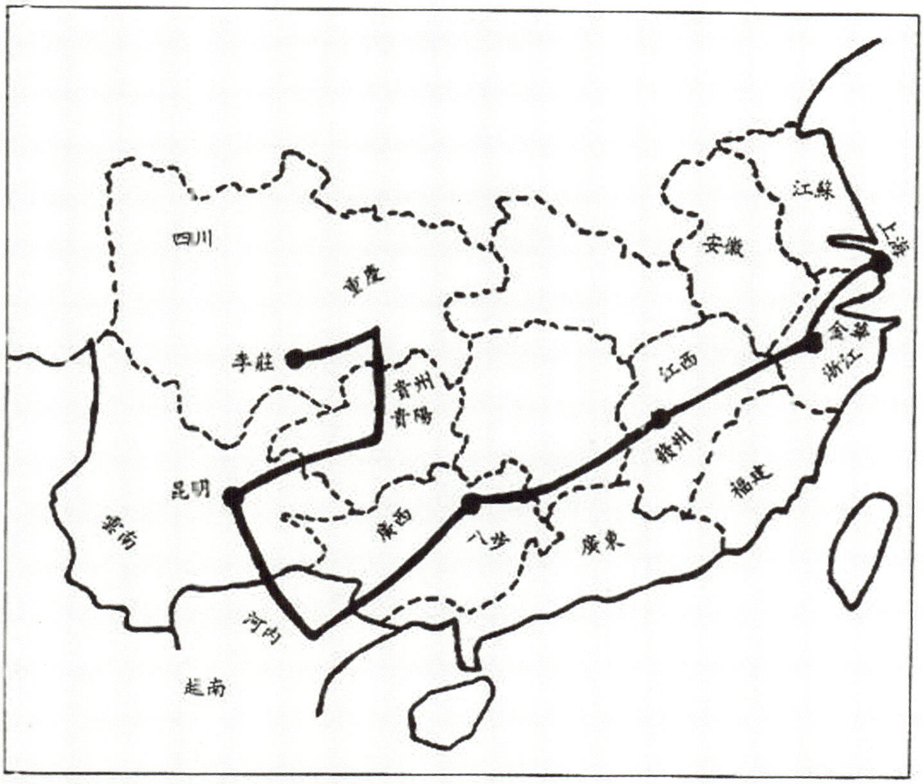

二次大戰期間學校遷移路線・代表遷校地點

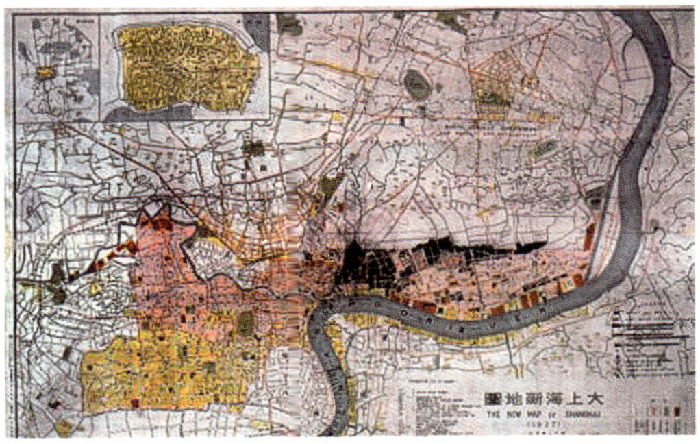

1937 年《大上海地图》，粉红色区域为公共租界。同济首次迁校就是从吴淞迁至公共租界内的地丰路 121 号（今乌鲁木齐北路）。

Map of Greater Shanghai in 1937 with the pink area representing the Public Concessions. Tongji moved first from Wusong to No. 121 of Difeng Road inside the Public Concessions (the current North Urumchi Rd.).

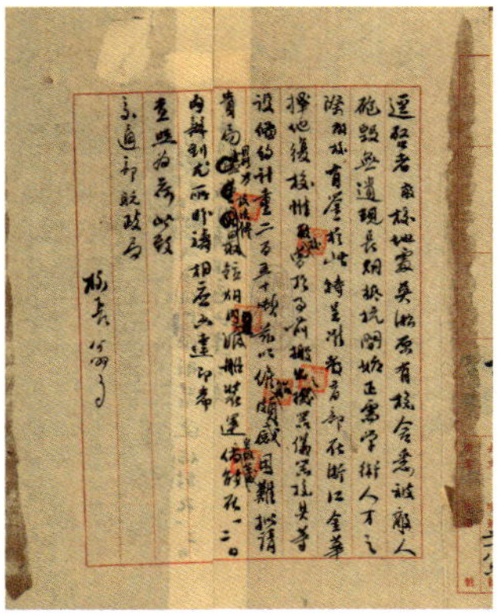

学校迁校金华的布告

Announcement on Tongji's relocation to Jinhua

迁校金华时期的校门

Main entrance of Tongji University at Jinhua

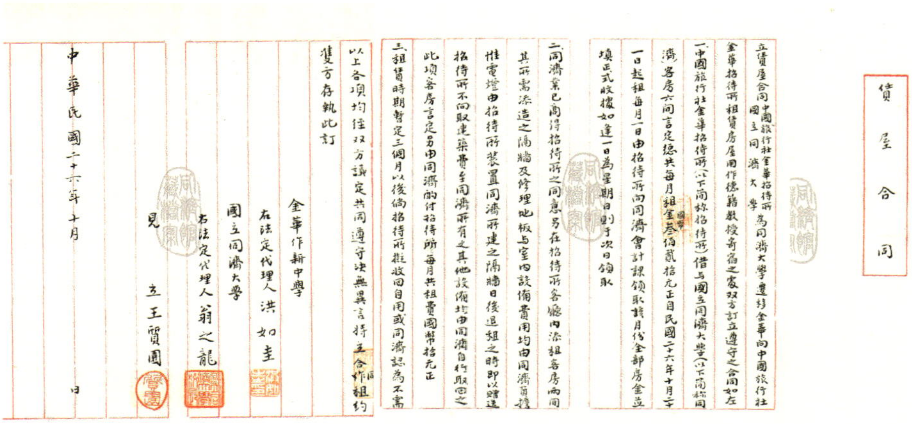

賃屋合同

迁校金华时期学校租赁金华作新中学房屋的合同

A lease between Tongji and Jinhua Zuoxin High School for the arrangement of classrooms

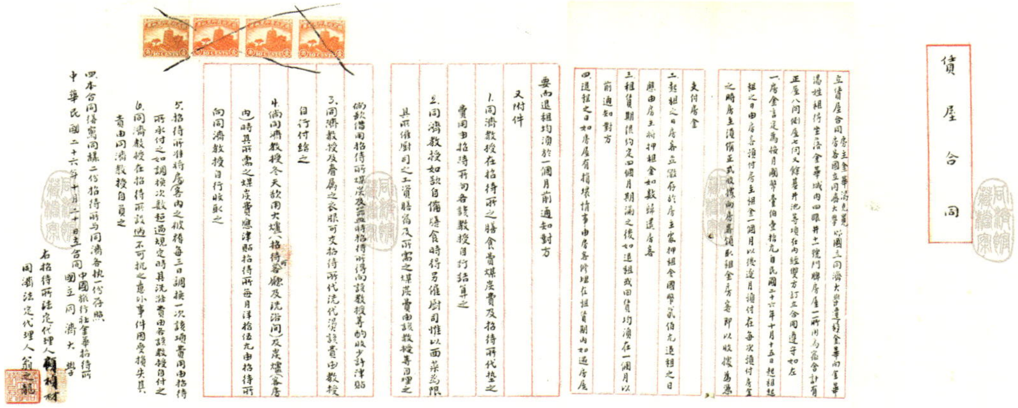

賃屋合同

迁校金华时期学校租赁中国旅行社金华招待所客房作为宿舍的合同

A lease between Tongji and China Travel Agency of renting guestrooms of Jinhua Hotel as dormitory of Tongji University

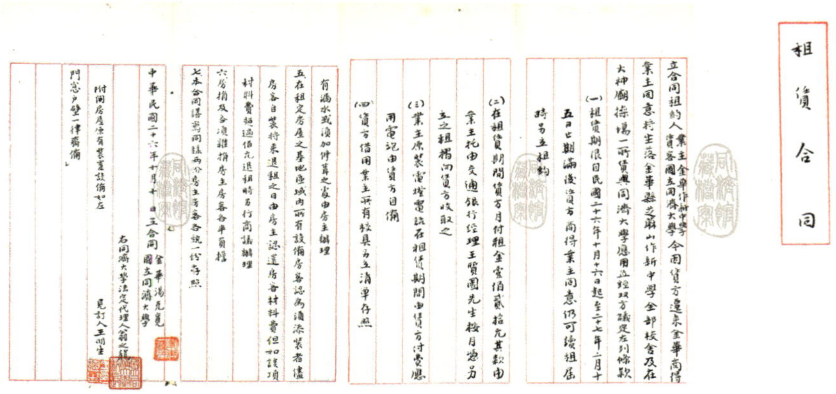

迁校金华时期学校与金华当地居民汤客宽签订的租赁房屋合同

A lease between Tongj and local resident Mr. Tang at Jinhua

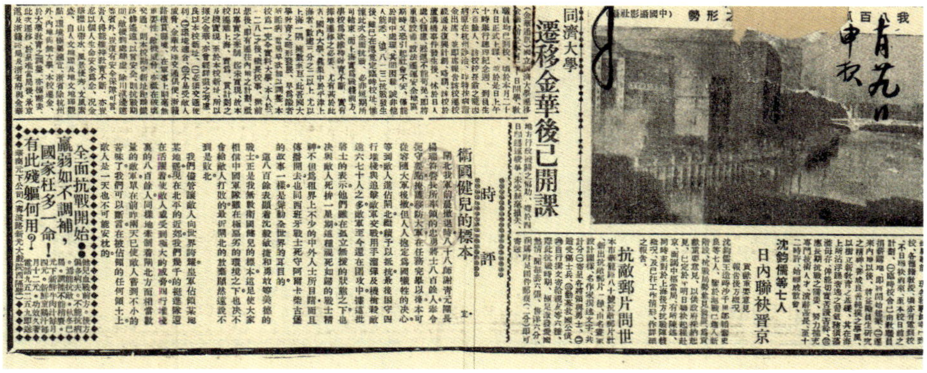

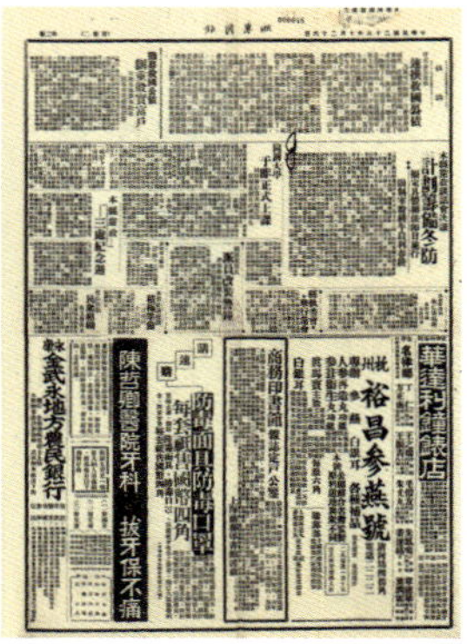

新闻媒体刊载的同济迁校金华后开课的消息

A newspaper report about Tongji's resumption of its teaching after its move to Jinhua

同济师生在金华坚持抗战救亡

Tongji teachers and students showing their strong will in fighting against the Japanese at Jinhua

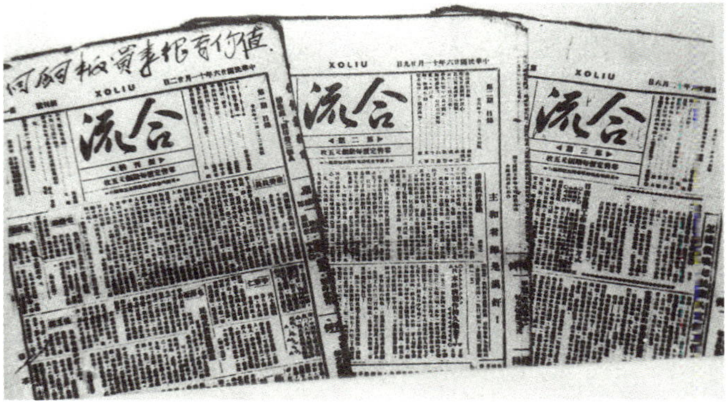

迁校金华时期同济学子创办的爱国刊物《合流》

A patriotic journal *Heliu* initiated by Tongji students during their stay at Jinhua

跋山涉水，千里八步

Relocation to Babu after Thousands of Miles

学校在金华度过了短暂的两个月。由于日机不断空袭，1937 年 11 月 12 日，学校决定第三次迁校至江西赣州和吉安。1938 年 7 月，九江危急，同济开始第四次迁校，工学院从赣州迁往广西贺县八步镇，10 月下旬借到一所中学正准备复课时，日军进攻华南，广州沦陷，广西不保。1938 年冬，学校决定迁往昆明。

The university stayed in Jinhua for only two months due to the frequent disruption of Japanese air attacks. On Nov. 12th 1937, Tongji decided to move for the third time to Ganzhou and Ji'an of Jiangxi Province. In July 1938, Tongji was forced to move for the fourth time, since the neighboring city Jiujiang of Jiangxi Province was on the verge of losing to Japanese. The Engineering School of Tongji University moved from Ganzhou to Babu Town, Hexian County of Guangxi Province. In late October when Tongji got ready to resume teaching in a local high school, the Japanese army invaded southern China and occupied Guangzhou. Guangxi, next to Guangzhou, was thus threatened. In the winter of 1938, Tongji decided to move again to Kunming.

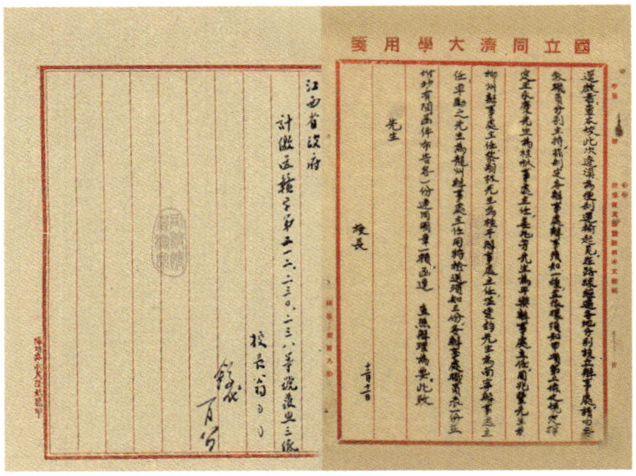

学校第四次迁校时，令金又民、陆志龙、冯承植（冯至）率师生由南昌乘船至赣州的校长函。
A letter from the university President requesting that Mr. Jin Youmin, Mr. Lu Zhilong, Mr. Feng Chengzhi (Feng Zhi) be responsible for organizing the move of teachers and students from Nanchang to Ganzhou by boat before the fourth relocation of the university

德国教授从上海前往赣州，途经广州时的合影 (1938 年)。
German professors with their Chinese counterparts at Guangzhou on their way to Ganzhou (1938)

赣江上的老帆船
Old sailboats along the Ganjiang River in Ganzhou

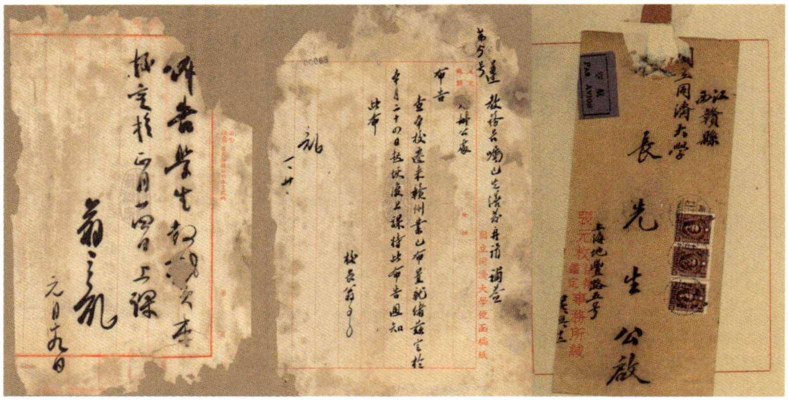

迁校赣州时发布的上课通知
Announcement of Tongji's resumption of teaching in Ganzhou

史图博教授与学生在赣州

Professor Stübel with students in Ganzhou

1938 年赣州通天岩上的“同济”石刻

Characters of “Tongji” engraved on the Tongtian Rock of Ganzhou , 1938

从赣州迁往广西贺县八步镇途中

On the way from Ganzhou to Babu Town

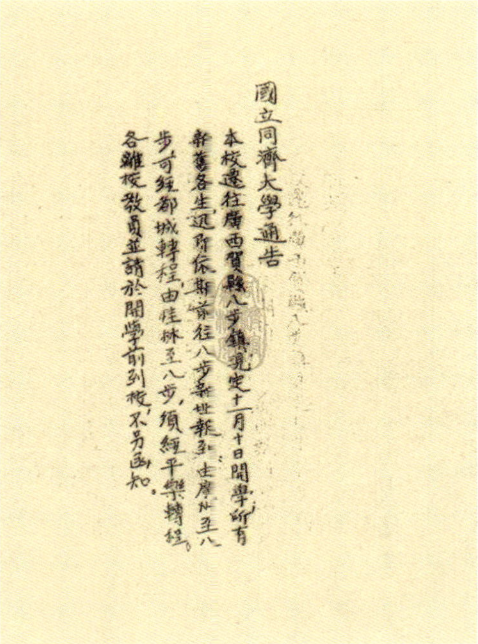

國立同濟大學通告

本校遷往廣西賀縣八步鎮，現定十一月十日開學，所有新舊各生，仰依期前往八步報到；由廣州至八步可經都城轉程，由桂林至八步，須經平樂轉程。各離校教員並請於開學前到校，不另函知。

迁往八步镇后的开学通告

Announcement of Tongji 's resumption of teaching after its relocation in Babu Town

在八步镇的校舍

Campus of Tongji University in Babu Town, Hexian County, Guangxi Province

蛰居昆明，满城工学

Engineering Programs of Tongji Scattered all over Kunming

1938 年冬，同济第五次迁校至云南昆明。昆明校址极为分散，工学院在富春街富春中学内；附属高级工业职业学校先在木行街，后迁至双塔寺女子师范学校，再迁至水晶宫、八省会馆，最后迁西仓坡 1 号；图书馆在富春街太阳巷 1 号；测量馆在富春街富春中学内；实习工厂先在八省会馆，后迁至龙翔街昆华工业学校。

In the winter of 1938, Tongji arrived in Kunming, Yunnan Province after its move for the fifth time. Engineering Programs of Tongji were scattered all over Kunming. The Engineering School was located inside Fuchun Middle School on Fuchun Street; the Affiliated Advanced Industrial Vocational School was moved first to Muxing Street, then to Girls' Normal School of Shuangta Tower, and later to Crystal Palace and Eight-Province House and eventually to No.1 Xicang Po; the library was located in No.1 Taiyang Lane on Fuchun Street; the Surveying Laboratory was located inside Fuchun Middle School on Fuchun Street; and the internship factory was relocated first to Eight-Province House and later to Kunhua Industrial School on Longxiang Street.

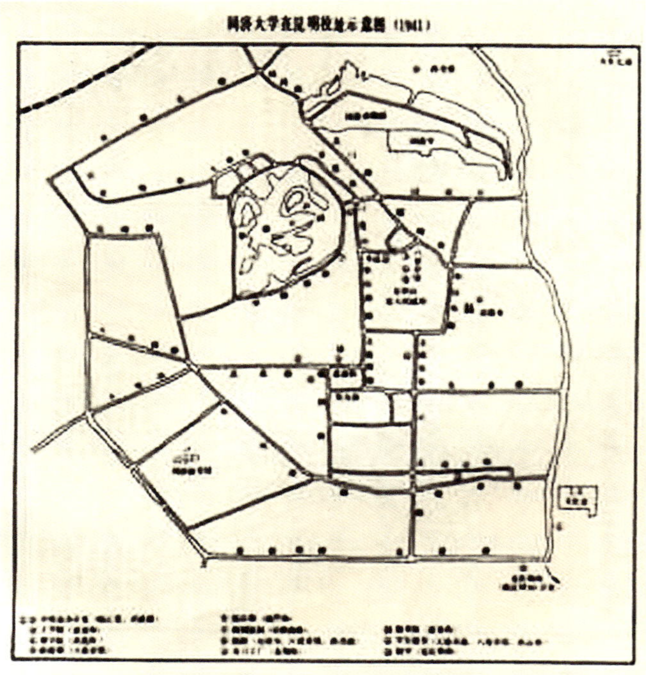

昆明校舍分布图
Map illustrating the distribution of Tongji in Kunming

昆明时期的宿舍
Dormitory in Kunming

昆明时期的校舍
Teaching building in Kunming

国立同济大学校长赵士卿，任期1939年4月至1940年7月。

Mr. Zhao Shiqin, president of National Tongji University from April 1939 to July 1940

国立同济大学校长周均时，任期1940年7月至1942年2月，主持学校迁川工作。

Mr. Zhou Junshi, president of National Tongji University from July 1940 to February 1942, was responsible for the relocation of Tongji to Sichuan Province.

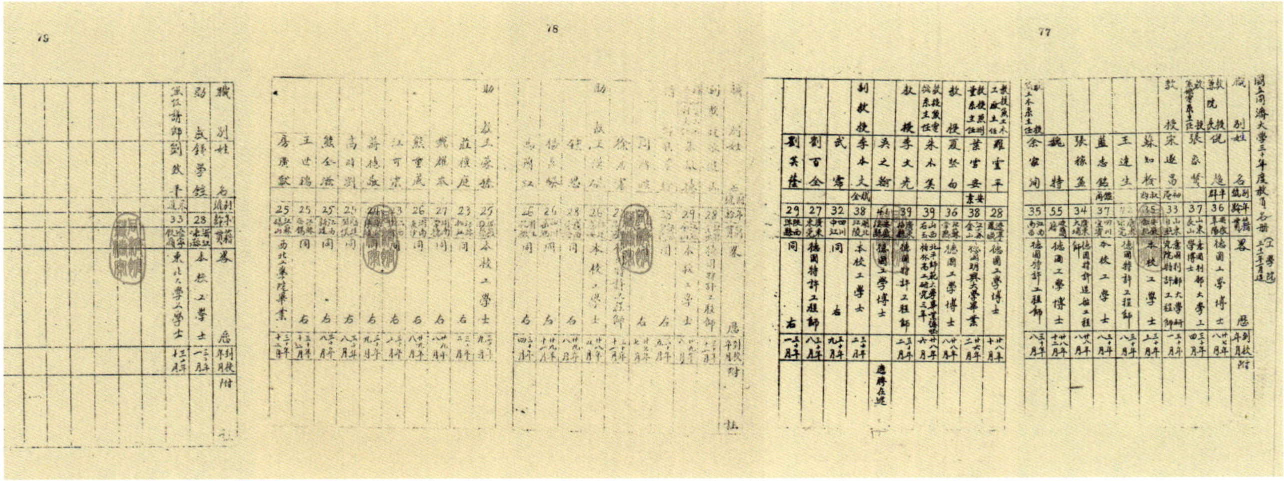

1940年工学院教职工名册

List of Faculty at Engineering School in 1940

师生在昆明报名参加抗战

Teachers and students in Kunming enthusiastic about joining the army to fight against the Japanese.

四系一组，工科壮大

Continuous Development of Engineering School with Four Departments and One Section

工学院初迁昆明时，设有机电、土木、测量3系和造船组。1940年机电系分拆为机械和电机两系，工学院发展为4系1组，是全校规模最大的学院，历任院长为叶雪安、吴之翰和倪超。1940年在校学生为478人，同济工程教育的规模进一步扩大。

The Engineering School was composed of three Departments of Electromechanics, Civil Engineering and Surveying, and a Shipbuilding Section when Tongji University first arrived in Kunming. In 1940, the Department of Electromechanics was divided into Mechanical Department and Electrical Department. Consequently, the Engineering School became the largest school of Tongji with four departments and one section.Ye Xue'an, Wu Zhihan and Ni Chao acted as deans of the school consecutively. The engineering education of Tongji University was futher expanded, and by 1940 the student number reached 478.

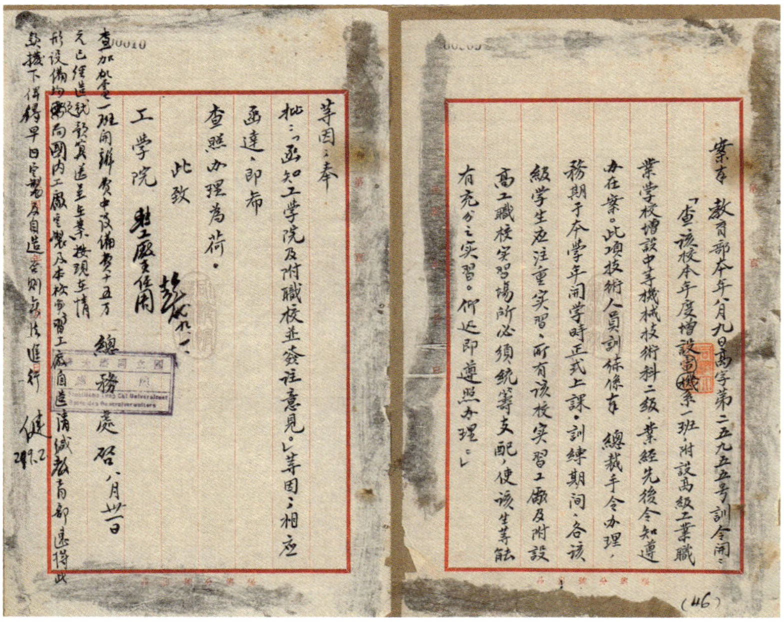
案奉
教育部本年八月九日高字第二五九五五号訓令開：
「查該校本年度增設高機第一班，附設高級工業職
業學校增設中等機械技術科二級，業經先後令知遵
办在案。此項技術人員訓練，係奉 總裁手令办理，
務期于本學年開學時正式上課。訓練期間，各該
級學生應注重實習，所有該校實習工廠及附設
高工職校實習場所，必須統籌支配，使該生等能
有充分之實習。仰迅即遵照办理。」
等因。奉
此。「函知工學院及附職校並簽注意見。」等因。相應
函達，即希
查照办理為荷。
此致
工學院
總務處啓 八月廿日

工学院转发教育部批复增设机械系的函
An official letter from the Ministry of Education authorizing the establishment of Mechanical Department forwarded by the Engineering School

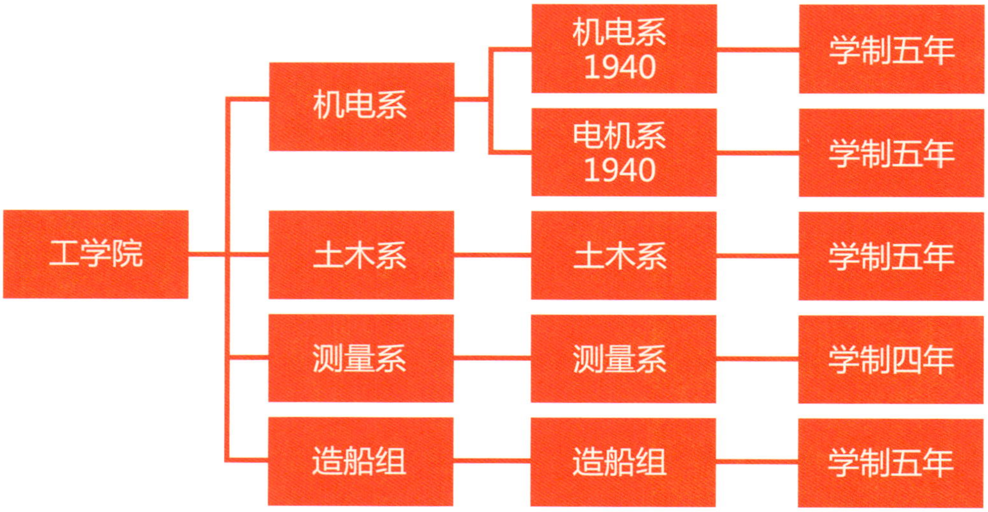

昆明时期工学院的学科发展及学制规定
Programs in relation with disciplinary development at the Engineering School of Tongji University in Kunming

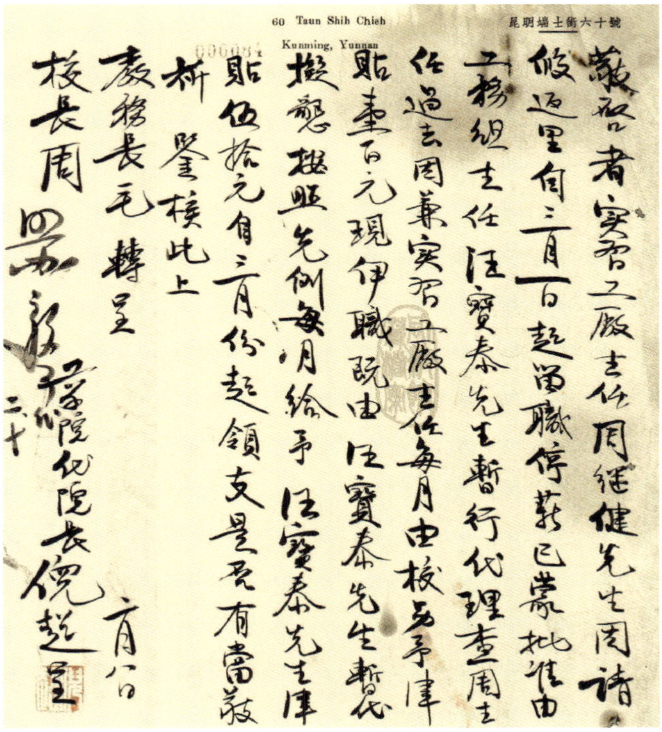

60 Taun Shih Chieh
Kunming, Yunnan
昆明靖土街六十號

敬启者 实习工厂主任周缉健先生因请
假返里自三月一日起留职停薪已蒙批准由
工务组主任汪宝泰先生暂行代理查周主
任过去因兼实习工厂主任每月由校另予津
贴壹百元现伊职既由汪宝泰先生暂代
拟恳按照先例每月给予汪宝泰先生津
贴伍拾元自三月份起领支是否有当敬
祈 鉴核此上
教务长毛 转呈
校长周
工学院院长倪超 呈 三月二十日

工学院院长倪超手书

A handwritten letter by Mr. Ni Chao, dean of Engineering School of Tongji University

机械系主任张象贤教授

Professor Zhang Xiangxian, dean of Mechanical Department

土木系主任陈士骅

Mr. Chen Shihua, head of Civil Engineering Department

1937 年陈士骅西迁途中赠送附中主任冯至的画作《松窦籀书图》

A painting by Mr. Chen Shihua which he presented to Mr. Feng Zhi, director of the Affiliated High School as a gift on his way westward in 1937

昆明时期，学校聘请有桥梁、铁路设计经验的林同炎担任兼课教师。

Mr. Lin Tongyan, experienced in bridge and railway design, was employed as part-time teacher by Tongji in Kunming.

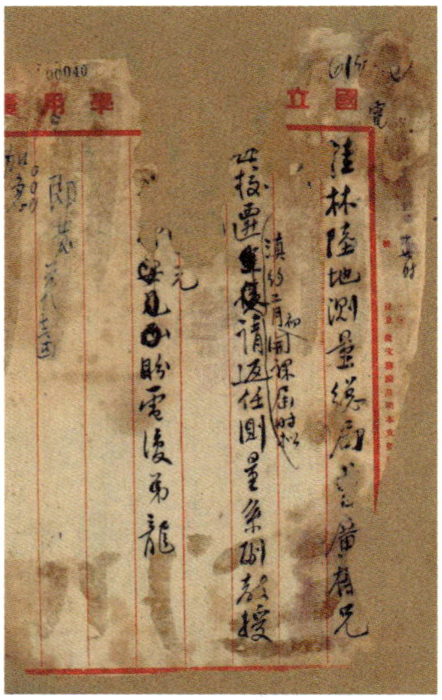

测量系曾广樑教授聘书

Appointment Letter of Professor Zeng Guangliang from the Department of Surveying

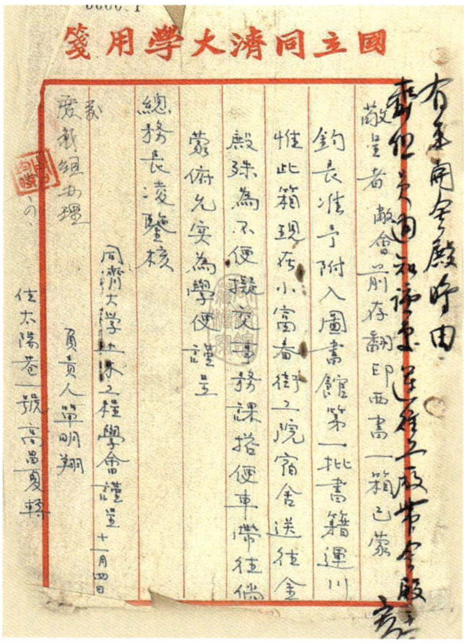
國立同濟大學用箋

1939 年 4 月在昆明成立了国立同济大学土木工程学会，出版定期刊物，交流学术成果，图为土木工程学会信函。

Civil Engineering Association of National Tongji University was established in Kunming in April of 1939. The association had regular issues of its newsletters for exchange of academic achievements. A letter endorsed by the association is on display.

昆明时期高职学生所用画板（由校友郑永录提供）

A drawing board used by students from the Affiliated Advanced Vocational School in Kunming (provided by Mr. Zheng Yonglu, an alumnus of Tongji University)

毕业高原，工程骨干

Backbones in Engineering from Graduates in Kunming

在昆明的两年，尽管条件非常艰苦，但师生们勤教勤学、保持严谨求实的学风，1939年与1940年两届共有126名毕业生。这些毕业生后来成为我国机械、造船、土木、电机、测绘领域的骨干，其中朱洪元、陶亨咸后来当选为中国科学院学部委员（院士）。

During the two years in Kunming, teachers and students overcame all kinds of difficulties and devoted themselves to teaching and learning. A total of 126 students graduated from Tongji in Kunming in 1939 and 1940. Those graduates later played important roles in the fields of mechanical engineering, shipbuilding, civil engineering, electrical engineering and surveying in China. Among them, Mr. Zhu Hongyuan and Mr. Tao Hengxian became members (of the Academic Division) of Chinese Academy of Sciences.

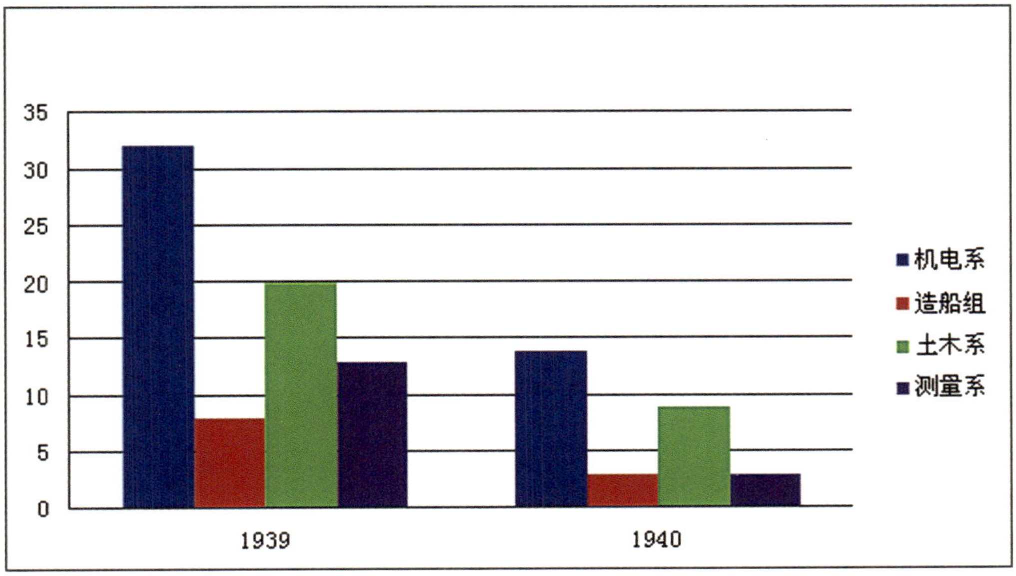

昆明时期工学院毕业人数

Number of graduates of Engineering School during the time in Kunming

朱洪元（1917-1992），江苏宜兴人，1939年工学院机电系毕业，1980年当选为中国科学院学部委员（院士），物理学家。

Mr. Zhu Hongyuan (1917-1992), from Yixing of Jiangsu Province, graduated from Electromechanical Department of Engineering School in 1939. He was a physicist and became a member of the Chinese Academy of Sciences in 1980.

陶亨咸（1914-2003），浙江绍兴人，1939年工学院机电系毕业，1955年当选为中国科学院学部委员（院士），机械工程专家。

Mr. Tao Hengxian (1914-2003), from Shaoxing of Zhejiang Province, graduated from Electromechanical Department of Engineering School 1939. He was an expert in mechanical engineering and became a member of the Chinese Academy of Sciences in 1955.

程望（1916-1991），1940 年工学院造船系毕业，曾任交通部副部长，中国船舶工业总公司副董事长。

Mr. Cheng Wang (1916-1991) graduated from Department of Shipbuilding of Engineering Schoool in 1940. He was appointed as vice minister of Ministry of Transportation and vice director of the board of China Corporation of Shipping Industry.

刘应虎（1915-　），1940 年工学院造船系毕业，船舶工业总公司 611 所总工程师。

Mr. Liu Yinghu (1915-) who graduatec from Department of Shipbuilding of Engineering School in 1940 was an engineer-in-chief of 611 Institute of China Corporation of Shipping Industry.

韦永宁（1915-2004），1940 年工学院造船系毕业。曾任台湾经济主管部门负责人，中华造船公司董事长。

Mr. Wei Yongning (1915-2004) graduated from Department of Shipbuilding of Engineering School in 1940. He worked in government bodies in Taiwan responsible for economic issues and acted as board director of China Shipbuilding Company later.

戚荣普（1916-1967），1939 年工学院机械工程系毕业，历任上海汽轮机厂设计科长、总设计师、副总工程师等职，负责新中国第一台 6000 千瓦汽轮机试制。

Mr. Qi Rongpu (1916-1967), graduated from Department of Mechanical Engineering of Engineering School, Tongji University in 1939. He was employed in Shanghai Steam Turbine Factory and acted as head of the Design Section, General Designer and deputy engineer-in-chief responsible for the development of the first 6000 kw steam turbine in China.

杨长骙（1916-2003），1940 年工学院机械工程系毕业，中国起重机行业创始人之一，大连理工大学机械系建系元老之一。

Mr. Yang Changkui (1916-2003) graduated from Department of Mechanical Engineering of Engineering School, Tongji University in 1940. He was one of the founders of the crane sector in China and one of the people who established Department of Mechanical Engineering, Dalian University of Technology.

落户李庄，魁星闪耀

Settlement of Tongji in Lizhuang Town

1939 年夏，日寇对昆明实行“疲劳轰炸”，以周均时校长为主席的迁建委员会，决定第六次迁校。1940 年 10 月，学校从昆明迁至四川南溪李庄镇。工学院在李庄东岳庙，附设高级工业职业学校在罗家祠，同济工科在李庄度过了五年相对安定的教学生活。

In the summer of 1939, the Japanese army conducted “continuous bombardment” in Kunming. The Relocation Committee led by President Zhou Junshi decided another move of the university: for the sixth time. In October 1940, the university was forced to move from Kunming to Lizhaung Town of Nanxi County, Sichuan Province. The Engineering School was relocated in Dongyue Temple and the Affiliated Advanced Vocational School in Luojia Temple of Lizhuang. Then Tongji University spent five stable years on its engineering education in Lizhuang.

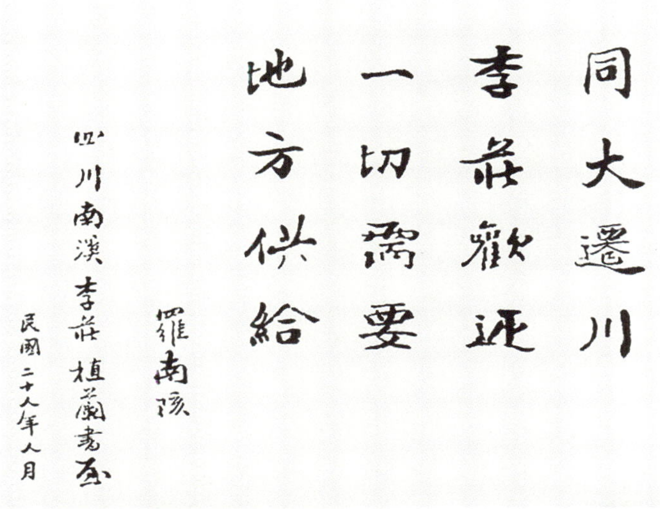

李庄乡绅罗南陔发给同济的十六字电文

A telegraph sent to Tongji University by Mr. Luo Nangai, a squire from Lizhuang which expressed a warm welcome to the relocation of Tongji University in Sichuan and a promise to provide all necessities

在同济迁往李庄过程中起了重要作用的校友钱子宁（1906-1974），祖籍浙江绍兴，中元造纸厂厂长，我国现代造纸工业的开拓者。

Mr. Qian Zining (1906-1974), a native of Shaoxing of Zhejiang Province and an alumnus of Tongji University, played an important role in Tongji's relocation to Lizhuang. He acted as director of Zhongyuan Papermaking Factory and was a pioneering figure of the modern paper industry in China.

时任国民党李庄区党部书记罗南陔，以他为首的当地乡绅对同济大学的迁入出力不少，提供诸多便利。

Mr. Luo Nangai, secretary of the Lizhuang branch of Kuomintang, made great contributions to the relocation of Tongji University in Lizhuang by leading the local squires to provide help needed by the university.

丁文渊，同济大学校长，任期 1942 年 2 月至 1944 年 7 月。
Mr. Ding Wenyuan, president of Tongji University from February 1942 to July 1944

徐诵明，同济大学校长，任期 1944 年 7 月至 1946 年 6 月。
Mr. Xu Yongming, president of Tongji University from July 1944 to June 1946

设在李庄禹王宫的学校总办公处
General Office of Tongji University located inside Yuwang Palace of Lizhuang

李庄禹王宫大戏台
Performance Stage of Yuwang Palace in Lizhuang

■ 位于李庄东岳庙的工学院
Engineering School of Tongji University in Dongyue Temple of Lizhuang

■ 1942 年 35 周年校庆时的工学院大门
Entrance of Engineering School in Dongyue Temple Decorated for the 35th anniversary of Tongji University

■ 李庄时期，工学院部分师生在东岳庙前合影。
Teachers and students of Engineering School in front of Dongyue Temple in Lizhuang

五系一科，扩充职校

Expansions of Engineering School and Affiliated Advanced Vocational School

1945 年，造船组扩建为造船系，并增办了机械专修科，工学院扩充为机械、电机、土木、测量、造船 5 个系 1 个机械专修科。附设高级工业职业学校开设机械、土木职业训练班，扩大职业教育规模。学校逐步设立了实习工厂、测量馆、电工试验馆、材料试验馆、机械试验馆等，确保各项实习均能进行。

In 1945, the Shipbuilding Teaching Group was expanded to be Department of Shipbuilding and a professional program in mechanics was set up. By far, the Engineering School of Tongji University was composed of five departments of Mechanical Engineering, Electromechanical Engineering, Civil Engineering, Surveying and Shipbuilding and a professional program in mechanics. In addition, the Affiliated Advanced Industrial Vocational School was also expanded with vocational training classes in mechanical engineering and civil engineering. In the meantime, the university gradually established an internship factory, a surveying laboratory, an electrical laboratory, a material laboratory and a mechanical laboratory to ensure the quality of engineering education.

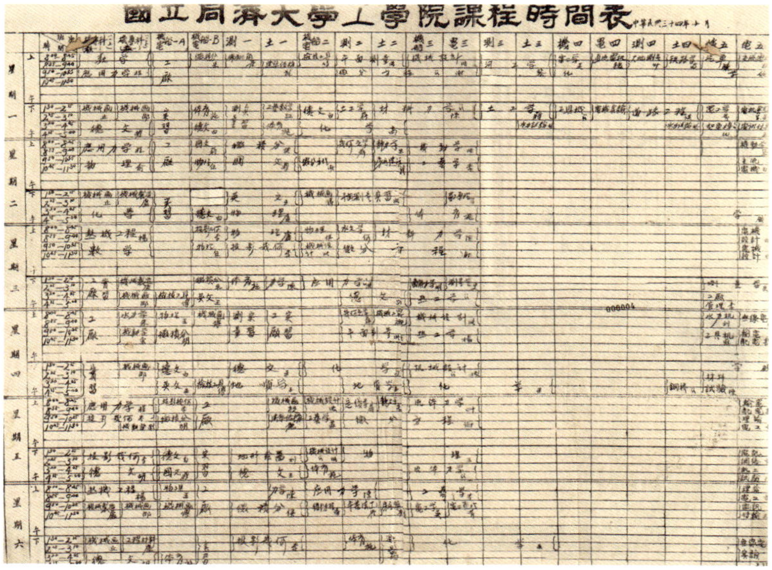
國立同濟大學工學院課程時間表

1945 年 10 月工学院授课时间表

Timetable of courses with Engineering School in October 1945

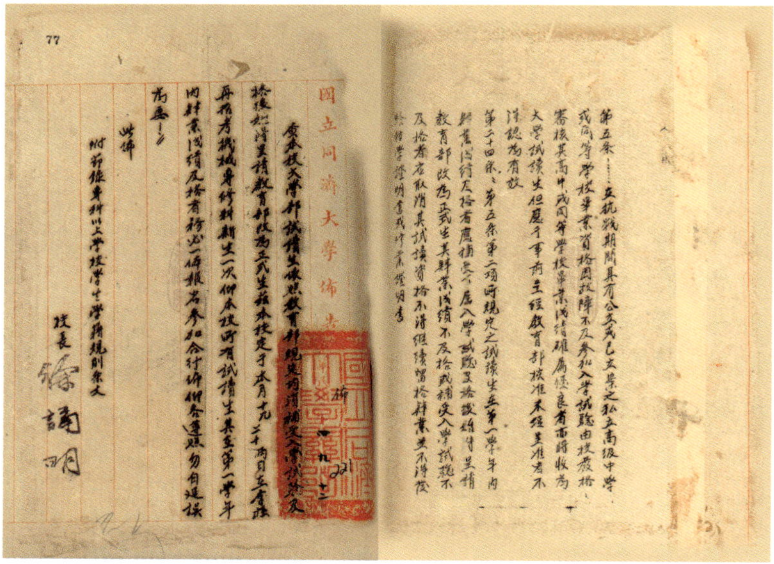

机械专修科招考布告及招考说明

Recruitment Promotion of the professional program in mechanics

名师荟萃，教授从军

Gathering of Leading Professors and Professors Joining the Army

李庄时期同济大学工科，汇集了叶在馥、夏坚白、王之卓、陈永龄、叶雪安、倪超、杨槱、黄席椿、朱木美、吴之翰、石声汉、波兰籍教授魏特等大批学术精英。1944 年冬天，日本进犯贵州独山，四川震动，国家告急，国民政府提出了“一寸山河一寸血，十万青年十万军”的口号，李庄时期同济以工科教授杨宝林为首的 364 名师生从军，奔赴抗日前线。

A number of leading academic figures including Ye Zaifu, Xia Jianbai, Wang Zhizhuo, Chen Yongling, Ye Xue'an, Ni Chao, Yang You, Huang Xichun, Zhu Mumei, Wu Zhihan, Shi Shenghan and the Polish professor Weit gathered for the engineering education of Tongji University in Lizhuang. In the winter of 1944, the Japanese army invaded Dushan Mountain of Guizhou Province adjacent to Sichuan. Sichuan was severely affected and the nation was in danger. The national government advocated a slogan of “a drop of blood for an inch of land; thousands of youth as thousands-of- people army”. A total of 364 teachers and students of Tongji University led by Professor Yang Baoling from engineering joined the army and fought bravely in the frontline for the country.

叶在馥（1888-1957），广东番禺人，李庄时期同济大学造船系教授兼系主任。中国造船工程学会创始人之一，川江轮设计的奠基人。

Mr. Ye Zaifu (1888-1957), from Fanyu of Guangdong Province, was a professor and head of Department of Shipbuilding, Tongji University in Lizhuang. He was one of the founders of Shipbuilding Engineering Society of China and an initiator of the design of Chuanjiang River Ferry.

杨槱（1917- ）江苏省句容县人，李庄时期同济大学造船系教授，1981 年当选为中国科学院技术科学部学部委员（院士），中国船舶设计学科的开拓者。

Mr. Yang You (1917-), from Jurong County of Jiangsu Province, was a professor of the Shipbuilding Department of Tongji University in Lizhuang. He became a member of the Science and Technology Division of Chinese Academy of Sciences in 1981 and was a pioneering member of the Discipline of Shipping Design in China.

电机系主任朱木美，解放后为华中工学院一级教授。

Mr. Zhu Mumei, head of Department of Electromechanical Engineering, Tongji University, became a First-grade Professor of Huazhong Institute of Technology.

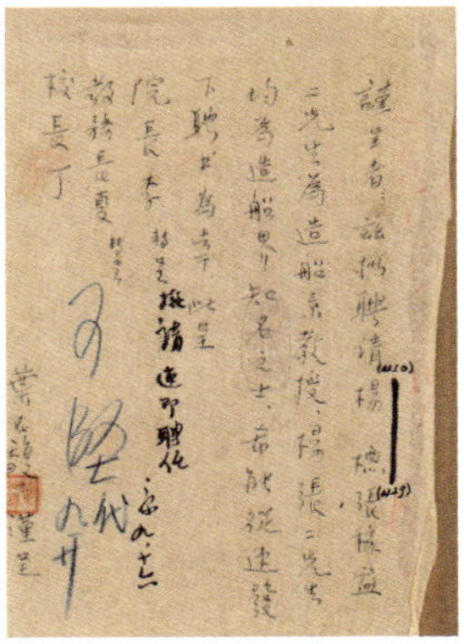

聘请杨槱为造船组教授的函

An employment letter to Mr. Yang You as professor of Shipbuilding Teaching Group

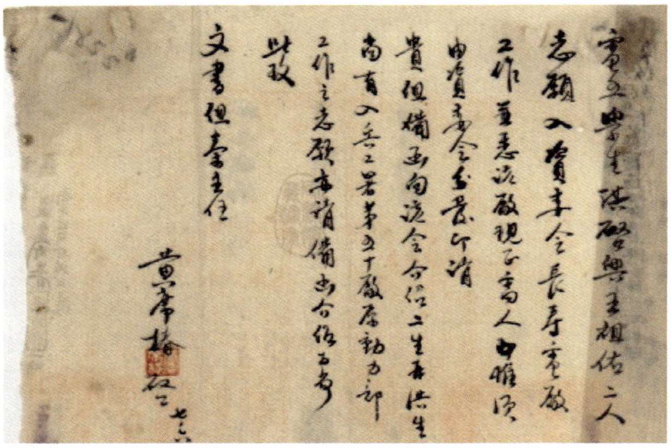

■ 电机系主任黄席椿手稿。黄席椿（1912-1986），江西九江人，1938 年赴德国留学，1943 年任同济大学工学院授兼电机系主任，著名电机专家。

Script of Mr. Huang Xichun, head of Department of Electromechanical Engineering Huang Xichun (1912-1986), from Jiujiang of Jiangxi Province, studied in Germany in 1938. He was appointed as professor of Engineering School and head of Department of Electromechanical Engineering in 1943. He was known as an expert of electromechanics.

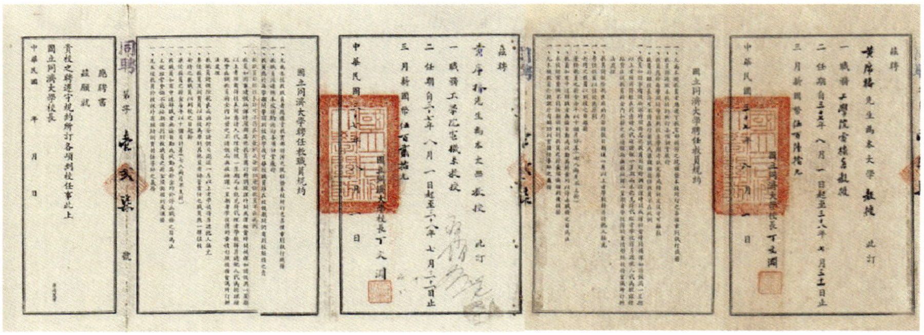

■ 电机系黄席椿教授聘书

Employment letter to Professor Huang Xichun from Department of Electromechanical Engineering

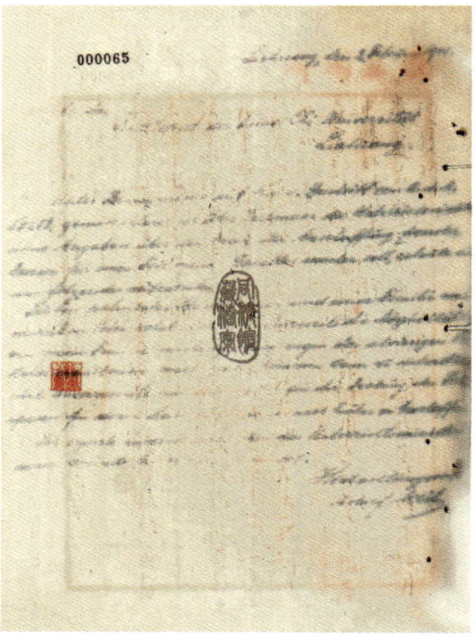

000065

■ 土木系波兰籍教授魏特签呈。魏特，波兰籍教授，犹太裔，德国工学博士，1939 年 12 月任同济工科教授，1946 年 1 月在李庄病世，葬于李庄。

A letter signed by Mr. Weit, a Polish professor of Department of Civil Engineering

Professor Weit, PhD in engineering, of Jewish origin, taught in Tongji as an engineering professor from November 1939. He died of illness and was buried in Lizhuang in January 1946.

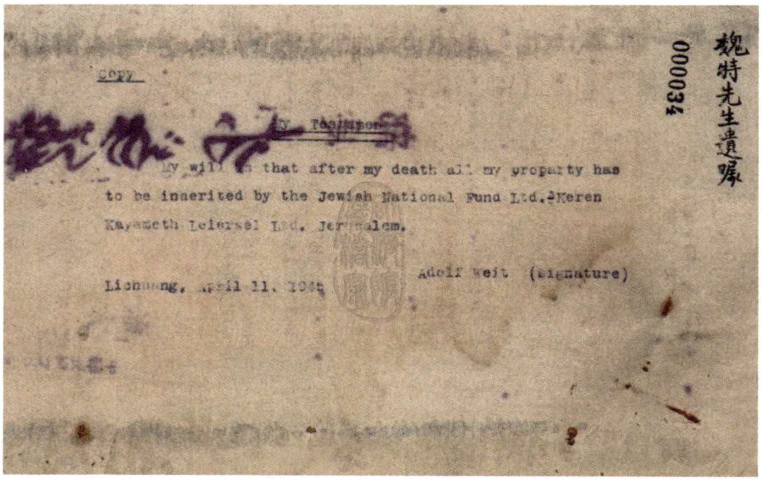

魏特先生遗嘱

000034

COPY

My Testament

My will is that after my death all my property has to be inherited by the Jewish National Fund Ltd. Keren Kayemeth Leisrael Ltd. Jerusalem.

Lichuang, April 11. 1945 Adolf Weit (signature)

■ 魏特教授遗嘱

Will of Professor Weit

王之卓（1909-2002），河北丰润人，柏林工业大学航空摄影测量博士，航空摄影测量与遥感专家。1941年至1943年为同济大学兼职教授，1980年当选为中国科学院学部委员（院士）。

Mr. Wang Zhizhuo (1909-2002), from Fengrun of Hebei Province, Ph.D. in Aerial Photogrammetry of TU Berlin, Germany was employed as part-time professor of Tongji University from 1941 to 1943. He was an expert of aerial photogrammetry and remote sensing and became a member of the Academic Division of Chinese Academy of Sciences.

陈永龄（1910-2004），北京人，柏林工业大学测量系博士，1943年至1945任同济大学工学院兼职教授，中国科学院院士，原国家测绘总局总工程师。

Mr. Chen Yongling (1910-2004), a native of Beijing, Ph.D. from the Department of Surveying, TU Berlin, Germany, was appointed as part-time professor of Engineering School of Tongji University from 1943 to 1945. He was a member of Chinese Academy of Sciences and acted as engineer-in-chief of the National Surveying Bureau.

李庄时期附设高级工业职业学校校长祝元青（右）夫妇在李庄时期的合影

Mr. Zhu Yuanqing (right), principal of Affiliated Advanced Industrial Vocational School and his wife in Lizhuang

同济大学杨宝林授代表从军师生接受宜宾各界献旗

Professor Yang Baoling of Tongji University accepting complimentary banners from people of Yibin, Sichuan Province, on behalf of teachers and students who joined the army

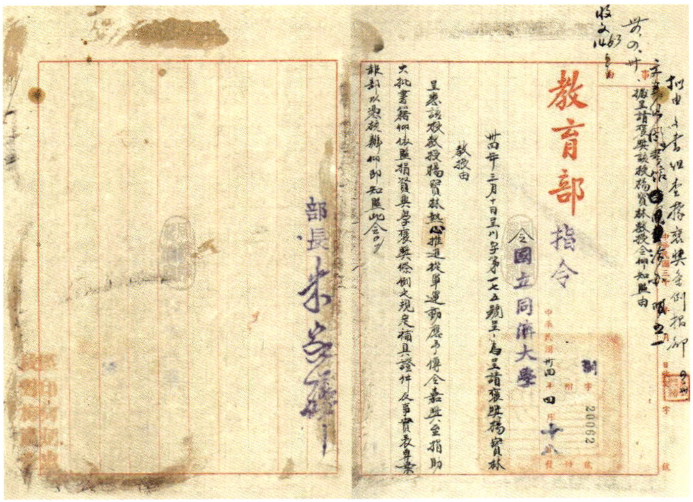

教育部褒奖杨宝林教授的指令

Commendation of Professor Yang Baoling from Ministry of Education

栉风沐雨，一心向学

Fully Devoted to Work During Hard Time

在相对平静的李庄，经过一段时间的恢复和发展，同济工科的师资、生源、硬件设施和实习环境都得到一定保障，师生们负隅一方，专心问学，在教学、科研各方面取得了一系列成果。

After some time of recovery in the peaceful Lizhuang, the engineering education of Tongji University had gradual improvement in its teaching resources, student recruitment, facilities and internship venues. Teachers and students were fully devoted to their work and study during the time of hardship against the background of war and made achievements in teaching and research.

李庄时期工学院做实验的滑轮

Pulley for experiments at Engineering School during the time in Lizhuang

李庄时期各系部分科研成果

Research Achievements in Lizhuang

名称 Name	部分科研成果 Research Achievements
机械系 Department of Mechanical Engineering	张象贤《钢球轴承原理》获教育部 1945 年（第五届）全国应用科学类学术发明三等奖 张景贤《机构之数量及其形态变化之理论基础》获全国应用科学类学术发明奖励 *Principles for Steel Ball Bearing* by Mr. Zhang Xiangxian awarded with a 3rd prize of 5th National Academic Invention in Applied Sciences in 1945 by Ministry of Education. *Theoretical Bases of Quantity of Units and Its Formal Transformation* by Zhang Jingxian awarded for Academic Invention in Applied Sciences.
电机系 Department of Electromechanical Engineering	1945 年成立国立同济大学电机工程学会，并编印年刊。 The Electromechanical Engineering Society of National Tongji University was established in 1945 and an annual report was published.
土木系 Department of Civil Engineering	王恒守《浮游选矿剂两种》获教育部 1942 年全国应用科学类学术发明二等奖 *Two Floating Mill Agents* by Wang Hengshou awarded with a 2nd prize of the National Academic Invention in Applied Sciences by Ministry of Education in 1945. 王志鹄《荆峪沟土壤之性状与水土保持》获教育部 1945 年全国应用科学类学术发明三等奖 *Nature and Water Preservation of Soil in Jinggu Vally* awarded with a 3rd prize of the National Academic Invention in Applied Sciences by Ministry of Education in 1945.
测量系 Department of Surveying	与中国地理研究所大地测量组合作出版《测量》杂志 20 期，专刊 11 册。 Twenty issues and eleven offprints of *Surveying* jointly published with Geodetic Surveying Team of China Geographic Science Institute.

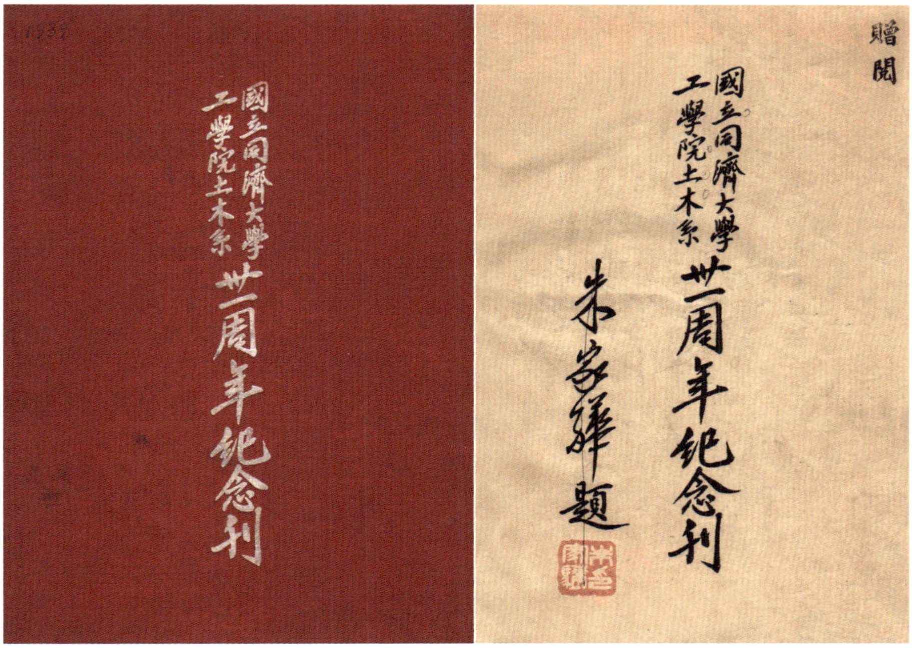

1942 年，土木系编印的建系三十一周年纪念刊（同济土木科始建于 1914 年，但土木系的前身为 1911 年建校的青岛德华高等专门学堂土木科，故按照 1911 年建系算起，三十一周年为 1942 年）。

A Commemorative Issue for the 31st Anniversary of Department of Civil Engineering in 1942 (The Civil Engineering School was established in 1914 on the basis of the Civil Engineering program of Deutsch-Chinesische Hochschule in Qingdao which was founded in 1911. Therefore it was 31 years between 1911 and 1942.)

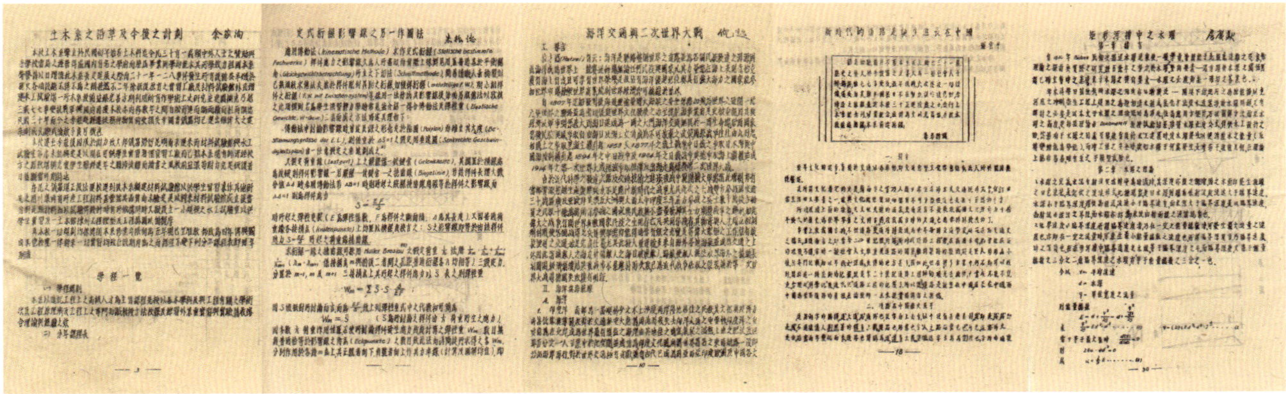

左一：余家洵的学术论文《水利与近代水利工程》

1st from left: An academic paper on *Hydraulics and Modern Hydraulic Engineering* by Mr. Yu Jiaxun

左二：朱振德的学术论文《定式桁樑影响线之另一作图法》

2nd from left: An academic paper on *Another Method of Drawing the Influence Line of Formulary Folding Beam* by Zhu Zhengde

左三：倪超的学术论文《海洋交通与二次世界大战》

3rd from left: An academic paper on *Ocean Transportation and World War II* by Mr. Ni Chao

左四：罗云平的学术论文《新时代的道路是诞生滋长在中国》

4th from left: An academic paper on *Roads in New Age in China* by Luo Yunping

左五：房广猷的学术论文《矩形河槽中之水跃》

5th from left: An academic paper on *Water Jumps in Rectangular River Channels* by Mr. Fang Guangyou

兵工栋梁，科技抗战

Military Elites with Knowledge of Science and Technology

1941 至 1946 年，因西迁沿途招生，工科毕业人数大幅增长，且吸收了大量四川、云南、贵州籍的学子，为改善西南地区的教育作出了巨大贡献。李庄同济工科毕业生理论联系实际、重技能、重实践，受到社会各界，尤其是战时急需的军工部门的欢迎。大部分学子就地毕业，在解放后成为领导西南地区建设的骨干力量。

The number of engineering graduates increased substantially from 1941 to 1946 due to an expansion of student recruitment along the way westward of relocation. Tongji recruited a large number of students from Sichuan, Yunnan and Guizhou, which made great contributions to the education in the southwestern area of China. Tongji University advocated a balanced engineering education between theory and practice with an emphasis on skills. Therefore, its engineering graduates during the time in Lizhuang were warmly welcomed by all walks of life, esp. by the military departments during war time. Most students stayed to work in the local areas upon their graduation and became the backbone in construction of southwestern area after liberation.

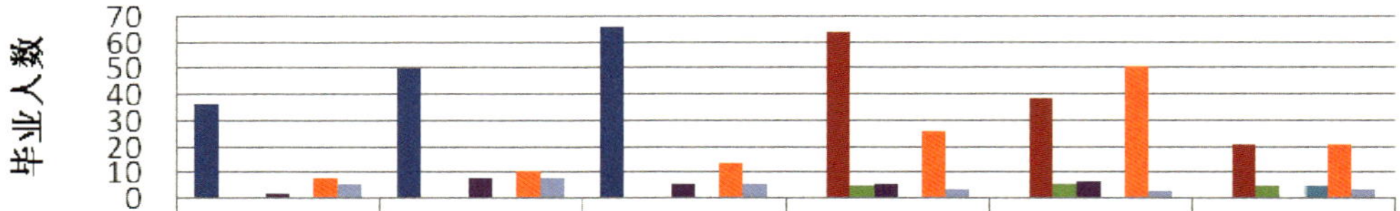

	1941	1942	1943	1944	1945	1946
■机电系	37	50	66			
■机械系				64	39	21
■电机系				5	6	5
■造船组	2	8	6	6	7	
■造船系						5
■土木系	8	11	14	26	51	21
■测量系	6	8	6	4	3	4

李庄时期工学院历届毕业生人数

Number of graduates from Engineering School during the time in Lizhuang

同济大学工学院机械系1946级全体师生合影。前排为教师，后两排为学生。

第一排左起：李本文 苏知检 张象贤 王志鹄 江 鸿 谢苍璃 刘百浩 施之千 张景贤 陈延年 史惠顺 黄厚锡

1946 年机械系毕业生全体师生合影

Teachers and all graduates of the Year 1946 from Department of Mechanical Engineering

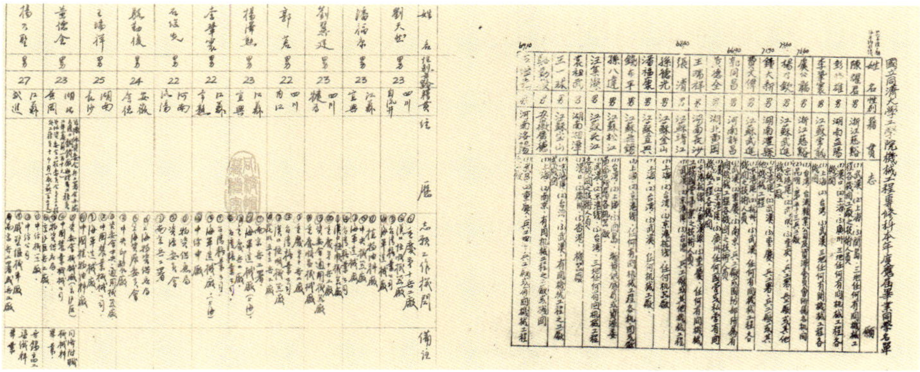

国立同济大学工学院机械专修科毕业生名单，表明大多毕业生在兵工部门就职。

The list of graduates from the Professional Program in Mechanics of Engineering School, National Tongji University showed that most graduates were employed by the military departments.

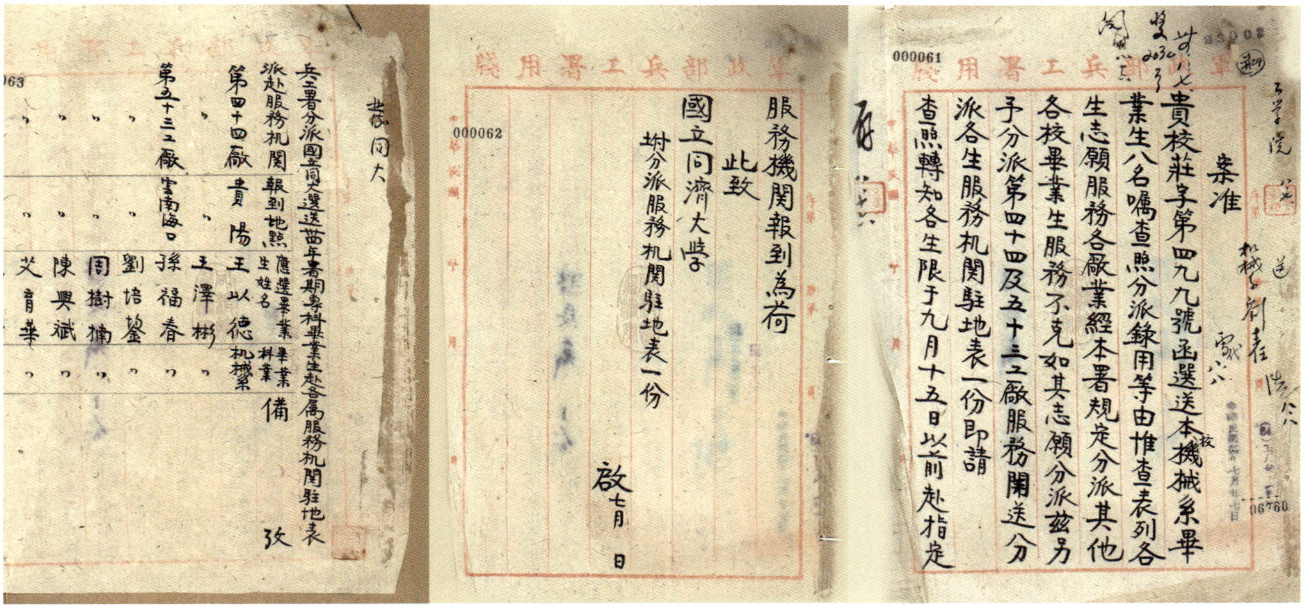

軍政部兵工署用箋

案准
貴校莊字第四九九號函選送本校機械系畢
業生八名囑查照分派錄用等由准查表列各
生志願服務各廠業經本署規定分派其他
各校畢業生服務不克如其志願分派茲另
予分派第四十四及五十三工廠服務開送分
派各生服務机關駐地表一份即請
查照轉知各生限于九月十五日以前赴指定

服務機関報到為荷
此致
國立同濟大學
附分派服務机關駐地表一份
啟 七月 日

兵工署分派國立同濟大學選送卅四年暑期專科畢業生赴各屬服務机關駐地表

第四十四廠 貴陽 王以德 機械

1945 年军工部兵工署选派同济毕业生赴各属服务机关驻地表

A list of Tongji graduates sent by the Army Office of Military Department to subordinate branches in different places in 1945

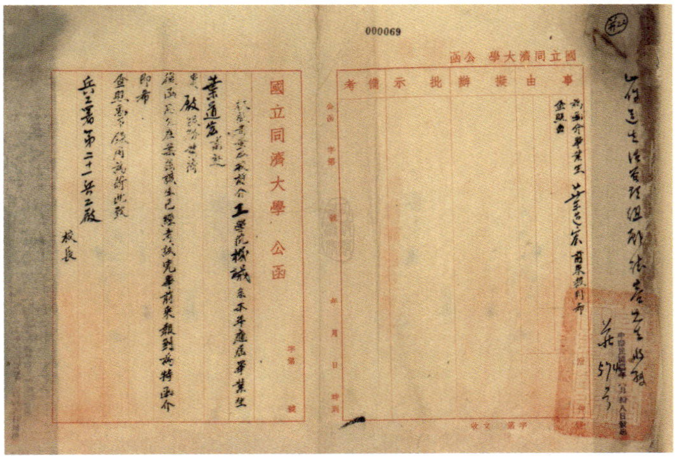

國立同濟大學公函

学校为毕业生进入兵工厂工作开出的证明函

An official letter of Tongji University introducing its graduates to work in the military factory

王守武，1919 年生，1941 年毕业于工学院机电系，半导体器件物理学家，1980 年当选为中国科学院学部委员（院士）。

Mr. Wang Shouwu, born in 1919, graduated from Department of Electromechanical Engineering of Engineering School in 1941. He was a physicist in semiconductor devices and became a member of Chinese Academy of Sciences in 1980.

吴式枢，1923 年生，1944 年工学院机械系毕业，1980 年当选为中科院学部委员（院士），著名理论物理学家。

Mr. Wu Shishu, born in 1923, graduated from Department of Mechanical Engineering of Engineering School in 1944. He was a famous theoretical physicist and became a member of Chinese Academy of Sciences in 1980.

张浩，1920 年生，1944 年工学院土木系毕业。北京市建筑设计研究院副院长、副总工程师，人民大会堂结构设计负责人之一。

Mr. Zhang Hao, born in 1920, graduated from Department of Civil Engineering of Engineering School in 1944. He was vice director and associate engineer-in-chief of Beijing Architectural Design and Research Institute. He was one of engineers responsible for the structural design of the Great Hall of the People in China.

吴几康，1918 年生于上海市，1943 年工学院机电系毕业，计算机专家，指导研制成功中国第一台 104 型计算机，对创建和发展中国计算机研究事业作出了重要贡献。

Mr. Wu Jikang, born in Shanghai in 1918, graduated from Department of Electromechanical Engineering, Tongji University in 1943. As an expert in computer, he supervised the research and development of the first 104-model computer in China, and made great contributions to the development of research in computer in China.

江可宗（1918-1997），江西临川人，1941 年毕业于工学院土木系，力学教育家，建立了上海交通大学流体力学教研室，上海力学学会筹建人。

Mr. Jiang Kezong (1918-1997), from Linchuan of Jiangxi Province, graduated from Department of Civil Engineering of Engineering School, Tongji University in 1941. He set up the Teaching and Research Group of Hydromechanics, Shanghai Jiaotong University. He was an educationalist of mechanics and an initiator of Shanghai Society of Mechanics.

俞载道，浙江奉化人，1944 年毕业于工学院土木系，历任同济大学讲师、副教授、教授、《同济大学学报》主编。

Mr. Yu Zaidao, from Fenghua of Zhejiang Province, graduated from Department of Civil Engineering of Engineering School, Tongji University in 1944. He worked as a lecturer, an associate professor, a professor and chief-editor of *Journal of Tongji University*.

史惠顺，1926 年生，1943 年工学院测量系毕业，台湾成功大学测量工程学创始人、工学院院长。

Mr. Shi Huishun, born in 1926, graduated from Department of Surveying, Engineering School in 1943. He was the founder of Surveying Engineering in Cheng Kung University, Taiwan and acted as Dean of Engineering School of the university.

高时浏，1915 年生于福建福州，1941 年毕业于工学院测量系，到达磁北极的第一位中国人，测量学家、教育家。

Mr. Gao Shiliu, born in Fuzhou of Fujian Province in 1915, graduated from Department of Surveying of Engineering School in 1941. He was the first Chinese who stepped his feet on the North Magnetic Pole. He was an expert in surveying and an educationalist.

高时浏 1950 年就职于加拿大联邦大地测量局天文科期间，进入北极圈执行勘测任务所使用的加拿大地图。

Map of Canada used by Mr. Gao Shiliu on his surveying mission within the Arctic Circle in 1950 during his employment with the Astronomy Section of Federal Geographic Surveying Bureau of Canada.

回迁上海，恢复建设

University Restoration after its Return to Shanghai

抗战胜利后，学校开始部署回迁上海。经过一年多的辗转，1946年新学年在上海开学。工学院位于其美路（今四平路），现同济大学四平路校本部。八年离乱，工学院办学规模不缩反增，是全校规模最大，师生人数最多的学院。回迁上海后，同济保持了重视实践的传统，为当时国内实习设备最齐全的大学之一。

After the Anti-Japanese war, Tongji University started to relocate back to Shanghai. In 1946, a new semester eventually started in Shanghai following a rough return journey for over a year. The Engineering School was relocated on Qimei Road (the current Siping Road), the main campus of the current Tongji University. Despite of the eight- year turmoil during the war, the Engineering School was expanded in its size and became a school with the largest number of teachers and students at Tongji University. After its return to Shanghai, Tongji University managed to keep its tradition of practice-oriented education and was one of the universities with most comprehensive facilities for student internship in China.

董洗凡校长，任期1946年6月至1947年9月。

Mr. Dong Xifan, president of Tongji University from June 1946 to September 1947

夏坚白校长（1903-1977），江苏常熟人。1939-1946年和1948-1956年先后两次任教于同济大学，著名大地测量和天体测量学家，中国测绘界第一位学部委员（院士），同济大学第一届校务委员会主任委员（校长）。

President Xia Jianbai (1903-1977), from Changshu of Jiangsu Province, taught in Tongji University from 1939 to 1946 and from 1948 to 1956. He was a famous expert in geodesy and astrometry and the first member of the Surveying Division of Chinese Academy of Engineering and the chairman (president) of the First University Council.

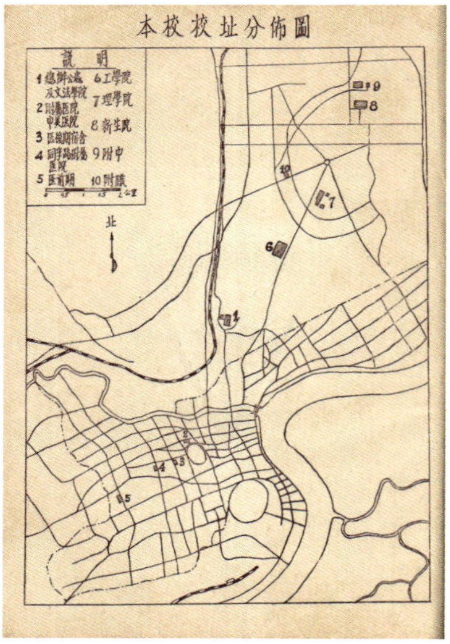

回迁上海后的校址分布图

Distribution of Tongji University after its return to Shanghai

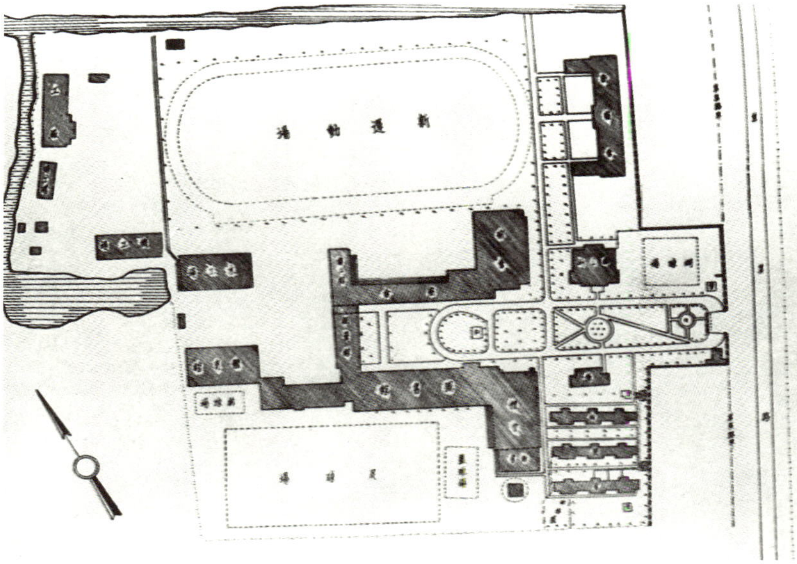

工学院平面图

Plan of Engineering School

工学院大门
Entrance of Engineering School

工学院“一·二九”大楼
1. 29 Building of Engineering School

工学院校舍
Campus of Engineering School

助教宿舍
Hall of Residence for assistant lecturers

工学院教室
Teaching building of Engineering School

附设高级工业职业学校校址，在新市区江湾魏德迈路 370 号（现邯郸路）
Affiliated Advanced Industrial Vocational School on No. 370 of Weidemai Road, New Jiangwan Zone of Xinshi District (the current Handan Road)

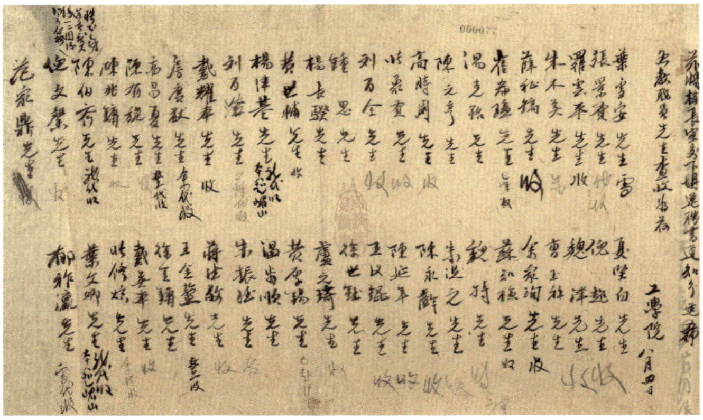

回迁上海后工学院教授名录

A list of professors of Engineering School after its relocation to Shanghai

1947 年工学院院长江鸿

Mr. Jiang Hong, dean of Engineering School in 1947

1948 年工学院院长兼测量系主任叶雪安，任期 1947 年 9 月至 1948 年 7 月。

叶雪安（1905-1966）上海金山人，1929 年毕业于同济大学土木系， 1935 年获慕尼黑工业大学特许工程师学位，回国后一直在同济大学任教授兼测量系主任，1956 年迁武汉，任武汉测量制图学院测量系主任。中国民用测量学科奠基人。

Mr. Ye Xue'an, Dean of Engineering School and head of Surveying Department from September 1949 to July 1948

Ye Xue'an (1905-1966), born in Jinshan of Shanghai, graduated from Civil Engineering Department of Tongji University in 1929. He got his degree in Chartered Engineer from Technical University of Munich in 1935. After his return to China, he was appointed as professor and head of Surveying Department of Tongji University. He moved to Wuhan with the Surveying Department in 1956 and was appointed as head of Surveying Department of Wuhan Surveying and Mapping Institute. He was the founder of the Civil Surveying Discipline in China.

回迁上海后各系主任，其中李国豪 1948 年 7 月起任工学院院长。

Heads of departments after Tongji's relocation back to Shanghai, among whom Li Guohao was appointed as dean of Engineering School since July 1948

工學院上課情形聚精會神！

閱覽室裏，靜！

■ 工学院学生上课及自习

Students of Engineering School in class and in a reading room after class

實習工廠

鉗工間

車床——工具機之母

機工間

■ 实习工厂

Internship factory

师生协力，教学相长

Mutual Improvement Between Teaching and Learning

1946 年电机工程系分为电力、电讯两组；1948 年土木工程系分为道路、结构、水利三组，学科布局进一步细化，测量学科仍属全国唯一。除本科教育外，机械专修科续招一届，附属高级工业职业学校进一步扩大。同济工科的学科规模、师资力量、学生人数较内迁前大幅提升，社会影响力大幅增强。

In 1946, Electromechanical Department was divided into two groups of electricity and telecommunications. In 1948, Civil Engineering Department was divided into three groups of road construction, structure engineering and hydraulic engineering. Surveying remained its No.1 ranking in China with the further development of academic programs at Tongji. In addition to the undergraduate education, the professional program in mechanics recruited students for one more year and the Affiliated Advanced Industrial Vocational School was further expanded. Tongji University had substantially enhanced its academic programs, faculty capacity and student number and became more and more influential in the society.

电机工程系实习与考察

Students from Electromechanical Engineering Department on internship and investigation trips

「如果號誌樓要火車從這股軌道進站，這是可以搬動的。你們看…」（上海北站）

李先生說：「這個Auflager Kraft……我ganz Kurz的erzaehlen一下」（參觀蘇州河各橋工程時攝）

我們鋼橋課的Beispiel—外灘白渡

你再仔細看這次多少？

先把儀器調整好

參觀滬西污水處理工程（金經昌教授攝）

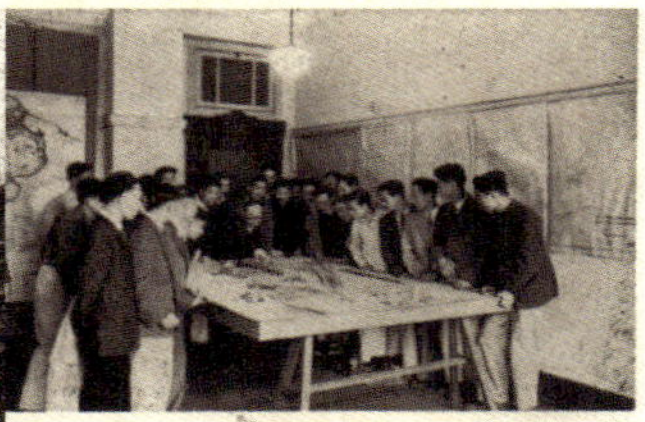

土木工程系实习与考察

Students from Civil Engineering Department on internship and investigation trips

机械工程系实习与考察
Students from Mechanical Engineering Department on internship and investigation trips

船五同學在民俗輪上

參觀中華造船放樣間

留連在黃浦江中

在江南造船所裏王先生為同學講解

楊槙先生與本班同學

我們要造出各式各樣的船舶

未來的航海家

未來的工程師在審慎檢查工人的工作

造船工程系实习与考察

Students from Shipbuilding Engineering Department on internship and investigation trips

測量蘇州天平山在一線天途中

天平山御碑亭小憩

多麼年青的一羣

實習開始了，先將儀器校正，水平，準備工作。

為了提高精度，王助教不厭煩地指導，在學習中，他和我們永遠在一起。

縱烈日當空，我們仍聚精會神的觀測讀數。

夕陽西下；小心地收檢儀器，面對精確的成果，雖有整日的辛勞，也掩不住內心的愉快。

测量工程系实习与考察

Students from Surveying Engineering Department on internship and investigation trips

交流合作，社会欢迎

Popularity with Employers with More Exchange and Cooperation

回迁上海后，李庄时期相对封闭的教学环境被打破，学校对内对外的科研合作以及学术交流活动日益频繁。1947、1948、1949 三届毕业生共 466 人，受到用人单位的热烈欢迎。其中，赵清澄和高佩荪是第一批获得本校工学学士学位的女同学。

When the peaceful yet closed academic environment in Lizhuang was broken in Shanghai, more and more academic exchange and cooperation activities were organized at both national and international levels at Tongji. A total of 466 students graduated from the university in 1947, 1948 and 1949, among whom were two girl students Zhao Qingcheng and Gao Peisun, the first female students who obtained their Bachelor's degree in Engineering from Tongji University. Graduates of the university were very popular with employers.

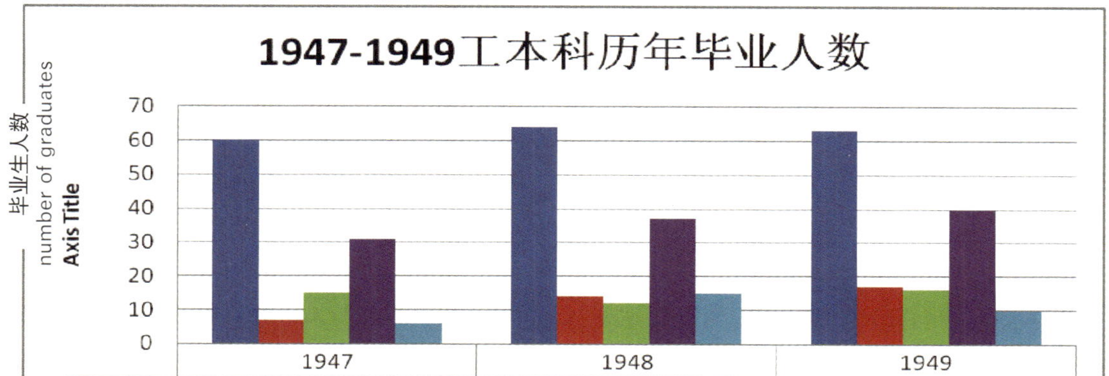

	1947	1948	1949
机械系	60	64	63
电机系	7	14	17
造船系	15	12	16
土木系	31	37	40
测量系	6	15	10

回迁上海至解放前工学院本科历年毕业人数

Number of graduates from Engineering School per year after Tongji's return to Shanghai and before liberation of China

工学院首届女毕业生赵清澄

Miss Zhao Qingcheng one of the first two female graduates of Engineering School from Tongji

工学院首届女毕业生高佩荪

Miss Gao Peisun, one of the first two female graduates from Engineering School of Tongji

王守觉，1925 年生，江苏苏州人，1949 年工学院电机系电讯组毕业，中国科学院院士，为中国制造电子仪器设备降低成本、提高发展速度开辟了新途径。

Mr. Wang Shoujue, born in Suzhou of Jiangsu Province in 1925, graduated from Telecommunications Section of Electromechanical Department of Engineering School in 1949. As a member of Chinese Academy of Sciences, he succeeded in finding a new way to produce electronic apparatus and equipment at a higher speed and a lower cost in China.

杜同（左一），生于 1927 年，四川南充人，1947 年毕业工学院机械系，著名水利专家，三峡工程专家，新中国水轮机之父，曾任四川工业学院院长。

Mr. Du Tong (first from left), born in Nanchong of Sichuan Province in 1927, graduated from Mechanical Department of Tongji University in 1947. He acted as president of Sichuan Industrial Institute and was hailed as father of water turbine in New China. He was well-known for his expertise in hydraulics and for his involvement in the megaproject of Three Gorges in China.

杨益言，生于 1925 年，四川武胜人，1944-1948 就读于同济大学电机系，当代文学经典《红岩》的作者之一。

Mr. Yang Yiyan, born in Wusheng of Sichuan Province in 1925, studied in Electromechanical Department of Tongji University from 1944 to 1948. He was one of the authors of the *Red Rocks*, a contemporary classical novel.

上海解放，同济新生

Rebirth of Tongji after Liberation of Shanghai

1949 年 5 月 27 日，上海解放，6 月 25 日，上海市军管会接管同济，同济大学的发展迈入了新时代。1949 年 9 月 2 日，工学院招生 175 名，学校还新聘了著名水利学家郑肇经等知名学者充实工学院，全体师生迎着朝阳，满怀信心，以崭新的精神面貌，庆祝新中国的到来。

Shanghai was liberated on May 27th 1949. On June 25th, Tongji University was taken over by Shanghai Military Control Commission, which marked a new era of the development of Tongji University. On September 2nd 1949, while 175 new students were admitted into Engineering School, leading scholars including famous hydraulic expert Zheng Zhaojing joined the school. Teachers and students of Tongji University felt overwhelmed with the tremendous changes in China and was filled with confidence to embrass the coming of new China.

1949 年 6 月 25 日，上海市军管会接管同济大学。

Tongji University was handed over to Shanghai Military Control Commission on June 25th 1949.

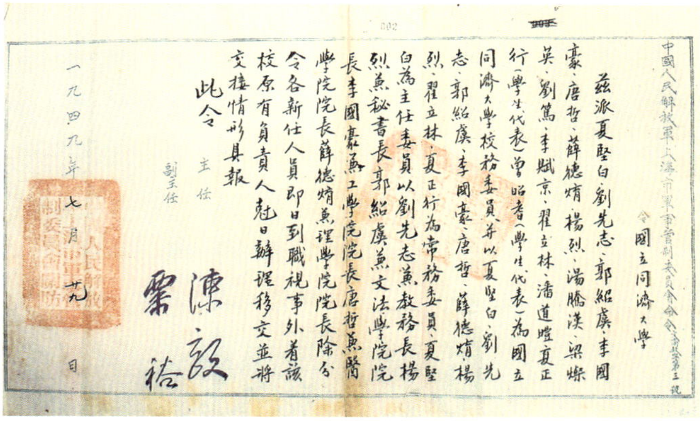

中國人民解放軍上海市軍事管制委員會命令

令 國立同濟大學

茲派夏堅白、劉先志、郭紹虞、李國豪、唐哲、薛德焴、楊烈、湯騰漢、梁嶸英、劉篤、李賦京、翟立林、潘道皚、夏正行（學生代表）、曾昭耆（學生代表）為國立同濟大學校務委員，並以夏堅白、劉先志、郭紹虞、李國豪、唐哲、薛德焴、楊烈、翟立林、夏正行為常務委員，夏堅白為主任委員，以劉先志兼教務長，楊烈兼秘書長，郭紹虞兼文法學院院長，李國豪兼工學院院長，唐哲兼醫學院院長，薛德焴兼理學院院長。除分令各新任人員即日到職視事外，著該校原有負責人剋日辦理移交，並將交接情形具報。

此令

主任 陳毅

副主任 粟裕

一九四九年七月十九日

军管会接管同济大学的命令

Authorization for Shanghai Military Control Commission to take over Tongji University

毛主席与李国豪等知识分子亲切交谈

Chairman Mao (first from left) in conversation with Li Guohao and other intellectuals

造船系主任李永庆
Mr. Li Yongqing, head of Shipbuilding Department

电机系主任黄席椿
Mr. Huang Xichun, head of Electromechanical Department

实习工厂主任郑兆益
Mr. Zheng Zhaoyi, director of the internship factory

附设高职校长朱振德
Mr. Zhu Zhende, Principal of Affiliated Advanced Vocational School

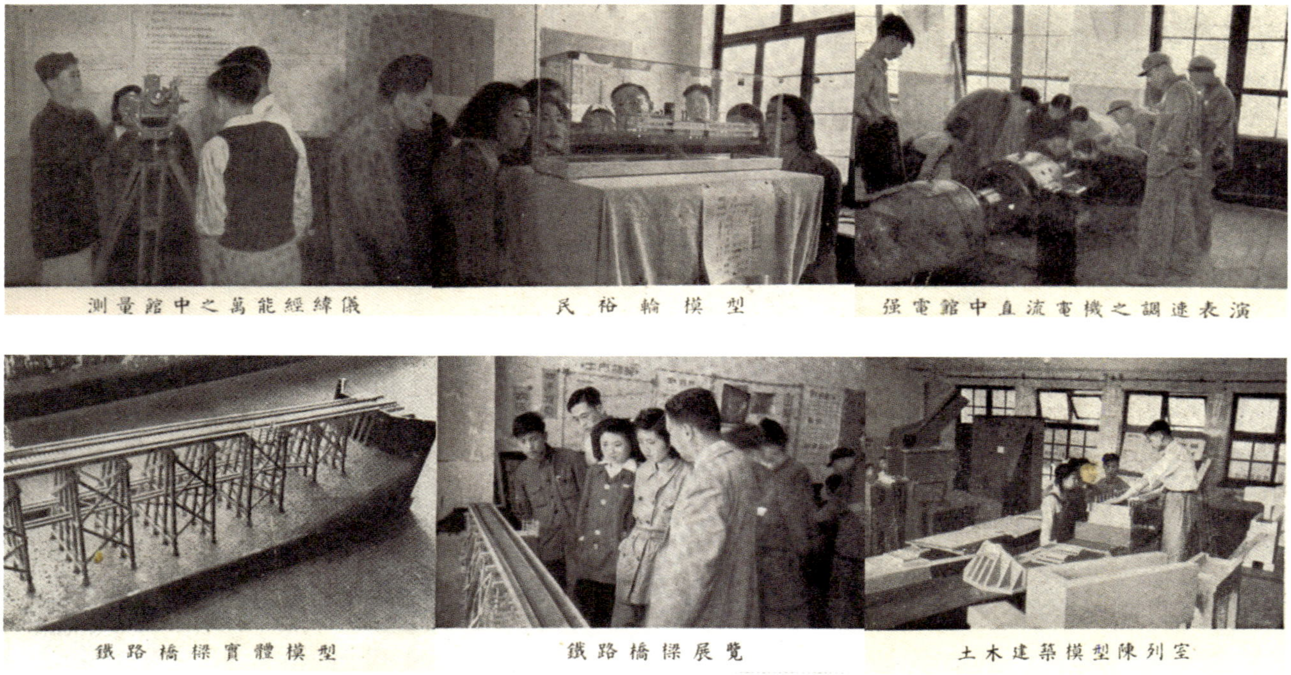

工学院概况
Engineering School

Planmeter

精簡課程系代表會議

課　堂

繪　圖　室

造船系概况

Shipbuilding Department

在他們的教導下

聽溝管如何製造

繪圖室裏

在教室中

土木系概况

Civil Engineering Department

机械系概况
Mechanical Department

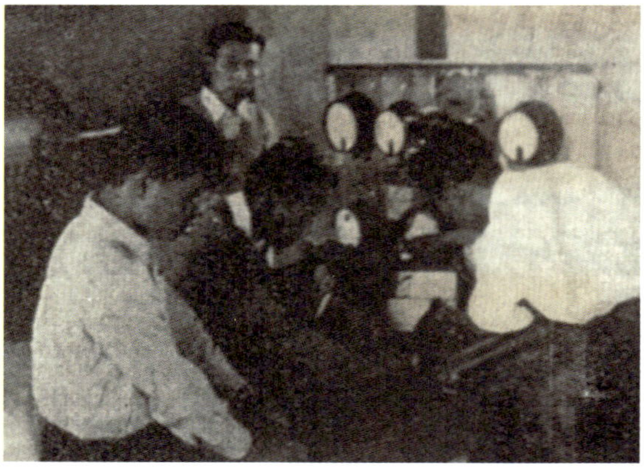

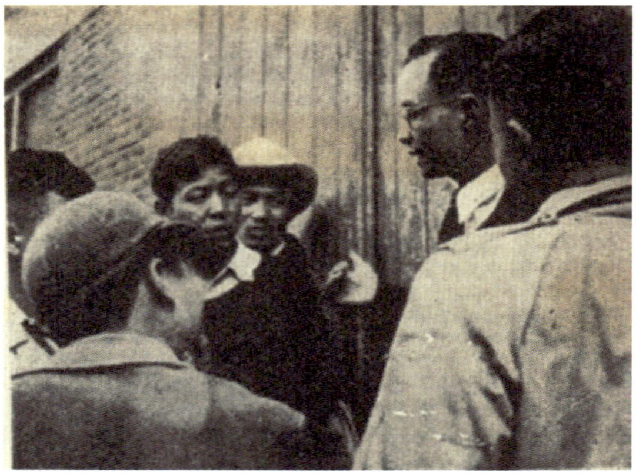

电机系概况
Electromechanical Department

建设祖国，多方贡献

Active Participation in Construction of New China

上海解放后不久，同济学生踊跃报名参加“南下服务团”、“西南服务团”，积极参与上海市政建设，投入到建设新中国的洪流中去。1950 年 6 月朝鲜战争爆发，10 月 19 日，中国人民志愿军赴朝鲜作战，学校开展了“抗美援朝、保家卫国”的参军参干运动。

Shortly after the liberation of Shanghai, Tongji students took an active part in the construction of New China campaign by joining in the Southward Service Delegation and, Southwestern Service Delegation and in participating in civil construction of Shanghai, making contributions to the construction of new China. In June 1950, Korean War broke out. On October 19th, the Chinese army went to Korea for a fight against the enemy. Tongji University started campaigns to “fight against the US, support Korea and safeguard the nation” and called on students to join the army.

南下服务团

Southward Service Regiment

“华东随军南下服务团”南下动员大会，大学部共有 50 名学子参加南下服务团，附中有 9 人参加。

A meeting to encourage more people to join the Southward Service Delegation. Fifty undergraduate students from the university and nine students from Affiliated High School joined in the army.

西南服务团

Southwestern Service Regiment

张彩珍，1930 年生，浙江宁波人，在李庄时就读于同济，抗战结束后随同济回到上海，积极从事革命运动，1949 年 10 月报名参加西南服务团，获得解放大西南胜利纪念章，是中国历史上第一位获得奥林匹克勋章的女性。

Ms. Zhang Caizhen, born in Ningbo of Zhejiang Province in 1930, studied at Tongji during the time in Lizhuang. She returned to Shanghai with Tongji's relocation after the liberation. She joined Southwestern Service Delegation in Oct. 1949 and won Memorial Badge for the liberation of southwestern China. She was the first female winner of an Olympic Medal in China's history.

刘敬光烈士 (1928-1950)，1943 年至 1949 年先后在同济附中和工学院机械系学习，后参加西南服务团，在激战中壮烈牺牲。

Mr. Liu Jingguang (1928-1950), studied in Affiliated Tongji High School and Mechanical Department of Tongji University from 1943 to 1949. He joined the Southwestern Service Delegation and sacrificed his life in the battle field.

参军参干运动

Join the Army

整隊入禮堂簽名

1950年12月，华东教育部发出了“加强国防建设，招收青年学生参加军事干部学校”的指示。同济129名学生参加军事干部学校，5名职工参加支前运输队。

In December 1950, the Ministry of Education of Eastern China issued an instruction of “strengthening national defense and recruiting young students for military cadre’s schools”. A total of 129 students of Tongji University were enrolled in military cadre’s schools and five staff members joined the transportation team to support the frontline.

歡送會上

参加治淮，建功立业

Great Contribution to Hydraulic Engineering Project of Huaihe River

在新中国第一波建设高潮中，同济大学师生担负了“学好本领，建设祖国”的任务。1950 年暑假，测量系参加了大上海三角网测量工作，土木系参加了江西福建支前公路的抢修工作，水利组参加了华东水利部海塘突击测量队。1950 年 10 月，土木系测量系 62 人响应政府号召，参加了历史性的治淮工程。

At the peak of the first wave of constructing New China, teachers and students of Tongji University assumed the responsibility of “learning to build the motherland”. During the summer vacation of 1950, teachers and students from the Surveying Department participated in a trigonometric survey of greater Shanghai; those from the Civil Engineering Department participated in the emergency repair of roads to the frontline in Jiangxi and Fujian, while those from the Hydraulic Group joined the seawall rapid response surveying team of Eastern China’s Ministry of Water Resources. In October 1950, sixty two students of Civil Engineering Department and Surveying Department participated the historical Hydraulic Engineering Project of Huaihe River.

同濟大學治淮工程人員訓練班全體師生合影

1951 年 9 月，同济先后派土木系和测量系 400 多名师生参加了治淮工程。

In September 1951, over 400 teachers and students of Civil Engineering Department and Surveying Department were sent to participate in the Hydraulic Engineering Project of Huaihe River.

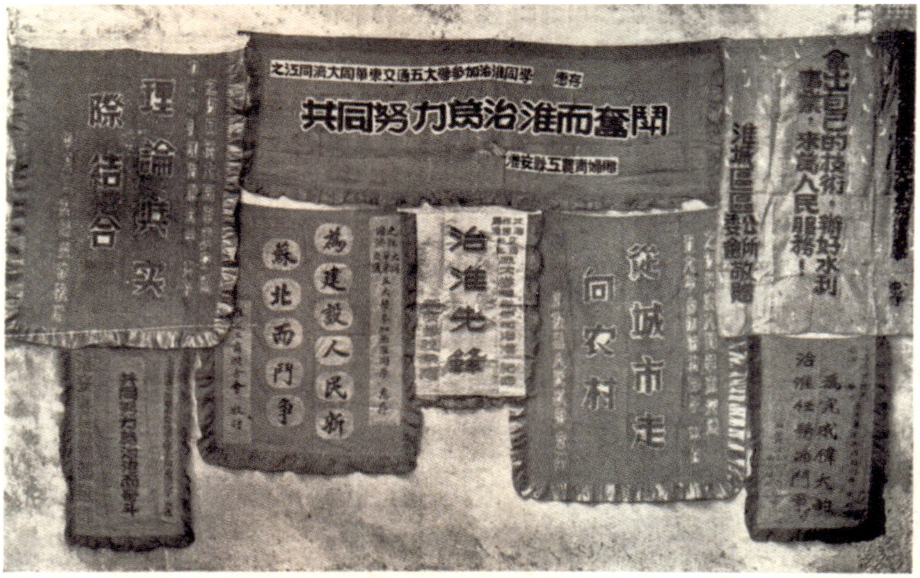

淮河兩岸人民對我們的熱望——各界所贈旗之一部

淮河两岸人民赠予同济师生的部分赠旗

Complimentary banners to teachers and students from Tongji University on the Hydraulic Engineering Project of Huaihe River from people along Huaihe River

在蘇北一望無際的平原上工作

測量出發前同學們趕製標桿及地形尺

寒嚴中，踏着冰雪前進在蘇北的原野上，入海測量隊出發了

测量入海水道
Surveying of waterway to the ocean

頭閘—中國古老的船閘船過閘口用岸上絞盤控制，淮陰船閘竣工後即要廢止

合龍時最後的一剎間

廢黃河楊莊草埧施工全景，背面是楊莊活動埧殘跡

同济学子在废黄河杨庄草坝
Students of Tongji University on the straw embankment of Yangzhuang along the abandoned Yellow River

運堤護岸工程及涵洞

施工第一步清除淤泥

飛硪（又名天硪）及火盆架打樁，這是運河綫上獨創的技術

高郵城外架設臨時浮橋至運河西取土

新填改修堤身，由蘇北監獄勞動改造隊拔出舊樁

高郵南八里松涵洞翼牆背面模板架設情形

运堤护岸工程及涵洞

Bank-protection dam project and culverts

閘室條石護坡施工情形

閘基鋼筋已經紮好

開關井口模板在裝置

模板完成

混凝土澆入模板後再搗實

淮阴船闸

Locks at Huaiyin

下　篇
Part II
1952-2012

粹大道而动
Making Progress to Keep Abreast of Time

本时期工程教育分三个阶段：第一阶段为 1952 至 1976 年，同济由综合性大学调整为以土木建筑为主的单科性工程院校；第二阶段为 1976 年至 1991 年，完成了由单一土木建筑类工科大学向多科性大学和从封闭型办学向对外开放型办学的两大转变；第三阶段为 1992 年至 2012 年，工程教育呈现了学科设置集成化、人才培养复合化、合作办学国际化、科研创新产业化的大繁荣特征。

The engineering education of Tongji University at this time was divided into three stages. During the first stage from 1952 to 1976, Tongji was restructured from a comprehensive university to a specialized university with a focus on civil engineering. During the second stage from 1976 to 1991, the university made two transformations from a closed university to an open one and from civil engineering-focused university to one with multiple engineering disciplines. During the third stage from 1992 to 2012, the engineering education of Tongji University was characterized by interdisciplinary integration, complex student cultivation, international cooperation and technology transfer.

100

第四章 Chapter IV（1952.6 - 1976.9）

土建单科，局部发展

Further Development Against All Odds

1952 年开始院系调整后，同济大学整合为结构、测量、建筑、上下水道和铁路公路 5 个系，其它专业停招，成了以土木建筑为主的单科大学。经过劳动建校、学习苏联、开门办学和五七公社等历次运动，甚至在十年文革相对艰难的政治环境中，工程教育某种程度上延续了重实践的传统教学特色，为国家建设培养了大批工程技术人才。

After the nationwide restructuring among colleges and universities in 1952, Tongji University became a university that specialized in civil engineering with five departments of structure, surveying, architecture, water supply and drainage and railway and road. Although the university went through such political movements as School Development through Labor, Learning from the Soviet Union, Open-ended School Operation and May Seventh Communes as well as the Cultural Revolution, engineering education managed somehow to keep its tradition of emphasizing on practice and produced a large number of engineering personnel for the country.

院系调整，单科大学

Nationwide Restructuring Leading to Specialization in Civil Engineering

1949 年开始，根据中央统一部署，同济文、法、理、医科和工科中的机械、电机和造船等专业调出，附设高级工业职业学校迁往南京。同时清华大学、上海交通大学、浙江大学、厦门大学等校的土木、建筑、测量各系、科、组陆续调入。1956 年下半年，同济大学测量系调往武汉，成立武汉测量制图学院。调整后的同济大学，从全国知名的综合性大学变成以土建为主的单科性工科大学。

From 1949, following the unified deployment of the central government, some schools and departments of Tongji were merged into other universities, including those of Literature and Arts, Law, Sciences, and Medicine, as well as such engineering programs in Mechanical Engineering, Electrical Engineering and Shipbuilding. The Affiliated Advanced Industrial Vocational School was moved to Nanjing. Meanwhile, divisions and departments of Civil Engineering, Architecture and Surveying from Qinghua University, Shanghai Jiaotong University, Zhejiang University and Xiamen University were merged into Tongji University. In the second half of 1956, Department of Surveying of Tongji University was relocated to Wuhan for the establishment of Surveying and Cartography Institute of Wuhan. Tongji University, a well-known comprehensive university at that time, was thus restructured to a university that in civil engineering.

■ 院系调整时的宣传条幅

Promotional banners encouraging restructuring among colleges and departments in China

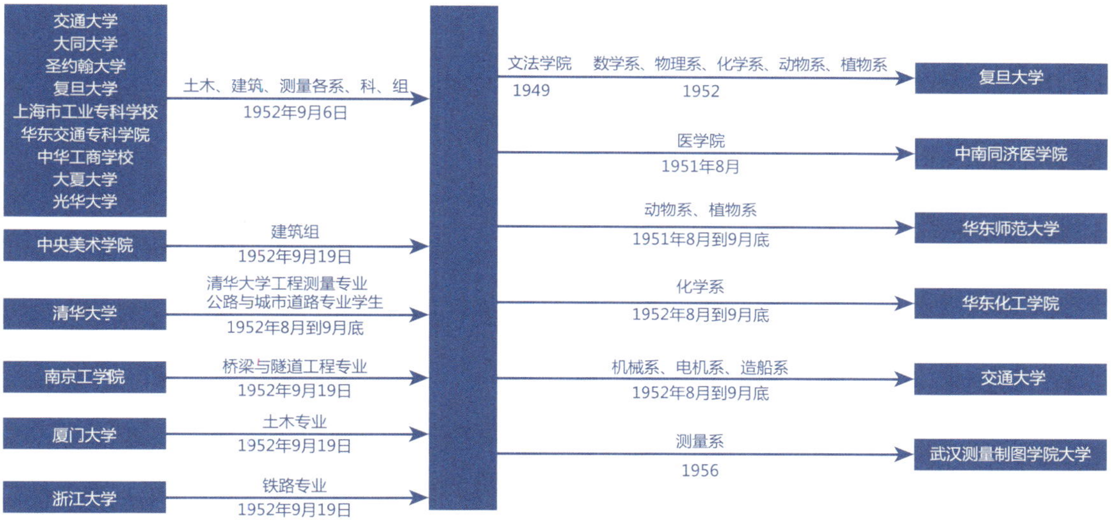

■ 1949 年至 1956 年同济大学院系调整示意图

Restructuring of colleges and departments of Tongji University from 1949 to 1956

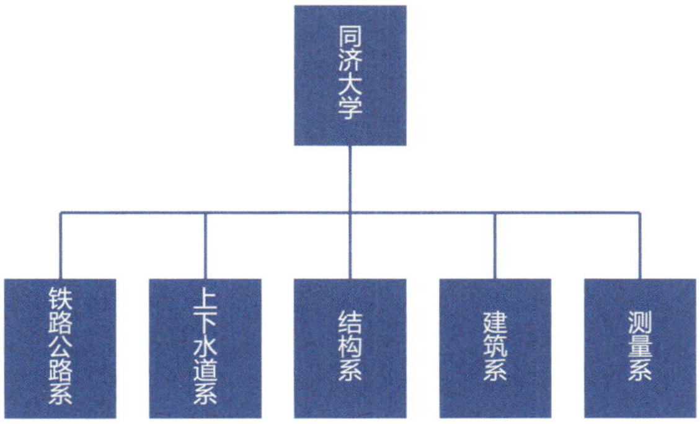

■ 1952 年大规模院系调整后同济大学院系组织结构图

Organizational structure of schools and departments in Tongji University after the nationwide restructuring in 1952

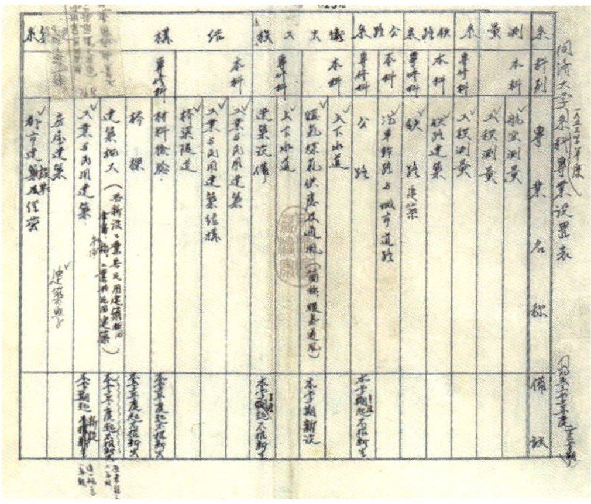

■ 同济大学 1953 年系科专业设置表

Programs of Tongji University in 1953

名师荟萃，兼容并包

Learned Scholars from Home and Abroad

院系调整中，同济大学调入教授 33 人、副教授 6 人，调出教授 36 人，副教授 10 人，共计调入教职工 191 人，调出教职工 172 人。调整结束后，全校师生员工共 3165 人，其中教职工 422 人，汇集了十多所高校一大批著名的学者和教授，这些教授大多留学欧美，也有本土培养的才俊，为同济的工科教育带来了兼容并包的学风。

During the nationwide restructuring of colleges and departments, 33 professors and 6 associate professors were transferred to Tongji University while 36 professors and 10 associate professors out of the university. A total of 191 teaching and administrative staff joined Tongji University while 172 were relocated to other universities. After the restructuring, the number of staff and students amounted to 3165, among which 422 were teaching and administrative staff. A number of established scholars and professors, most of whom with overseas education background, gathered at Tongji from over ten leading universities. They brought with them different styles of teaching and learning and made great contributions to the engineering education of Tongji University.

1952 年 12 月同济大学教授、副教授留学情况览表
(Associate) Professors with overseas Education in Tongji University in December 1952

留学国家 Countries of study	结构系 Department of Structural Engineering	铁路公路系 Department of Rail and Road Engineering	上下水道系 Department of Water Sewage	建筑系 Department of Architecture	测量系 Department of Surveying	其他教研室 Other teaching and research division
英国 UK	丁燮和、俞调梅、康时清 Ding Xiehe, Yu Diaomei, Kang Shiqing	童大埙 Tong Daxun		黄作燊 Huang Zuoshen		张国隆 Zhang Guolong
美国 US	王兴、王达时、王龙甫、朱宝华、沈君敏、祝永年、俞徵、孙绳曾、张问清、曹敬康、黄蕴元、杨培琫、钱钟毅 Wang Xing, Wang Dashi, Wang Longfu, Zhu Baohua, Shen Junmin, Zhu Yongnian, Yu Zheng, Sun Shengzeng, Zhang Wenqing,Cao Jingkang, Huang Yunyuan, Yang Peifeng, Qian Zhongyi	李秉成、陈本瑞、潘承梁 Li Bingcherg, Chen Benrui, Pan Chengliang	李善道、杨钦、裴冠西、谢光华 Li Shandao, Yang Qin, Pei Guanxi, Xie Guanghua	哈雄文、陈植、黄家骅、谭垣、罗邦杰 Ha Xiongwen, Chen Zhi, Huang Jiahua, Tan Yuan, Luo Bangjie	刘宸伟 Liu Chenwei	樊映川 Fan Yingchuan
德国 Germany	李国豪、贾成和 Li Guohao, Jia Chenghe	吴之翰 Wu Zhihan		金经昌、唐英 Jin Jingchang, Tang Ying	夏坚白、叶雪安、顾葆康 Xia Jianba , Ye Xuean, Gu Backang	廖馥君 Liao Fujun
法国 France	周念先 Zhou Nianxian			吴景祥、周方白 Wu Jingxiang, Zhou Fangbai		张镇谦 Zhang Zhenqian
日本 Japan				陈盛铎 Chen Shengduo		
奥地利 Austria				冯纪忠 Feng Jizhong	陈适 Chen Shi	
加拿大 Canada					高时浏 Gao Shiliu	

此时期在同济工科担任专任教师后来成为院士的同济人
Academicians who used to teach engineering course in Tongji

■ 张煦（1913- ），1949 年至 1956 年曾在同济任教（兼职），中国科学院院士。

Professor Zhang Xu (1913-), a part-time teacher with Tongji University from 1949 to 1956, is a member of the Chinese Academy of Sciences.

■ 沙庆林（1930- ），1952 年至 1954 年同济大学任教，中国工程院院士。

Professor Sha Qinglin（1930-), a teacher with Tongji University from 1952 to 1954, is a member of Chinese Academy of Engineering.

■ 戴复东（1928- ），1952 年南京大学工学院建筑系毕业后任教于同济大学，中国工程院院士。

Professor Dai Fudong (1928-), a teacher with Tongji University upon his graduation from the Department of Architecture of Engineering school, Nanjing University in 1952, is a member of the Chinese Academy of Engineering.

1956 年国家确定的一级教授
First-Grade Professor authorized by the State in 1956

■ 李国豪

Professor Li Guohao

1956 年国家确定的二级教授
Second-Grade Professors authorized by the State in 1956

王达时
Professor Wang Dashi

冯纪忠
Professor Feng Jizhong

朱宝华
Professor Zhu Baohua

吴景祥
Professor Wu Jingxiang

童大埙
Professor Tong Daxun

李秉成
Professor Li Bingcheng

陈本端
Professor Chen Benduan

杨钦
Professor Yang Qin

俞调梅
Professor Yu Diaomei

钱钟毅
Professor Qian Zhongyi

谭垣
Professor Tan Yuen

樊映川
Professor Fan Yingchuan

吴之翰
Professor Wu Zhihan

康时清
Professor Kang Shiqing

王龙甫
Professor Wang Longfu

1956 年国家确定的三级教授
Third-Grade Professors authorized by the State in 1956

曹敬康
Professor Cao Jingkang

柴志明
Professor Chai Zhiming

陈超
Professor Chen Chao

丁燮和
Professor Ding Xiehe

杜庆萱
Professor Du Qingxuan

胡家俊
Professor Hu Jiajun

黄家骅
Professor Huang Jiahua

黄学渊
Professor Huang Xueyuan

黄蕴元
Professor Huang Yunyuan

黄 足
Professor Huang Zu

黄作燊
Professor Huang Zuoshen

江之永
Professor Jiang Zhiyong

蒋汉文
Professor Jiang Hanwen

金经昌
Professor Jin Jingchang

李寿康
Professor Li Shoukang

马地泰
Professor Ma Ditai

裴冠西
Professor Pei Guanxi

沈 诚
Professor Shen Cheng

孙青羊
Professor Sun Qingyang

王 兴
Professor Wang Xing

翁朝庆
Professor Weng Chaoqing

吴沈钇
Professor Wu Shenyi

谢光华
Professor Xie Guanghua

许德纪
Professor Xu Deji

许应期
Professor Xu Yingqi

薛卓斌
Professor Xue Zhuobin

俞征
Professor YuZheng

张国隆
Professor Zhang Guolong

张问清
Professor Zhang Wenqing

郑大同
Professor Zheng Datong

周方白
Professor Zhou Fangbai

周念先
Professor Zhou Nianxian

朱振德
Professor Zhu Zhende

祝永年
Professor Zhu Yongnian

庄秉权
Professor Zhuang Bingquan

学习苏联，邦交东德

Learning from JSSR and Linking with DDR

自1952年下半年起，全国高校全面学习苏联，同济大学也不例外。1954年10月，苏联专家陆续来校，担任校、系、专业顾问，对教学、科研工作进行指导。学校组织了大批骨干教师，翻译出版苏联教材，并根据我国的实际情况，在培养目标、专业设置、教学计划、教学大纲、课程设置、教材内容、教学方法和教学组织等方面作了较大调整。同时，学校还加强同东德的学术联系，邀请东德专家来校交流访问。

Since the second half of 1952, universities throughout China were involved in a campaign of all-round learning from the former USSR. There was no exception with Tcngji University. In October 1954, experts from the former USSR joined Tongji University one after another as specialized consultants for teaching and research. Teachers were organized to translate texts from Russian to Chinese and had them published. Meanwhile, substantial adjustments were made in teaching objectives, program planning, guidance and program design, curriculum provision, teaching materials, teaching methods and teaching organization based on the situation in China. In addition, experts from the DDR (the former East Germany) were invited to Tongji University for academic exchanges.

为聘请苏联专家，1954年学校选派专业教师九人为业务翻译员，前往上海俄文专科学校培训，俄专委派外藉教师二人进行小班教学。照片中后排从左起为：江景波、曹善华、俄语老师、孙钧、袁国干、李青岳，前排为朱照宏、郑伟宗、赵骅、皮明才。

In preparation for the coming of experts from the former USSR, nine teachers of Tongji University were selected to receive training in translation for special purposes in Shanghai Russiar Training school. Training was conducted by two Russian teachers in a small class. From left to right in the back row: Jiang Jingbo, Cao Shanhua, a Russian teacher, Sun Jun, Yuan Guogan and Li Qingyue; from left to right in the front row: Zhu Zhaohong, Zheng Weizong, Zhao Hua and Pi Mingcai.

苏联专家来校工作时同校内专家合影，前排左四为苏联专家萨多维奇，左三为结构系主任王龙甫教授，左五为结构系副主任黄蕴元教授，后排左一为结构系副主任张问清教授。

Teachers from the former USSR with their Chinese colleagues at Tongji University. Fourth from left in the front: Mr. Saduoweiqi, an expert from USSR; third from left in the front: Professor Wang Longfu, head of the Department of Structural Engineering; fifth from left in the front: Professor Huang Yunyuan, vice head of the Department of Structural Engineering; first from left in the left: Professor Zhang Wenqing, vice head of the Department of Structural Engineering

在同济大学的苏联专家

Experts from the former USSR at Tongji University

土木系施工组织与计划专家维托希金及翻译汪定国同教职工交流讨论。

Mr. Vitohin, an expert in construction organization and planning from the former USSR, in communication with staff from the Department of Civil Engineering with the help of his interpreter Mr. Wang Dingguo.

苏联专家在给青年教职工上课

An expert from the former USSR teaching with the help of interpreter

苏联桥梁专家斯尼特柯
Mr. Cnitko, an expert in Bridge Engineering from the former USSR

苏联学生与建筑系学生联欢
A friendship party staged by students from the former USSR and the Department of Architecture, Tongji University

建筑系苏联专家克涅亚谢夫
Mr. Kniacef, an expert from the former USSR, teaching at the Department of Architecture

1957 年建筑系邀请民主德国雷德尔教授来同济讲学，为金经昌先生、李德华先生与雷德尔教授在一起。
Professor Raeder from the former DDR, in discussion with Professor Jin Jingchang and Professor Li De, on his lecture tour at Tongji University at the invitation of the Department of Architecture in 1957

1957 年金经昌先生接待民主德国建筑师代表团访问同济
Professor Jin Jingchang receiving a delegation of architects from the former DDR on their visit to Tongji University in 1957

劳动建校，设计先锋

Campus Built with a Distinctive Style

院系调整后，根据新中国经济建设的需要，学校招生规模扩大，师生员工扩增近 1000 人，加之学科方面的变化，校舍日益紧缺。从 1952 年下半年开始，学校开展了劳动建校活动，师生们自己规划、设计、施工，兴建了一大批极具特色的优秀校园建筑，形成了今天四平路校区的雏形。

After the nationwide restructuring of colleges and departments, Tongji University increased its student enrollment in response to the economic development of new China. As a result, the number of staff and students grew to 1,000. The large number of people coupled with disciplinary adjustments brought about a shortage in buildings on campus. From the second half of 1952, a campaign of Building Our Campus with Our Own Hands was launched. Teachers and students of the university planned, designed and constructed a number of buildings with distinctive styles on campus, which shaped the initial landscape of the current Siping Campus of Tongji University.

劳动建校，师生热情高涨

Teachers and students enthusiastic about building a campus with their own hands

■ 1954 年校门设计方案之一

One of the design proposals for entrance of the university in 1954

■ 1955 年校门

Entrance of the university in 1955

■ 1959 年校门

Entrance of the university in 1959

1952 年建成的大草棚，具有礼堂、食堂多种功能。
A duel-functional thatched building, an auditorium and a dining hall, completed in 1952

1950 年代校园规划模型
A campus model of the 1950s

解放楼旁的草棚教室
Thatched classrooms beside Jiefang Building

1953 年学校成立校舍设计处，部分教师和建筑学毕业班学生参与设计华东地区多所院校校舍，图为 1953 年黄毓麟和哈雄文设计的文远楼，是我国最早、也是唯一的典型包豪斯风格建筑，被列为第四批受保护的“上海市优秀历史建筑”，被载入《世界建筑史》和《中国建筑史》。
Wenyuan Building, built in 1954, has been the earliest and the only Bauhaus-style building in China. It has been listed as one of the Outstanding Historical Buildings in Shanghai, and recorded in *History of World Architecture* and *History of China Architecture*.

■ 青年楼和解放楼

Qingnian Building and Jiefang Building

■ 胜利楼

Shengli Building

■ 1955 年吴景祥、戴复东、吴庐生合作设计的中心大楼，即今天的南北楼，是学院派代表作，建筑外貌简洁匀称，具有中西古典建筑韵味。

The Central Buildings (the current South and North Teaching Buildings), co-designed by Wu Jingxiang, Dai Fudong and Wu Lusheng, were representative of academic architecture: simple and symmetrical with a classical styles from both Chinese and western buildings.

1956 年李德华、王吉螽、陈琬、童勤华、赵汉光、郑肖成等教师合作设计的同济工会俱乐部开始兴建。该建筑采用现代建筑空间处理手法。1993 年中国建筑学会四十周年时授予该作品“中国建筑学会优秀建筑创作奖”。

Tongji Staff Club co-designed by teachers of architecture Li Dehua, Wang Jizhong, Chen Wan, Tong Qinhua, Zhao Hanguang, Zheng Xiaocheng, started its construction in 1956. The modern planning of architectural space was embodied in this building. In 1993, the building was awarded with an Outstanding Architectural Design by the Architectural Society of China in celebration of the society's fortieth anniversary.

陈从周教授设计的三好坞

Sanhaowu Garden designed by Professor Chen Congzhou

1961 年建成的大礼堂，采用当时最先进的薄壳拱型结构屋架，全场没有一根立柱，建成时被称为“远东第一拱”，被列入上海市第四批优秀历史建筑。

The auditorium built in 1961 was referred to as the First Arch in the Far East, for there was not a single column inside the auditorium with the application of the most advanced shell-arch structure for the roof truss. It has been included in the fourth group of Outstanding Historic Buildings in Shanghai.

工程试验馆

Engineering laboratory

旭日楼

Xuri Building

百废待兴，热情高涨

Reconstruction with High Spirit

新中国成立后，百废待兴。院系调整后至“文化大革命”开始前，以知名教授牵头的土建各专业，师资队伍充实，教学态度认真。学校不时邀请各专业领域内的知名学者来校讲座，在培养方法上继续秉持课堂学习、工厂操作和课外实习相结合的原则，呈现出朝气蓬勃的气象。

After the founding of new China, full-scale reconstruction was under way. During the time between the nationwide restructuring of colleges and departments and the launch of the Cultural Revolution, programs in civil engineering led by famous professors had thrived with joint efforts made by hard working and responsible teachers. Well-known experts from different fields were invited to give lectures in Tongji. The university was filled with flourishing vitality with implementation of integrating classroom study with factory internship and field work.

结构系俞载道教授（左三）正在指导学生

Professor Yu Zaidao (third from left) from the Department of Structural Engineering supervising students

黄家骅教授指导学生设计大礼堂多用餐桌

Professor Huang Jiahua instructing a student to design a multi-functional dining table for an auditorium

樊映川教授编写的《高等数学讲义》

Lecture Notes on Advanced Mathematics compiled by Professor Fan Yingchuan

程守洙、江之永教授编写的《普通物理学》

General Physics compiled by Professor Cheng Shouzhu and Professor Jiang Zhiyong

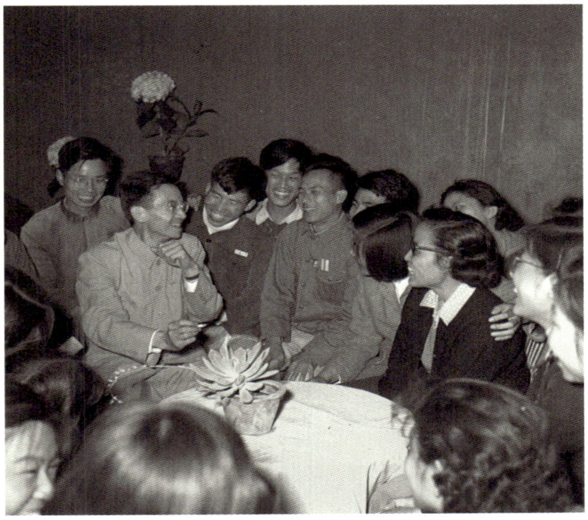

著名建筑学家梁思成（左二）来校访问

Mr. Liang Sicheng (second from left), a famous architect, with teachers and students on his visit to Tongji University

理论学习
Theoretical study

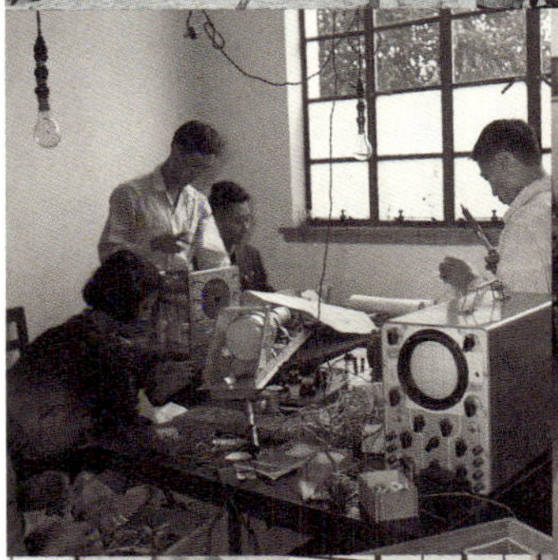

操作实践
Practice

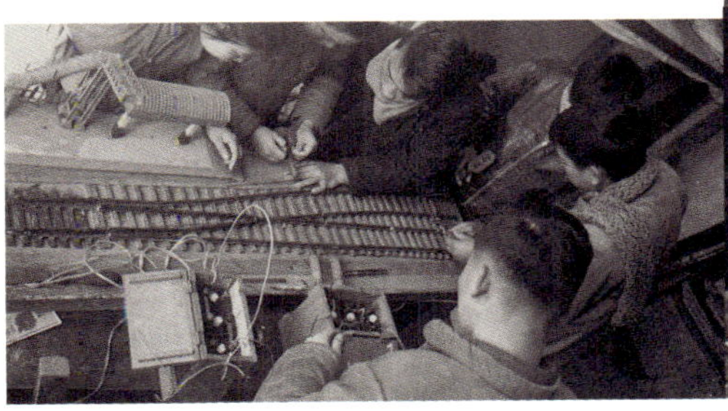

学生在工厂实习

Student at the internship factory

毕业设计、答辩

Graduation designs and oral defense

广开学路，多方探索

Exploration of Graduate and Correspondence Programs

1953 年底，同济大学根据高教部《高等学校培养研究生暂行办法（草案）》，招收了第一届 9 名研究生。1956 年，学校效仿苏联在全国首次举行副博士研究生入学考试。同年 9 月，函授部举行开学典礼，是较早开展函授教育的高校之一。此阶段，学校遵循国家对外政策，以土建学科优势招收友好邻国及非洲国家的留学生，为这些国家培养建设人才。

At the end of 1953, Tongji University enrolled nine graduate students in accordance with the *Interim Procedure for Graduate Study of Higher Education (Draft)*. Tongji University held the First Entrance Examination for Pre-doctoral Program in China after the fashion of the former USSR in 1956. In September of the same year, an opening ceremony was held for a correspondence program at Tongji University, the first of its kind in China. During this time, following a national foreign policy, the university provided training to students from friendly neighboring countries and from Africa in the field of civil engineering and architecture.

■ 1956 年，同济大学举行副博士研究生入学考试，在全国尚属首次，前排左一为结构系主任王龙甫，左二位副主任黄蕴元，左三、左四以及第二排左一为苏联专家。

The First Entrance Examination for Pre-doctoral Program in China was organized by and held at Tongji University in 1956. First from left in the front: Mr. Wang Longfu, head of the Department of Structural Engineering; second from left: Mr. Huang Yunyuan, vice head of the Department of Structural Engineering; third and fourth from left and first from left in the back: experts from the former USSR

■ 道路系副博士初试

Preliminary examination for the Pre-doctoral program at the Department of Road Engineering

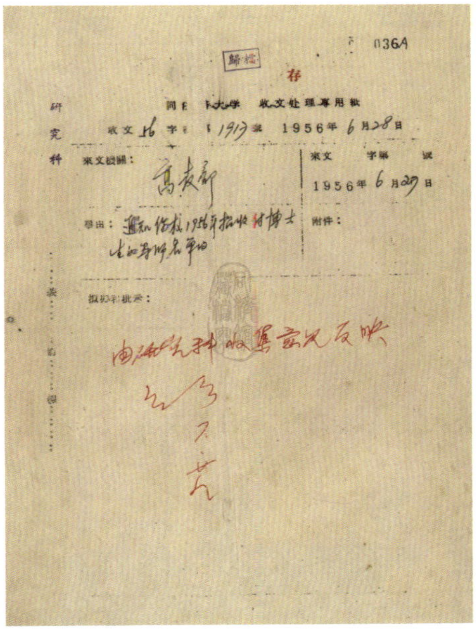

0364

存

1956年6月28日

1956年6月29日

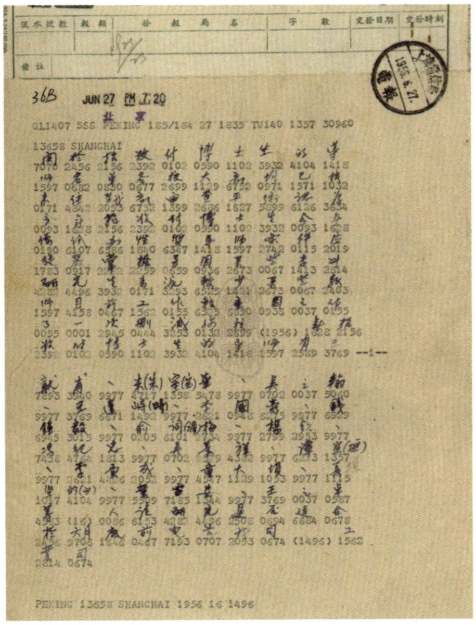

PEKING 13658 SHANGHAI 1956 16 1496

■ 高教部批准同济大学第一批副博士导师名单的电报

A list of first supervisors of the pre-doctoral candidates endorsed by the Ministry of Higher Education

1956 年 9 月，函授部开学典礼。

Opening ceremony for the correspondence program in September 1956

首届函授生毕业设计答辩

Oral examination on graduation designs of the first correspondence students

工民建首届函授毕业生毕业典礼

Graduation ceremony for the first correspondence program graduates of Civil Engineering

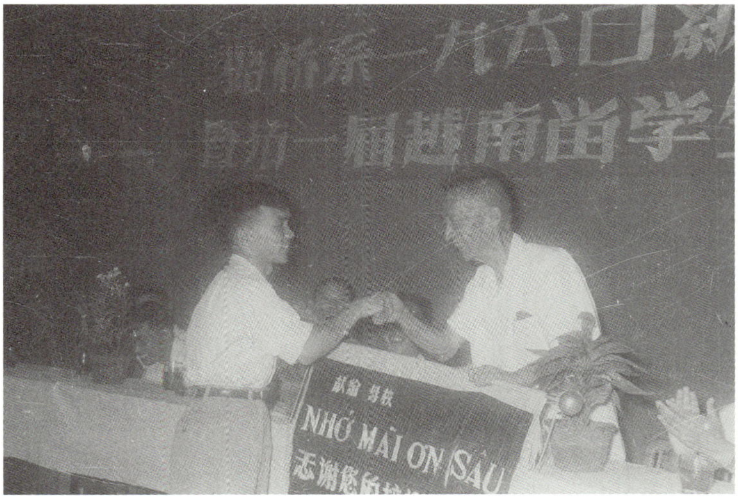

第一届越南留学生毕业，副教务长吴之翰代表学校接受留学生致谢赠旗。

Mr. Wu Zhihan, Vice Dean of the university, receiving a pennant from the first Vietnamese graduates.

越南留学生从同济毕业后回国成为技术骨干

Vietnamese graduates from Tongji University working as engineers in Vietnam

苏联学生来同济交流

Students from the former USSR on a visiting tour to Tongji University

整合设备，专人专管

Integrated Facilities Under Special Care

院系调整的同时，相应学科的教学实验设备一并调整。同济大学先后成立了材料试验馆、工程试验室、暖通实验室、道路材料实验室、结构实验室、水工实验室等，为教学及科研工作提供基础。1954 年，为加强教学上的科学研究工作，学校成立专门科研管理机构，鼓励教职工和学生开展科研创新。

During the restructuring of colleges and departments, facilities for teaching and experiments for various disciplines were reallocated accordingly. Tongji University established laboratories for material science, engineering, HVAC, road material, structural engineering and hydraulics, which laid a firm foundation for teaching and research. In 1954, a research management section was founded to encourage research in teaching among teachers and students.

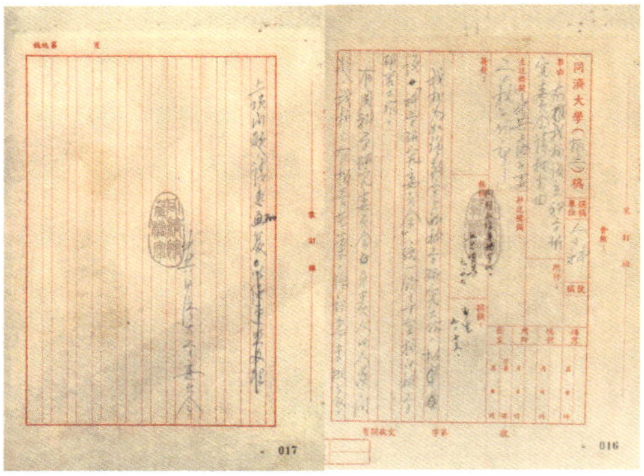

1954 年，同济大学请示设立科学研究委员会的函。

Tongji University submitted an application letter of Application for the establishment of a Scientific Research Committee in 1954

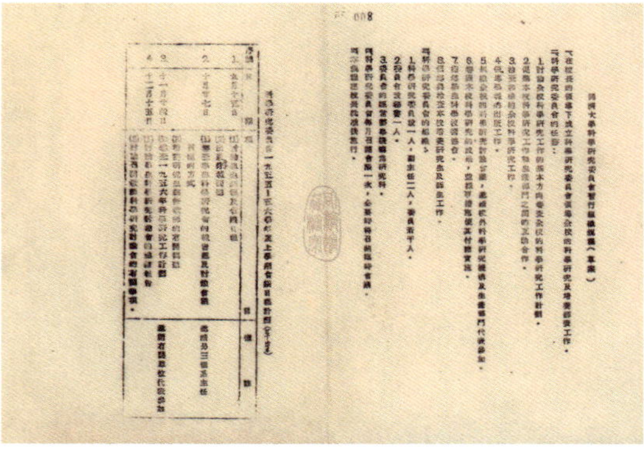

《同济大学科学研究委员会暂行组织规程（草案）》

Provisional Organizational Regulations of the Scientific Research Committee of Tongji University (Draft)

材料实验室

Material laboratory

暖通实验室

HVAC laboratory

道路材料实验室

Road material laboratory

工程试验馆压力实验

A pressure test in the engineering laboratory

■ 水利实验室

Hydraulic laboratory

■ 材料力学实验室

Material mechanics laboratory

■ 声学实验室

Acoustic laboratory

■ 水工实验室

Hydro-engineering laboratory

■ 结构实验室

Structural Engineering laboratory

■ 力学实验室

Laboratory of Mechanics

师生互动，交流学术

Academic Interaction Among Teachers and Students

随着科研制度的完善，科研交流活动日益频繁。1955 年 11 月，同济大学召开上海高校第一次学生科学技术讨论会，会上报告了 60 位本科生和 8 位研究生的研究成果，1956 年 5 月，学校召开第一次教师科学研究讨论会，全国 110 多个单位及 800 多名代表参加了会议。此外，学校不定期举行各种研究讨论会、成果展览会，交流科研经验及最新成果。

With the improvement of scientific research system, communications in scientific research were increasingly active. In November 1955, Tongji University hosted the First Student Conference in Science and Technology for institutions of higher learning in Shanghai. Sixty undergraduate students and eight postgraduate students reported their research findings during the conference. Tongji University hosted the First National Teachers' Conference in Science and Technology in May 1956. More than 800 representatives from 110 institutions of higher learning participated in the conference. Besides, seminars and achievement exhibitions were held in Tongji University for exchange and display of research results.

1955 年 11 月，同济大学在上海高校中第一次召开学生科学技术讨论会。

The first Student Conference in Science and Technology for institutions of higher learning in Shanghai was held in Tongji University in November 1955.

鉄路系同學在張景豐教授的幫助下，認眞修改着自己的報告。↑

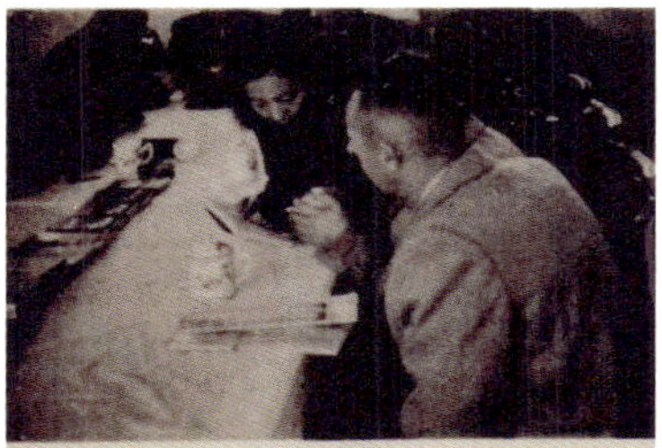

對討論會中的優良報告將給予獎勵、圖爲蘇聯專家在評獎會前，觀看即將發下的奬品的一部分。↑

蘇聯專家阿格羅斯金對如何召開學生科學技術討論會，介紹了寶貴的經驗。↑

十九日下午，廿一日上午各系分別舉行了分組討論會。圖爲道路與橋梁分組討論會會場。↑

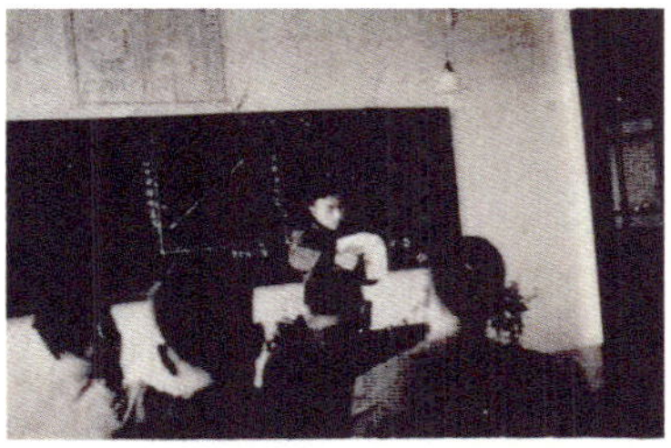

同學的科學報告準備好了之後，先在教研組內提出初步報告。上圖是工業與民用建築結構專業四年級張雪亮同學在教研組試講情形。↑

結構建築分組施工技術及組織計劃小組會會場的一角。↑

■ 同济大学第一次学生科学技术讨论会会场

Panel discussions during the First Student Conference in Science and Technology for institutions of higher learning in Shanghai

■ 1956 年 5 月，学校召开第一次科学讨论会。

The First National Teachers' Conference in Science and Technology was held in Tongji University in May 1956.

■ 1956 年第一次科学讨论会竹材第一分组会

A presentation on bamboo materials in Session One of the First National Teachers' Conference in Science and Technology

■ 1956 年第一次科学讨论会施工分组会

A presentation at the Construction Session of the First National Teachers' Conference in Science and Technology

■ 1959 年路桥系科学研究报告会

A seminar at the Department of Road and Bridge in 1959

■ 城建系学生科研报告会，发言者为李国豪教务长。

Dr. Li Guohao, dean of the university, delivering a speech to students at a seminar in the Department of Urban Construction

■ 在大草棚举办高校科技成果展览会

Exhibition of research achievements of institutions of higher learning in the thatched hall

■ 1950 年代同济科学研究展览

Exhibition of research achievements of Tongji University in the 1950s

■ 1960 年，研制成功全国第一台液压挖掘机，获得建工部嘉奖。

Commendation by the Ministry of Construction and Engineering for the first hydraulic excavator developed in 1960

■ 师生一起发明群钻

Drill cluster invented by teachers and students

■ 1958 年，上海拟建三千人歌剧院，建筑系师生参与，黄作燊、王宗瑗主持。所提交方案功能合理、室内声学达到很高标准，并采用了新型悬索挑台和屋盖结构。图为学生们在歌剧院模型前。

Model of a 3000-seat opera house in Shanghai, design of which was led by Mr. Huang Zuoshen and Mr. Wang Zongyuan with participation of students from the Department of Architecture in 1958. The proposed design of the opera house which had a structure with a suspended terrace and roof, was reasonable in its function and sophisticated in its indoor acoustics.

师生一起搞科研

Teachers and students active in research

1956 年，学校举行首次科研成果表彰会

The First Research Achievement Commendation Ceremony in 1956

1955 年陈从周先生带领学生在苏州园林进行古建筑测绘，他们的测绘成果后来编录在《苏州园林》一书中。

Mr. Chen Congzhou, on top of the building, with students on a mapping investigation of classical buildings in gardens at Suzhou in 1955, results of which were incorporated into the his book *Gardens in Suzhou* later

建筑系谭垣教授主持设计的上海人民英雄纪念碑，获设计竞赛一等奖。

Monument to People's Heroes of Shanghai, designed by Professor Tan Yuan from Department of Architecture, won the first prize in a design competition.

教育革命，摸索前进

Educational Revolution and Great Leap Forward

1957 年开始，顺应全国政治形势，同济大学开展“整风整改”、“大跃进”“教育大革命”等系列政治运动，跃进风、浮夸风盛行，大学的正常秩序遭破坏。但这一阶段，学校尝试增设了机、电、数理方面的专业，在打基础、建队伍、摸方向等方面也做了一些符合教育发展规律的工作。

Since 1957, in response to the national political situation, Tongji University launched a series of political campaigns of Rectification, Great Leap Forward and Educational Revolution. The tendency of great leap forward and exaggeration prevailed and the normal order of the university was destroyed. In spite of the turmoil, Tongji University managed to expand its size of engineering by setting up programs in mechanics, electrics, mathematics and physics, and therefore laid a firm foundation in staff capacity building and in further development of the university.

■ 1959 年“大跃进”动员大会

Meeting to launch the campaign of Great Leap Forward in 1959

■ 技术革新现场会

A talk on technological innovation

■ “跃进炉”，大炼钢铁。

A self-made steel furnace for steelmaking during the Great Leap Forward

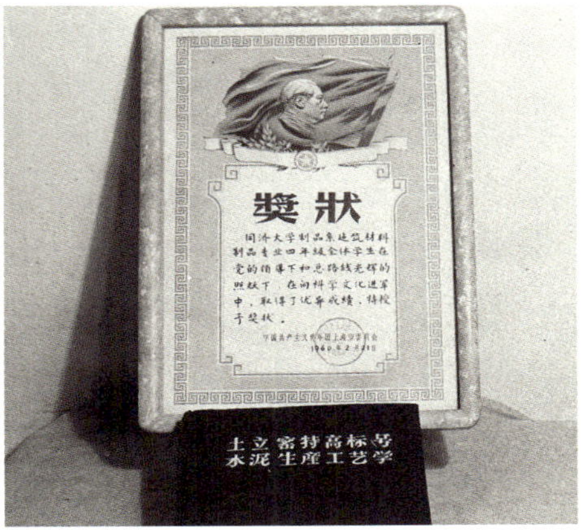

■ “大跃进”中制成高强度水泥

High-strength cement made during the Great Leap Forward

■ 测量系工农班学员上课

A teacher demonstrating a surveying device to Class of Workers and Peasants at the Department of Surveying

1958 年，建工系 300 余名师生去戚墅堰机车厂工地，开展教育与生产相结合工作，参加扩建厂房。

Over 300 teachers and students from the Department of Construction Engineering working on the construction site of the Qi Shuyan Locomotive Factory to promote the combination of education with production and participating in the construction of factory buildings in 1958

1958 建筑系部分青年教师提出成立建筑设计院作为师生实习场所，校部同意，于是成立同济建筑设计院。图为后来在设计院实习的学生们。

Students on internship at the Tongji Institute of Architectural Design, which was established by the university at the suggestion of a group of young teachers from the Department of Architecture in 1958

“大跃进”中的评比喜报

Commendations during the Great Leap Forward

1958 年学生在马桥镇参加劳动

Students active in the field of Maqiao Town in 1958

1958 年人民公社运动时期，学生去郊区为当地居民做人民公社规划，图为学生为解放公社进行规划设计。

Students doing planning and design of people's commune for the local peasants from Jiefang Commune during the commune movement in 1958

路桥系“教育革命”鸣辩园地

Discussions on Educational Revolution on the walled posters at the Department of Road and Bridge

1958 年王吉螽先生在马桥镇给学生现场上课，介绍规划设计方案。

Mr. Wang Jizhong teaching on site introducing a planning and design proposal in 1958

城规专业“跃进大会”

Launch of Leap Forward at the Department of Urban Planning

文革十年，逆水行舟

Hard Time During Cultural Revolution

1966 年 5 月，全国开始“无产阶级文化大革命”，同济大学大批教职工、学生遭受迫害，正常的教学科研秩序被破坏。此阶段的“教育革命”，由学校与施工单位、设计单位三结合成立“五七公社”；教职员进“五七干校”接受贫下中农再教育；派出教改实践队探索“办学方向”；工农兵“上大学、管大学、改造大学”和“厂校挂钩”等为主要内容。

Great Proletarian Cultural Revolution started throughout the country in May 1966. The normal teaching order was disrupted when a large number of teaching and administrative staff and students from Tongji University were under political persecution. During this period, the Educational Revolution was carried out in the following ways. A May Seventh Commune was jointly organized by Tongji University, a construction unit and a design unit; the teaching and administrative staff were sent to the May Seventh Cadres' School to receive re-education from poor peasants; an education reform group was dispatched to explore Educational Direction; workers, peasants and soldiers entered, managed and reformed universities; and universities were linked with factories.

在安徽“五七干校”劳动的教师们

Teachers at work in the May Seventh Cadres' School

1970 年部分教师被送往安徽“五七干校”劳动，休息时间集体合唱自娱自乐。

Teachers singing in chorus to entertain themselves during break time in the May Seventh Cadre School in 1970

1970 年，首届“工农兵学员”入学

The first group of worker-peasant-soldier students on a welcoming ceremony at Tongji University in 1970

工农兵学员在学习

Worker- peasant-soldier students in study

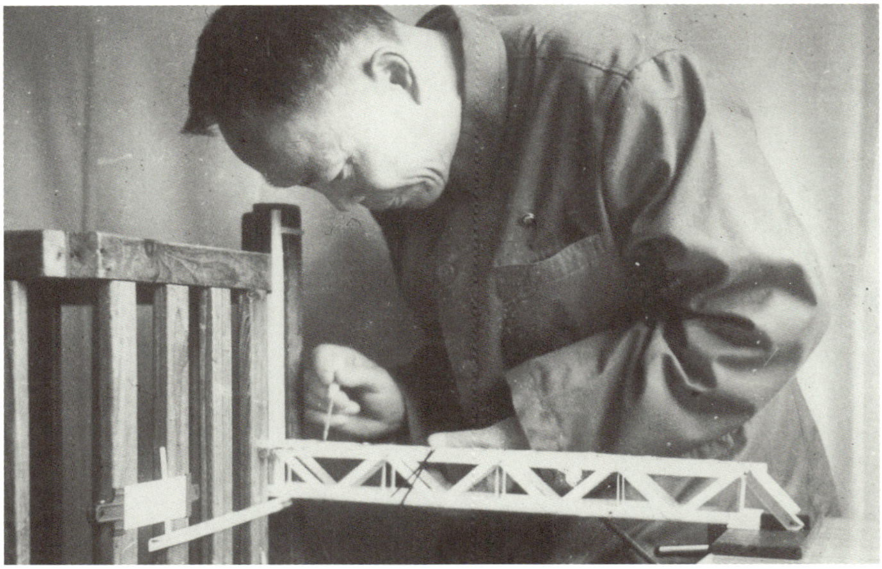

李国豪受禁期间，凭记忆分析武汉长江大桥产生晃动的原因，在家进行模拟试验演算抖振问题并获得1978年全国科学大会重大科技成果奖。

Mr. Li Guohao, during his imprisonment, analyzed the cause of the shiver of Wuhan Yangtze River Bridge out of his memory and conducted simulation test at home to calculate buffeting of the bridge, for which he won a prize for significant achievement in science and technology in the National Science and Technology Conference 1978.

1974年同济参与设计的万人体育馆

The 10,000-seat Stadium of Shanghai co-designed by Tongji University in 1974

1971年由同济大学电视塔设计小组设计的上海电视塔，1974年建成，高210米，位于南京西路青海路，该塔在东方明珠电视塔建成后拆除。

Shanghai TV Tower designed by Tongji University in 1971 completed its contruction in 1974. The tower was 210m tall and was located on Nanjing West Road off Qinghai Road. It was dismantled after the completion of the Oriental Pearl TV Tower in Pudong.

多才多艺，积极乐观

Keeping Optimistic Against the Odds

"惟有健康之身体，方能阐发深邃之学理"，为保证在德、智、体、美方面得到发展，师生们每天都有一定的时间进行课余文化娱乐和体育锻炼。20 世纪五、六十年代的同济校园，汇集了一批多才多艺的教师和爱好广泛的学生。

"Deep thoughts reside in only healthy bodies". In order to ensure all-round development of students, teachers and students took part in cultural and recreational activities and did exercises after school every day. There were a large number of teachers and students with versatile interests at Tongji University during the 1950s and 1960s.

校长夏坚白参加校运会铅球比赛

President Xia Jianbai doing a shot put at a university sports meeting

建筑系黄作燊教授参加学校短跑比赛

Professor Huang Zuoshen from Department of Architecture taking part in a short race

1955 年新年师生舞会

A dance party on the New Year's Eve of 1955

建筑系陈从周教授在联欢会上吹笛子

Professor Chen Congzhou from Department of Architecture playing flute in a party

建筑系金石声教授的摄影作品。金经昌教授以金石声为笔名，长期从事业余摄影，解放前参加三友影会，主编《飞鹰》摄影杂志，任中国摄影家协会第三届理事、上海分会副主席。

Photograph by Professor Jin Shisheng from the Department of Architecture

Professor. Jin Jingchang, under the penname of Jin Shisheng, was engaged in amateur photography for many years. He joined the Sanyou Photography Society before liberation and served as the editor-in-chief of *Eagle*, a photo magazine of photography. He was a board member on the third Session of China Photographers Association and the Vice Chairman of Shanghai branch of the association.

学生赛诗、赛歌、赛画大会

Students at competition for poem composing, singing and painting

建筑系陈从周教授的画作，陈从周教授不仅是闻名的古建筑、园林艺术家，还擅长文、史、兼工诗词、绘画。

A painting by Professor Chen Congzhou from the Department of Architecture Professer Chen, a renowned classical Chinese garden designer, was good at literature, history, poetry and painting.

建筑系学生在排练舞蹈

A rehearsal of dancing by students from the Department of Architecture

建工系学生画漫画

Cartoons drawn by students from the Department of Construction

师生与南斯拉夫客人间的友谊足球赛

A friendship football match between teachers and students from Tongji University and visitors from Yugoslavia

建筑系朱膺教授的画作

A painting by Professor Zhu Ying from the Department of Architecture

学校举行国庆十周年油画展

An exhibition of oil paintings organized by the university to mark the 10th Anniversary of the National Day

学生在建筑工地上同工人进行篮球比赛

Students playing basketball with workers on a construction site

课间广播体操

Exercises between classes

烈火年代，百炼成钢

Rebirth During Hard Times

尽管受到政治运动的影响，但由于同济传统的影响和一批精英教师的存在，严谨求实的精神得以承传。某种程度上，生产与劳动相结合的时代风气使同济工程教育重视实践的特点得以保持。在相对艰难的条件下，同济学子积极上进，好动手，勤钻研，涌现了一批杰出人才，其中有 22 位工科学子后来成为中国科学院和中国工程院院士。

Although the political movement had adverse impact across the nation, the university managed to remain its spirit of pursuing integrity and truth under the influence of the time-honored tradition of Tongji University and the persistence of some honest teachers. To some extent, the combination of education with production played a positive role in the Tongji's preservation of its practice-oriented policy in engineering education. Under the harsh conditions, the self-motivated students never gave up their efforts in practice and exploration, which helped produce a number of outstanding engineers in China. Twenty two of them later became members of Chinese Academy of Sciences and/or Chinese Academy of Engineering.

李猷嘉，1953 年毕业于同济大学结构系工业与民用建筑结构专业，中国工程院院士。

Mr. Li Youjia who graduated from the Industrial and Civil Construction program, Department of Structural Engineering of Tongji University in 1953 is a member of Chinese Academy of Engineering.

沈世钊，1953 年毕业于同济大学结构系工业与民用建筑结构专业，中国工程院院士。

Mr. Shen Shizhao who graduated from the Industrial and Civil Construction program, Department of Structural Engineering of Tongji University in 1953 is a member of Chinese Academy of Engineering.

陈新，1953 年毕业于同济大学结构系桥梁隧道专业，中国工程院院士。

Mr. Chen Xin who graduated from the Bridge and Tunnel program, Department of Structural Engineering of Tongji University in 1953 is a member of Chinese Academy of Engineering.

项海帆，1955 年毕业于同济大学道路与桥梁系道路桥梁与隧道专业，中国工程院院士。

Mr. Xiang Haifan who graduated from the Bridge and Tunnel program, Department of Structural Engineering of Tongji University in 1955 is a member of Chinese Academy of Engineering.

沈祖炎，1955 年同济大学结构系工业与民用建筑结构专业本科毕业，中国工程院院士。

Mr. Shen Zuyan who graduated from the Industrial and Civil Construction program, Department of Structural Engineering of Tongji University in 1955 is a member of Chinese Academy of Engineering.

魏敦山，1955 年于同济大学建筑系建筑设计专业毕业，中国工程院院士。

Mr. Wei Dunshan who graduated from architectural design, Department of Architecture of Tongji University in 1955 is a member of Chinese Academy of Engineering.

■ 邹德慈，1955 年毕业于同济大学建筑系城市规划专业，中国工程院院士。

Mr. Zou Deci who graduated from architectural design, Department of Architecture of Tongji University in 1955 is a member of Chinese Academy of Engineering.

■ 许厚泽，1955 年毕业于同济大学测量系，中国科学院院士。

Mr. Xu Houze who graduated from the Department of Surveying of Tongji University in 1955 is a member of Academic Divisions of Chinese Academy of Engineering.

■ 范立础， 1955 年毕业于同济大学道路与桥梁系道路桥梁与隧道专业， 中国工程院院士。

Mr. Fan Lichu who graduated from the Bridge and Tunnel program, Department of Structural Engineering of Tongji University in 1955 is a member of Chinese Academy of Engineering.

■ 董石麟，1955 年毕业于同济大学结构系工业与民用建筑结构专业，中国工程院院士。

Mr. Dong Shilin who graduated from the Industrial and Civil Construction program, Department of Structural Engineering of Tongji University in 1955 is a member of Chinese Academy of Engineering.

■ 宁津生，1956 年毕业于同济大学测量系，中国工程院院士。

Mr. Ning Jinsheng who graduated from the Department of Surveying of Tongji University in 1955 is a member of Chinese Academy of Engineering.

■ 钟万勰，1952 年至 1956 年在同济大学攻读桥梁与隧道工程专业，中国工程院院士。

Mr. Zhong Wanxie who was on the Bridge and Tunnel program from 1952-1956, Department of Structural Engineering of Tongji University is a member of Chinese Academy of Engineering.

■ 钱易，1956 年毕业于同济大学卫生工程系，中国工程院院士。

Ms. Qian Yi who graduated from the Department of Health Engineering in 1956 is a member of Chinese Academy of Engineering.

■ 张祖勋，1955 年考入同济大学测绘系，1956 年随测绘系迁往武汉，中国工程院院士。

Mr. Zhang Zuxun who was admitted to study at the Department of Surveying of Tongji University in 1955 and moved to Wuhan following the relocation of the department in 1956, is a member of Chinese Academy of Engineering

■ 陈俊勇，1955 年考入同济大学测绘系，1956 年随测绘系迁往武汉，中国科学院院士。

Mr. Chen Junyong who was admitted to study at the Department of Surveying of Tongji University in 1955 and moved to Wuhan following the relocation of the department in 1956, is a member of Chinese Academy of Engineering.

■ 朱能鸿，1960 年毕业于同济大学建筑系城市规划专业，中国工程院院士。

Mr. Zhu Nenghong who graduated from Urban Planning program, Department of Architecture of Tongji University in 1960 is a member of Chinese Academy of Engineering.

■ 叶可明，1962 年毕业于同济大学函授部工业与民用建筑专业，中国工程院院士。

Mr. Ye Keming who graduated from Correspondence program in Industrial and Civil Engineering of Tongji University in 1962 is a member of Chinese Academy of Engineering.

■ 郑颖人，1961 年 9 月至 1962 年 9 月在同济大学地下工程专业进修，中国工程院院士。

Mr. Zheng Yingren who pursued his further study in Underground Engineering of Tongji University from September 1961 to September 1962 is a member of Chinese Academy of Engineering.

■ 梁文灏，1964 年毕业于同济大学铁道建筑专业， 中国工程院院士。

Mr. Liang Wenhao who graduated from the Railway Construction program of Tongji University in 1964 is a member of Chinese Academy of Engineering.

■ 郑时龄，1965 年毕业于同济大学建筑系建筑学专业，中国科学院院士。

Mr. Zheng Shiling who graduated from the architecture program, Department of Architecture of Tongji University in 1965 is a member of Chinese Academy of Sciences.

■ 潘云鹤，1970 年毕业于同济大学建筑系建筑学专业，中国工程院院士。

Mr. Pan Yunhe who graduated from the architecture program, Department of Architecture of Tongji University in 1970 is a member of Chinese Academy of Engineering.

■ 段宁，1975 年毕业于同济大学环境工程专业，中国工程院院士。

Duan Ning who graduated from the Environmental Engineering program of Tongji University in 1975 is a member of Chinese Academy of Engineering.

第五章 Chapter V（1976.10-1991.12）

两个转变，承前启后
Two Transformations Bridging Past and Future

1976 年 10 月“文化大革命”结束，学校提出了“向以对德联系及德语教学为主转变，逐步从土建类为主向理工多科性方向转变”的指导方针，迎来了工程教育史上第二个发展高峰。尤其在工科布局和多学科建设上取得重要进展，为世纪之交工程教育的繁盛打下了坚实基础。

The Cultural Revolution came to an end in October 1976. Tongji University proposed to take two transformations as the guideline for university development to transform to a German-focused development, i.e. teaching in German and building links with Germany; and to transform from civil engineering-focused university to a university with multiple engineering disciplines. The successful implementation of the two transformations helped the university enter the second phase of rapid development in its history of engineering education. In particular, the university made great progress in developmental planning of engineering education and in its multi-disciplinary construction, which laid a firm foundation for the prosperity of engineering education at the turn of the century.

拨乱反正，两个转变

Two Transformations after the Cultural Revolution

“文化大革命”结束后，李国豪校长提出了“两个转变”的历史性决策，即由“向以对德联系及德语教学为主转变，逐步从土建类为主向理工多科性方向转变”，作为新时期的办学思想。

After the ten-year Cultural Revolution, President Li Guohao made the historic decision of taking Two Transformations as a guiding principle for the university development in the new era: to transform to a German-focused development, i.e. teaching in German and building links with Germany; and to transform from a university that specialized in civil engineering to a university with multi-disciplines in science and engineering,

拨乱反正

Bringing Order out of Chaos

■ 同济师生愤怒声讨“四人帮”罪行

Teachers and students of Tongji University denouncing the Gang of Four for their flagrant crimes

■ 同济师生庆祝粉碎“四人帮”游行

Teachers and students of Tongji University on demonstration in celebration of the demise of the Gang of Four

1978 年 3 月，在我国科学事业发展史上具有重大历史意义的全国科学大会在北京人民大会堂举行，同济有四项科技成果获奖。图为参加全国科学大会的四位教师（左起：翁智远、冯纪忠、李国豪、王开发）

Tongji professors attending the National Science Conference held in the Great Hall of the People in Beijing in March 1978. Tongji University received four awards of scientific and technological achievements on the conference, which played a vital role in the development of sciences and technology in China. The picture shows the four professors attending the conference (from left: Weng Zhiyuan, Feng Jizhong, Li Guohao and Wang Kaifa).

1978 年校学术委员会建立，各系建立了学术小组。

Academic groups set up in each department following the establishment of the Academic Committee of Tongji University in 1978

1978 年全校科技表彰大会

Science and Technology Commendation Conference of Tongji University in 1978

金经昌教授文革后第一次上课

Professor Jin Jingchang teaching the first class after the Cultural Revolution

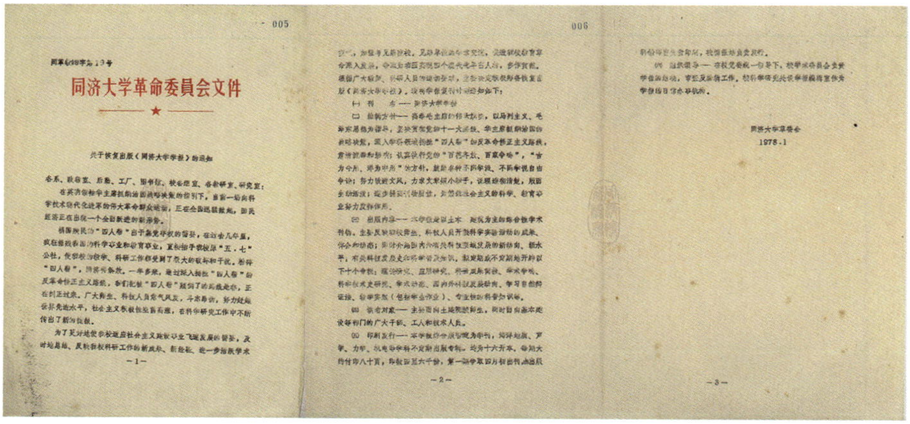

005

同济大学革命委员会文件

关于恢复出版《同济大学学报》的通知

-1-

006

-2-

-3-

"文革"中被迫停刊的《同济大学学报》复刊通知

Notice of resuming the publication of *Journal of Tongji University* which was suspended during the Cultural Revolution

两个转变
Two Transformations

■ 1978 年，方毅副总理来校视察，校领导对其谈到“两个转变”的设想。
Vice Premier Fang Yi on an inspection tour to the university in 1978, during which he was briefed on the Two Transformations

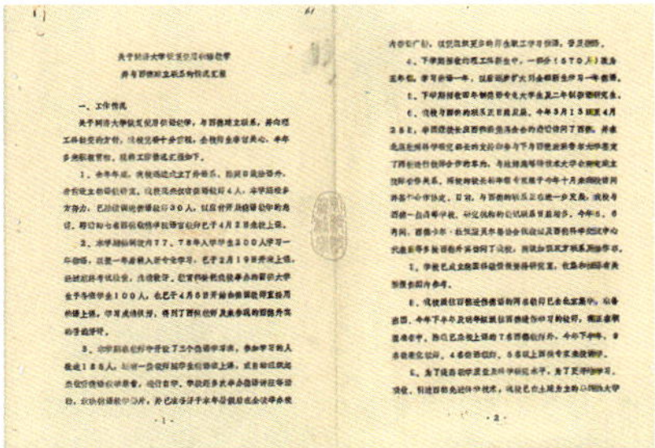

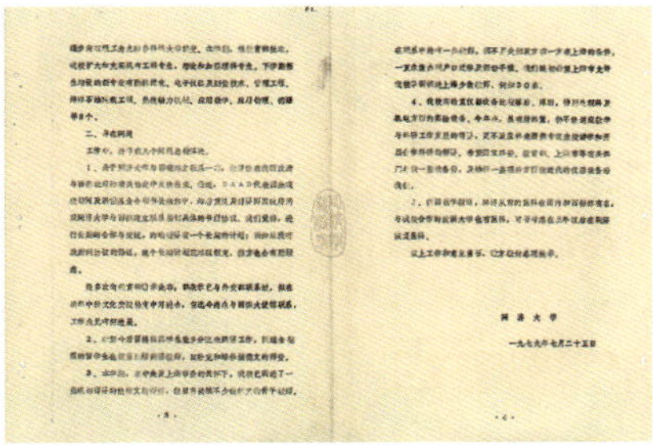

■ 1979 年 7 月 25 日《关于同济大学恢复使用德语教学并与西德建立联系的情况汇报》
Report on *Tongji University's Establishing Links with West Germany and Resuming Teaching in German* dated on July 25, 1979

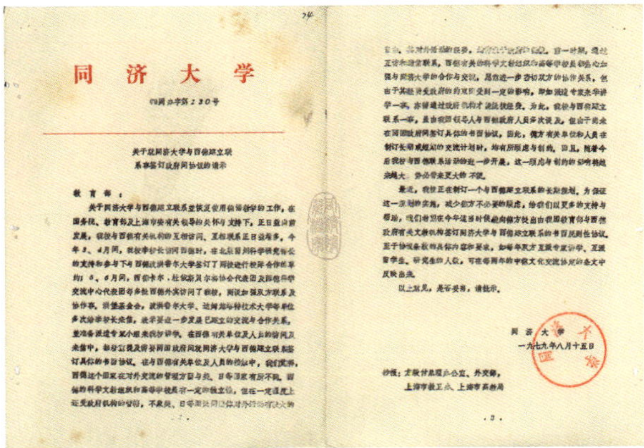

同 济 大 学

■ 1979 年 8 月《关于就同济大学与西德建立联系签订政府间协议的请示》
Request for Signing an Intergovernmental Agreement of Establishing Links Between Tongji University and West Germany in August 1979

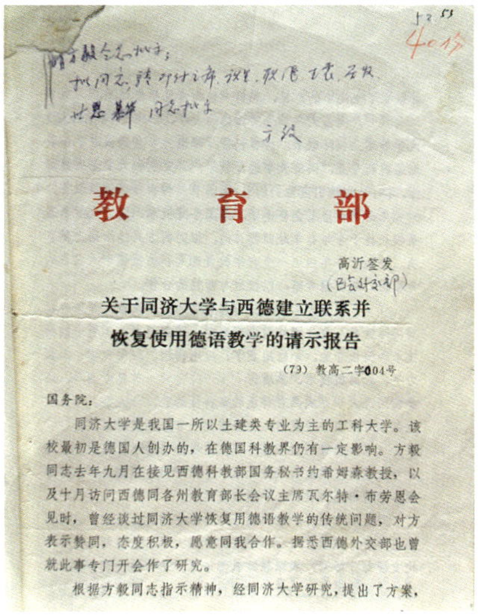

教 育 部

高沂签发

关于同济大学与西德建立联系并
恢复使用德语教学的请示报告

(79) 教高二字004号

国务院：

同济大学是我国一所以土建类专业为主的工科大学。该校最初是德国人创办的，在德国科教界仍有一定影响。方毅同志去年九月在接见西德科教部国务秘书约希姆森教授，以及十月访问西德同各州教育部长会议主席瓦尔特·布劳恩会见时，曾经谈过同济大学恢复用德语教学的传统问题，对方表示赞同，态度积极，愿意同我合作。据悉西德外交部也曾就此事专门开会作了研究。

根据方毅同志指示精神，经同济大学研究，提出了方案，

■ 1978 年 11 月 16 日，国务院副总理方毅在同济大学《关于恢复用德语教学传统的请示报告》上批示。
On November 16, 1978, Vice Premier Fang Yi gave his instructions on the *Request for Resuming the Tradition of Teaching in German* proposed by Tongji University.

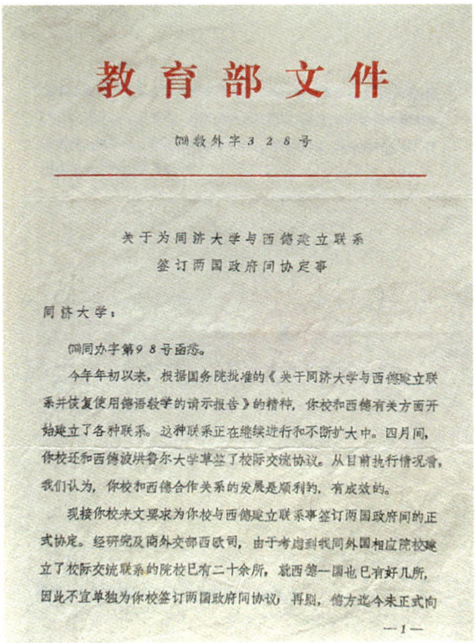

教 育 部 文 件

(79) 教外字 3 2 8 号

关于为同济大学与西德建立联系
签订两国政府间协定事

同济大学：

(79)同办字第 9 8 号函悉。

今年年初以来，根据国务院批准的《关于同济大学与西德建立联系并恢复使用德语教学的请示报告》的精神，你校和西德有关方面开始建立了各种联系。这种联系正在继续进行和不断扩大中。四月间，你校还和西德波洪鲁尔大学草签了校际交流协议。从目前执行情况看，我们认为，你校和西德合作关系的发展是顺利的，有成效的。

现接你校来文要求为你校与西德建立联系事签订两国政府间的正式协定。经研究及商外交部西欧司，由于考虑到我同外国相应院校建立了校际交流联系的院校已有二十余所，就西德一国也已有好几所，因此不宜单独为你校签订两国政府间协议，再则，德方迄今未正式向

—1—

■ 1979 年 2 月 26 日，教育部请示国务院《关于同济大学与西德建立联系并恢复使用德语教学的报告》，邓小平等八位副总理圈阅同意。
On February 26, 1979, report on Tongji University's *Establishing Links with West Germany and Resuming Teaching in German* submitted by the Ministry of Education to the State Council for authorization consented by eight vice premiers including Deng Xiaoping.

庚续传统，对德交流

Resumption of Communication with Germany

1979 年 3 月，李国豪校长应洪堡基金会邀请率团访问德国，恢复了与德国教育、科研等领域的合作，开辟了同济大学全面振兴的道路。1980 年开始，同济大学派出大批教师到德国进修，并聘请德国专家来校授课，建立不同类型、不同层次的德语教学组织，快速成为全国德语教学和研究的重要基地。

At the invitation of Alexander von Humboldt Foundation, President Li Guohao led a delegation to Germany in March 1979, which marked the resumption of cooperation with Germany in education and research and paved the way for overall revitalization of Tongji University. Since 1980, Tongji University had start send a large number of teachers for further education in Germany, hired German experts, established organizations of different types and levels for teaching in German, and thereby quickly became an important base in China for the teaching and research in German.

恢复对德联系传统

Resumption of communication with Germany

■ 1979 年，李国豪校长受邀访德，上海市领导及学校领导到机场送行。

Leaders of Shanghai Government and Tongji University seeing President Li Guohao off at the airport before his visit to Germany in 1979

■ 1979 年李国豪校长访问西德

President Li Guohao on a visiting tour to West Germany in 1979

■ 1982 年西德总统卡斯滕斯在汪道涵市长的陪同下来校访问

Mr. Carstens, President of West Germany, on a visit to Tongji University at the company of Mr. Wang Daohan, Mayor of Shanghai in 1982

■ 1984 年联邦德国总理科尔访问同济

Mr. Helmut Kohl, Chancellor of the Federal Republic of Germany, at Tongji University in 1984

■ 1980 年，波鸿鲁尔大学代表团与李国豪校长签订第一个合作协议。

Delegation of Ruhr-Universität Bochum signing a cooperation agreement with Tongji University in 1980, which was the first agreement Tongji signed with its counterparts in Germany.

■ 1981 年张德龙常务副校长与达姆斯塔特工业大学签订协议书

Executive Vice President Zhang Delong of Tongji University signing an agreement with TU Darmstadt in 1981

■ 1983 年西德银行向王达时副校长校赠书

Westdeutsche Landesbank Girozentrale (Bank of West Germany) donating books to Tongji University in 1983

恢复德语教学传统
Resumption of teaching in German

■ 金经昌教授给教师上德语课
Professor Jin Jingchang teaching German to teachers

■ 由德国捐赠的德语听力教学设备
Facilities donated by Germany for German listening courses

■ 西德教师组长波隆博士
Dr. Bolong, leader of German Teachers Group

■ 西德教师纶丝夫人
Mrs. Luns, a teacher from West Germany

■ 西德教师凯普夫博士
Dr. Kapfu, a teacher from West Germany

■ 1986 年科技德语培训中心成立大会
Inaugural Meeting of Training Center of Science German in 1986

■ 1979 年 6 月西德科学文化交流中心来校交流
The delegation from the Scientific and Cultural Exchange Center of West Germany visiting Tongji University in June 1979

■ 1980 年西德专家弗鲁克博士来校讲学
Dr. Fulukas, an expert form West Germany, giving a lecture in 1980

■ 1980 年西德韦贝尔教授为自动化教师讲课
Professor Weber from West Germany giving a lecture to teachers of automation in 1980

■ 1980 年西德缪恩教授来校作学术报告
Professor Mioen from West Germany making an academic report in Tongji University in 1980

■ 1980 年西德波恩绍尔教授来校讲学
Professor Sauer of Bonn University giving a lecture in Tongji University in1980

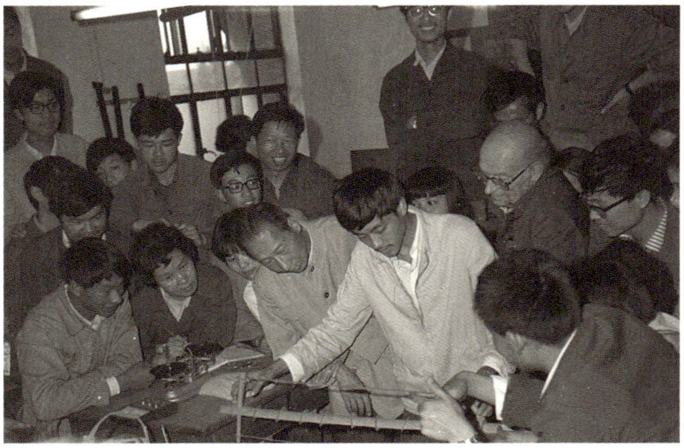

■ 1981 年西德贝歇尔教授考建筑系学生

Professor Becher from West Germany testing the students from the Department of Architecture in 1981

■ 1981 年西德电工教授梅因特尔给师生讲学

Professor Mayinteer of electrical engineering from West Germany doing a presentation to the students and teachers of Tongji University 1981

■ 1983 年西德阿亨大学 U. 鲁德维希教授来校讲学

Professor U. Ludwig from Rheinisch-Westffalische Techr ische Hochschule of West Germany giving a lecture in Tongji University in1983

■ 1988 年西德汉沙航空公司总裁来校讲学

President of Lufthansa Aviation Group of West Germany giving a lecture in Tongji University in1988

走向多科，综合发展

Towards Multidisciplinary Development

以"两个转变"为指导思想，自 1978 年始，学校在原有工科系所的基础上恢复、改建和充实，先后成立了机械工程系、电气工程系、建筑材料工程系、物理系、数学力学系、环境工程系、工程地质与水文地质系、结构工程系、道路与交通工程系；新成立了管理工程系、测量系、计算中心、化学系、外语系、留德预备部和高教研究所等，向以理工为主的多科性大学发展。

Since 1978, under the guiding principle of Two Transformations, Tongji University restored, reorganized and enriched its disciplines in engineering. As a result, the university had Departments of Mechanical Engineering, Electrical Engineering, Building Materials Engineering, Physics, Mathematics and Mechanics, Environmental Engineering, Engineering Geology and Hydrogeology, Structural Engineering, Road and Traffic Engineering. Moreover, the university established Departments of Management Engineering, Surveying, Chemistry and Foreign Languages, and a Computing Center, a Pre-departure German Training Center and the Research Institute on Higher Education. Tongji was developing towards a multidisciplinary university with strength in science and engineering.

1977 年院系结构示意图

Schools and departments in 1977

1988 年院系结构示意图

Schools and departments in 1988

学科发展树状成长图

■ 1978 年结构理论研究所成立大会

Inaugural meeting of the Institute of Structure Theories in 1978

■ 1986 年建筑与城市规划学院成立大会

Inaugural meeting of the School of Architecture and Urban Planning in 1986

■ 1987 年结构工程学院成立

The School of Structure Engineering established in 1987

■ 1989 年防灾救灾研究所成立

The Shanghai Institute of Disaster Prevention and Relief established in 1989

■ 测量系学生在校园内实习

Students of the Department of Surveying doing internship on campus

■ 地下工程系科研人员在工作

Researchers of the Department of Underground Engineering at work

老骥伏枥，新帅出征

Dedicated and Concerted Efforts by Old and New Teachers

“文革”结束后，学校为蒙冤的干部、教师平反，广大教师重新焕发了工作热情。1981 年冯纪忠、朱伯龙、孙钧、杨钦、黄蕴元、李国豪被批准为首批博士生导师。1991 年，孙钧、马在田、汪品先 3 位教授当选为中国科学院院士。

After the ten-year Cultural Revolution, the wrongly accused administrators and teachers were rehabilitated. Teachers resumed their work with renewed enthusiasm. Feng Jizhong, Zhu Bolong, Sun Jun, Yang Qin, Huang Yunyuan and Li Guohao were approved as the first PhD supervisors in 1981. Sun Jun, Ma Zaitian and Wang Pinxian were elected as members of the Chinese Academy of Sciences in 1991.

■ 李国豪院士和中青年教师一起讨论

Professor Li Guohao with young and middle-aged teachers

■ 建筑系主任冯纪忠教授在查阅资料

Professor Feng Jizhong, head of the Department of Architecture, reading literature

■ 建材系祝永年教授在做实验

Professor Zhu Yongnian of the Department of Building Materials doing an experiment

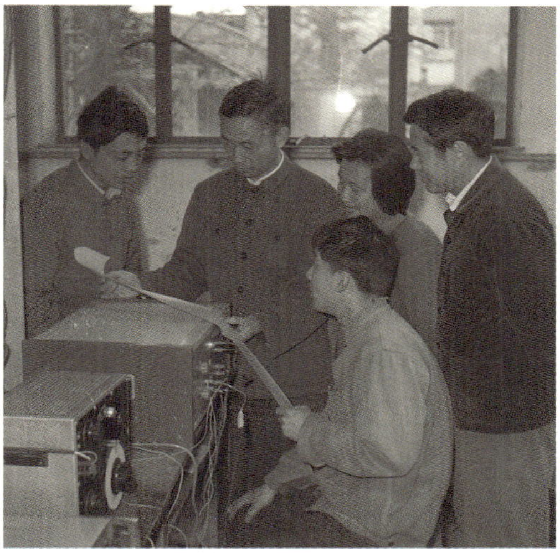

■ 结构理论研究所副所长徐植信教授（左二）等进行地震波工作研究

Professor Xu Zhixin (second from right), deputy director of the Institute of Structure Theories, analyzing seismic waves with colleagues

■ 建筑系陈从周教授与研究生
Professor Chen Congzhou with his postgraduate student

■ 徐次达教授指导研究生
Professor Xu Cida supervising his postgraduate student in1984

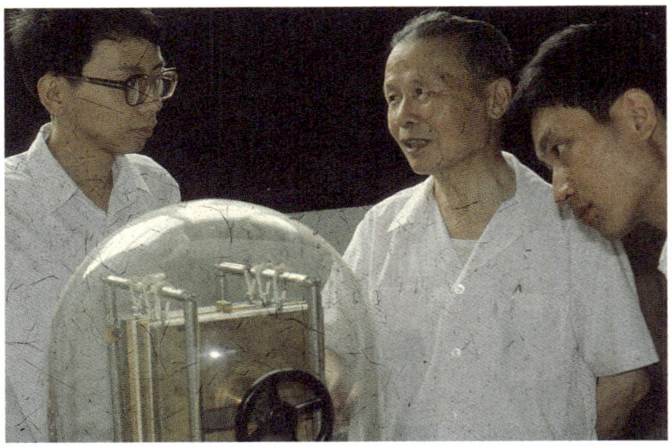

■ 机械系蒋汉文教授与研究生
Professor Jiang Hanwen of the Department of Mechanical Engineering with his postgraduare students 1984

■ 建材系黄蕴元教授与研究生
Professor Huang Yunyuan with his postgraduare students

■ 朱伯龙教授和博士生吕西林
Professor Zhu Bolong with his PhD student Lv Xilin

■ 孙钧教授与博士生李永盛
Professor Sun Jun with with his PhD student Li Yongsheng

■ 1991 年，学校为孙钧、 马在田、汪品先三位新当选的中国科学院学部委员（院士）举行庆祝会。

Professors Sun Jun, Ma Zaitian and Wang Pinxian at a meeting in celebration of their being elected as members of the China Academy of Sciences in 1991

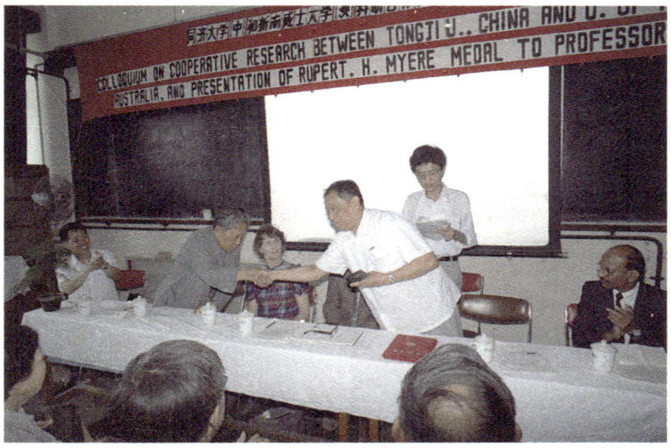

■ 1985 年俞调梅教授获梅耶尔奖

Professor Yu Diaomei receiving the Meyer Award in 1985

■ 马在田教授获 1991 年陈嘉庚地球科学奖、1992 年上海市第一届科技功臣。

Professor Ma Zaitian won the Tan Kah Kee Earth Science Award in 1991, and title of Shanghai's Great Contributor of Science and Technology 1992.

固本培元，教材建设

Compilation of Textbooks for Consolidation of Engineering Foundation

根据教学需要，1977 年全国恢复高考后，同济大学共承担了 1978-1980 年全国统编教材任务 123 门，参加编写的教师多达 500 余人，占全校教师的三分之一。另外，同济主编、主审及参编 1978-1980 年高校建筑专业教材 60 余门，教材建设迈入新台阶。

After the Higher Entrance Examinations were resumed in 1977, Tongji University was commissioned to compile 123 textbooks from 1978 to 1980 for universities in China. More than 500 teachers participated in the compilation, accounting for one-third of all teachers in the university. In addition, more than 60 textbooks in architecture were edited, co-edited or proofread by teachers from Tongji from 1978 to 1980. All this marked a new phase for textbook development.

■ 同济教师编写的各类教材、参考书

Textbooks and books compiled by teachers of Tongji University

■ 1985 年高等工业学校八个教材委员会成立大会

Inaugural meeting of eight Textbook Compilation Committees for Advanced Industrial School in 1985

■ 1987 年教材科出版的部分新书

New books published by the Textbook Division in 1987

1987 年教书育人成果发布会

A meeting in commendation of Teaching Achievements in 1987

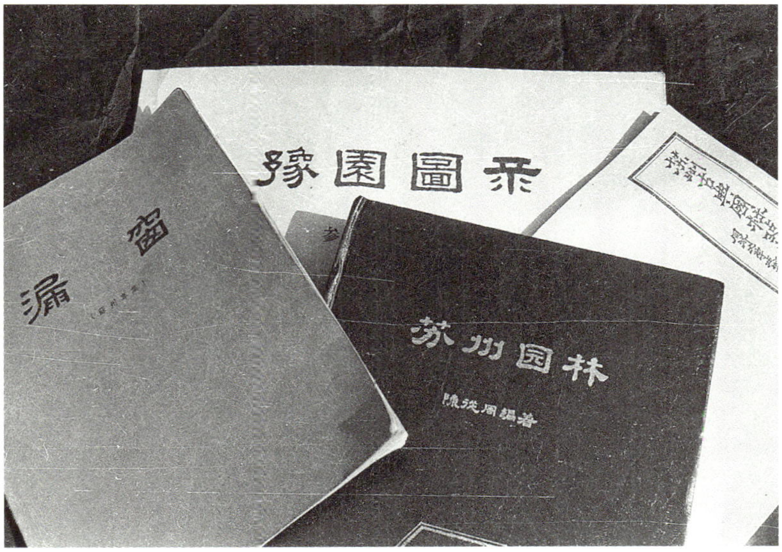

同济大学教师编写的园林类书籍

Books on landscape architecture compiled by teachers of Tongji University

同济大学 1987-1991 获奖教材

Award-winning Textbooks of Tongji University (1987-1991)

获国家级优秀教材及全国高等学校部委级优秀教材一等奖书目 Al isto fT extbooks of Excellence at National Levela nd First-prizeT extbooks forI nstitutionso fH igherL earninga tM inisterialL evel		
书名 Book Titles	编（著）者 Editors(Authors)	获奖年份 Yearso fA wards
高等数学讲义(第二版)(上、下册)Lecture Noteso fA dvancedM athematics (VolumeI andV olumeI I) (Second Edition)	樊映川等 FanYingchuan,e ta l1	1987
高等数学(第二版)(上、下册) Advanced Mathematics(Second Edition) (Volume Ia nd Volume II)	王福楹 邱伯驺等 Wang Fuying,Q iu Bozou, et al	1987
机械设计基础(第二版) F undamentalso f Mechanical Design (SecondE dition)	喻怀正 Yu Huaizheng	1987
普通物理学（第三版） GeneralP hysics (Third Edition)	程守洙 江之永等 ChengS houzhu, JiangZ hiyong,e ta l	1987
机械制图及习题集(第二版) C ollectiono f Mechanical Drawings andE xercises (SecondE dition)	何铭新 李名纪 关震荣 李耀群 洪钟德等 He Mingxin, Li Mingji, Guan Zhenrong, Li Yaoqun, Hong Zhongde	1987
多层及高层房屋结构（上、下册） Structures of Multi-layerB uildings and High-rises (VolumeI andV olumeI I)	沈祖炎主编 Editor-in-chief Shen Zuyan	1987

建筑施工 Building Construction	江景波 赵志缙等 Wang Jingbo, Zhao Zhijin, et al	1987
桥梁工程 Bridge Engineering	姚玲森主编 Editor-in-chief: Yao Lingsen	1987
中国城市建筑史（第二版） History of Chinese Urban Architecture (second edition)	董鉴泓 阮仪三 Dong Jianhong, Ruan Yisan	1991
钢结构（上、下）册 Steel Structure (Volume I and Volume II)	欧阳可庆 沈祖炎 王肇民 潘士劼 宗听聪等 Ouyang Keqing, Shen Zuyan, Wang Zhaomin, Wang Shijie, Zong Tingcong	1991
给水工程（第二版）（上、下册） Water Supply Engineering (Volume I and Volume II) (Second Edition)	杨钦 严煦世主编 Editor-in-chief: Yang Qin, Yan Xushi	1991
金属工艺学 Metallurgical Technology	钱增新 陈全明 Qian Zengxin, Chen Quanming	1991
水污染控制工程（上、下册） Water Pollution Control Engineering (Volume I and Volume II)	高廷耀主编 Editor-in-chief: Gao Tingyao	1991

学位教育，步入正轨

Education with Academic Degrees

1981 年 12 月，国务院学位委员会公布《关于下达首批博士和硕士学位授予单位的通知》，同济大学 5 个专业获得博士学位授予权，23 个专业获得硕士学位授予权，成为全国首批获得博士、硕士学位授予权的单位。当年招收博士生 6 名。1982 年 2 月，成立学位评定委员会；1986 年 4 月，试办研究生院。

In December 1981, the Academic Degree Committee of the State Council issued its Notification of First Institutions Eligible for Conferring Doctorate and Master's Degrees. Five majors of Tongji University were authorized to confer PhD degrees and eighteen majors to confer Master's degrees, making Tongji University one of the first universities in China that were entitled to confer Master's and PhD degrees. Six PhD candidates were enrolled in the same year. In February 1982, the Academic Degree Evaluation Committee was set up, and in April 1986, the Graduate School was informally established on a trial basis.

■ 第一批工学博士学位授权学科、专业（1981）

First PhD Degree Programs in Engineering (1981)

学科门类 Category of Disciplines	一级学科名称 First-levelD isciplines	二级学科、专业名称 Programs for Second-level Disciplines
工学　Engineering	建筑学 Architecture	城市规划与设计 UrbanP lanninga nd Design
		建筑设计 ArchitecturalD esign
	土建、水利 CivilE ngineering, Hydraulics	结构工程 Structural Engineering
		市政工程 MunicipalE ngineering
	非金属材料 Nonmetallicm aterials	无机非金属材料 InorganicN onmetallic Materials

■ 第二批工学博士学位授权学科、专业 (1984)

Second PhD Degree Programs in Engineering (1984)

学科门类 Category of Disciplines	一级学科名称 First-levelD isciplines	二级 学科 、专 业名称 Programs for Second-level Disciplines
工学 Engineering	土建、水利 Civile ngineering Hydraulics	岩土工程 Geotechnical Engineering
		环境工程 EnvironmentalE ngineering
		地震工程及防护工程 Earthquake and Protection Engineering

■ 第三批工学博士学位授权学科、专业 (1986)
Third PhD Degree Programs in Engineering (1986)

学科门类 Category of Disciplines	一级学科名称 First-levelD iscipline	二级学科、专业名称 Programs forS econd-level Discipline
工学 Engineering	动力 机械及 工程 热物理 Power Machinery and Engineering Thermophysics	热能工程 ThermalP ower Engineering
	建筑学 Architecture	建筑历 史与现代建筑 理论 Architectural History and Modern Architecture Theories
	土建、水利 CivilE ngineering, Hydraulics	道路工程 Road Engineering
	管理工程 EngineeringM anagement	工业管理工程 Industrial of Disciplines

■ 第四批工学博士学位授权学科、专业 (1990)
Fourth PhD Degree Programs in Engineering (1990)

学科门类 Category of Disciplines	一级学科名称 First-level Discipline	二级学科、专业名称 Programs for Second-level Discipline	学科门类 Category of Disciplines
工学 Engineering	力学 Mechanics	固体力学 Solid Mechanics	
	建筑学 Architecture	建筑技术科学 Building Technology Science	
	铁道、公路与水运 Railway Road and Watertransportation	桥梁与隧道工程 Bridge and Tunnel Engineering	因专业目录调整，从第一批的结构工程分出来 Derived from Structural Engineering in the First PhD Degree Programs as a result of amendment to First-level Disciplines

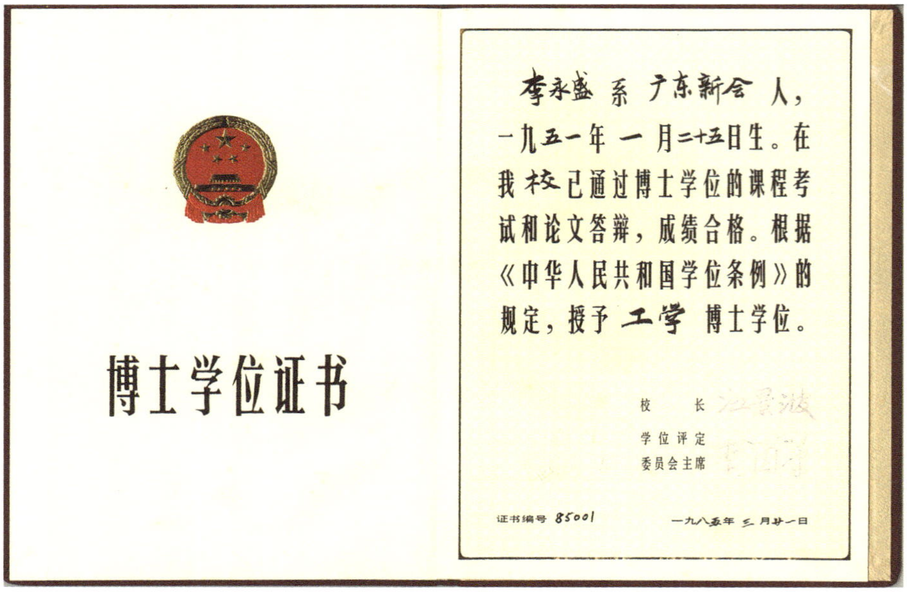

博士学位证书

李永盛 系 广东新会 人，一九五一年 一 月二十五日生。在我校已通过博士学位的课程考试和论文答辩，成绩合格。根据《中华人民共和国学位条例》的规定，授予 工学 博士学位。

校　长

学位评定
委员会主席

证书编号 85001　　一九八五年 三 月廿一日

■ 实行学位制度以来，同济大学发出的第一份博士学位证书。
The first PhD degree certificate issued by Tongji University after the implementation of the degree system

■ 1984 年同济第一位论文答辩的博士研究生吕西林，导师为朱伯龙教授。
Mr. Lv Xilin, the first PhD candidate of Tongji University doing his oral examination
Professor Zhu Bolong was his PhD supervisor.

■ 1985 年结构系首届博士论文答辩会
The first PhD theses oral examinations at the Department of Structural Engineering in 1985

■ 1981 年首次颁发硕士学位证书大会
The first Master's Degree Awarding Ceremony in 1981

■ 1981 年桥梁专业 1978 级研究生毕业论文答辩会

Oral examinations of Postgraduate Graduation Theses in 1981 for students of Bridge Engineering of Year 1978

■ 1984 年测量系研究生毕业答辩

Oral Examination of a Postgraduate Graduation Thesis at the Department of Surveying in 1984

■ 1984 年机械系曹善华进行研究生毕业答辩

Mr. Cao Shanhua doing his oral examination of his Postgraduate Graduation Thesis at the Department of Surveying in 1984

■ 1985 年同济大学学术委员会会议

A meeting of the Academic Committee of Tongji University in 1985

■ 1986 年研究生院成立大会

The Graduate School of Tongji University was established in 1986

■ 1984 年第三世界一批留学生来校学习

A group of students from the third world countries studying in Tongji University in 1984

■ 1987 年来同济进修的苏联留学生

Students from the former USSR pursuing further study at Tongji University in 1987

■ 1988 年建筑系陈从周教授和他的日本研究生久保田雅代

Professor Chen Congzhou from the Department of Architecture and his Japanese graduate student Ms. Kubota Masayo in 1988

■ 1990 年尼泊尔留学生通过博士论文答辩

A Nepalese student doing his PhD thesis defense in 1990

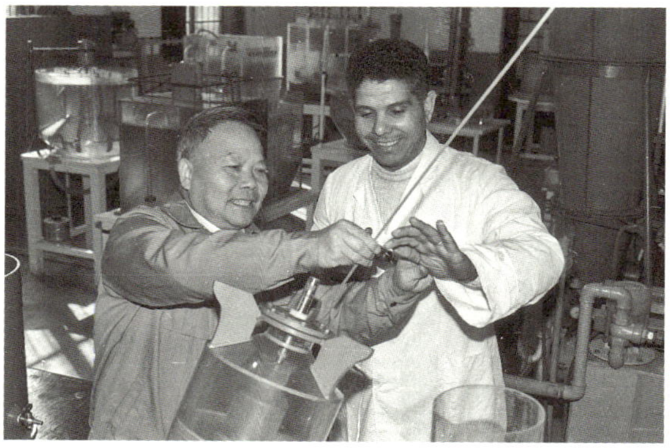

■ 1991 年环境实验室老师教留学生制作教具

A teacher from the Environmental Laboratory showing an overseas student how to make teaching aids in 1991

函授夜大，朝气蓬勃

Prosperity of Correspondence Programs and Night Schools

1978 年同济大学恢复函授招生，1979 年招生地区扩大到华东六省一市，1980 年学校成立业余教育处，1983 年函授招生专业由“文革”前的 4 个发展到 9 个，学生达到 3366 人。当年还设立了夜大。1984 年 7 月，学校为 64 名函授毕业生举行授予学士学位仪式，是新中国成立以来全国第一次授予函授生学士学位，国家教育部专门发来贺电。

In 1978, Tongji University resumed enrolling students into correspondence programs; and in 1979, university started to enroll students from six provinces and one city (Province of Shandong, Jiangsu, Anhui, Zhejiang, Jiangxi, and the city of Shanghai) in East China. In 1980, the Office of Correspondence Education was set up; and in 1983, the number of correspondence programs increased from four before the Cultural Revolution to nine, with up to 3366 students. The Night School was set up in the same year. In July 1984, 64 correspondence students obtained their Bachelor's degrees, which were the first of its kind since the founding of new China; the Ministry of Education sent a letter of congratulations to Tongji University for the success of the correspondence programs.

■ 1980 年学校成立函授教育处

The university set up the Office of Correspondence Education in 1980

■ 1980 年函授生进行混凝土试验

Correspondence students doing a concrete test in 1980

■ 1986 年电气工程系函授生进行翻砂实验

Correspondence students of the Department of Electrical Engineering doing the foundry experiment in 1986

■ 1984 年函授毕业设计指导教师会议

Correspondence supervisors at a meeting on how to supervise graduation designs in 1984

■ 1984 年参加上海成人教育讨论会的亚非欧美 23 个国家与地区代表来校了解函授教育情况

In 1984, representatives from 23 countries and regions in Asia, Africa, Europe and America on an Adult Education Conference in Shanghai visiting Tongji University to learn about its correspondence education

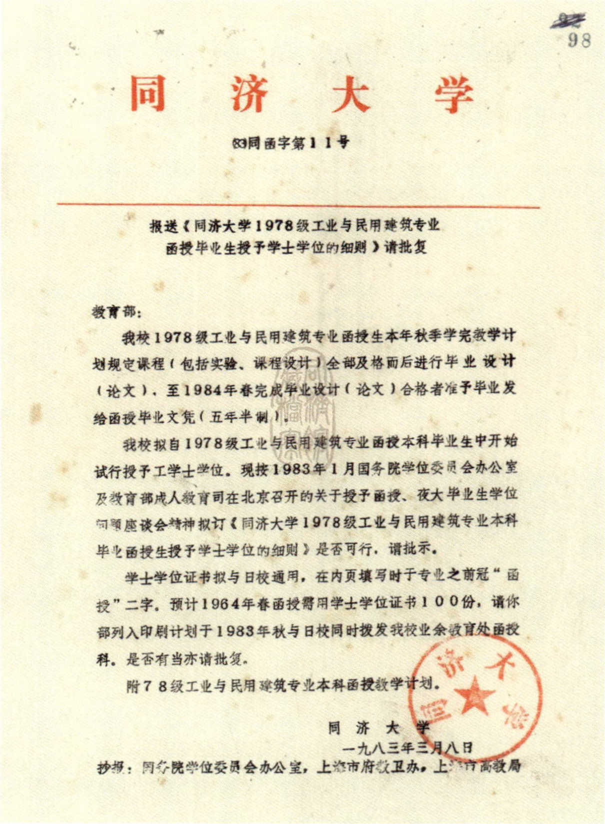
98

同 济 大 学

83同函字第11号

报送《同济大学1978级工业与民用建筑专业函授毕业生授予学士学位的细则》请批复

教育部：

我校1978级工业与民用建筑专业函授生本年秋季学完教学计划规定课程（包括实验、课程设计）全部及格而后进行毕业设计（论文），至1984年春完成毕业设计（论文）合格者准予毕业发给函授毕业文凭（五年半制）。

我校拟自1978级工业与民用建筑专业函授本科毕业生中开始试行授予工学士学位。现按1983年1月国务院学位委员会办公室及教育部成人教育司在北京召开的关于授予函授、夜大毕业生学位问题座谈会精神拟订《同济大学1978级工业与民用建筑专业本科毕业函授生授予学士学位的细则》是否可行，请批示。

学士学位证书拟与日校通用，在内页填写时于专业之前冠“函授”二字。预计1964年春函授需用学士学位证书100份，请你部列入印刷计划于1983年秋与日校同时拨发我校业余教育处函授科。是否有当亦请批复。

附78级工业与民用建筑专业本科函授教学计划。

同 济 大 学

一九八三年三月八日

抄报：国务院学位委员会办公室，上海市府教卫办，上海市高教局

学校关于“1978级工业与民用建筑专业函授毕业生授予学位的细则”的请示。

Request for Rules of Conferring Bachelor's Degrees to Correspondence Students of Industrial and Civil Engineering of year 1978

1983年“文革”后第一届函授生毕业合影

First graduates from correspondence programs after the Cultural Revolution in 1983

1984年7月25日，同济首批函授生学士学位证书颁证典礼。

Graduation ceremony of the first correspondence students of Tongji University on July 25, 1984

1981年夜校高中电子班毕业典礼

Graduation Ceremony for the High School Electronics Class at Night School in 1981

1983年夜大首届学生入学

Orientation for the first students enrolled in Night School in 1983

建章立制，分散实习

Regulations Established and Internships at Different Venues

20世纪80年代，同济大学教务处下设实践教学科，成立校外实习和社会实践指导委员会，制订《关于生产实习（毕业实习）暂行条例》，将工程教育重实践的传统特色进一步制度化。1982年，学校进行实习改革试点，将过去的集中实习改为分散实习，鼓励学生开展业余兴趣活动小组，至1987年，已建立实习基地近30个，可安排2500名学生实习。

In the 1980s, the Practice Teaching Office was up under the Teaching Affairs Office of Tongji University. The newly established Steering Committee of Off-campus Intership and Social Practice made Provisional Regulations on Practice (Graduation intership), which further systematized the tradition of emphasizing practice in engineering education. In 1982, the university carried out pilot practice - changes from intership in one venue in the past to practice in different venues, and encouraged students to participate in extracurricular activities. By 1987, nearly 30 internship bases had been established for 2500 students.

■ 江景波校长（右二）赴安徽巢湖和阜阳实习基地慰问师生

President Jiang Jingbo (second from right) visiting teachers and students in internship bases of Chaohu and Fuyang, Anhui Province

■ 1981年工民建学生测量实习

Students of the Department of Industrial and Civil Engineering on surveying internship in 1981

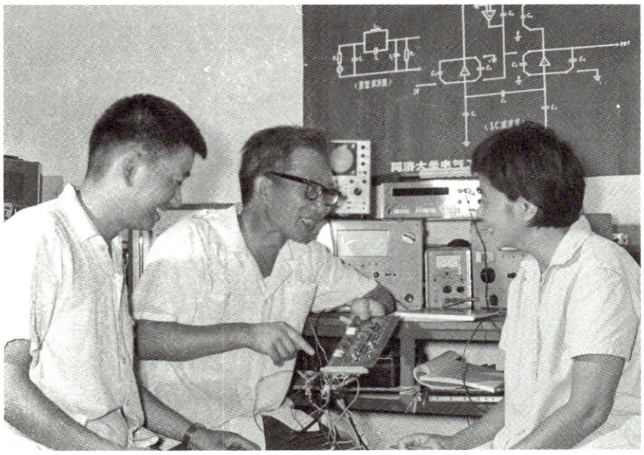

■ 1981年电工教研组师生在上海通风厂实习

Teachers and students of Electrical Engineering Teaching and Research Group on internship in Shanghai Ventilation Factory in 1981

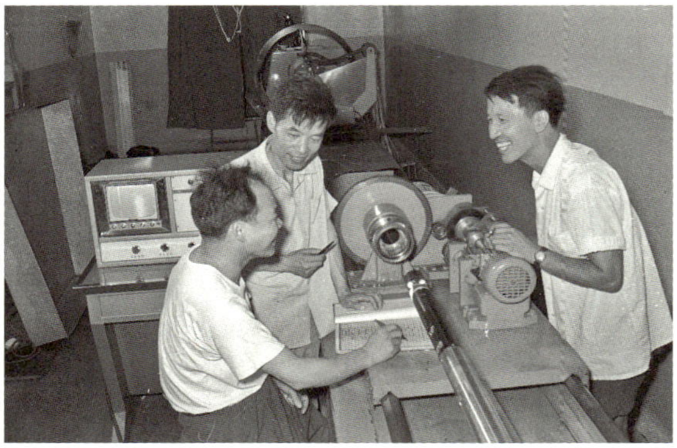

■ 1981 年电仪教研室师生在长征机械厂实习

Teachers and students of the Electrical Instruments Teaching and Research Group on internship in Changzheng Machinery Factory in 1981

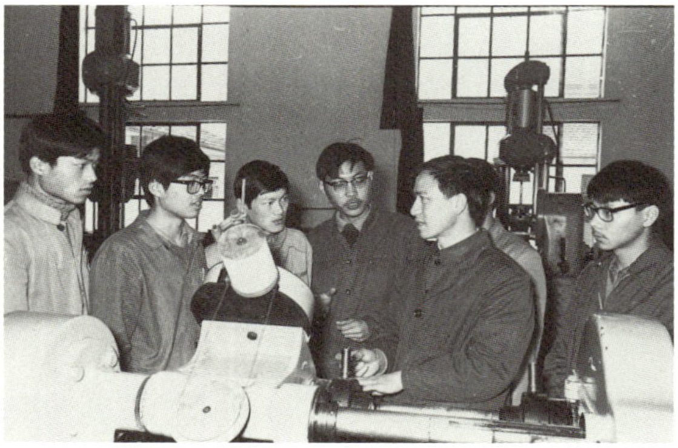

■ 1983 年工民建学生在材料力学试验室做实验

Students of the Department of Industrial and Civil Engineering conducting experiments in the laboratory of material mechanics in 1983

■ 1983 年建筑系、机械系学生制图作业展览

Homework Display of drawings by students of architecture and mechanics in 1983

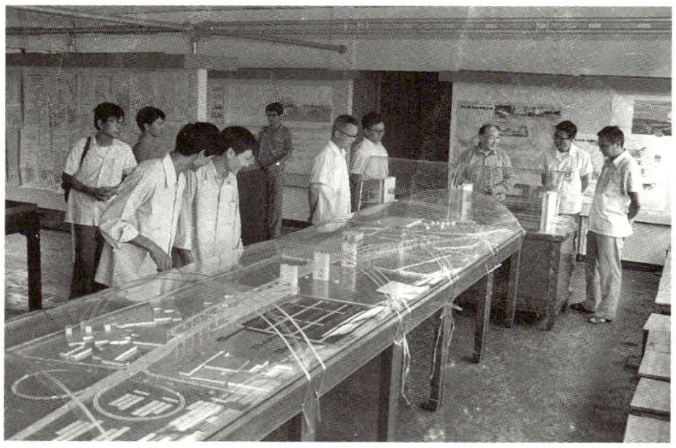

■ 1983 年建筑系学生成果展览

Exhibition of the works by students from the Department of Architecture in 1983

■ 建筑系教授指导建筑学专业学生赴青阳县九华山进行古建筑测绘实习，编写成《传统建筑测绘手册》

Students of architecture doing surveying and mapping of classical buildings under the guidance of their professors in Jiuhua Mountain, Qingyang County for compilation of *Surveying and Mapping Manual of Traditional Buildings*

■ 1984 年道路与交通工程系学生在浙江嵊县山区进行公路选线

Students of the Department of Road and Traffic Engineering selecting the route for high ways in mountainous areas of Shengxian County in Zhejiang Province in 1984

■ 机械系在宝钢石洞口实习

Students of the Department of Mechanical Engineering on internship in Shidongkou of Baosteel

■ 1990 年学生课外实践交流表彰大会

Commendation for Student Extracurricular Activities in 1990

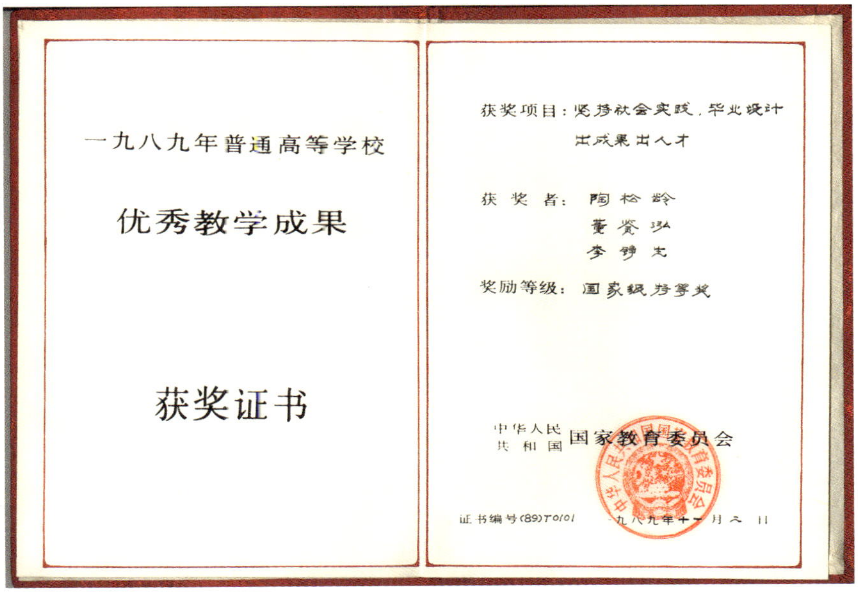

一九八九年普通高等学校

优秀教学成果

获奖证书

获奖项目：坚持社会实践，毕业设计出成果出人才

获 奖 者：陶松龄
董鉴泓
李铮生

奖励等级：国家级特等奖

中华人民共和国 国家教育委员会

证书编号(89)T0101　一九八九年十一月六日

■ 1989 年，陶松龄、董鉴泓、李铮生在城市规划专业“坚持社会实践毕业设计出成果、出人才”的课题中，获国家教委颁发的“优秀教学成果国家级特等奖”。

Project of Cultivating Talents Through Practice in Graduation Design conducted by Mr. Tao Songling, Mr. Dong Jianhong and Mr. Li Zhengsheng of the Department of Urban Planning won a National Special Award for Outstanding Teaching Achievements issued by the State Education Committee in 1989.

实验教学，牢固基础

Learning in Laboratories to Consolidate Fundamentals

实验室是工科高校教学、科研的重要场所，是人才培养的基地，同济大学通过多种渠道筹集资金，实验室建设得到不断加强，1980 年有给排水、暖通、城市燃气、热工、自动化、工程结构、地下建筑、测量等 28 个实验室。1990 年开始筹建污染控制和资源化研究、混凝土材料研究 2 个国家重点实验室和城市规划现代化技术国家专业实验室。

Laboratories formed an important part of teaching and research for engineering universities, and therefore became the base for student education. Tongji University raised funds through various channels for continuous improvement of laboratories. In 1980, there were 28 laboratories covering drainage, HVAC (Heating, Ventilation and Air Conditioning), urban gas, thermal engineering, automation, engineering structure, underground construction and surveying. In 1990, Tongji University began the construction of two national key laboratories for research in pollution control and resourcing, and in concrete materials, and a national laboratory of modern technologies for urban planning.

1980 年实验室设置基本情况表

Table of Laboratories in 1980

年份 Year	实验室数 Number of Laboratories	实验室名称 Names of Laboratories
1980	28	1.给排水 2.暖通 3.城市燃气 4.热工 5.自动化 6.电工 7.无线电 8.工机 9.金工 10.化学 11.硅酸盐 12.制品 13.建材 14.物理 15.声学 16.土工 17.道路 18.桥梁 19.实验力学 20.工程结构 21.水力水文 22.材料力学 23.海洋地质 24.海洋物探 25.建筑光照 26.工程地质 27.地下建筑 28.测量 1. Drainage 2. HVAC 3. Urban Gas 4. Thermal Engineering 5. Automation 6. Electrical Engineering 7. Wireless Radio 8. Construction Machinery 9. Metalworking 10. Chemistry 11. Silicate 12. Product Making 13. Building Materials 14. Physics 15. Acoustics 16. Soil Engineering 17. Roads Engineering 18. Bridges Engineering 19. Experimental Mechanics 20. Engineering Structure 21. Hydraulics and Hydrology 22. Material Mechanics 23. Marine Geology 24. Marine Geophysical Exploration 25. Lighting for Buildings 26. Engineering Geology 27. Underground Construction 28. Surveying

■ 土木工程防灾国家重点实验室（1991）
National Key Laboratory of Disaster Prevention in Civil Engineering (1991)

■ 污染控制与资源化研究国家重点实验室在做污水排海扩散实验
An experiment on the diffusion of sewage in the sea in the National Key Laboratory of Pollution Control and Resourcing Research

■ 道路与交通工程国家教委开放实验室
The Open Laboratory of Road and Traffic Engineering funded by the State Education Committee.

■ 固体力学国家教委开放实验室
The Open Laboratory of Solid Mechanics funded by the State Education Committee

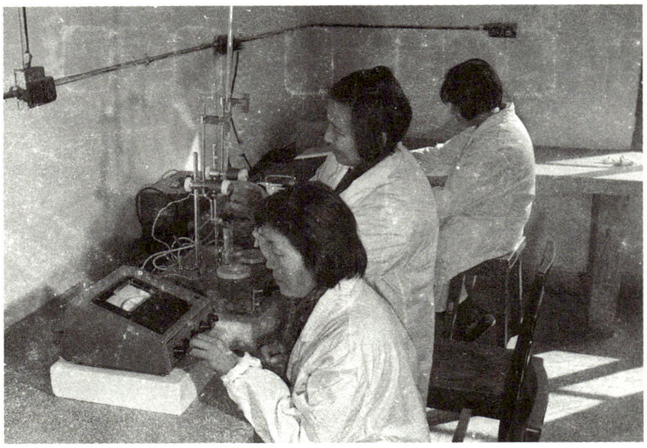

■ 给水排水实验室（1979）
Laboratory of Water Supply and Drainage in 1979

■ 工程结构实验室（1979）
Laboratory of Construction Structure in 1979

■ 水利水文实验室（1980）
Laboratory of Hydraulics and Hydrology in 1980

■ 暖通实验室（1980）
HVAC Laboratory in 1980

■ 暖通实验室通风试验（1986）
A ventilation test in HVAC Laboratory in 1986

■ 电工电子实验（1986）
An electrical and electronic experiment in 1986

■ 路桥实验室路面试验（1980）
A pavement test in the Laboratory of Road and Bridge in 1980

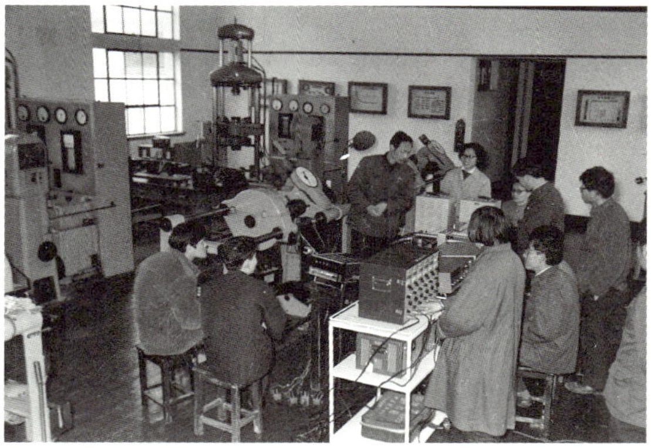

■ 材料力学试验室（1987）
Laboratory of Material Mechanics in 1987

■ 土动力学试验室（1987）
Laboratory of Soil Dynamics in 1987

■ 风洞实验室（1990）
Laboratory of Wind Tunnels in 1990

■ 环境实验室（1991）
Environmental Laboratory in 1991

科研改革，推陈出新

Reform and Innovation in Scientific Research

1979 年至 1984 年，学校陆续建立了 17 个科研班子，在稳定科研方向、形成学科优势、促进专业建设、培养新的学术带头人方面起了积极作用。1985 年 7 月，学校根据中央科技体制改革决定的精神和学校存在的问题，制定了《同济大学科研改革方案》，在此方案指导下，科研工作迅速发展，1985 年至 1991 年底，635 项科研成果达到国际或国内先进水平，有的属国内首创。

From 1979 to 1984, Tongji University established 17 research groups which played an active role in keeping research directions, developing disciplinal advantages, promoting professional development and producing new academic leaders. Based upon the decision of reform in science and technology system made by the central government, Research Reform Program of Tongji University was formulated to address the issues of Tongji in July 1985. Guided by the program, rapid progress was made in research. From 1985 to the end of 1991, 635 research achievements reached internationally standards, some of which were pioneering ones in china.

1981-1991 年科研课题及经费表

Research Projects and Funds from 1981 to 1991 (unit: 10,000 *yuan*)

年份 Year	当年在研课题总数/项 Number of research programs	当年拨入经费合计/万元 Research funds Received /¥10000	科研事业费/万元 Research Expenses /¥10000	国务院有关部门专项费/万元 Specialized funds from departments under the State Council /¥10000	国家自然科学（中科院）基金/万元 National funds for natural science (CAS) /¥10000	省、市、自治区专项费/万元 Specialized funds from provinces, municipalities and autonomous regions /¥10000	企、事业单位委托经费/万元 Funds from commissioned projects of industry or other sources /¥10000	其他 Miscellaneous /¥10000
1981	250	207.85	50.00	81.60		34.65	41.60	
1982	280	219.6	60.00	131.40	0.10	22.10	78.00	
1983	334	389.80	80.00	87.60	63.00	52.30	106.95	
1984	384	386.26	102.00	121.00	55.96	42.60	63.70	
1985	463	901.00	108.50	164.70	38.80	54.50	534.50	
1986	403	1005.6	107.4	199.0	3.0	64.1	570.7	61.2
1987	697	1366.7	108.9	487.4	27.7	185.1	525.2	32.4
1988	1245	1235.2	106.2	319.5	58.1	176.7	532.9	41.8
1989	878	1299.7	108.4	299.5	71.4	215.2	578.4	26.8
1990	893	1573.7	129.5	593.1	97.9	114.1	567.7	71.4
1991	1086	1971.7	131.10	216.60	89.40	191.60	1310.50	32.50

1977-1991 同济大学所获各类奖项情况

Awards Won by Tongji University from 1977 to 1991

1978 全国科学大会成果奖 AchievementA wardsa tN ationalC onferenceo nS cience in 1978	30 项
国家自然科学奖 National NaturalS cience Awards	2项
国家发明奖 National InventionA wards	6项
国家科技进步奖 National Awards forP rogressi nS cience andT echnology	12 项
国家教委（教育部）科技进步奖 Sciencea nd Technology Progress Awards of StateE ducation Commission (Ministry of Education)	44 项
上海市人民政府科技进步奖 Sciencea nd Technology Progress Awards of Shanghai MunicipalG overnment	124项
其他省部科技进步奖 Sciencea nd technology progress awards at provincial or ministeriall evel	109项
1986-1991 科技攻关奖 Awards forS cience andT echnologyB reakthroughA chievementsf rom1 986t o 1991	17 项
设计竞赛及设计奖 Design Contests andD esignA wards	20 项

■ 1979 年上海电视大楼模型试验

Test on the model of Shanghai TV Tower in 1979

■ 1979 年模拟抗震研究

Anti-earthquake simulation research in 1979

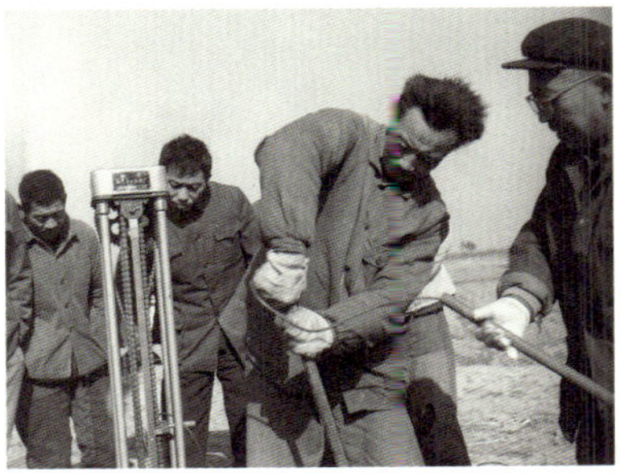

■ 1979 年 11 月溧阳抗震研究

Anti-earthquake research in Liyang City in November 1979

■ 1980 年芜湖市规划方案讨论

Demonstration of the planning scheme of Wuhu City, Anhui Province in 1980

■ 1980 年工程结构研究所研制全息条纹读数仪

A holographic stripe reader developed by the Research Ins:itute of Structural Engineering in 1980

■ 1980 年桥梁试验

A bridge test in 1980

■ 1981 年建筑系戴复东教授设计的四平大楼

Siping Building designed by Professor Dai Fudong from the Department of Architecture in 1981

■ 1981 年建筑系得奖者和农林住宅模型

Award-winners from the Department of Architecture and their models of residential buildings in agricultural and forested areas in 1981

■ 1981 年科研成果鉴定会

An appraisal meeting on research achievements in 1981

■ 1983 年胜利油田规划方案讨论

Discussion about the planning scheme of Shengli Oilfield in 1983

■ 1984 年结构所房屋抗震试验

Anti-earthquake test by the Research Institute of Structural Engineering in 1984

■ 1983 年热工教研室研制的科研成果水卡计

Water calorimeter developed by the Department of Thermal Engineering in 1983

■ 城市规划与设计现代化技术专业实验室开发的三维模拟设计系统

3D simulation design system developed by the Laboratory of Urban Planning and Modern Design Technologies

■ 1991 年同济设计的南浦大桥引桥

Approach Bridge of Nanpu Bridge designed by Tongji University in 1991

■ 1991 年，同济设计的吴淞新客运大楼

New Wusong Passenger Terminal designed by Tongji University in 1991

1986 年周庄镇总体规划报告会

Symposium on overall planning of Zhouzhuang Village in 1986

1988 同济建筑系教师设计的人民英雄纪念碑模型

Model of Monument to the People's Heroes designed by a teacher of the Department of Architecture, Tongji University in 1988

1990 年工程机械研制小型挖土机在江阴开鉴定会

Evaluation meeting of small excavators designed by Institute of Construction Machinery in Jiangyin in 1990

1991 年机械系完成宝钢石洞二期电厂烟道管顶升工艺科研项目

Research project of smoke pipe workmanship on the second phase of Shidong Power Plant of Baosteel was completed by the Department of Mechanics in 1991.

1991 年地下建设开发产品展示会

Exhibition of products of underground construction in 1991

科技产业，学科交叉

Technological Enterprises and Inter-disciplinary Collaboration

同济大学为适应国家经济快速发展需要，在过去校办工厂辅助教学、实习、科研并接受部分生产订单的基础上，创办了一批科技企业，促进科技成果产业化。此外，学校先后成立 13 个横向协作组织，多方位、多层次参与全国现代化建设，培育交叉学科生长点。

In order to meet the needs of rapid economic development in China, Tongji University founded a number of hi-tech enterprises to promote the industrialization of research achievements on the basis of the existing factories which had taken orders in addition to provided assistance to teaching, research and student practice. Moreover, Tongji gradually set up 13 organizations, which fully participated in the modernization of the country as well as cultivating inter-disciplinary programs.

■ 1980 年与上海内燃机研究所合作会议

Meeting on cooperation with the Shanghai Internal Combustion Engine Research Institute in 1980

■ 1981 年与上海内燃机研究所第二次合作会议

The second meeting on cooperation with the Shanghai Internal Combustion Engine Research Institute in 1981

■ 1984 年同济与厦门华侨大学签订互助协议

Tongji signing a mutual aid agreement with Huaqiao University in Xiamen in 1984

■ 1984 同济和城乡建设部合办的“建筑管理干部培训中心”成立

The Construction Management Cadres Training Center jointly organized by Tongji University and the Ministry of Urban and Rural Construction was established in 1984

1984 年校党委书记王零与杭州市副市长签定科技合作协议

Mr. Wang Ling, Chairman of the University Council, signing a cooperation agreement of science and technology with a vice mayor of Hangzhou in 1984

1984 年同济大学机械技术开发公司靖江建筑机械厂成立大会

Inaugural meeting of the Jingjiang Construction Machinery Factory of the Tongji Machinery Technology Development Company in 1984

1984 年“中国同济工程机械研究开发中心”在徐州成立

Tongji Engineering Machinery R & D Center was established in Xuzhou in 1984

1984 年同济锌铂合金开发中心九亭五金厂成立大会

Inaugural meeting of the Jiuting Hardware Factory of Tongji Zinc-platinum Alloy Development Center in 1984

1984 年同济大学湖州市环保设备技术联合开发公司成立大会

Inaugural meeting of the Tongji-Huzhou Environmental Protection Equipment Technology Co-development Company in 1984

1985 年同济材料技术研究开发公司成立大会

Inaugural meeting of the Tongji Materials Technology Development Company in 1985

多向交流，世界视野

Multinational Cooperation and Global Vision

在恢复与德国全面合作的同时，学校加强了与美、日、法、意、奥、澳等国的合作与交流。仅 1982 年就有 23 个国家 139 批 514 人来校访问、讲学及作专题报告。同时，学校聘请了贝聿铭、林同炎、许靖华、李斯特、哈斯、帕尔、梅尔巴赫和默恩等一大批国际著名学者为名誉教授、顾问教授和兼职教授。

In addition to the resumption of all-round cooperation with Germany, Tongji University also stepped up cooperation and exchanges with the United States, Japan, France, Italy, Austria, Australia and other countries. In the year 1982, 514 people in 139 groups from 23 countries visited Tongji University, gave lectures and made themed reports. Furthermore, a large number of internationally renowned scholars such as Ieoh Ming Pei, Tung-yen Lin, Jingkwa Hsu, Liszt, Haas, Pahl, Mel Bach and Mons were employed as honorary professors, advisory professors and adjunct professors.

■ 1978 年日本城市规划代表团来校讲学

The Japanese urban planning delegation giving a lecture on a visit to Tongji University in 1978

■ 1979 世界抗震学会主席武藤清来校讲学

Mr. Muto Kiyoshi, President of World Anti-earthquake Society, doing a presentation on his visit to Tongji University in 1979

■ 1980 年结构所请美籍华人来校上课

A Chinese-American invited by the Research Institute of Structural Engineering giving a lecture in 1980

■ 1981 年 4 月底贝聿铭（中）来校讲学

Ieoh Ming Pei doing a presentation in Tongji University at the end of April, 1981

■ 1982 年与美国乔治亚理工学院签署校际合作协议

Tongji signing a cooperation agreement with Georgia Institute of Technology, USA in 1982

■ 1979 年美国堪萨斯大学教授麦金尼讲授给排水课程

Mr. McKinney, Professor of the University of Kansas, giving a lecture on water supply and drainage in 1979

■ 1981 年瑞典专家在建材系讲课

A Swedish expert giving a lecture to the Department of Building Materials in 1981

■ 1980 年美国女建筑师访华团作报告

A U.S. female architect delegation to China making a report in 1980

■ 1984 年美国普渡大学土木系姚治平教授来校讲学

Mr. Yao Zhiping, Professor of the Department of Civil Engineering of Purdue University, USA giving a lecture in Tongji University in 1984

■ 1984 年澳大利亚欧文教授为力学毕业班讲授结构力学

Australian Professor Owen giving a lecture on structural mechanics to the graduating class of mechanics in 1984

■ 1984 年联合国教科文成人教育代表团参观震动台

UNESCO adult education delegation visiting the Vibration Center in 1984

■ 1984 年东京大学杯松笕次郎来校讲课

Mr. Kakehi Jiro from University of Tokyo giving a lecture in Tongji University in 1984

■ 1984 年 10 月 29 日日本抗震专家来校作学术报告

A Japanese anti-earthquake expert making an academic report in Tongji University on October 29, 1984

■ 1985 年布伦瑞克工业大学与同济签订合作协议

TU Braunschweig signing a cooperation agreeemnt with Tongji University in1985

1985 年与法国煤气公司签订合作协议

Tongji signing a cooperation agreement with a French gas company in1985

1986 年同济与日本大阪积水房屋株式会社联合召开第一届工业化住宅研讨会

Tongji University and the SEKISUI, a Japanese corporation based in Osaka, co-held the First Seminar on Industrialized Housing in 1986

1987 年与澳大利亚大学签订协议

Tongji signing an agreement with an Australian University in 1987

■ 1987 年中日建筑声学交流会

Sino-Japan Seminar on Architectural Acoustics in 1987

■ 1987 年中美居住形态比较国际讨论会

International Symposium on Habitat in US and China in 1987

■ 1987 年中日超精加工学术研讨会

Sino-Japan Superfinishing Symposium in 1987

第六章 Chapter VI（1992.1-2012.5）

百年辉煌，继往开来
Exploration of a Brighter Future in Centennial Glory

1992 年以来，随着改革开放的进一步深化，同济大学抓住“211 工程”和“985 工程”建设契机，通过三次并校，调整学科结构，学习国际一流大学工科教学经验，重实践，重创新，重产业，重合作；服务杨浦、服务上海，服务全国，服务世界，确立了具有国际背景和同济特色的卓越工程师系统培养模式。

Since 1992, with the further development of economic reform and opening up to the outside world in China, Tongji managed to optimize the structure among different disciplines following its three mergers with other universities by taking advantage of the 211 Project and 985 Project for its construction. It emphasized on practice, innovation, industry and cooperation by learning from the experience of engineering education in leading universities abroad. The university built a systematic educational model with distinctive Tongji features for cultivating excellent engineers with international perspectives while actively involved in serving Yangpu, Shanghai, China and the whole world.

两大工程，加快振兴

Rapid Development Stimulated by Two National Projects

同济大学 1996 年成为全国“211 工程”首批启动学校，2001 年进入“面向 21 世纪教育振兴行动计划”(985 工程）行列，通过“九五”、“十五”、“十一五”期间的持续建设，学校发展成为拥有医、工、理、法、文、哲、经、管、教、农、艺等十一大学科门类的综合性现代大学，工科教育迈入优势带头、综合迈进的新阶段。

Tongji University was among the first national 211 Project universities in 1996, and later was included in the Action Plan for Education Revitalization known as 985 Project in 2001. Through continuous efforts during the ninth, tenth and eleventh five-year plans, Tongji University has become a comprehensive university with eleven disciplines including medicine, engineering, sciences, law, literature, philosophy, economy, management, education, agriculture, and arts. Its engineering education has also stepped into a new phase with strong engineering disciplines leading its development in a comprehensive way.

■ 1995 年 11 月，同济大学通过国家教委“211 工程”部门预审。

Tongji University passed the 211 Project pre-examination by the State Education Commission in November 1995.

■ 2002 年 6 月 26 日，教育部与上海市人民政府重点共建同济大学签字仪式举行，标志着学校进入“985 工程”重点建设高校。

On the June 26th, 2002, the Ministry of Education signed an agreement with the Shanghai Municipal Government for joint construction of Tongji University, signifying that Tongji was included in the Action Plan for Education Revitalization.

■ 2004 年 7 月，同济大学被列为由中央管理的普通高等学校。

In July 2004, Tongji became a university under direct leadership of the central government.

■ 2010 年 12 月，教育部与上海市签约，继续重点共建同济大学。

In December 2010, the Ministry of Education signed an agreement with the Shanghai Municipal Government to continue the joint construction of Tongji University

三次并校，优势增强

Advantages Strengthened by Three Mergers of Universities

1996 年 9 月，上海城市建设学院、上海建筑材料工业学院并入同济大学，此次并校被喻为“同济模式”，成为中国高等教育界具有示范意义的标志性工程。2000 年 4 月 27 日，上海铁道大学并入；2003 年 11 月 14 日，上海航空工业学校并入。通过并校，吸收了几所高校的特色专业，学科结构得到改善，工科类优势学科变得更强。

In September 1996, the Shanghai Institute of Urban Construction and Shanghai Institute of Building Materials merged with Tongji University. The merger was hailed as Tongji Model, which became a landmark with pioneering significances for the higher education in China. On April 27th 2000, Shanghai Railway University also joined the merge. On November 14th 2003, Shanghai Aviation Industrial School followed. Through such incorporations, Tongji absorbed the characteristic specialties of the above four schools and improved its disciplinary structure. This strengthened the advantages of its engineering discipline.

■ 1996 年 9 月 4 日，国家教委主任朱开轩来校宣布上海市城市建设学院、上海建筑材料工业学院正式并入同济大学。

On September 4th 1996, Zhu Kaixuan, Director of the State Education Committee, announced the official incorporation of Shanghai Institute of Urban Construction and Shanghai Institute of Building Materials into Tongji University at Tongji University.

■ 上海建筑材料工业学院创建于 1953 年，并入后为同济大学沪东校区。

The Shanghai Institute of Building Materials, which was established in 1953, became the Hudong Campus of Tongji University after the incorporation.

■ 上海城市建设学院创建于 1978 年，并入后为同济大学南校区。

The Shanghai Institute of Urban Construction, which was established in 1978, became the South Campus of Tongji University after the incorporation.

2000 年 4 月 27 日，同济大学与上海铁道大学合并大会

Conference for the incorporation of Shanghai Railway University into Tongji University on April 27th, 2000

上海铁道大学创建于 1958 年，是我国铁路工程高层次人才培养和科学研究的重要基地，并入后为同济大学沪西校区。

The Shanghai Railway University established in 1958 as an important base for the cultivation of high-level professionals and research of railway engineering, became the Huxi Campus of Tongji University.

2003 年 11 月 14 日，上海航空工业学校划归同济大学管理。

On November 14th, 2003, Shanghai Aviation Industrial School was incorporated into Tongji University.

上海航空工业学校创建于 1951 年，其前身为民航第三学校，创办以来为国家培养了中等专业或技工人才 13000 余名，并入后为同济大学彰武路校区。

Shanghai Aviation Industrial School (formerly known as No.3 Aviation School), which was established in 1951 and cultivated more than 13,000 technicians for the nation, became the Zhangwu Campus of Tongji University.

嘉定新区，产学链接

Cooperation Between University and Industry in Jiading Campus

为支持“上海国际汽车城”的建设，同济大学提出“紧密结合产业链来建设学科链”的发展理念，2001 年起开始建设总建筑面积 40 万平方米的嘉定校区，汽车学院、软件学院、电子与信息工程学院、机械与能源工程学院、交通运输工程学院、材料科学与工程学院、中德工程学院、轨道交通研究院等 8 个工科学院整体迁入，构筑以地面交通工具为核心、以汽车为龙头的现代装备制造学科链。

To support the construction of the Shanghai International Automobile City, Tongji University proposed a developmental concept of “building a disciplinary chain through close cooperation with industrial chains”. It started the construction of the 2500-mu (1 mu=666.7) Jiading Campus in 2001. Engineering schools of Automotive Engineering, Software Engineering, Electronics and Information Engineering, Mechanical and Energy Engineering, Traffic & Transportation Engineering, Material Science and Engineering, the Sino-German College of Applied Sciences, and the Institute of Railway Transportation were relocated to the Jiading Campus in 2004. A disciplinary chain of modern equipment manufacturing took its initial shape with automotive engineering as the head and ground transport in the central core.

■ 2001 年 9 月 28 日，同济大学汽车学院奠基仪式举行。

The Foundation-laying Ceremony for the School of Automotive Engineering of Tongji University on September 28th, 2001

■ 2001 年 9 月 28 日，嘉定校区打下第一根桩，正式开工建设。

The first pile of Jiading Campus was laid on September 28th 2001, marking the beginning of its construction

■ 嘉定校区校名石

Stone inscribed with Tongji University on Jiading Campus

■ 2004 年 9 月，嘉定校区一期工程建成，首批师生入驻。

The first group of teachers and students moved to Jiading Campus following the completion of its first-phase construction in September 2004.

■ 嘉定校区规划全图
Master Plan of Jiading Campus

■ 嘉定校区图书馆
Library in Jiading Campus

■ 交通运输工程学院

■ 汽车学院
School of Automotive Engineering

■ 材料科学与工程学院
School of Material Science and Engineering

■ 上海地面交通工具风洞中心
Shanghai Wind Tunnel Center for Ground Transport

■ 电子与信息工程学院
School of Electronics and Information Technology Engineering

■ 中德工程学院
The Sino-German College of Applied Sciences

■ 软件学院
School of Software Engineering

■ 机械与能源工程学院
School of Mechanical and Energy Engineering

学科协同，规模效应

Scale Effects from Interdisciplinary Coordination

同济大学按强势学科核心化、优势学科体系化、新兴学科交叉化、人文学科特色化的建设思路，构筑以科技战略和产业布局为优势的学科群和学科链，四平、嘉定校区分别形成了“城市建设与防灾”、“清洁能源地面交通装备制造”两大学科群落。工科协同已见雏形，规模效应开始显现。

Guided by the idea of “centralizing the strong disciplines, systematizing the advanced disciplines, intercrossing the emerging disciplines and characterizing the liberal arts”, Tongji University constructed disciplinary clusters and chains that excel in technological strategy and industrial layout. The two clusters of Urban Construction and Disaster Prevention, and Clean Energy & Ground Transport Equipment Manufacturing were formed in the Siping Campus and Jiading Campus respectively. The coordination among engineering disciplines took its initial shape and scale effects thus came into being.

■ 四平路校区“城市建设与防灾学科群”

Disciplinary Cluster of Urban Construction and Disaster Prevention in Siping Campus

■ 嘉定校区“清洁能源地面交通装备制造学科链”

Disciplinary Cluster of Clean Energy & Ground Transport Equipment Manufacturing in Jiading Campus

■ 桥梁与隧道工程研究成果（左：上海卢浦大桥设计与施工关键技术研究；右：崇明越江桥隧通道工程风险分析研究）

Achievements in bridge and tunnel engineering (left: research on key technologies in the design and construction of Shanghai Lupu Bridge; right: research on key construction technology of Jiangyin Yangtze River Bridge)

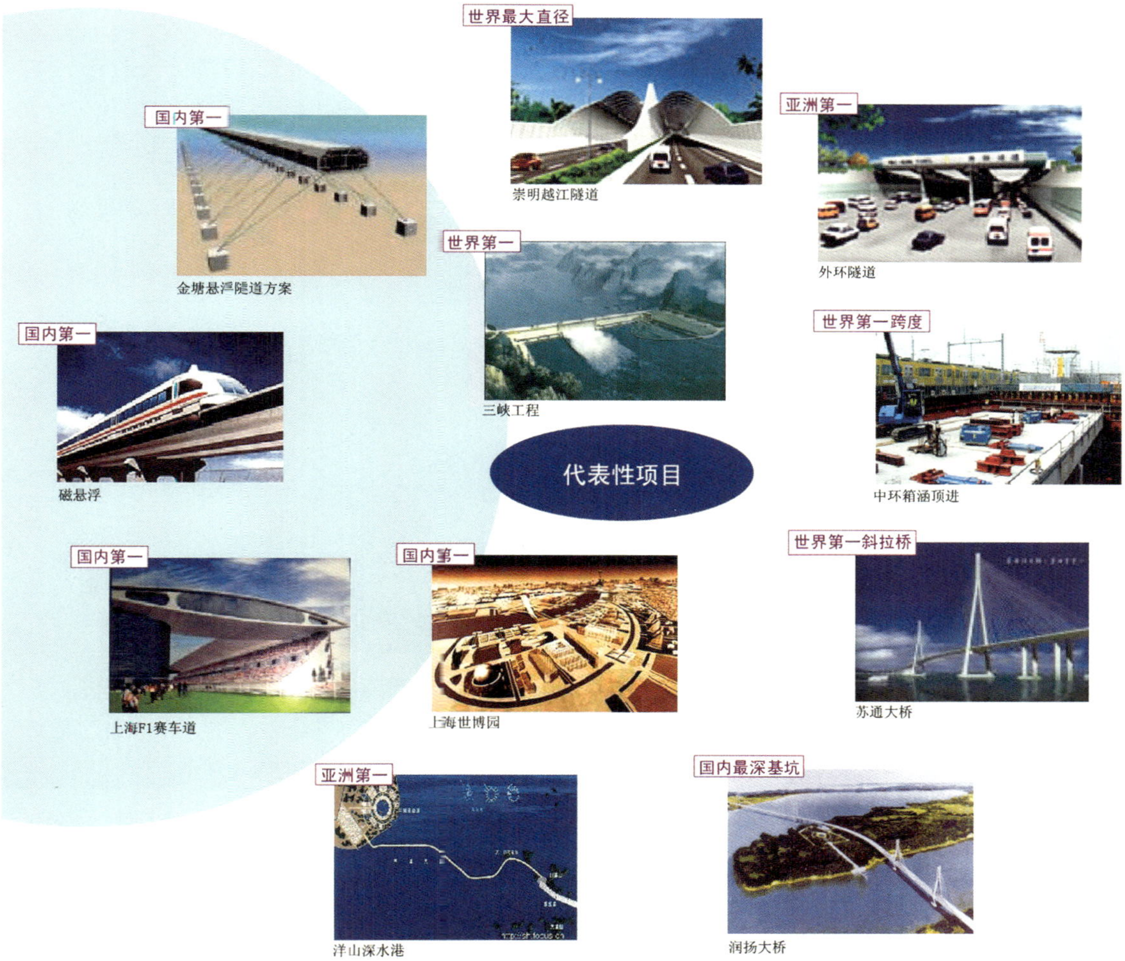

■ 岩土工程成果展示

Projects of geotechnical engineering

■ 工程力学研究成果（左：缠绕式增强夹砂管在上海市污水治理工程中的应用试验研究；右：建筑结构在强风作用下的动力影响研究）

Research achievements of engineering mechanics (left: experimental research on the application of winding reinforced mortar pipes in sewage treatment of Shanghai; right: research on dynamical influence on building structures against strong wind.)

■ 交通运输规划与管理专业研究成果（左：交通运输系统仿真平台；右：模块化交通控制及智能交通集成实验）

Research achievements of transport planning and management (left: A simulation platform of road transport system; right: An integrated experiment on modularized transport control and intelligent transport)

■ 结构工程成果展示

Achievements in structural engineering

■ 环境工程学科团队承担的国家 863 项目“化学 - 生物絮凝组合技术与设备”的相关研究成果在上海、北京等多家城市污水处理厂应用。

Research results of the National 863 Project of Technologies and Equipment of Integrated Chemical-biological Flocculation undertaken by the research team of environmental engineering have been applied in urban sewage treatment factories in Shanghai, Beijing and other cities.

■ 城市规划与设计成果展示（左：2010 世博会总体规划设计研究；右：2008 奥运乒乓球馆方案设计）

Achievements in urban planning and design (left: master plan of the Expo 2010 Park; right: design of the Table Tennis Stadium for the Olympics Games 2008)

院士领衔，济济一堂

Faculty Capacity Building Led by Academicians

同济大学坚持培养与引进并重政策，大力加强教师队伍建设，目前全校工科教授中有多名中国科学院、中国工程院和其他国家科学院院士，以及多名国家级突出贡献中青年专家、百千万人才工程专家、长江学者奖励计划特聘教授、讲座教授，2 个国家自然科学基金创新群体，4 个教育部创新团队，形成了一支素质高、眼光远、专业强、作风硬的人才队伍。

Tongji University has made great efforts in strengthening its faculty capacity building by adhering to a policy of “emphasis on cultivation and introduction of talents”. So far, among the professors in engineering disciplines there are a number of members of Chinese Academy of Sciences, of Chinese Academy of Engineering and of equivalent academies of other countries. There are also a number of Young and Middle-aged National Experts with Merits, experts on the Hundred, Thousand and Ten Thousand Talents Project, distinguished professors on the Cheung Kong Scholars Program and chair professors. Meanwhile, two science and technology innovation groups supported by the National Natural Science Fund and four innovation teams supported by the Ministry of Education have been established. A pool of specialists of high competence with global perspectives has been built up to ensure a sustainable development of the university.

■ 孙钧，1926 年 10 月生于江苏苏州，祖籍浙江绍兴，同济大学岩土工程研究所教授，工程力学家、隧道与地下结构工程专家，1991 年当选为中国科学院院士。

Sun Jun, born in Suzhou, Jiangsu Province in October 1926 (of Shaoxing origin, Zhejiang Province). He is a professor of the Research Institute of Geotechnical Engineering of Tongji University and expert in engineering mechanics and tunnel and underground structure engineering. He became a member of the Chinese Academy of Sciences in 1991.

■ 姚熹，1935 年 9 月生，江苏武进人，同济大学功能材料研究所所长，我国在铁电陶瓷研究方面的主要奠基人之一，1991 年当选为中国科学院院士，国际陶瓷科学院院士，美国工程院外籍院士。

Yao Xi, a native of Wujin, Jiangsu Province, born in September 1935, is director of the Research Institute of Functional Materials of Tongji University and a pioneering figure in research on ferroelectric ceramics in China. He was elected as a member of the Chinese Academy of Sciences in 1991. He is also a member of the World Academy of Ceramics and a foreign associate of US National Academy of Engineering.

■ 李同保，1942 年 10 月生，河南温县人。1963 年毕业于同济大学物理系，同济大学声学研究所教授，我国计量测试领域的著名专家，1994 年当选为中国工程院院士。

Li Tongbao, a native of Wenxian County, Henan Province, born in October 1942, graduated from the Physics Department of Tongji University in 1963. He is a professor of the Research Institute of Acoustics of Tongji University and a well-known expert in the field of metrology in China. He was elected as a fellow of the Chinese Academy of Engineering in 1994.

■ 郭重庆，1933 年 6 月生，陕西富平县人，同济大学机械与能源工程学院教授，著名工程设计大师，1995 年当选为中国工程院院士。

Guo Chongqing, a native of Fuping County, Shannxi Province, born in 1933, is a professor of the School of Mechanical and Energy Engineering, and a renowned master of engineering design. He was elected as a member of the Chinese Academy of Engineering in 1995.

■ 项海帆，1935 年 12 月生于上海，祖籍浙江杭州，1955 年毕业于同济大学桥梁与隧道专业，土木工程学院教授，著名桥梁及结构工程专家，1995 年当选为中国工程院院士。

Xiang Haifan, born in Shanghai in December 1935 (origin in Hangzhou, Zhejing Province), graduated from the Department of Bridge and Tunnel Engineering of Tongji University in 1955. He is a professor of the School of Civil Engineering and a well-known expert in bridge and structural engineering. He was elected as a member of the Chinese Academy of Engineering in 1995.

■ 卢耀如，1931 年 5 月生，福建福州人，同济大学土木工程学院地下建筑与工程系教授，著名地质学家，1997 年当选为中国工程院院士。

Lu Yaoru, a native of Fuzhou, Fujian Province, born in May 1931. He is a professor of the Department of Underground Architecture and Engineering, School of Civil Engineering of Tongji University and a famous geologist. He was elected as a member of the Chinese Academy of Engineering in 1997.

■ 戴复东，1928 年 4 月生于广州，安徽无为县人，同济大学建筑与城市规划学院教授，1999 年当选为中国工程院院士。

Dai Fudong, born in Guangzhou in April 1928 (origin in Wuwei County, Anhui Province), professor of the School of Architecture and Urban Planning of Tongji University, was elected as a member of the Chinese Academy of Engineering in 1999.

■ 范立础，1933 年 6 月生，浙江镇海人，1955 年毕业于同济大学路桥系桥梁与隧道工程专业，同济大学土木工程学院教授，2001 年当选为中国工程院院士。

Fan Lichu, born in June 1933, is a native of Zhenhai, Zhejiang Province. He graduated from the Bridge and Tunnel Engineering program at the Department of Road and Bridge Engineering of Tongji University in 1955. He is a professor of the School of Civil Engineering and was elected a member of the Chinese Academy of Engineering in 2001.

■ 郑时龄，1941 年 11 月生，广东惠阳人，1965 年毕业于同济大学，同济大学建筑与城市规划学院教授，2001 年当选为中国科学院院士，法国建筑科学院院士、美国建筑师协会海外荣誉院士。

Zheng Shiling, born in November 1941, is a native of Huiyang, Guangdong Province, He is graduated from Tongji University in 1965. He is a professor of the School of Architecture and Urban Planning, Tongji University and was elected as a member of the Chinese Academy of Sciences in 2001. He is also a member of the French Academy of Architecture, and an honorary foreign member of the American Society of Landscape Architects

■ 沈祖炎，1935 年 6 月生，浙江杭州人，1955 年毕业于同济大学工业与民用建筑结构专业，同济大学土木工程学院教授，2005 年当选为中国工程院院士。

Shen Zuyan, born in June 1935, a native of Hangzhou, Zhejiang Province, graduated from the Department of Industrial and Civil Architectural Structure of Tongji University in 1955. He is a professor of the School of Civil Engineering, Tongji University and was elected as a member of the Chinese Academy of Engineering in 2005.

■ 周兴铭，1938 年 12 月出生于上海，浙江余姚人，著名计算机专家，同济大学软件学院院长、教授，1993 年当选为中国科学院院士。

Zhou Xingming, born in Shanghai in December 1938 with origin in Yuyao, Zhejiang Province. He is a professor and Dean of the School of Software Engineering, Tongji University, and a well-known expert of computer. He was elected as a member of the Chinese Academy of Sciences in 1993.

中组部“千人计划”引进人才

Professors introduced by The Thousand Talents Program of the Organizational Department of the Central Government

■ 杨志刚（汽车学院）

Yang Zhigang (School of Automotive Engineering)

■ 章桐（汽车学院）

Zhang Tong (School of Automotive Engineering)

■ 戴晓虎（环境科学与工程学院）

Dai Xiaohu (School of Environmental Science and Engineering)

■ 张伟贤（环境科学与工程学院）

Zhang Weixian (School of Environmental Science and Engineering)

■ 黄文锐（土木工程学院）

Huang Wenrui (School of Civil Engineering)

■ 李荣兴（土木工程学院）

Li Rongxing (School of Civil Engineering)

■ 吴俊（电子与信息工程学院）
Wu Jun (School of Electronics and Information Technology Engineering)

■ 周孟初（电子与信息工程学院）
Zhou Mengchu (School of Electronics and Information Technology Engineering)

■ 林峰（电子与信息工程学院）
Lin Feng (School of Electronics and Information Technology Engineering)

■ 崔玉军（土木工程学院）
Cui Yujun
(School of Civil Engineering)

■ 张红军 （交通与运输工程学院）
Zhang Hongjun
(School of Traffic and Transportation Engineering)

■ 张永和（建筑与城市规划学院）
Zhang Yonghe
(School of Architecture & Urban Planning)

三位一体，复合培养

KAP Model of Talent Cultivation

同济大学以"本科教育为立校之本，研究生教育为强校之路"，确立了"知识、能力、人格"三位一体的全面素质教育和"校内培养、企业培养和国际化培养"的复合型人才培养模式，严抓管理，确保质量，努力培养具有"工程基础、科学精神、人文素养、国际视野"的高级专门人才。

Guided by the university principle of "having the undergraduate education for its firm foundation and the postgraduate education for its competitive strength", Tongji University has adopted a quality-oriented, three-in-one educational model for all-round development of students known as the KAP (Knowledge, Ability and Personality) model. This model coupled with another model of "cultivating students with an international perspective jointly by the university and the industry" helped the university to achieve its goal of producing advanced personnel who have "engineering knowledge, scientific spirit, cultural literacy and international perspective".

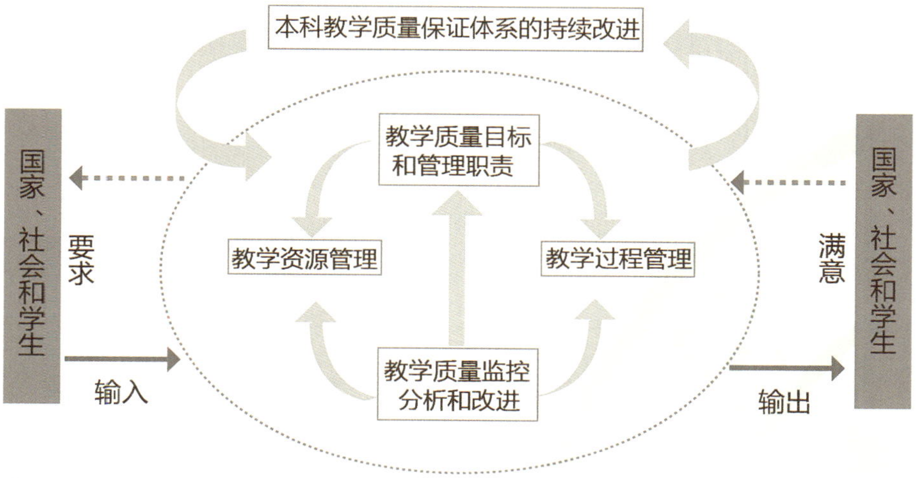

■ 教学质量保证体系

Teaching Quality Assurance System

1993 — 2009 国家级教学成果奖：教材与专题（一等奖）

Awards for National Teaching Achievements (1993-2009): Textbooks and Themed Programs (First Prize)

年度 Year	教学成果 Teaching achievements	获奖者 Award winners
1997	高等数学（第三版）（教材） Advanced Mathematics (3rd edition) (textbook)	王福楹、邱伯驺、骆承钦、王章炎 Wang Fuying, Qiu Bozou, Luo Chengqin, Wang Zhangyan
	突出创新能力培养，努力创建有特色的大学物理课程教学体系 Establishment of a distinctive teaching system for undergraduate physics courses with distinctive features	顾牡、吴於人、陈铭南、羊亚平、毛骏健 Gu Mu, Wu Yuren, Chen Mingnan, Yang Yaping, Mao Junjian
	我国高等口腔医学教育课程体系和教学模式改革 Reform of the curriculum and teaching mode of China's advanced medical education in Stomatology	潘可风 Pan Kefeng
2005	土建类专业工程素质和实践能力培养的研究与实践 Research and practice on the cultivation of engineering and practical abilities of students in civil engineering disciplines	蒋永生 邱洪兴 陈以一 郭正兴 黄晓明 单 建 何敏娟 Jiang Yongsheng, Qiu Hongxing, Chen Yiyi, Guo Zhengxing, Huang Xiaoming, Shan Jian, He Minjuan
2009	土木工程本科学生创新型、国际化人才培养体系与实践 Teaching system and practice for cultivating innovative and civil engineering undergraduates with an international perspective	何敏娟、顾祥林、熊海贝、赵宪忠、林峰、丁文其、吴迅 He Minjuan, Gu Xianglin, Xiong Haibei, Zhao Xianzhong, Lin Feng, Ding Wenqi, Wu Xun

国家级教学团队
National Teaching Teams

年度 Year	国家级教学团队名称 Titles of Teams	带头人 Leader	类别 Target Students	所属院系 Affiliated Organizations
2008	大学计算机基础教学团队 Teaching Team of College Computer Basis	龚沛曾 Gong Peizeng	本科 Undergraduates	电子与信息工程学院 School of Electronics and Information Engineering
	钢结构教学团队 Teaching Team of Steel Structure	陈以一 Chen Yiyi	本科 Undergraduates	土木工程学院 School of Civil Engineering
	城市与区域规划理论与方法教学团队 Teaching Team of Urban and Regional Planning Theories and Techniques	赵 民 Zhao Min	本科 Undergraduates	建筑与城市规划学院 School of Architecture & Urban Planning
2009	建筑历史与理论教学团队 Teaching Team of Architectural History and Theories	郑时龄 Zheng Shiling	本科 Undergraduates	建筑与城市规划学院 School of Architecture and Urban Planning

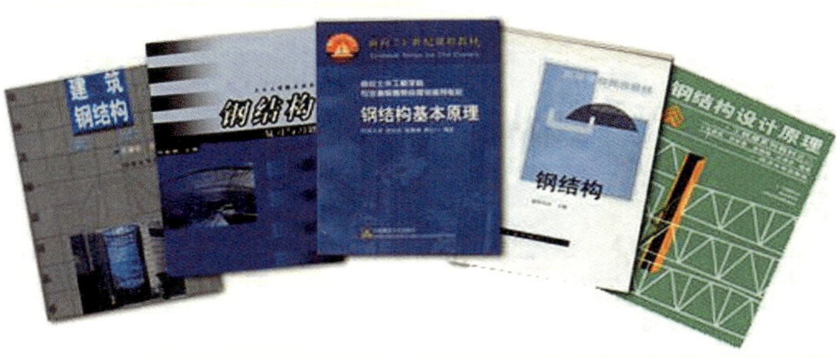

● 钢结构教材

● 老师带领学生到现场讲解，让同学得到感性认识

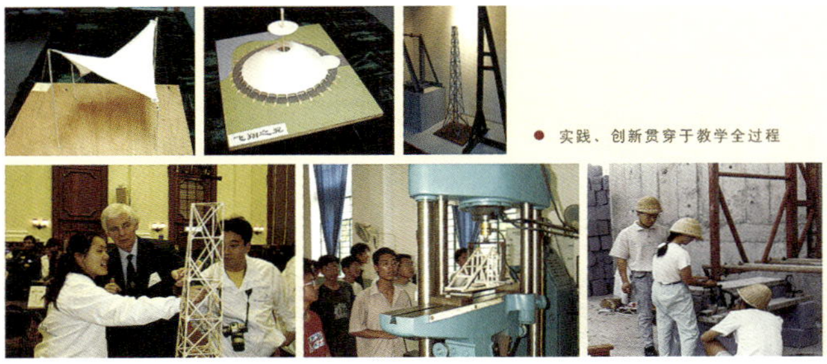

● 实践、创新贯穿于教学全过程

■ “钢结构”教学

Teaching of the Steel Structure

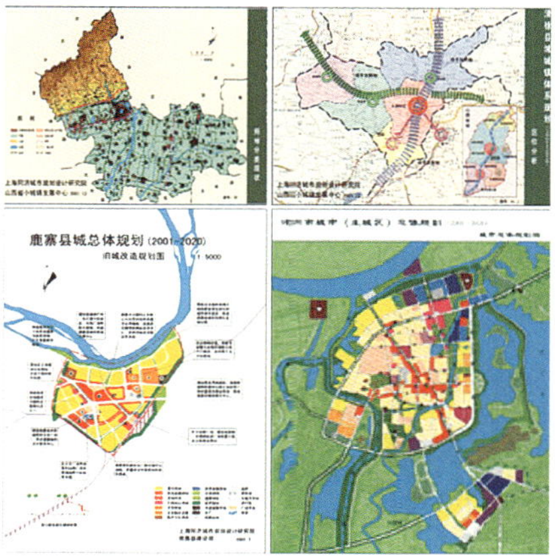

● 学生作业

● 研讨

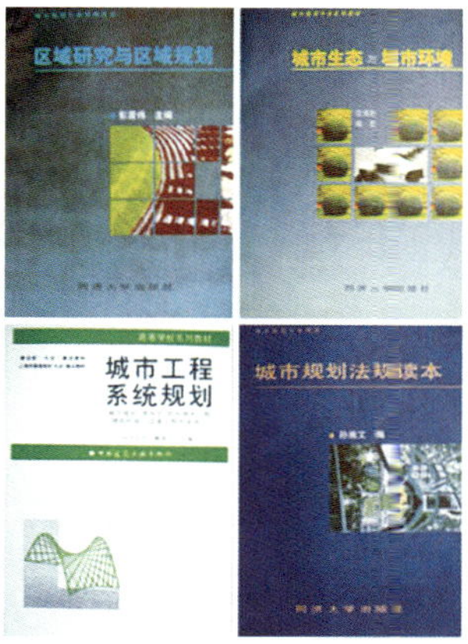

● 课程教材

■ “城市与区域规划理论与方法”教学

Teaching of “Theories and Techniques of Urban and Regional Planning”

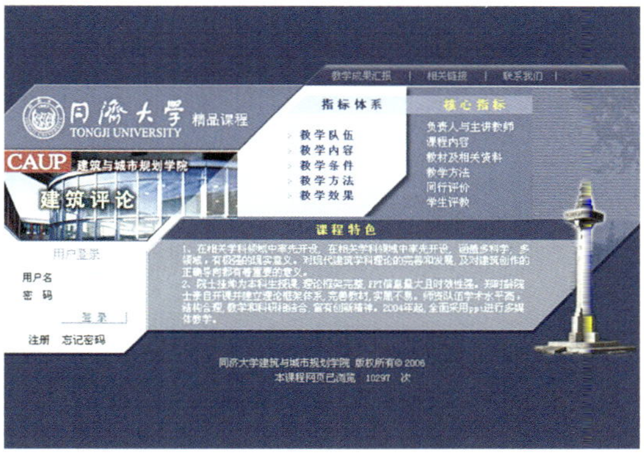

■ “大学计算机基础”教学

Teaching of College Computer Basis

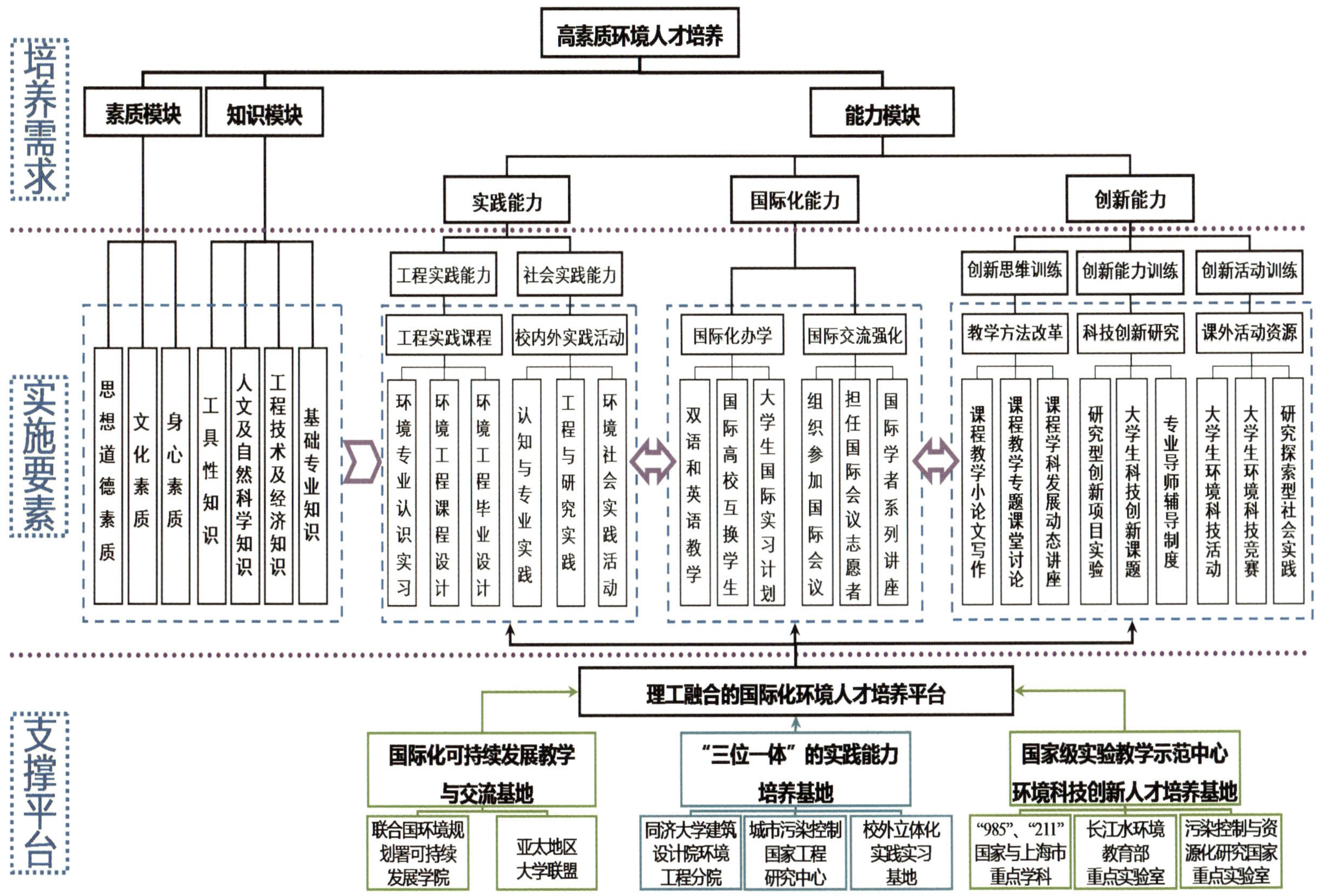

■ 环境科学与工程学院融合的国际化环境人才培养体系

The International Sciences and Engineering Integrated Talents Cultivation System of the School of Environmental Science and Engineering

创新计划，加大投入

Innovative Projects with Increased Investments

同济大学将创新训练纳入培养计划和课程体系，建立“学院（系）项目 - 校级项目 - 上海市级项目 - 国家级项目”四级大学生创新训练计划体系，学校从 2004 年开始，先后投入 4000 万元进行“本科教学创新人才培养基地建设”工程，共申请获得国家大学生创新性试验计划项目 305 个，上海市大学生创新活动计划项目 400 个，校级项目 1373 个，每年约有 36000 人次的学生参与完成各层次的创新计划。

Innovation has been integrated into the teaching plan and curriculum of Tongji University and this leads to the establishment of an undergraduate innovation cultivation system which contains projects at four levels of, i.e. the levels of department or school, university, Shanghai government and the state. Since 2004, Tongji University has invested 40 million RMB on the project of Construction of Cultivation Base for Innovative Undergraduates, and was successful in its applications for 305 national innovative experimental projects for the undergraduates, for 400 undergraduate innovative activity project of Shanghai and 1373 projects of the university. A total of 36,000 students were involved in the innovative projects at various levels.

工科创新教育基地

Innovative Base for Engineering Education

序号 No.	项目负责单位 Organizations Concerned	创新基地名称 Titles of Innovative Base	成立时间 Time of Commencement	基地级别 Levels
1	物理系 Physics Department	国家工科物理基础课程教学基地 State Base for Engineering Physics Basic Courses Instruction	1996年11月 November of 1996	国家级 State
2	数学系 Mathematics Department	国家工科数学基础课程教学基地 National Base for Engineering Mathematics Basic Course Instruction	2004年9月 September of 2004	国家级 State
3	土木工程学院 School of Civil Engineering	土木工程教学创新基地 Base for Civil Engineering Instructional Innovation	2003年7月 July of 2003	校级 University
4	环境科学与工程学院 School of Environmental Science and Engineering	环境科技创新人才培养基地 Base for Cultivation of Environmental Technology Innovative Talents	2003年7月 July of 2003	校级 University
5	汽车学院 School of Automotive Engineering	大学生汽车科技创新实践基地 Base for Undergraduate's Automobile Technology Innovation Practice	2003年7月 July of 2003	校级 University
6	交通运输工程学院 School of Traffic and Transportation Engineering	大学生实验交通科技创新基地 Base for Undergraduate's Experimental Transportation Technology Innovation	2003年7月 July of 2003	校级 University
7	电子与信息工程学院 Electronics and Information Engineering School	大学生电子信息科技创新基地 Base for Undergraduate's Electronics and Information Technology Innovation	2003年7月 July of 2003	校级 University
8	建筑与城市规划学院 School of Architecture & Urban Planning	建筑与城市规划学院教学创新基地 Instructional Innovation Base of School of Architecture & Urban Planning	2004年6月 June of 2004	校级 University
9	机械工程学院 School of Mechanical Engineering	大学生机械与热能创新实践基地 Base for Undergraduate's Mechanical and Thermal Energy Innovation Practice	2004年6月 June of 2004	校级 University
10	航空航天与力学学院 School of Aerospace Engineering and Mechanics	力学本科教学创新基地 Base for Undergraduate's Mechanics Instructional Innovation	2007年3月 March of 2007	校级 University
11	材料科学与工程学院 School of Material Science and Engineering	材料科学与工程学院创新基地 Innovative Base of School of Material Science and Engineering	2009年1月 January of 2009	校级 University
12	软件学院 School of Software Engineering	软件学院大学生创新基地 Innovative Base for Undergraduates of School of Software Engineering	2009年1月 January of 2009	校级 University

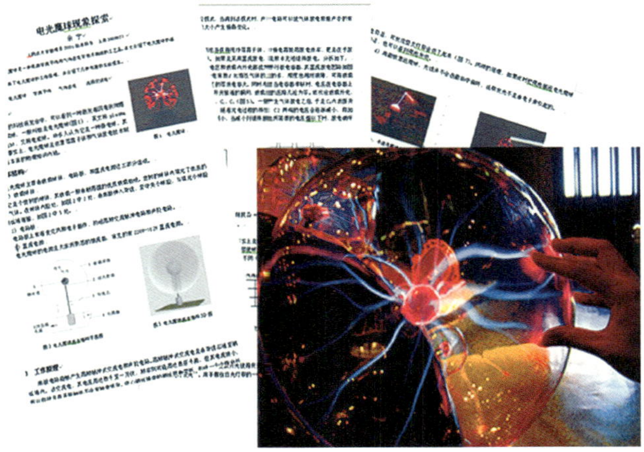

■ 国家级工科物理基础教学基地
National Teaching Base for Basic Courses in Engineering Physics

■ 大学生电子信息科技创新实践基地
Innovation and Practice Base of Electronics and Information Technology for Undergraduates

■ 国家级工科数学基础教学基地
National Teaching Base for Basic Courses in Engineering Mathematics

■ 大学生实验交通科技创新基地
Innovation Base of Experimental Transportation Technology for Undergraduates

■ 力学本科教学创新基地
Innovation Teaching Base of Mechanics for Undergraduates

■ 大学生机械与热能创新实践基地

Innovation and Practice Base of Mechanical and Thermal Energy for Undergraduates

■ 土木工程教学创新基地

Innovation Teaching Base of Civil Engineering

■ 建筑与城市规划学院教学创新基地

Innovative Teaching Base of the School Architecture and Urban Planning

■ 环境科技创新人才培养基地

Innovative Talent Cultivation Base of Environmental Science and Technology

■ 大学生汽车科技创新实践基地

Innovation and Practice Base of Automotive Technology for Undergraduates

■ 2003 年校长万钢迎接参加全国大学生“挑战杯”课外科技作品竞赛获奖返校的学生

President Wan Gang meeting the winners of Challenge Cup, a national contest of extracurricular technological works for college students in 2003

■ 2011 年同济大学学生在第十二届“挑战杯”全国大学生课外学术科技作品竞赛勇夺团体“优胜杯”

Students of Tongji University winning the Best Team Award of the 12nd Challenge Cup in 2011

■ 自 2007 年开始每年一度的建造节活动

Annual Construction Activities since 2007

■ 2004 年大学生课外活动展示

Student extracurricular activities on display in 2004

■ 校内创意设计大赛

Innovative Design Contest of Tongji University

■ 仿真机器人展示

A simulation robot on display

创业教育，带动就业

Better Employment from Entrepreneurial Education

同济大学积极开展大学创业教育与培训，带动大学生就业。2006 年 9 月，与上海市大学生科技创业基金会联合设立同济分基金，至 2010 年底，55 个项目获得立项资助注册公司，入驻大学生创业园。学生创业企业已成功申请国家专利 67 项，2 家被认定为上海市高新技术企业，19 个创业项目得到科技部和上海市中小企业创新基金立项资助，资助金额 570 万元。

Tongji University has actively practiced entrepreneurial education and training to increase the employment rate of graduates. Shanghai Technology Entrepreneurship Fund for Graduates helped establish a Tongji branch of the fund at Tongji University in September 2006. By the end of 2010, fifty five projects supported by the fund had turned into registered companies which subsequently moved into the Incubation Park for College Students. These companies had successfully obtained 67 state patents, two of which being recognized as Shanghai High-tech Companies. In addition, nineteen pioneering projects received funds from the Ministry of Science and Technology and the Shanghai Small and Medium-size Enterprises Innovative Funds, totaling 5.7 million RMB.

■ 2007 年 11 月 8 日，科技部高技术研究发展中心副主任陈志敏与同济大学党委副书记马锦明共同为“同济大学大学生创业园揭牌”

Mr. Chen Zhimin, deputy director of the High-tech R&D Center of the Ministry of Science and Technology unveiling a plate for the Student Incubation Park of Tongji University jointly with Ms. Ma Jinming, vice Party secretary of Tongji University, on November 8th 2007

■ 科技部颁发的“大学生科技创业见习基地”牌

Plate of the College Student Technology Incubation Observation Base issued by the Ministry of Science and Technology

■ 教育部、科技部颁发的“高校学生科技创业实习基地”牌

Plate of the College Student Technology Incubation Internship Base jointly issued by the Ministry of Education and Ministry of Science and Technology

■ 中央电视台记者王小丫（前排中）采访学生创业者

CCTV reporter Wang Xiaoya (first middle) interviewing students who started their high-tech businesses

■ 学生创业产品展示

Hi-tech products produced by student start-up companies on display

■ 2008 年，同济大学校团委与上海市大学生科创基金会同济分基金于 11 月 18 日至 27 日联合举办同济大学首届大学生创业文化节，图为开幕式的企业家演讲论坛。

An entrepreneur doing a presentation at the opening ceremony of the First Student Entrepreneurship Festival co-organized by the University Youth League and the Tongji Branch of the Shanghai Technology Entrepreneurship Fund for Graduates from November 18th to 27th, 2008

■ 2010 年同济大学第一期大学生创业基础培训班结业合影

Students upon their completion of the First Student Entrepreneurship Training Course of Tongji University in 2010

社会实践，增长才干

Experience from Social Practice

同济大学把社会实践作为工程教育的重要内容和有效手段，引导大学生走出校门，在实践中“受教育、长才干、做贡献”。学校围绕“创设项目，凝练主题，组建团队，建设基地”的思路，基本形成常规化、系列化、制度化、基地化的社会实践体系，学生参与率提高至 100%，并逐步提高重复参与率，形成具有时代特征、同济特色的项目链、团队簇、基地群。

Tongji University takes social practices an integral part of engineering education and encourages students to go out of the campus to receive education, improve their capabilities and make contributions. A standard systematic social practice system has been built with 100% participation of students.

■ 郑时龄副校长暑假期间到工厂看望学生实习（1996）

Vice President Zheng Shiling visiting students on internship in a factory during summer vacation (1996)

■ 学生在内燃机公司，浦东水泥厂等地实习（1996）

Students doing internship at Internal-Combustion Engine Company and Pudong Concrete Factory in 1996

■ 校外实习基地会议（1997）

Meeting at an off-campus Internship Base in 1997

■ 建筑系在乌镇实习（1998）

Students of the Architecture Department doing internship in Wuzhen in 1998

■ 暖通专业 95 年级学生在上海凯灵空调设备有限公司实习（1998）

Students of Year 1995 doing internship in Shanghai Kailing Air Conditioner Co., Ltd in 1998

■ 建筑与城市规划学院学生生产实习（2000）

Model making practice of students from the School of Architecture and Urban Planning in 2000

■ 环境科学与工程学院学生在三峡进行环境考察实习

Students of the School of Environmental Science and Engineering doing investigation in the Three Gorges

■ 2002 年同济赴青藏线"三个代表"社会实践服务团在青藏铁路施工现场

Tongji social practice service group on the construction site of Qingzang Railway in 2002

■ 土木工程学院开展暑期调研

Summer investigation by students of the School of Civil Engineering

■ 古建筑测绘实习

Surveying of classical buildings

■ 学生暑期走进企业

Summer internship in companies

■ 机械工程学院师生在上海振华港口机械（集团）股份有限公司实习

Teachers and students of the School of Mechanical Engineering practicing at Shanghai Zhenhua Port Machinery Co., Ltd.

■ 师生进行测量实习

Teachers and students doing field work of surveying

■ 本科生参加为期 5 至 6 周的金工实习

Metal work practice for undergraduates for 5-6 weeks

科研成果，与时俱进

Scientific Research Abreast of Latest Developments

同济大学以科研条件和科研成果作为提高工程教育师资水平的重要手段，以重点科研基地、重大项目、重大成果为抓手，构筑科技创新平台，提供完善的科研设备和良好的学术氛围，让学生在紧密结合国家科技发展战略和社会需求的前瞻视角中攀登学术高峰，培养与时俱进的新型工程人才。

Tongji University takes the advantage of research conditions and research achievement to improve the teaching quality of engineering education; it also makes good use of major state laboratories, major research projects and major research achievements to build new platforms of science and technology and to provide sophisticated research facilities and create good academic atmosphere. In this way, students are well motivated to embark on frontier academic research in line with the national development strategies and the social needs, and will become engineering professionals who keep abreast of the latest development of technology.

1992-2010 年科研经费及高水平论文情况表

Research funds and papers published in top academic journals (1992-2010) (UNIT: 10,000 RMB)

	2002	2003	2004	2005	2006	2007	2008	2009	2010
科研经费（万）research funds	50309.5	60106.1	78664.5	98515.7	105735.4	116854.8	129182.9	139603.7	163885.1
SCI 论文（篇）SCI papers	203	232	292	374	441	495	671	853	1056
EI 论文（篇）EI papers	276	292	391	909	892	1043	1271	1374	1680

	1992	1993	1994	1995	1996	1997	1998	1999	2000	2001
科研经费（万）research funds	4249.1	6419.3	10466.7	11510.6	12626.7	15720.2	17171.5	20084.8	28428.0	42372.0
SCI 论文（篇）SCI papers					26	41	53	83	135	159
EI 论文（篇）EI Papers					36	28	44	75	197	203

■ 上海环球金融大厦抗震防灾试验
Anti-seismic and disaster prevention experiments of Shanghai World Financial Tower

■ 独立研制国内第一个快速道路智能交通管理系统
Independent research on the first expressway intelligent transport management system in China

■ 承担东方明珠电视塔抗风、抗震研究和天线顶升工程。
An anti-wind and anti-seismic research and an antenna lifting project of the Oriental Pearl TV Tower

■ 研究并参与上海苏州河水环境治理
Research on Suzhou Creek's water treatment of Shanghai

■ 万钢教授领衔研发的洁净能源汽车，被评为2005年中国高校十大科技进展之一。
The clean energy vehicle project led by Professor Wan Gang was selected as one of Ten Major Scientific Achievements of Universities in China in 2005.

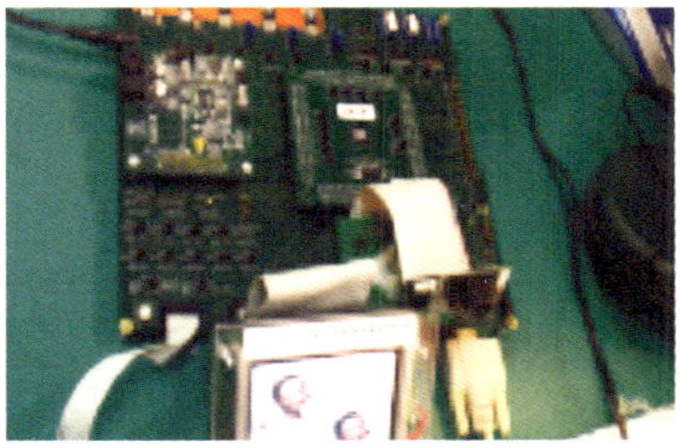

■ 大规模集成电路研究所自主研究设计“神芯”系列第三代多媒体手机核心芯片
The 3rd generation CMOS chip of the “Magic Core” series for multimedia cell phones developed by Research Institute of Large-scale Integrated Circuits

■ 环境工程与科学学院主持的“863”项目——大型源水生物处理技术
Large-scale Biological Treatment Technology of Source Water, an “863 Project” led by the School of Environmental Science and Engineering

■ 2005年航空航天与力学学院师生研制的水上轻型飞机“蜻蜓一号”。
“Dragonfly No.1” developed by teachers and students from the School of Aerospace and Mechanics in 2005

■ 土木工程防灾国家重点实验室承担的江阴长江大桥的抗风、抗震研究工作。

Anti-wind and anti-seismic research on Jiangyin Changjiang Bridge undertaken by the State Key Laboratory of Civil Engineering Disaster Prevention

同济大学近年所获国家级科研奖项名称

List of national awards for scientific research won by Tongji University in recently years

授奖单位	成果名称
国家科技进步奖 一等奖	大跨、高墩桥梁抗震设计关键技术
国家科技发明奖 二等奖	耦合式城市污水处理新技术及应用 基于虚拟超市技术的大规模网络资源管理及其应用
国家自然科学奖 二等奖	特大桥梁颤振和抖振精细化理论
国家科技进步奖 二等奖	重交通沥青路面设计的理论体系、关键技术与工程应用 软土盾构隧道设计理论与施工控制技术及其应用 燃料电池轿车动力平台关键技术 国产化智能温室及其环境控制系统等配套设施的研制 城市交通智能诱导系统与关键技术 结构抗震防灾新技术研究及其工程应用

同济大学“工博会”参展项目/展品获奖一览表

List of the exhibits and awards of Tongji University on the Industry Fair

年份	奖项	项目/展品
2010	大会金奖	直径11.22米泥水平衡盾构
	大会铜奖	高端印刷机控制系统
	大会铜奖	用于污水和污泥处理的平板膜生物反应器
	中国高校展区优秀作品奖	能源自足型太阳能竹屋
		DJK-T1无线调车机车信号和监控系统
		新一代节能环保永磁电驱动全液压叉车
2009	大会创新奖	耦合式城市污水处理新技术及应用
	大会铜奖	校园节能监管平台系统
	中国高校展区优秀作品奖	自主驾驶电动场馆车
		软土遁构隧道设计理论与施工控制技术及其应用
		NOx选择性催化还原一体化装置及复合型催化剂
2008	大会银奖	系列功能化水处理剂
	大会创新奖	轻量化燃料电池微型车
	大会铜奖	国产化智能温室及其环境控制系统等配套设施的研制
	中国高校展区优秀作品奖	东海大桥斜拉桥抗风性能及颤动控制研究及应用
		TJWX-2006TD信号微机监测系统
2007	中国高校展区优秀作品奖	NVPG电动汽车平台
		基于三维实体模型的钢结构制作设计系统
		处理城市污水及回用集装式膜生物反应器成套技术装备
2006	大会创新奖	玉米塑料-聚乳酸
	中国高校展区优秀作品奖	同济曙光软件
		液压爬行机器人成套技术及装备（tjg-1000型)
	最具技术交易潜力奖	钢结构防火防腐蚀双功能涂料

校园节能，高校典范

Energy-saving Campus Leading Universities in China

同济大学在全国率先创建节约型校园，从宣传教育、制度管理、科学研究、建筑节能等方面着手，建立起多层次节能科教基地。学校提高节约意识、普及节能科技、开放示范技术、支持引导学生开展节能主题活动，使校园建设成为工程教育实践的一大基地，被建设部列为全国节约型示范校园。

Tongji University has taken the lead in building an energy-saving campus in China and in establishing an energy-saving educational base for the promotion, education, system management, scientific research and practice of the concept of energy saving. The university has improved student awareness of energy saving, promoted energy-saving technologies, made available demonstration technologies and encouraged students to do energy-saving activities, thus making the campus itself a base for engineering education. The campus was selected as a National Energy-saving Model Campus by the Ministry of Construction.

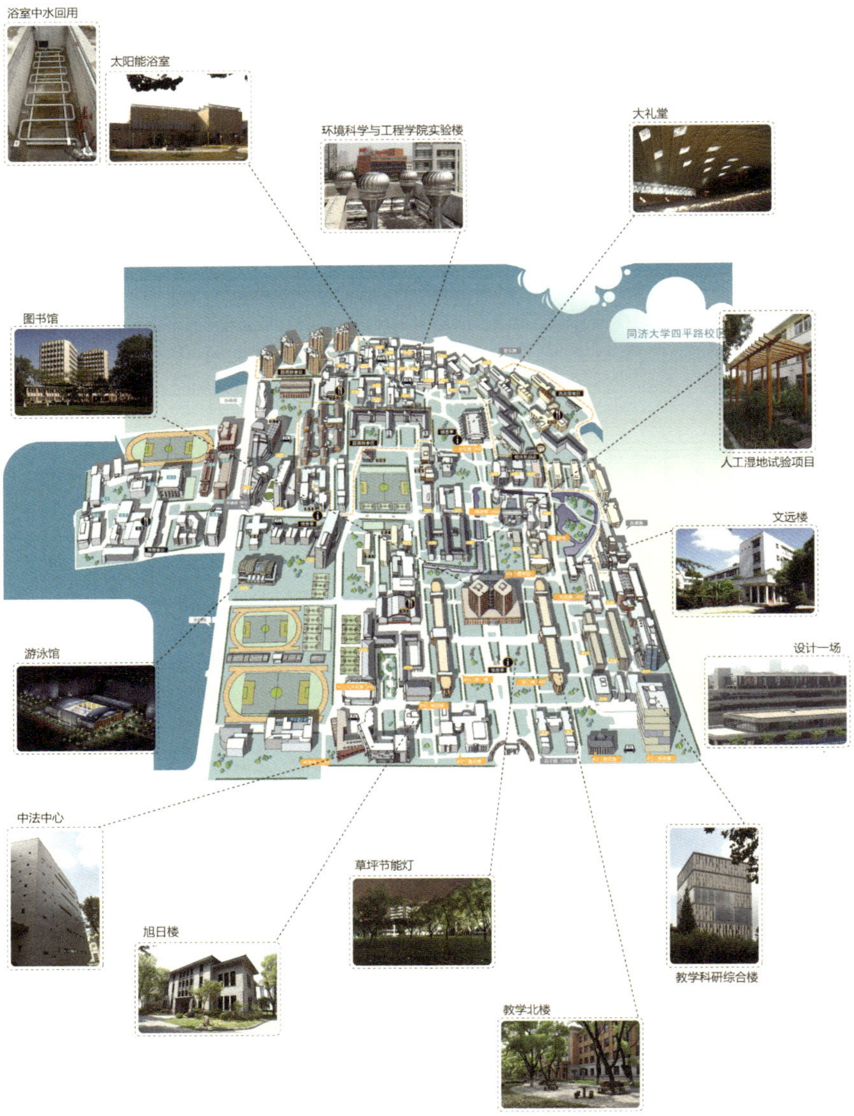

■ 四平路校区节能项目分布图

Distribution of energy-saving projects in Siping Campus

■ 嘉定校区的节能建设，重点突出节能和生态技术

Construction of Jiading Campus focusing on energy-saving and biological technologies

■ 2010 年 12 月 29 日，“同济大学人居环境与节能联合研究中心”揭牌，图中从左到右依次为校长裴钢，副校长蒋昌俊、伍江。

President Pei Gang and vice presidents Jiang Changjun and Wu Jiang (from left to right) unveiling plate of the Research Center of Habitat & Energy Saving of Tongji University on Dec. 29, 2010

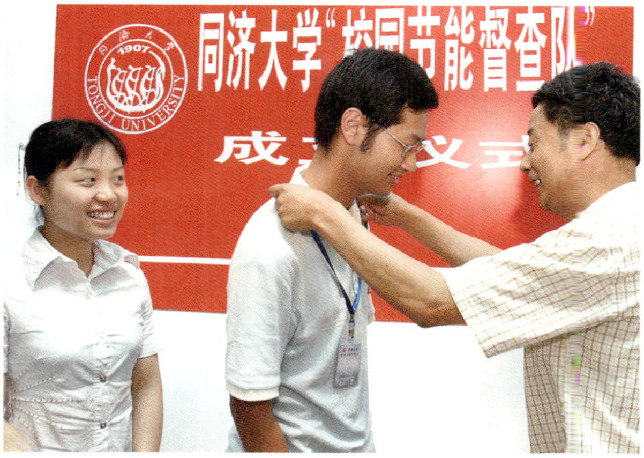

■ 同济大学成立“校园节能督查队”

An initiation ceremony of Energy Saving Supervision Team on Campus

■ 2010 年，同济大学太阳竹屋出征太阳能十项全能欧洲赛场，这是太阳能十项全能竞赛自举办以来首次中国高校也是首次亚洲高校参赛。

Solar-Energy Bamboo House of Tongji University attending the First European Solar-energy Decathlon Omnipotence Competition in 2010. Tongji was the first team from China even from Asia to attend the event.

■ 学生创新团队参加节能车大赛

Student Innovation Group in the Energy-saving Automobile Contest

■ 关于“同济大学节约型校园建设”的媒体报道

Media reports on energy-saving campus construction of Tongji University

■ “节约型校园建设监管平台”接受专家评估

Assessment on Tongji's Supervision Platform of Energy-saving Campus Construction by external experts

■ 陈小龙副校长在国际论坛介绍同济大学可持续校园建设经验

Vice president Chen Xiaolong introducing the experiences of building a sustainable campus in Tongji University in an international forum

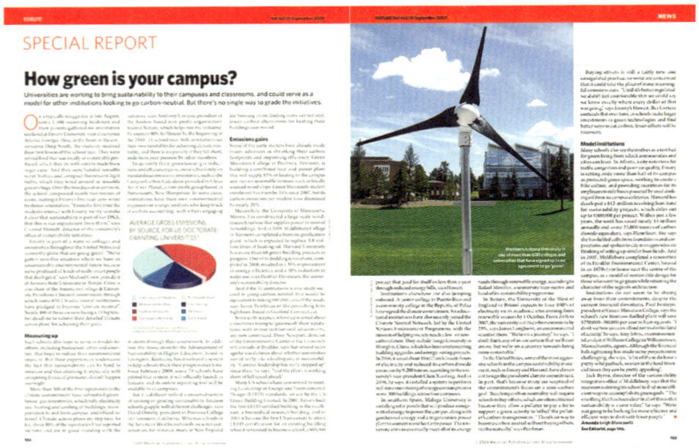

■ 《Nature》杂志介绍同济大学节能型校园建设

Report on *Nature* introducing the energy-saving campus of Tongji University

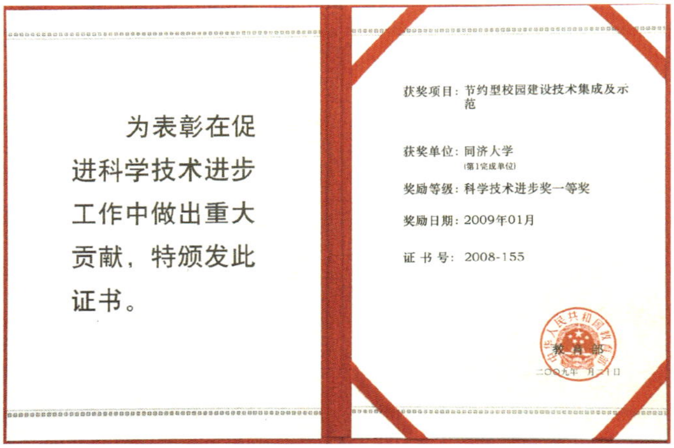

■ 同济大学“节约型校园建设技术集成及示范”项目获教育部科技进步一等奖

Project of Energy-saving Campus Technology Integration and Demonstration of Tongji University won the first-prize Scientific Advancement Award by the Ministry of Education in 2009

■ 同济大学节约型校园示范工程被评为“2007中国建筑节能年度代表工程”

The Energy-saving Campus Demonstration Project of Tongji University was awarded 2007 Annual Representative Project of Architectural Energy Saving in China.

重大工程，同济品牌

Tongji Brand in Major Projects

秉持“以服务为宗旨，在贡献中发展”的信条，同济工科凭借在建筑、土木、环境、车辆、交通等专业的领先水平，使“同济”二字成为城乡建设、装备制造等国家重大工程质量与信誉的品牌保证。自1992年以来，同济人主持或参与的国家重大工程近百项，这些工程不仅铸造了同济工程技术的品牌，而且为同济工科学生参与工程实践创造了宝贵机会。

Tongji University firmly believes in Service-oriented Contributions for Development and successfully makes the two characters of Tong and Ji a brand name of quality and credibility in national major projects of urban planning and equipment manufacturing by taking advantage of its strength in architecture, civil engineering, environmental engineering, automotive engineering and transport. Since 1992, staff from Tongji have led or participated in nearly a hundred national major projects, which has not only helped cast the brand of Tongji engineering technology, but also provided valuable practice opportunities for engineering students of Tongji University.

■ 东方明珠电视塔天线顶升工程，同济教授们运用自己研发的“超大构件计算机控制液压提升、顶升技术”，顺利地完成顶升安装的经典示范。

The "computer-controlled hydraulic lifting technology for super-size components" developed by professors of Tongji employed in the antenna jacking-up of Oriental Pearl Tower in Shanghai, a typical case of successful lifting installation.

■ 平遥古城总体规划，由城市规划与建筑学院阮仪三教授主持，开创了中国规划保古城建新城的先河。

A design project of the master plan of ancient city Pingyao led by Professor Ruan Yisan from the School of Architecture and Urban Planning. The master plan marked the beginning of preservation of old cities while building new cities.

■ 上海大剧院特大型钢屋面液压整体提升工程，顶升安装的另一经典案例。

Hydraulic-pressure large-scale roof lifting project of Shanghai Grand Theatre, another typical case of lifting installation

■ 上海八万人体育场钢屋盖模型试验

An integral steel roof model experiment of Shanghai 80,000-seat Stadium

■ 上海浦东国际机场张弦梁足尺试验

Beam string structure full scale test of Shanghai Pudong International Airport

■ 中央电视台新址大楼“含钢率超限的特殊形状 SRC 结构”

Special SRC structure of over-limit steel ratio of the new CCTV building

■ 上海国际会议中心球体工程

Sphere structure of Shanghai International Conference Center

■ 苏州河治理工程，上海的“母亲河”苏州河曾污臭难当，同济人“标本兼治”的治污理念，让她神奇地变为鱼虾竞现的“源头活水”。

Suzhou River treatment project: Shanghai's "Mother River" Suzhou River was heavily polluted in the past. Tongji has magically turned the river into flowing water suitable even for fishes by following the sewage treatment idea of “treating both the symptoms and their root causes simultaneously”.

■ 同济参与系统规划、架构设计及核心软件开发的南北高架

South-North Elevated Expressway of Shanghai: Tongji University participated in the system planning, structure design and core software development.

■ 苏通大桥获美国土木工程师协会“2010 年度 ASCE 杰出工程成就奖”，该奖项是我国桥梁工程在国际上获得的最高荣誉。同济大学有中国工程院院士 4 人、正高级职称 65 人、副高级职称 76 人、中级职称 54 人、博士和硕士研究生逾两百人参与建设，是学校参与国内外同一工程建设投入人力、物力、财力最多，系统最庞大，组织协调最完善的一次。

Sutong Bridge awarded with 2010 ASCE Outstanding Engineering Achievements Award by the American Society of Civil Engineers. The award is the highest honor a bridge project in China has ever won in the international arena. More than two hundred people from Tongji University, including 4 members of the Chinese Academy of Engineering, 65 teachers with senior titles, 76 with vice senior titles, 54 teachers with intermediate titles, doctors and graduates, participated in the project. Among all the projects Tongji ever did at home and abroad, Sutong Bridge was the one that required the most investment in manpower, material and financial resources. It also stands out for its most complicated system, and best organization and coordination that Tongj has ever seen.

■ 同济合作设计的上海中心

Shanghai Center co-designed by Tongji University

■ 同济设计的非盟会议中心

African Union Conference Center designed by Tongji University

■ 同济主持研制的北京奥运氢燃料电池轿车

Inaugurating Ceremony of fuel-cell cars for the Olympic Games Beijing 2008 designed by Tongji University

■ 同济设计的北京奥运乒乓球馆

Table Tennis Stadium of the Olympic Games Beijing 2008 designed by Tongji University

■ 北京奥运会主会场“鸟巢”的施工设计

Construction design of the Bird's Nest, the main track and field stadium of Beijing Olympic Games

■ 被誉为世纪工程的洋山深水港及其配套工程的建设中，同济人承担了“东海大桥的海上超常距离”、“深水港的巨大填海面积”、“临港新城的交通控制管理”等重大项目。

In the Yangshan deep-water port project and its supporting projects, Tongji solved the problems of "super distance of the East Sea Bridge on the sea", "huge reclamation area of the deep-water port", and "city traffic control and management of the new harbor city".

科技园区，产业孵化

Technological Parks for Industrial Incubation

同济大学对校办企业进行改制、重组，形成了具有同济特色的科技产业集群，2009年4月环同济知识经济圈被授牌为“环同济研发设计服务特色产业基地”，成为国内首个以现代服务业为主的特色产业基地，直接推动教学科研成果的转化和产业化，助力学生创业和城市经济提升。

Tongji University has reformed and regrouped the university-owned companies and established a technological industrial cluster with distinctive Tongji features. In April 2009, the Knowledge Economy Circle around Tongji was authorized to be a Research, Design and Service Base around Tongji, which has become China's first featured industrial base of modern service industry. It could directly promote the transformation and industrialization of teaching and research achievements, boost students' entrepreneurship and urban economic development.

■ 2004年1月13日，校党委书记周家伦、杨浦区副区长马杰富共同为“同济大学国家大学科技园”揭牌。

The party secretary Zhou Jialun and vice governor of Yangpu District Ma Jiefu unveiling the plate of National Science and Technology Park of Tongji University on Jan. 13, 2004.

■ 同济大学科技园图示

Map of Tongji Science and Technology Park

■ 位于赤峰路上的同济大学国家大学科技园总部

Headquarters of National Science and Technology Park of Tongji University located on Chifeng Rd.

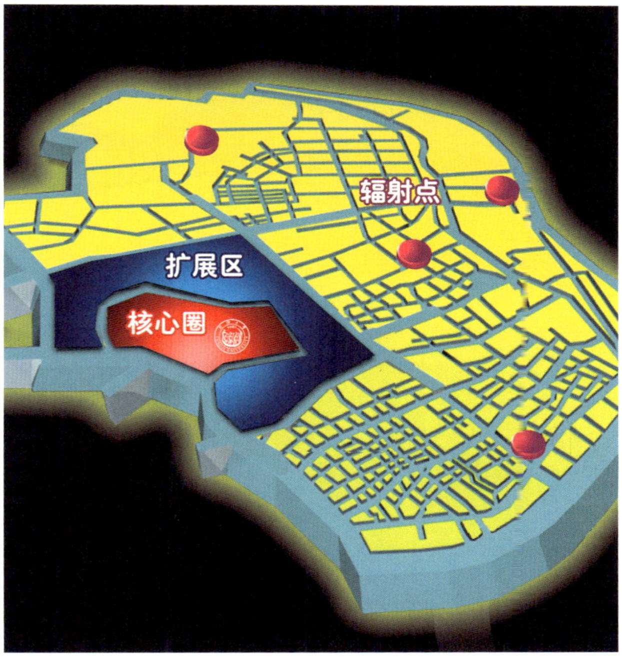

■ 环同济知识经济圈示意图

Map of Knowledge and Economy Circle around Tongji

■ 2007 年 6 月 16 日，“杨浦环同济知识经济圈建设启动仪式”举行，图为科技部部长万钢（左）、上海市副市长杨定华（右）为“同济杨浦新技术创新基地”揭牌。

Minister Wan Gang(left) of the Ministry of Science and Technology and Vice Mayor of Shanghai Yang Dinghua(right) unveiling the plate of the Yangpu New Technology Innovation Base of Tongji University at the initiation ceremony of Construction of Yangpu Knowledge and Economy Circle around Tongji on June 16, 2007.

■ 2009 年 4 月 18 日，科技部部长万钢（左）、上海市副市长沈晓明（右）为国家火炬计划“环同济研发设计服务特色产业基地”揭牌，该基地是国内首个以现代服务业为主的特色产业基地。

Minister Wan Gang of the Ministry of Science and Technology and Vice Mayor of Shanghai Shen Xiaoming unveiling the plate of Research & Design and Service Base around Tongji, which was the first featured industrial base with focus on modern service on April 18, 2009.

■ 2009 年 9 月 12 日，上海市首个由市、区、校三方共建的创意产业集聚区“上海环同济设计创意产业集聚区”正式揭牌。

Signing Ceremony of Industrial Cluster District around Tongji on Sep. 12, 2009, which was the first of its kind that was co-established by the city, district and university parties.

■ 2010 年 5 月 28 日，同济与杨浦区政府签署《上海国际设计一场项目合作协议》。

Signing Ceremony of “Shanghai No. 1 International Design Plaza Project Cooperative Agreement” between Tongji University and the government of Yangpu District on May 28, 2010.

■ 2010 年 9 月 17 日，“上海国际设计中心落成典礼暨入驻仪式”举行，图中从左至右依次为：同济大学常务副校长李永盛、同济大学党委书记周家伦、杨浦区区委书记陈寅、区长金兴明。

Opening Ceremony of Shanghai International Design Center on Sep. 17, 2010. From left to right: the executive vice president of Tongji University Mr. Li Yongsheng, party secretary of Tongji University Mr. Zhou Jialun, party secretary of Yangpu District Mr. Chen Yin, head of the district Mr. Jin Xingming.

国内合作，层层推进

Further Development through More Cooperation at Home

同济大学加强与各地方政府及企业的合作，与政府共建科研实习基地，搭建校企合作平台，形成紧密的产学研联盟，为工程人才的培养提供多途径、多层次发展平台，为国家和地方发展作出重要贡献。

Tongji University has attached great importance to the cooperation with local governments and companies by establishing scientific and technological internship bases together with the governments, building up academy-enterprise cooperative platforms. The practice has formed close industry-academy-research associations, provided various multi-level development platforms for the cultivation of engineering talents and made great contributions to the national and local development.

校地合作

Cooperation with Local Governments and Industry

■ 2006 年 6 月 1 日，“同济大学与苏州市全面科技合作协议暨同济大学科技园苏州基地项目签约仪式”举行，苏州市副市长周伟强与同济大学副校长杨东援代表双方签约。

Signing Ceremony of Scientific & Technological Cooperation between Suzhou Municipal Government and Tongji University on June 1, 2006. The vice mayor of Suzhou City Mr. Zhou Weiqiang, and Mr. Yang Dongyuan, the vice president of Tongji University, signing the agreement on behalf of the two parties.

■ 2010 年 1 月 19 日，同济大学与铁道部签署科研合作协议，铁道部科学技术司司长季学胜与同济大学副校长蒋昌俊代表双方签约。

Mr. Ji Xuesheng, the director of the Division of Science and Technology of the Ministry of Railway, and Mr. Jiang Changjun, the vice president of Tongji University signing an agreement at the signing ceremony of Scientific & Technological Cooperation between Ministry of Railway and Tongji University on Jan. 19, 2010.

■ 2010 年 3 月 19 日，同济大学与昆明市签订合作协议，昆明市委常委、常务副市长李文荣与同济大学副校长董琦代表双方在协议书上签字。

Signing Ceremony of Cooperation between Kunming Municipal Government and Tongji University on March 19, 2010. Member of the Standing Committee of the CPC Kunming Municipal Committee, Deputy Mayor, Mr. Li Wenrong, and Dong Qi the vice president of Tongji signing the agreement on behalf of the two parties.

■ 2011 年 6 月 18 日，同济大学与天津市政府签署全面合作协议，天津市副市长张俊芳与同济大学校长裴钢代表双方在协议书上签字。

Vice Mayor of Tianjin Zhang Junfang, and President Pei Gang of Tongji University signing the agreement at the signing ceremony of Cooperation between Tongji University and Tianjin Municipal Government on June 18th, 2011.

■ 2012 年 3 月 29 日，同济大学与宁波市签订战略合作协议，宁波市副市长成岳冲、同济大学副校长董琦代表双方签字。

Signing Ceremony of Strategic Cooperation between Ningbo Government and Tongji University on March 29, 2012. The vice mayor of Ningbo City Mr. Cheng Yuechong, and Dong Qi, the vice president of Tongji University, signing the agreement on behalf of the two parties.

■ 同济大学与黑龙江教育厅、科技厅签约

Signing Ceremony of Cooperation between Heilongjiang Ministry of Education, Ministry of Science & Technology and Tongji University

■ 同济大学与丽水市科技合作交流签约

Signing Ceremony of Technological Cooperation between Tongji Universtiy and Lishui City

校校合作
Cooperation among Universities

■ 2006 年 4 月 29 日，同济大学与山东大学共同签署两校校际合作协议，同济大学李国强副校长、山东大学樊丽明副校长代表双方签字。

Signing Ceremony of Cooperation between Tongji University and Shandong University on April 29, 2006. The vice president of Tongji University, Mr. Li Guoqiang and the vice president of Shandong University Ms. Fan Liming signing the agreement on behalf of the two parties.

■ 2010 年 12 月 13 日，同济大学与第二军医大学共同签署合作框架协议，同济大学校长裴钢、第二军医大学校长刘振全代表双方签约。

Signing Ceremony of Cooperation between Tongji University and the Second Military Medical University on Dec. 13, 2010. The president of Tongji University Mr. Pei Gang and the president of the Second Military Medical University Mr. Liu Zhengquan signing the frame agreement on behalf of the two parties.

■ 2011 年 12 月 20 日，同济大学与解放军理工大学在南京签订校际战略合作协议，解放军理工大学副政委周争光与同济大学副校长董琦分别代表两校签署协议。

Signing Ceremony of Cooperation between Tongji University and PLA University of Science and Technology on Dec. 20, 2011. Mr. Zhou Zhengguang, deputy political commissar of the PLA University and Dong Qi, the vice president of Tongji University, signing the agreement on behalf of the two parties

■ 2010 年 6 月 2 日，同济大学与潍柴动力签署校企合作协议，潍柴动力执行总裁孙少军、同济大学副校长陈小龙代表双方签字。

Signing Ceremony of Academy-Enterprise Cooperation between Weichai Power and Tongji University on June 2, 2010. The CEO of the company, Mr. Sun Shaojun and the vice president of Tongji Mr. Chen Xiaolong signing the agreement on behalf of the two parties.

■ 2009 年 9 月 22 日，同济大学校长裴钢与永久自行车股份公司签订产学合作协议。

Signing Ceremony of Industry-Academy Cooperation between Forever Co., Ltd and Tongji University on Sep. 22, 2009.

■ 2010 年 7 月 2 日，同济大学与北新集团建材股份有限公司“校企合作协议”签约暨“同济大学——北新建材学生实习基地”揭牌仪式举行。

Signing Ceremony of Academy-Enterprise Cooperation between Beixin New Building Material (Group) Co., Ltd and Tongji University and the establishment of Tongji - Beixin New Building Material Internship Base on July 2, 2010.

■ 2007 年 5 月 20 日，同济大学与新奥集团签署成立“清洁能源联合研究所”合作协议，新奥集团副总裁甘中学博士和同济大学汽车学院院长余卓平博士代表双方在合作协议上签字。

Signing Ceremony of Co-construction of Clean Energy Research Institute between Xin'ao Group and Tongji University on May 20, 2007.The vice president of the Group Dr. Gan Zhongxue and the dean of the Department of Automobiles of Tongji, Dr. Yu Zhuoping signing the agreement on behalf of the two parties.

■ 2007 年 5 月 19 日，同济大学与浙江吉利控股集团有限公司联合投资创办的“吉利—同济汽车工程研究院”合作签字暨揭牌仪式举行，开创了我国以资本合作为纽带的“产学研”合作模式之先河。

Geely-Tongji Institute of Automobile Engineering Research, co-invested by Geely-Tongji was established on May 19, 2007. The cooperation model is the first of its kind in terms of the bridging role capital plays in the "manufacturing-learning-research" cooperation.

■ 2010 年 4 月 17 日，同济大学与香港经纬集团合作成立的“经纬不动产研究院”揭牌成立，同济大学常务副校长李永盛和经纬集团董事局主席陈经纬为研究院揭牌。

TongjiUniversity and Hong Kong KINGWORLD Group established "KINGWORLD ResearchInstitute", unveiled by the executive vice president of Tongji Mr. Li Yongshengand the chairman of the board of the Group on April 17, 2010.

■ 2007 年 2 月 6 日，同济大学与光大国际有限公司签订合作协议，光大国际有限公司总经理范仁鹤、同济大学副校长杨东援代表双方在协议书上签字。

Signing Ceremony of Cooperation between China Everbright Group and Tongji University on Feb. 6, 2007. The general manager of the Company Mr. Fan Renhe and the vice president of Tongji Mr. Yang Dongyuan signing the agreement on behalf of the two parties.

■ 2009 年 1 月 20 日，同济大学与上海磁浮交通工程技术研究中心战略合作协议签字仪式举行，上海磁浮交通工程技术研究中心主任吴祥明、同济大学党委书记周家伦代表双方签字。

Signing Ceremony of Cooperation between Shanghai Maglev Research Center and Tongji University on Jan. 20, 2009. The director of the Center Mr. Wu Xiangming and the party secretary of Tongji Mr. Zhou Jialun signing the agreement on behalf of the two parties.

国际交流，纵深发展

Development Through International Exchanges and Communications

同济大学坚持国际化办学，与国外高校和企业的交流与合作日益增强。从以德为主转向对欧为主，拓展北美、辐射亚非、联合国际组织。国际政要和学术大师相继来访，承担政府间合作项目不断增加，形成了具有同济特色的国际化发展模式。

Tongji University adheres to the internationalization of school-running and increasingly strengthens communications and cooperations with overseas universities and companies. Tongji has shifted the focus from Germany to Europe, extending to North America, Asia, Africa and international organizations. A large number of International political celebrities and academic masters have come to visit Tongji. The number of inter-government cooperative projects undertaken by Tongji University keeps growing. An international development mode with Tongji features comes into being.

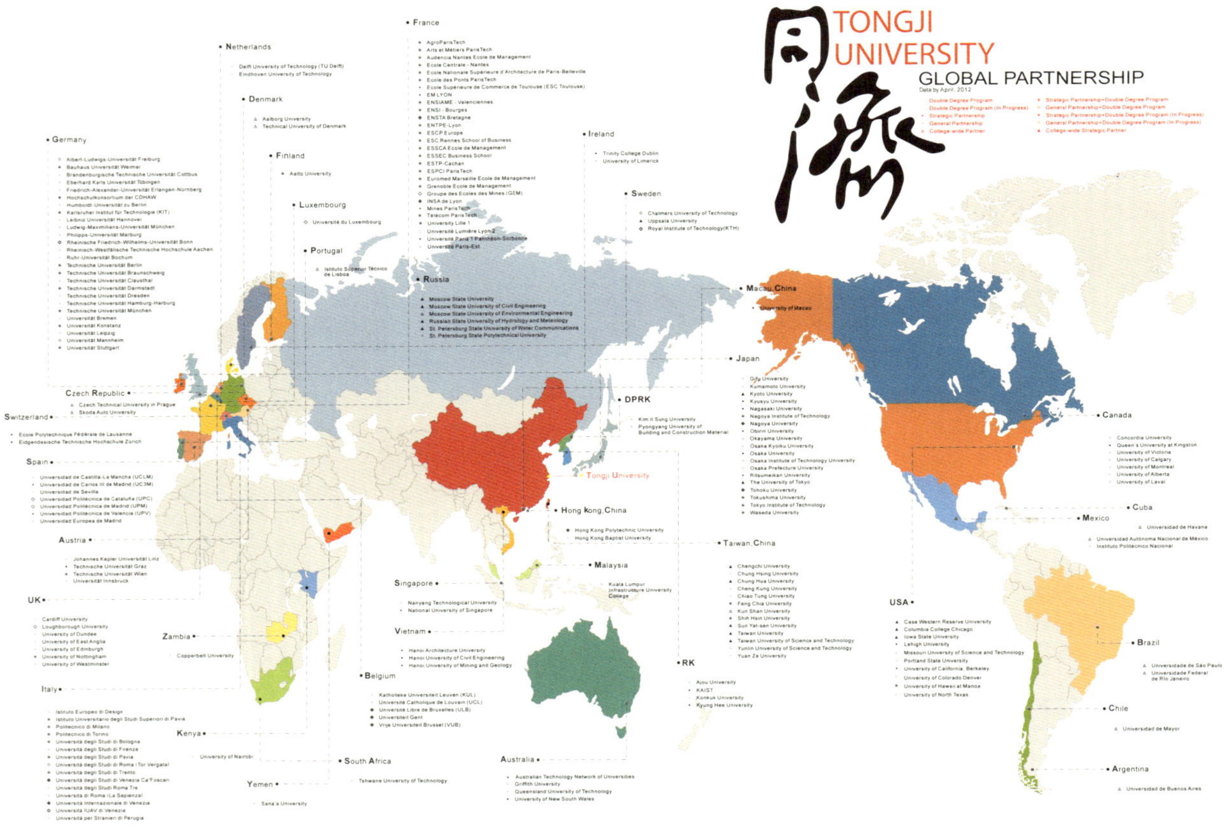

■ 同济大学全球合作地图

Map of global parternership of Tongji University

校校合作
Cooperation among Universities

■ 2007 年 3 月 21 日，同济大学与意大利博洛尼亚大学合作协议签署仪式举行，意大利博洛尼亚大学副校长罗贝托·戈冉迪教授与同济大学副校长李国强代表双方签字。

Signing Ceremony of Cooperation between Tongji University and University of Bologna of Italy on March 21, 2007. The vice president of the University of Bologna, Roberto and the vice president of Tongji Mr. Li Guoqing signing the agreement on behalf of the two parties.

■ 2008 年 11 月 14 日，同济大学校长裴钢与法国国立桥路大学校（ENPC，现更名为 Ecole des Ponts-ParisTech）校长 Philippe Courtier 博士共同签署了两校双文凭（同济大学硕士 + 法国工程师文凭）合作协议。

Signing Ceremony of Double Degree Cooperation (master degree from Tongji and engineer certificate from ENPC) with Paris ENPC on Nov. 14, 2008 by the presidents Mr. Pei Gang and Mr. Philippe Courtier.

■ 2010 年 6 月 25 日，同济大学副校长郑惠强在米兰与欧洲设计学院董事 Carlo Valerio 先生签署校际框架合作协议。

Signing Ceremony of Cooperation between Tongji University and European Design Institute on June 25, 2010 by the vice president of Tongji Mr. Zheng Huiqiang and the chairman of European Design Institute Mr. Carlo Valerio.

■ 2011 年 5 月 31 日，同济大学举行为期三天的首届"同济—伯克利合作联盟研讨会"，标志着同济大学与加州大学伯克利分校结盟合作实质性启动。

The first Tongji-Berkeley Cooperation Seminar was opened on May 31, 2011 and lasted for 3 days. It signalized the start of cooperation between Tongji University and University of California, Berkeley.

■ 2011 年 9 月 27 日，同济大学与美国芝加哥哥伦比亚学院签署校际合作协议，芝加哥哥伦比亚学院校长 Warrick Carter、同济大学副校长陈以一代表双方签字。

Signing Ceremony of Cooperation between Tongji University and Columbia College Chicago on Sep. 27, 2011. The president of Columbia College Chicago Mr. Warrick Carter and the vice president of Tongji Chen Yiyi signing the agreement on behalf of the two parties.

国际学术会议
International Academic Conferences

■ 国际桥梁与结构工程协会（IABSE）“当代大桥”学术研讨会（2009）
IABSE's academic forum "Modern Bridge" in 2009

■ 中国上海国际建筑科技大会（2009）
Shanghai International Conference on Technology of Architecture and Structure in 2009

■ 国际氢能燃料电池技术及汽车发展论坛（2010）
International Hydrogen Fuel Cell Technology Forum in 2010

■ 中日城市建设与再生国际学术研讨会（2006）
Sino-Japanese International Academic Symposium on Urban Construction and Regeneration in 2006

■ 第三届中法可持续发展城市交通系统论坛（2010）
The 3rd Sino-French Sustainable Urban Transportation System Forum in 2010

■ 中德城市道路交通安全研讨会（2009）
Sino-Germen Symposium on Urban Road Traffic Safety in 2009

■ 中非可持续发展论坛（2008）

Sino-African Sustainable Development Forum in 2008

■ 拜耳 - 同济 -UNEP 可持续发展论坛（2009）

Bayer-Tongji-UNEP Sustainable Development Forum in 2009

■ 2008 年 7 月 8 日，同济大学副校长陈小龙、同济大学汽车学院院长余卓平与法国标致雪铁龙集团中国事务部 CEO 华日曼共同签署了标致雪铁龙（中国）与同济大学汽车学院合作框架协议，决定成立“标致雪铁龙—同济合作中心”。

Signing Ceremony of Cooperation Framework Agreements between Tongji University and PSA Peugeot Citroen on July 8, 2008 to establish the PSA Peugeot Citroen-Tongji Cooperation Center. The vice president of Tongji University, Mr. Chen Xiaolong and the Dean of the Department of Automobiles, Mr. Zhao Zhuoping, CEO of the Department of Chinese Affairs of the French PSA Peugeot Citroen Group signed the agreement.

校企合作

Cooperation with Industry

■ 2007 年 5 月 10 日，通用汽车公司、电子资讯系统公司、太阳计算机公司、优集系统公司等四家全球跨国公司在同济大学设立的“教育推进伙伴计划（PACE）”中心在嘉定校区揭牌成立，中心获赠 700 套产品生命周期管理软件、50 台工作站等硬件设备以及技术培训，总价值超过 4.7 亿美元。

General Motors, Electronic Data Systems Corporation, Sun Microsystems, and UGS started Education Promotion Partnership Project in Jiading campus, Tongji University on May 10, 2007. The center received 700 sets of product lifecycle management software, 50 workstations and other hardware equipment and technical training, with a total value of more than 470 million U.S. dollars.

■ 2007 年 6 月 11 日，同济大学与德国汉高股份公司签署合作协议，汉高股份公司执行副总裁 Krautter 和同济大学副校长陈小龙分别代表双方在协议上签字。

Signing Ceremony of Cooperation between Tongji University and Germany Henkel Group on June 11, 2007. The executive vice president of the Company, Mr. Krautter and the vice president of Tongi Mr. Chen Xiaolong signing the agreement on behalf of the two parties.

■ 2010年9月26日，同济大学校长裴钢会见了欧洲宇航防务集团（EADS）首席技术官 Jean BOTTI 博士一行4人，双方将在“系统工程师”人才培养和生物燃料领域开展合作。

The president Mr. Pei Gang receiving the delegation from the European Aeronautic Defense and Space Company led by the chief technology officer, Dr. Jean BOTTI on Sep. 26, 2010. The two parties will start cooperation on the cultivation of “systems engineers” and the development of biofuels.

■ 2010年10月15日，同济大学副校长董琦与德国大众人事董事纽曼博士（Dr. Horst Neumann）、大众汽车（中国）投资有限公司总裁范安德博士（Dr. Winfried Vahland）共同签署《关于同济大学与大众汽车股份公司联合培养留德学生意向书》。

Signing Ceremony of Further Study in Germany between Tongji University and Volkswagen Group on Oct. 15, 2010. The vice president of Tongji, Dong Qi, the Volkswagen personnel director Dr. Horst Neumann, the CEO of Volkswagen (China) Investment Co., Ltd Dr. Winfried Vahland signed “the letter of intent on joint training of Chinese overseas students in Germany by Tongji University and Volkswagen Group ”.

■ 2008年11月21日，日本三菱集团资助同济大学研究生留学日本成蹊大学奖学金签约仪式举行，同济大学亚洲太平洋研究中心主任蔡建国和日本成蹊大学国际交流中心主任井上智夫作为协议执行方签约。

Signing Ceremony of Mitsubishi Scholarship for Tongji Students' Study in Seikei University on Nov. 21, 2008. Mr. Cai Jianguo, director of the Asia-Pacific Research Center of Tongji University and Mr. Inoue Chi-fu, director of the International Exchange Center of Seikei University signed as the implementation parties of the agreement.

■ 2009年11月24日，同济大学副校长董琦和法国泰雷兹集团研发与亚洲总监杜思奇（Serge DRUAIS）博士、泰雷兹中国集成中心总经理唐小龙（Serge BERTRAND）、上海济安交通咨询有限公司汪涛总经理，签署了“同济大学－泰雷兹－济安”合作备忘录。

Signing Ceremony of Cooperation Memorandum between Tongji University, Thales Group and Ji'an Group on Nov. 24, 2009.
The vice president of Tongji University Dr. Dong Qi, the director of the Department of R & D and Asian Affairs of the French Thales Group Dr. Serge DRUAIS, the general manager of Thales Integration Center (China) Serge BERTRAND, the general manager of Shanghai Ji'an Traffic Consulting Co., Ltd., Wang Tao signed the MOU.

■ 2008 年 7 月 2 日，“同济大学 - 美国 PTC 公司教育合作备忘录”签约仪式举行，PTC 公司全球高级副总裁 John Stuart 与校长助理余卓平教授代表双方签署了合作备忘录。

Signing Ceremony of MOU between Tongji University and Parametric Technology Corporation on July 2, 2008. PTC's global senior vice president Mr. John Stuart and principal assistant prof. Yu Zhuoping signed the memorandum of cooperation on behalf of the two sides.

■ 2010 年 8 月 26 日，欧直公司总裁兼首席执行官 Lutz Bertling 博士、欧直中国公司首席执行官 Bruno Boulnois 与同济大学党委书记周家伦签署“同济大学与欧洲直升机公司签署合作协议”。

Dr. Lutz Bertling, the president and CEO of Eurocopter, Mr. Bruno Boulnois, the CEO of Eurocopter China, and the party secretary of Tongji University Mr. Zhou Jialun signed an agreement at the signing ceremony between Tongji University and Eurocopter on Aug. 26, 2010.

■ 2010 年 9 月 16 日，同济大学党委副书记方守恩与世界顶级健身器材厂商意大利泰诺健公司总裁内里奥·亚历山大签署了合作备忘录。

Signing Ceremony of Cooperation between Tongji University and Italian Technogym Group 2010 on Sep. 16, 2010. The deputy party secretary of Tongji University, Mr. Fang Shou'en with the president of the world's top fitness equipment manufacturers Mr. Rio Alexander.

■ 2011 年 7 月 28 日，同济大学副校长伍江与普莱克斯高级副总裁兼首席技术官 Ray Roberge 代表双方签署合作备忘录。

The vice president of Tongji Wu Jiang and Mr. Ray Roberge, senior vice president of Praxiar signed a Memorandum of Understanding at the signing ceremony of cooperation between Tongji University and Praxiar on July 28, 2011.

中外基地，合作办学

Educational Bases Established for More International Cooperation

随着国际交流的纵深拓展，同济大学逐步探索出中外合作办学的成功模式。自 1998 年开始，先后成立了中德学院、中德工程学院、中法工程与管理学院、联合国环境规划署 - 同济大学环境与可持续发展学院、中意学院、中芬中心、中西中心等国际合作办学基地。开展以双学位为主，多种交流形式并存的合作方式，致力于培养富有国际竞争力的杰出工程人才。

With the further development of international exchange and cooperation, Tongji University has successfully built a model of joint international education. Since 1998, Tongji University has established Sino-German College for Postgraduate Studies, Sino-German College of Applied Sciences, Sino-French Institute of Engineering and Management, UNEP - Tongji Institute of Environment for Sustainable Development, Sino-Italian Campus, Sino-Finnish Center and other joint international education bases. This model is dedicated to producing excellent engineering talents with international competitiveness.

中德学院

Sino-German College for Postgraduate Studies

■ 1998 年 2 月 18 日，同济大学中德学院正式成立。

Sino-German College for Postgraduate Studies of Tongji University officially established on 18th February, 1998.

■ 2012 年 1 月 10 日德国教育和科研部部长沙万教授受邀访问同济大学中德学院，并在学院做专题报告。

Professor Annette Schavan, Minister of the Ministry of Education and Research of Germany, on a visiting tour to Sino-German College for Postgraduate Studies at the invitation of Tongji University on January 10th 2012.

中德工程学院

Sino-German College of Applied Sciences

■ 2004 年 7 月 30 日，中德两国政府共同倡议和支持的高等教育合作项目“同济大学中德工程学院”成立，图为教育部曹国兴司长和德国教研部国务秘书 Dudenhausen 博士为学院揭牌。

Mr. Cao Guoxing from Ministry of Education, China and Dr. Dudenhausen from the Ministry of Education and Research, Germany, unveiling the plate of Sino-German College of Applied Sciences of Tongji University which was established at the joint proposal of and with joint support from both Chinese and German governments on July 30th, 2004.

■ 2006 年 1 月 20 日，在德国 HS Esslingen 举行中德工程学院在德十二所合作高校联盟协议签署仪式。

A cooperation agreement was signed between Sino-German College of Applied Sciences, Tongji University and the University Alliance of twelve German universities in HS Eslinggen, Germany on January 20th, 2006.

职业技术教育学院

Institute of Vocational and Technical Education

■ 2002 年 12 月 30 日，中德职教师资培养项目第二期意向书签约仪式。

Signing ceremony of Memorandum of Understanding for the second phase of the Sino-German Teacher Training Program of Vocational and Technical Education on December 30th, 2002.

■ 2007 年，德国总统克勒与职教学院中外学生合影。

Mr. Koehler, ex-president of Germany with Chinese and international students of Institute of Vocational and Technical Education on his visit to Tongji University in 2007.

■ 2004 年，法国总统希拉克和同济大学校长万钢为中法中心奠基。

President Jacques Chirac of France and President Wan Gang of Tongji University laid the cornerstone for the Sino-French Center at Tongji University in 2004.

中法工程与管理学院

Sino-French Institute of Engineering and Management

■ 2007 年 5 月 17 日，“中法科技合作展”开幕，同济大学副校长周祖翼、法国国立路桥大学校长教授、上海市科学技术委员会陈克宏副主任、法国驻沪总领事马捷利共同为展览揭幕。

Professor Zhou Zuyi, vice president of Tongji University, Professor Philippe Courtier, president of National University of Roads and Bridges Engineering (École des Ponts ParisTech), France, Mr. Chen Kehong, vice director from Science and Technology Committee of Shanghai and Mr. Thierry Mathou, Consul General from the Consulate General of France in Shanghai, unveiling the Exhibition of Sino-French Cooperation in Science and Technology at its opening ceremony on May 17th 2007.

中意学院
Sino-Italian Campus

■ 2006 年 9 月，意大利普罗迪总理（前排左五）于同济大学见证中意学院成立，教育部副部长吴启迪和意大利教育、大学、研究部部长为中意学院成立揭牌。

Professor Wu Qidi, vice minister of the Ministry of Education, China and Mr. Mussi, minister of the Ministry of Education, Universities and Research, Italy, unveiled the plate of Sino-Italian Campus at its opening ceremony, which was witnessed by Mr. Prodi (5th front left), premier of Italy in September 2006.

■ 2010 年 7 月，首届 PoliTong 项目本科双学位学生顺利毕业。

First students graduated from the double-degree PoliTong program in July 2010.

联合国环境规划署—同济大学环境与可持续发展学院
UNEP-Tongji Institute of Environment for Sustainable Development

■ 2002 年 5 月 9 日，联合国副秘书长、联合国环境规划署执行主任托普弗博士和同济大学校长吴启迪签署合作协议，共同建立联合国环境规划署—同济大学环境与可持续发展学院。

Dr. Klaus Töpfer, Under-Secretary-General of UN and the Executive Director of UNEP, and Professor Wu Qidi, President of Tongji University, signing an Agreement of Cooperation for the establishment of UNEP-Tongji Institute of Environment for Sustainable Development on May 9th, 2002.

■ 2007 年 5 月 18 日，联合国副秘书长、联合国环境规划署执行主任施泰纳先生、同济大学校长万钢为双方共建的“联合国环境规划署—同济大学环境与可持续发展学院”续签合作协议。

Mr. Achim Steiner, Under-Secretary General of UN and the Executive Director of UNEP, and Professor Wan Gang, President of Tongji University signed the renewed Agreement of Cooperation for UNEP-Tongji Institute of Environment for Sustainable Development on May 18th, 2007.

中芬中心

Sino-Finnland Centre

■ 2010 年 5 月，同济大学校长裴钢、副校长伍江出席同济阿尔托设计工厂成立仪式，粉刷最后一堵墙。

Pei Gang, president of Tongji University and Wu Jiang, vice president of Tongji University painting the last wall at the founding ceremony of Tongji Aalto Design Workshop in Sino-Finnish Centre in May 2010

■ 2011 年 11 月 3 日，同济大学党委书记周家伦与阿尔托大学副校长汉努共同为中芬中心揭牌。

Zhou Jialun, party secretary general of Tongji University and Mr. Hannu, vice president of Aalto University of Finland unveiled the plate of Sino-Finnish Centre on November 3rd 2011.

■ 2011 年 11 月 24 日 -25 日，第一次“中西学院”（筹）研讨会在加泰罗尼亚理工大学举行。

The first workshop on Sino-Spanish Campus (in preparation) held at Universidad Politécnica de Cataluña from November 24th to 25th, 2011.

■ 2012 年 5 月 25 日，《同济大学、马德里理工大学与加泰罗尼亚理工大学关于成立“中西学院”谅解备忘录》签署仪式举行，同济大学“中西学院”正式成立。

The signing ceremony of Memorandum of Understanding for the establishment of Sino-Spanish Campus between Tongji University and Polytechnic University of Madrid and Polytechnic University of Cataluna on May 25th, 2012, marking the establishment of the Sino-Spanish Campus.

教育反哺，对口支援

Support for Designated Schools to Repay Society

同济大学紧密结合高教需求，与全国多个学校积极开展了形式多样的对口支援工作。从师资援助、人才培养、管理水平和科研服务各方面推广工程教育的先进经验，为国家和地方的发展，特别是中国城市建设发展发挥了重要作用。

Tongji University has provided various support to designated schools across the country to keep abreast of the needs for higher education in China. The university has played an important role in the national and local development, especially in the development of urban construction in China by promoting its successful experiences in engineering education through teachers, student cultivation, research, management and service.

■ 同济大学支援西部部分重点项目分布示意图

Distribution of major projects supported by Tongji University in western China

■ 2005年7月18日，同济大学常务副校长李永盛与井冈山学院院长张泰城共同签署《同济大学对口支援井冈山学院协议书》。

Professor Li Yongsheng, executive vice president of Tongji University, and Professor Zhang Qincheng, president of Jinggangshan College signing an Agreement of Support to Jingangshan College by Tongji University on July 18th, 2005.

■ 2006年10月23日，同济大学党委副书记、副校长周祖翼与宜宾学院院长罗元松签署合备忘录，进一步加强两校在教育、科研等方面的合作交流。

Professor Zhou Zuyi, vice chairman of the University Council and vice president of Tongji University and Mr. Luo Yuansong, president of Yibin College, shaking hands after signing a Memorandum of Understanding for further cooperation in teaching and research on October 23rd, 2006.

■ 2007年6月5日，同济大学常务副校长李永盛与昆明理工大学副校长王华签署对口支援合作协议。

Professor Li Yongsheng, executive vice president of Tongji and Professor Wang Hua, vice president of Kunming University of Technology, signing an agreement of support on June 5th, 2007.

■ 2010年8月31日，同济大学建筑与城市规划学院与新疆大学建筑工程学院签署对口支援协议。

Signing ceremony of an agreement of support between School of Architecture and Urban Planning of Tongji University and College of Architecture Engineering of Xinjiang University on August 31st 2010

服务世博，为国争光

Service for Shanghai Expo 2010 Bringing Honors to the Country

2010 年，第 41 届世博会在上海隆重举行。以此为契机，同济工程教育接受了一次世界检阅。在世博会的申办、规划、建设、运营过程中，同济工科人完成各类规划设计任务 90 多项，先后承担 170 多个相关科技项目，参与世博园公共设施和多处场馆建设，展示了同济工程教育的雄厚实力和良好的国家形象。

The 41st World Expo was held in Shanghai in 2010. The engineering education of Tongji University received a world-level examination during the event. During the process of application, planning, construction and operation of the Expo, engineering teachers and students of Tongji University completed over 90 planning and design tasks of various nature, undertook over 170 technical projects, and participated in the construction of public facilities and many pavilions at the Expo Park, demonstrating the robust strengths in engineering education of Tongji University.

2002 年 12 月 16 日，上海市常务副市长蒋以任与吴启迪校长为同济大学"上海世博会"研究中心成立揭牌。

Mr. Jiang Yiren, executive vice mayor of Shanghai and Professor Wu Qidi, president of Tongji at the opening ceremony of Shanghai World Expo Research Center at Tongji University on December 16th, 2002

2005 年 6 月，同济大学校长万钢陪同上海市副市长周禹鹏到建筑与城市规划学院考察师生参与上海世博会规划设计工作。

Mr. Zhou Yupeng, vice mayor of Shanghai, at the company of President Wan Gang of Tongji University, inspecting the planning work of the Shanghai Expo 2010 at the School of Architecture and Urban Planning of Tongji University in June 2005.

2008 年 7 月 20 日，同济大学书记周家伦、校长裴钢向中央政治局委员刘延东、俞正声汇报同济参与世博工作情况。

Party secretary general Zhou Jialun, at the company of President Pei Gang of Tongji University, reporting to Mrs Liu Yandong, member of the Political Bureau of the CPC Central Committee and Mr. Yu Zhengsheng, Party secretary general of Shanghai about Tongji's participation in the Shanghai World Expo 2010 on July 20th, 2008.

同济大学校长裴钢主持同济世博工作研讨会

President Pei Gang chairing a seminar on Tongji's participation in Shanghai Expo 2010

■ 世博会同济大学方案鸟瞰图（竞赛阶段，2004 年），在园区规划方案国际竞标中，同济规划团队与 40 多家国际著名机构同场竞技，并以"世界眼"的独特创意最终胜出，成为与美国和英国团队并列的"三甲"方案之一。

A bird's view of the planning proposal of the Shanghai Expo Park by Tongji University (at the time of competition, 2004). In an international bidding of Shanghai Expo Park Planning, Tongji's planning team eventually won the bidding with their unique design of the World's Eye out of over 40 strong competitors from internationally renowned design firms. Their design along with two others from USA and UK turned out to be the Best Three Designs in the bidding.

■ 汇集了 5000 余张笑脸的同济大学世博志愿者之旗

Flag of Expo Volunteers of Tongji University composed of a collection of over 5000 smiling faces

■ 世博会开园首日校领导慰问同济志愿者

Leaders of Tongji meeting Tongji volunteers at the Expo Park on the first day when the Expo Park opened to the public

世博八总

Eight Experts of Shanghai World Expo 2010 from Tongji University

■ 郑时龄院士，世博会总策划师之一，建筑与城市规划学院教授

Zheng Shiling, professor of School of Architecture & Urban Planning and a member of Chinese Academy of Sciences, acting as one of the General Planners of Expo 2010

■ 吴志强，世博会园区总规划师，建筑与城市规划学院教授

Wu Zhiqiang, professor of School of Architecture & Urban Planning, acting as the General Planner of the Expo Park

■ 唐子来，世博会城市最佳实践区总策划师，建筑与城市规划学院教授

Tang Zilai, professor of School of Architecture & Urban Planning, acting as the General Planner of Urban Best Practice Area at the Expo Park

■ 乐云，世博会工程建设总体项目管理总负责，经济与管理学院教授

Le Yun, professor of School of Economics and Management, was responsible for the overall project management of engineering construction at the Expo Park

■ 曾群，主题馆总设计师，建筑设计研究院教授

Zeng Qun, professor of the Architectural Design and Research Institute, acting as Chief Designer of the Theme Pavilion at the Expo Park

■ 丁洁民，世博村总体规划及设计总协调，建筑设计研究院教授

Ding Jiemin, professor of the Architectural Design and Research Institute, acting as Chief Coordinator of the overall planning and design of the Expo Village

■ 郝洛西，世博会园区夜景照明总设计师，建筑与城市规划学院教授

Dr. Hao Luoxi, professor of School of Architecture & Urban Planning, acting as Chief Designer of night lighting at the Expo Park

■ 杨东援（上），陈小鸿（下），世博交通规划方案总策划，交通与运输工程学院教授

Yang Dongyuan (above), Chen Xiaohong (below), professors of School of Traffic and Transportation Engineering, acting as General Planners of the Transport Planning for Expo 2010

由同济主持设计的世博场馆
Expo Pavilions, designs of which were headed by designers from Tongji University

同济合作设计的世博场馆
Expo Pavilions Co-designed by Tongji University

科技支撑

Scientific & Technological Support

■ 世博园区专用燃料电池汽车

Fuel cell cars customized for the Expo Park

■ 屋面膜模型实验

An experiment on a roof film model

■ 施工现场测试

Testing at the construction site

■ 直饮水项目

Drinking Water Project

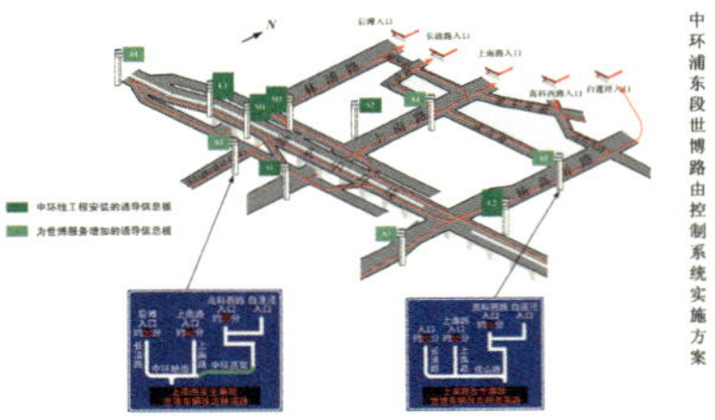

■ 中环浦东段世博路由控制系统实施方案

Implementation Proposal of the Expo Traffic Routing Control System for the Mid-Ring Elevated Roads in Pudong

■ 世博轴阳光谷节点试验

Experiment on the nodes of the Sunshine Valley along the Expo Axis

■ 世博园区废弃物资源化利用（废弃混凝土再生制造）

Recycling of waste materials from the Expo Park (regeneration of waste concrete)

■ 中国国家馆结构模型抗震试验

Anti-seismic experiment on the structure of China Pavilion

■ 由同济企业承建的信息通信馆

Communications Pavilion constructed by a Tongji-owned company

■ 同济在世博会上的监理队伍

The supervision team of Tongji University at the construction site of the Expo Park

抗震救灾，专业支援 100

Earthquake Relief with Professional Expertise

2008 年，“5.12”汶川地震发生后，同济师生发扬“同舟共济、自强不息”的精神，第一时间成立“同济大学抗震救灾专业技术志愿服务队”，发挥工科专业特长，提供地震灾评、房屋应急评估、临时安置规划等支援服务。在灾后重建中，组建科技特派团对口援建都江堰市，先后承担了 41 个重建和援建项目。

An earthquake hit Wenchuan, Sichuan Province on May 12th, 2008. Soon after the devastating earthquake, teachers and students established a Professional Anti-seismic and Disaster Prevention Volunteer Team of Tongji University and went to the earthquake-struck area in Sichuan. They made full use their strengths in engineering and provided on-site technical support on earthquake damage evaluation, housing emergency assessments and temporary relocation planning. After the earthquake, Tongji University set up a special technical support team to help Dujiangyan City in Sichuan with its reconstruction. They undertook 41 reconstruction projects in the city, some of which were sponsored by Tongji University.

■ 2008 年 5 月 16 日，同济大学紧急成立由 6 位土木工程相关学科领域专家组成的“抗震救灾专业技术志愿服务队”，奔赴抗震救灾第一线，以学科专业优势，为抗震救灾提供智力支援。

On May 16th 2008, Tongji University established a Professional Anti-seismic and Disaster Prevention Volunteer Team which was composed of six experts from civil engineering. They went to the earthquake-struck area in Sichuan and provided on-site technical support.

■ 同济大学规划专业师生奔赴灾区开展应急安置规划制订

Teachers and students of urban planning engineering of Tongji University ready to leave for the earthquake-struck area to provide their help with emergency relocation planning

■ 匡晓明老师带领学生使用红外线测距仪勘测现场

Tongji teacher Kuang Xiaoming and his the students doing a survey with an infrared range finder

■ 同济师生在灾区实地勘测

Teachers and students of Tongji University doing on-site surveys in the earthquake-struck area

■ 常青教授带领学生在二王庙大殿前完全垮塌的仿古建筑中察看

Professor Chang Qing and his students examining collapsed pseudo-classic buildings in front of the main hall of Erwang Temple

■ 吕西林教授带领学生现场检查承重构件的裂缝

Professor Lv Xilin examining cracks on the load-bearing structural elements

■ 陈保胜教授灾区现场工作

Professor Chen Baosheng at work on the site

■ 夏南凯教授率专业技术团实地调研

A professional technical team led by Professor Xia Nankai discussing on site about their disaster investigation

■ 2009 年 12 月，同济大学与绵阳市委签署《北川地震遗址保护及纪念馆建设项目设计合作框架协议》。

An Agreement on Preservation of Earthquake Relics in Beichuan and the Establishment of an Earthquake Museum was signed between Tongji University and Mianyang City of Sichuan Province in December 2009.

■ 同济大学设计的北川地震博物馆设计，以“永恒北川”为主题。
Beichuan Earthquake Museum designed by Tongji University was made on the theme of Eternal Beichuan

■ 同济主持设计的都江堰“壹街区”规划
Planning of Yijie Area at Dujiangyan City was headed by Tongji University

■ 同济对口援建的都江堰向峨小学主教学楼
Main teaching building of Xiang'e Primary School sponsored and built by Tongji

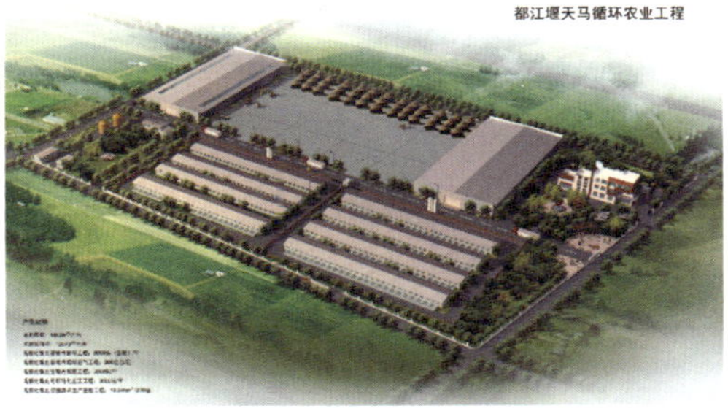

■ 同济主持规划的灾后特色农村重建项目“都江堰天马循环农业工程”
Planning of an agricultural reconstruction project of Tianma Circular Agricultural Engineering of Dujiangyan headed by Tongji University

卓越工程，卓越联盟

Excellent Engineering Education and University Alliance of Excellence

作为教育部首批“卓越工程师教育培养计划”试点高校，同济大学发起成立了卓越人才培养合作高校联盟，通过建设校际、校企和国际化合作交流平台，全方位开展卓越人才培养。此外，同济大学承担了由我国 18 所高校和欧洲 12 所高校共同成立“中欧工程教学平台”的中方秘书处工作，推动中欧工程类院校在卓越工程人才方面开展长期稳定合作。

As one of the first pilot universities on the Educational Program for Excellent Engineers launched by the Ministry of Education, Tongji University initiated to establish a University Alliance for Education of Excellent Talents for an overall cultivation of excellent talents through cooperation and exchanges among universities, between universities and the industry and at an international level. Besides, Tongji University has served as a secretariat in China for the Sino-Europe Engineering Education Platform jointly established by 18 Chinese universities and 12 European universities, to promote long-term stable cooperation in education of excellent engineering talents among higher institution of engineering in China and Europe.

卓越人才培养合作高校

Member Universities of University Alliance for Education of Excellent Talents

同济大学	Tongji University
北京理工大学	Beijing Institute of Technology
大连理工大学	Dalian University of Technology
重庆大学	Chongqing University
东南大学	Southwest University
哈尔滨工业大学	Harbin Institute of Technology
华南理工大学	South China University of Technology
天津大学	Tianjin University
西北工业大学	Northwest Polytechnic University
湖南大学	Hunan University

■ 2010 年 4 月，召开中意学院第三次理事会，同济大学裴钢校长与米兰理工、都灵理工大学校长签署“4+M”卓越工程师联合培养协议。

President Pei Gang, president of Politecnico di Milano and president of Politecnico di Torino signing a 4+M Agreement of Joint Education of Excellent Engineers at the third Board Meeting of the Sino-Italian Campus in April 2010

■ 2010 年 9 月 4 日，首届“中欧工程教育研讨会”在同济大学拉开帷幕，教育部与欧洲工程教育研究联盟共同签署了《关于中欧工程教育合作的谅解备忘录》，双方决定由与会的中方 18 所高校和欧方 12 所高校共同成立“中欧工程教育平台”。

The first Sino-European Engineering Education Forum was held in Tongji University on September 4th, 2010. The Ministry of Education of China and Research Alliance of European Engineering Education signed a Memorandum of Understanding on Engineering Education Cooperation between China and Europe. The two sides decided that a platform for engineering education in China and Europe be established jointly by the Forum participants of 18 universities from China and 12 universities from Central Europe.

■ 2010 年 11 月 25 日，卓越联盟九所高校在同济大学举行“卓越人才合作培养研讨会”，同意全方位合作并签署《卓越人才培养合作框架协议》。

On November 25th, 2010, nine universities from the University Alliance for Education of Excellent Talents were on a seminar on Joint Education of Excellent Talents in Tongji University and a Framework Agreement on Joint Education of Excellent Talents was signed for all-round cooperation.

■ 2010年12月9日，同济大学召开“卓越人才校企联合培养研讨会”，与到会的近 50 家企业代表达成合作共识：校企双方将共同承担人才培养重任，共建“工程实践教育中心”，共促卓越人才培养。

A Seminar on Joint Education of Excellent Talents between universities and businesses was held in Tongji University on December 9th, 2010. About 50 business representatives reached a consensus with Tongji on their cooperation: both universities and businesses will share the responsibility of talents cultivation by building an Education Center for Engineering Practice to promote the education of excellent talents.

■ “卓越人才培养合作高校”9 校自主选拔联考举行

Students attending the joint examinations for independent student recruitment by the nine member universities of the University Alliance for Education of Excellent Talents

■ 卓越联盟自主招生面试

An interview for independent student recruitment of the University Alliance for Education of Excellent Talents

■ “卓越人才培养合作高校”2011 年校长联席会议

A joint presidential meeting of the University Alliance for Education of Excellent Talents in 2011

■ 2011 年，同济大学中德学院、机械工程学院与 8 所德国大学联盟代表共同签署了《“卓越工程师培养计划 (4+M)”中德合作项目备忘录》。

Memorandum of Understanding for Sino-German Cooperation on 4+M Joint Education Program of Excellent Engineers signed between Sino-German College for Postgraduate Studies, Sino-German College of Applied Sciences of Tongji University and the university alliance of eight German universities in 2011.

后 记

《周礼·考工记》曰："天有时，地有气，材有美，工有巧，合此四者，然后可以为良"。1912年，于世界之中国，于中国之上海，于上海之同济，统天时地利美材与巧工，由德人贝伦子担历史之大任，创办了工科，数千年中外教育史上，第一次出现了"同济德文医工学堂"。

1918年《同济》第一期的《发刊词》说："厚国聚民，莫先乎工"。经济的落后，民生的羸弱，城乡的凋敝，促使百年来的知识分子寻找种种强国救民之道，同济人站在新世纪的高度创办工科和发展工学，无论是培养普通民众的科学精神，还是提升东方大国的工业力量，同济工科的一百年都是中国高教史上的一座高地，也是中华民族现代化进程中的一块路标。

同济工科是同舟共济的一百年，是协同创新的一百年，也是竭心尽力培养卓越工程师的一百年。同济大学培养的一代又一代卓越工程师们，为祖国规划和建设了一条条隧道、一片片园林、一道道长桥、一辆辆汽车甚至一艘艘舰船和一座座城市，以其严谨性、实用性、专业性、创造性、国际性和服务性，谱写了一曲曲"同心同德同舟楫，济人济事济天下"的同济之歌。

2012年5月，同济迎来了105周年校庆和百年工程教育纪念。在这百花盛开、青果连枝的季节，溯历史以求同济经验，展未来以追大学梦想，正是百多年来所有同济人的事业，更是工科人和历史记录者责无旁贷的任务。本此，我们策划了"同济大学百年卓越工程教育图片展"，按照时间顺序，分上下篇六个阶段，将同济百年工学的辉煌一一展现在你的面前。而这部请诸君打开的图史，就是我们建起的另一间永不拆卸的展览大厅。

展览以及书籍的多次修订得到了学校党政领导的高度重视，他们提出了很多具体的修改意见，也得到相关部门负责人和工科学院的大力支持。董鉴泓、范家骥、屠听泉、朱照宏、林章豪、朱月海、陆厚根、李乐曾、章仁彪、皋古平、钟勤等老同志和校史专家提出了修改意见。

外国语学院李梅教授承担了全书的英文翻译。土木工程学院刘曙光教授帮助翻译了苏联专家的姓名。

本书中的图片资料大多来源于同济大学档案馆馆藏档案和新闻中心历年的积累，新闻中心姜锡祥和江平提供了大量的帮助。德国问题研究所李乐曾教授提供了部分珍贵的历史照片。

档案馆王琍琍、王忞怡负责了展览版英文翻译稿的审校。林松、孙洁、王毓灵等同志做了部分辅助性工作。校史馆助管王文琳、韦苏宁、常雅如、李睿、周昕诸同学参与了部分材料的搜集整理工作。上海欣诚艺阁广告传播有限公司承担了本书的版面设计工作。同济大学出版社为此书顺利出版贡献良多。

特志于上。

编者

2012年5月

Epilogue

According to *the Chronicles of Works in Zhouli*, "one can only make the right thing when it is done at the right time and right place with the right material and the right skill". In 1929, Mr. Bernhard Berrens from Germany took the historical responsibility of making good use of the four right elements of time, place, material and skill in establishing an engineering program for Tongji, Shanghai, China. German Medical and Engineering School hence came into being in the thousand-year long educational history of China and the world.

As was put in the first issue of *Tongji* in 1918, "technology will make a country and its people stronger". Chinese intellectuals had tried every means possible to make their country and people strong in the face of backward economy, poor life and depressed cities for hundreds of years. At the turn of the century, Tongji people established and developed the engineering programs, which was of great significance both in raising the awareness of science and technology in Chinese people and enhancing the industrial power of the oriental country. The centennial engineering education of Tongji University meant a milestone not only in the history of higher education in China, but in the modernization of the Chinese nation.

The engineering education of Tongji Unviersity witnessed a hundred years of joint efforts marked with innovation and excellence. Over the hundred years, Tongji University produced generations of engineers who had planned and constructed countless tunnels, parks, bridges, vehicles, ships as well as cities for its country, thus composing a proud song of Tongji with the theme of "reaching the bank to serve the people and country in a boat with joint efforts".

The centennial anniversary of the engineering education of Tongji along with the 105th anniversary of the university fell in May 2012. At a time when flowers were in full blossom and trees full of fruits, it was the cause of Tongji people as well as the responsibility of the engineering people of Tongji to record the history for learning of lessons and to look into the future for pursuit of dreams. Therefore, we planned an Illustrated Exhibition of Centennial Engineering Education of Tongji University, which was arranged chronologically in six chapters. On the exhibition, we unfolded in front you the glory of engineering education of Tongji University whereas in the current illustrated history book, we led you into a hall of exhibition that we constructed and will never demolish.

Leaders of the university paid close attention to the exhibition and the publication of the book and had made detailed comments on the revised versions of the book. People from relevant administration offices and engineering schools of the university kindly lent their never-failing support. Dong Jianhong, Fan Jiaji, Tu Tingquan, Zhu Zhaohong, Lin Zhanghao, Zhu Yuehai, Lu Hougen, Li Lezeng, Zhang Renbiao, Gao Guping and Zhong Qin provided their elaborate accounts of the past of the university and gave their feedback for the draft and revisions of the book.

Professor LI May from the School of Foreign Languages translated the book into English and Professor Liu Chuguang from the School of Civil Engineering provided translation of Russian names.

The pictures in the book were mostly from the collections of the Archives of Tongji University and the News Centre of the university. Mr. Jiang Xixiang and Mr. Jiang Ping from the News Centre provided a lot of help in selecting the pictures, and Professor Li Lezeng from the Research Institute of Germany provided some historically valuable pictures.

Wang Lili and Wang Minyi from the Archives did the proofreading for the English translation of the exhibition and Linsong, Sun Jie and Wang Yulin also offered some help. Wang Wenlin, Wei Suning, Chang Yaru, Li Rui and Zhou Xin, who worked as students assistants helped with the data collection. Shanghai Xincheng Yige Advertising and Communicatons Co. Ltd. did the graphic design of book and the Tongji University Press made great contributions to the publication of the book .

We would like to take this opportunity to express our gratitude to the above-mentioned people and organizations.

Editors
May, 2012